State, Community and Neighbourhood in Princely
North India, c.1900–1950

State, Community and Neighbourhood in Princely North India, c.1900–1950

Ian Copland

Associate Professor School of Historical Studies
Monash University
Australia

First published 2005 by
PALGRAVE MACMILLAN
Houndmills, Basingstoke, Hampshire RG21 6XS and
175 Fifth Avenue, New York, N.Y. 10010
Companies and representatives throughout the world

PALGRAVE MACMILLAN is the global academic imprint of the Palgrave Macmillan division of St. Martin's Press, LLC and of Palgrave Macmillan Ltd. Macmillan® is a registered trademark in the United States, United Kingdom and other countries. Palgrave is a registered trademark in the European Union and other countries.

ISBN-13: 978–1–4039–4707–9
ISBN-10: 1–4039–4707–4 hardback

This book is printed on paper suitable for recycling and made from fully managed and sustained forest sources.

A catalogue record for this book is available from the British Library.

Library of Congress Cataloging-in-Publication Data
Copland, Ian, 1943–
    State, community and neighbourhood in princely North India,
    c.1900–1950 / Ian Copland.
        p.   cm.
    Includes bibliographical references and index.
    ISBN 1–4039–4707–4 (cloth)
    1. Communalism—India—History—20th century.   2. Religion and
    politics—India—History—20th century.   3. India—History—20th
    century.   I. Title.

    DS422.C64C68 2005
    305.6'0954'09041—dc22

                                                          2004062474

10   9   8   7   6   5   4   3   2   1
14   13   12   11   10   09   08   07   06   05

Printed and bound in Great Britain by
Antony Rowe Ltd, Chippenham and Eastbourne

For Matthew

Contents

List of Tables, Figures and Maps

Tables

Figures

Maps

List of Abbreviations

AGG	Agent-to-the-Governor-General
AICC	All-India Congress Committee
AISPC	All-India States Peoples' Conference
BJP	Bharatiya Janata Party
BJS	Bharatiya Jana Sangh
Br. Lib.	British Library
CC	Chief Commissioner
CI	Central India
CID	Criminal Investigation Department
CIO	Central Intelligence Officer
Col.	Colonel
Coll.	Collection
CR	Crown Representative
CWC	Congress Working Committee
DM	Deputy Magistrate
F&P	Foreign and Political
GOI	Government of India
HH	His Highness
IB	Intelligence Bureau
IG	Inspector-General
INA	Indian National Army
INC	Indian National Congress
IOR	India Office Records
MOS	Ministry of States
MP	Madhya Pradesh
MPSA	Madhya Pradesh State Archives
NAI	National Archives of India
NMML	Nehru Memorial Museum and Library
PA	Political Agent
P&S	Political and Secret
PEPSU	Punjab and East Punjab States Union
PM	Prime Minister
Pol.	Political
Pol. Sec.	Political Secretary

PS	Private Secretary
PSA	Punjab State Archives
RC	Regional Commissioner
RCO	Regional Commissioner's Office
RPM	Rajya Praja Mandal
RSA	Rajasthan State Archives
RSAB	Rajasthan State Archives, Bikaner Branch
RSS	Rashtriya Swayamsevak Sangh
SCR	Statutory Commission *Report*
Sec. State	Secretary of State
SP	Superintendent of Police
TF	*Towards Freedom*
TOI	*The Times of India*
TOP	*The Transfer of Power, 1942–7*
UP	United Provinces

Acknowledgements

I always begin the project of every new book with the fond expectation that it will take less time than the previous one; so far I have been disappointed. This one took all of eight years—albeit eight years in which there were other publications and many competing activities. During that long time anchored to the grindstone, I was sustained and kept focussed by the encouragement of a number of colleagues and friends, among whom I would like to acknowledge Professor Graeme Davison, Dr Eleanor Hancock, Dr David Garrioch my Head of School, Dr Dick Kooiman, Professor D.A. Low, A.G. Noorani and the late Professor Ravinder Kumar, whose office at Teen Murti was, at once, a place of welcome and a source of intellectual enrichment.

The research for the book was facilitated by two Australian Research Council grants, and a third from Monash University—which also granted me two extended periods of leave from my University duties. I was also well served by the labours of three very talented research assistants, namely Dr Kate Brittlebank, Dr Vrinda Mishra and Ms Lucy Sutherland and by the cartographical skills of Gary Swinton. I thank the Indian government and the governments of Punjab, MP, and Rajasthan for giving me access to their archives; and Mr Mohan Singh Kanota for allowing me to see transcripts of his grandfather Thakur Amar Singh's diaries. The service at the British Library was, as ever, pleasant and resourceful; and the Acting Director of the Punjab Archives branch at Patiala, Mr Shamshad Ali Khan, put other duties aside to help me find my way through that immense collection. Yet while archival work represented the backbone of the research for this project, the part I enjoyed most was talking to some of the former rulers and subjects from the region. I thank them all most sincerely for giving so freely of their time, and for sharing their priceless memories of life and politics in the erstwhile kingdoms.

1
Introduction

According to me, the Hindu–Muslim problem is a gift of the English after 1857 and more so, basically, in 1921. It was they who took steps to divide Hindu and Muslim, Hindu and Sikh,... 'Aryan' North and 'Dravidian' South. They got maximum success dividing the Hindus and Muslims. For them, communal riots were games to be relished.

The Shiv Sena's Bal Thackeray, 1998 ?

Unmasking the other

At the start of the second millennium, even as the world enters a new age of unparalleled globalism, local communities in many parts of our 'global village' are breaking up, sundering along the fault lines of ethnicity. In Ambon, Bosnia, Sri Lanka, East Timor and the former Soviet republics of Central Asia, populations once united by ties of respect, practicality, neighbourliness and mutual interdependence have become divided, estranged by recrimination, fear and death. Former neighbours have become strangers; old friends have turned into bitter enemies; people once looked up to as community stalwarts have been reduced to homeless, rootless refugees.

Looking back on our own lives, we tend to remember things as better than they actually were. So it is with societal pasts. It is often tempting, from our contemporary vantage point, surrounded by violence and urban crowding, and caught up in the frenetic pursuits of modern life, to romanticise the old ways, endow them with more innocence and rustic charm than they actually possessed. Yet some facts cannot be gainsaid. We have abundant evidence, from many sources, that in the former Yugoslavia people of different ethnic backgrounds managed not

1

only to co-exist peacefully, but also to interact socially in a variety of ways. Down to the late 1980s, for example, Albanian Muslims made regular pilgrimages to the Serbian Orthodox shrine at Zociste, and were welcomed as decent God-fearing people.[1] And Indonesia, too, has a history of Christian–Muslim amity. The Ambonese, for example, used to speak of themselves as coming from the *satu gandong*—one womb. Malaku had not witnessed bloodshed between Christians and Muslims for centuries. Placed against the backdrop of history, the current spate of violence seems at first sight bizarre, senseless—inexplicable.

Nevertheless there is a school of thought that holds that these out-of-the-blue outbursts of ethno-nationalist violence are comprehensible and rational. The argument runs as follows. Although individuals typically identify themselves with reference to a range of attributes and symbols, the key determinant of group-formation is ethnicity. Language, race and religion are ultimately the ties that bind—and divide. While 'mixed' communities built up upon a perception of shared political or economic interest might prosper for a time, they are inherently unstable, vulnerable to external threat or internal crisis. Ethnic groups, by contrast, are fixed, bounded, eternal formations patiently awaiting their political anointing, which occurs when people come to realise that their interests are better served by identifying with and joining with others culturally similar to themselves. Among scholars of South Asian ethnicity, Francis Robinson is probably the most eloquent exponent of this 'primordialist' viewpoint.[2]

Criticism of the primordialist position focusses principally on its imputation that ethnic groups are more or less homogeneous. In fact, the critics aver, almost all such groups in real life are characterised by wide variations in dialect, belief, ritual, occupation, wealth and taste. But another common criticism is that the primordialist view takes no account of the manifest changes that have occurred in recent time in the composition of many ethnic groups, which would indicate that ethnicity is not fixed by birth or inheritance but is instead rather fluid, a construct subject to changes in the criteria set for membership. Indeed some scholars, the so-called instrumentalists, insist that ethnic formation is an inherently political process occupying three distinct stages: first, the deliberate selection and assertion of one cultural marker, say religion, as *the* distinguishing marker of the group; second, the relegation of any other shared attributes to the domain of the private; and third, the mobilisation, through propaganda and other forms of mass manipulation, of potential constituents.[3] Still, on one matter the primordialists and the instrumentalists are of like mind. Both agree on the importance of ethnic affiliation (real or imagined) as a springboard for collective action in the modern world. Bosnia, Kosovo, Rwanda, Jaffna, Ambon, East Timor are just some of the more recent manifestations of ethnicity's terrible potential to, simultaneously, unite and exclude.

In India the process of ethnic or communal assertion (*communalism*, in local parlance)[4] began early and quickly became widespread: by the early twentieth century there were groupings of 'non-Brahmins', 'martial' Rajputs, Kayasthas, Telugu-speakers, 'tribals' claiming descent from the original inhabitants of the subcontinent, and many others. But from the start, communalism in its South Asian context was associated in particular with ethnic assertion based on the putative ties of religion; and by the 1920s the connection had been narrowed still further. Thereafter the 'communal problem' in India was always identified, both in the popular and the official mind, with 'the Hindu–Muslim problem'.

Needless to say, the dichotomy was an artificial one. As many scholars have pointed out, the terms 'Hindu' and 'Muslim' are little more than crude shorthand labels for two very complex and heterogeneous systems of belief and ritual practice. Even South Asian Muslims—rigorously monotheistic, devoted to one Prophet and one holy book, and mystically linked by the fellowship of the *ummah*—are deeply divided by sect (Sunni/Shi'a) and class (*ashraf/ajlaf*). Hindus, owing allegiance to a variety of gods, sectioned off vertically and horizontally by caste, are still more fractured. As for 'Hinduism', there was not even such a word until the nineteenth century. Yet once Muslim and Hindu elite leaders discovered that it was advantageous, in dealing with the British colonial government, to organise politically along communal lines, all reference to ethno-graphic diversity was conveniently expunged from the political discourse.

Probably the process of ethnic bifurcation began in the 1870s, with attempts by Hindu reformers such as Dayānanda Sarasvatī to revitalise their traditional religion by reducing it to a core of essential truths centred on the *Vedas*. Twenty years later the first Hindu *sabhas* were established in the Punjab, and in 1915 a political party, the All-India Hindu Mahasabha, was founded to represent the interests of a supposedly 'threatened' majority. But for the most part it was the Muslims who made the early running on the issue of communal representation, notably Muslims connected to the circle of Saiyyid Ahmad Khan at Aligarh. By the 1880s, Saiyyid was referring to the South Asian Muslims as a *qaum*, an Arabic word that can be translated either as 'community' or 'nation'. A generation later, a deputation led by the Aga Khan persuaded Lord Minto's government to the point of view that the Muslims constituted a distinct and separate political entity warranting preferential treatment, which resulted in the reservation of special electorates for Muslims in the colonial constitution. By the 1930s these aspirations to separatism had escalated into a demand for a territorial Muslim 'homeland', underpinned by a fully fledged theory of nationhood:

> A [territorial] redistribution of British India, calculated to secure a permanent solution to the communal problem, is the main demand of the Muslims of India.... We are seventy millions and far more homogeneous than any other people in India. Indeed the Muslims are the only Indian people who can fitly be described as a nation in the modern sense of the word.[5]

'Imagined' ethno-nationalist communities, to use Benedict Anderson's evocative term,[6] are, by definition, contestable communities; and invariably they *are* contested. Indeed, the instrumentalists would hold that a measure of confrontation between rival elites competing for territorial space and potential follower-citizens is absolutely integral to the process of ethnic- or nation-formation. Regularly, perhaps ineluctably, therefore, assertions of ethnicity have been accompanied by outbreaks of collective violence.

So it was in the case of India. From the start, the notion of Muslim separatism was hotly contested by the avowedly secularist, but dominantly Hindu and assiduously hegemonic, Indian National Congress (INC): first, at a philosophical and rhetorical level, but later, as the Muslim League became more of a mass-based party, at the grass roots as well. In particular, the Congress after 1940 set its face against any scheme of Muslim separatism that would compromise India's territorial integrity. Nevertheless in the end Congress was prevailed on to accept a scheme of partition which gave the league most, though by no means all, of what it had asked for in its Lahore resolution of 1940. It did so, basically, in the hope that the partition would put a break on Hindu–Muslim communal violence, which by 1947 was threatening to assume the proportions of a holocaust. However the theory that communalism could be eradicated from the Indian body politic by, in Sardar Vallabhbhai Patel's pungent phrase, 'cutting off the diseased limb'—by corralling the Muslims in Pakistan—was fundamentally flawed, if only because it took no account of the 40-odd million Muslims that the partition left stranded in India, people who could not or would not relocate. Whilst Hindu–Muslim communal riots were comparatively infrequent during the first decade or so of independence, the number and intensity of riots started to rise again quite steeply after 1962. In 1975 there were 238 such episodes; in 1983, 500 (Table 1.1). By the 1980s the annual death toll from communal riots was regularly pushing four figures; in 1993 riots claimed more than 3000 lives. More communal riots have occurred in Aligarh since independence than in the whole of the first half of the twentieth century—a statistic that, as Paul Brass notes, makes a mockery of the claim that communalism was simply a product of British divide-and-rule.[7] At first sight, the doleful narrative of post-independence inter-communal relations in India seems to suggest that Hindus and Muslims are doomed by their very nature to wage an endless struggle.

This essentialist view—that Hindus and Muslims were divided by irreconcilable cultural antagonisms—commends itself, however, to few modern scholars working in the South Asian area. Since the 1960s, dozens of field studies of communal riots have been carried out. They suggest that riots are overwhelmingly specific, planned, arguably even staged events that have tended to flourish in particular socio-economic environments, for example large industrial towns. Secondly, the statistical map of riot-distribution, as revealed by figures collected by the Home Ministry, shows that there is a close functional relationship between the intensity of riots and the prevailing socio-political ethos. As we have seen, riots were relatively rare in the post-partition period, but have increased in number and intensity every decade since. In particular, there was

Table 1.1 Major communal clashes in selected states, 1962/63–1986/87

	1962/63		1966/67		1970/71		1978/79		1986/87	
	I	D	I	D	I	D	I	D	I	D
Andhra Pradesh	12	–	582	13	34	na	59	na	82	17
Assam	49	14	25	1	56	na	27	na	23	8
Bihar	27	2	679	197	145	na	77	na	171	74
Gujarat	24	1	4	–	47	na	48	na	288	205
Jammu and Kashmir	–	–	–	–	1	na	2	na	24	2
Kerala	1	3	6	2	19	na	21	na	52	5
Madhya Pradesh	12	1	37	25	65	na	34	na	90	25
Maharashtra	47	11	411	38	199	na	29	na	164	76
Rajasthan	2	–	46	1	23	na	14	na	50	5
Uttar Pradesh	43	12	176	26	91	na	91	na	168	193
West Bengal	110	24	51	11	90	na	39	na	146	47
India	349	72	2035	295	842	401	534	368	1475	801

I = number of incidents; D = number of deaths
Sources: Krishna, 'Communal Violence In India', pp. 64, 71; *Muslim India*, Vol. 76 (1989), p. 419; Asghar Ali Engineer (ed.), *Communal Riots in Post-Independence India* (Bombay, 1984), pp. 54–5.

a very sudden rise during the late 1980s and the early 1990s. This would indicate that the socio-political climate of India in recent times has become more encouraging of communal confrontation.

How so? During the 1980s, a number of developments served to foment a climate of resentment towards Indian Muslims among sections of the country's Hindu population, especially the middle and 'Other Backward' castes (OBCs). Most commentators agree, however, that the most important change has been the emergence of the Hindu Right as a powerful and assertive force on the Indian political scene. Cobbled together in 1980 from the rump of the Bharatiya Jana Sangh (BJS), the Bharatiya Janata Party (BJP) did little in its first few years to indicate that it would improve upon the electoral performance of its predecessor. In 1984 it held just two Lok Sabha seats, and only 148 Vidhan Sabha seats across the country. But by the end of the decade it had increased its share of parliamentary seats to 85, and had become the majority party in several northern states (Table 1.2). Arguably, these electoral gains were achieved largely as a consequence of the BJP's adoption after 1984, under the presidency of Lal Kishanchand Advani, of a more overtly Hindu platform and campaigning style, epitomised by its choice of the lotus flower as its election symbol, by Advani's flamboyant cross-country *yātrā* (pilgrimage) in September 1990 in a Toyota truck decked out as an Aryan chariot,[8] and by the party's support for the campaign of the Vishwa Hindu Parishad

Table 1.2 BJS/BJP vote share, Lok Sabha polls, 1957/71–1984/99 (per cent)

Year	Gujarat	Madhya Pradesh	Rajasthan	Uttar Pradesh	Bihar	India
1957	–	14.0	11.1	14.8	0.1	5.9
1962	1.4	17.9	9.3	17.7	2.3	6.4
1967	[39.9]*	26.6	10.3	22.2	11.1	9.4
1971	7.7	33.6	12.4	12.3	12.1	7.4
1984	18.6	30.0	23.7	6.4	6.9	7.4
1989	30.5	39.7	29.6	7.6	13.0	11.4
1991	50.4	41.9	40.9	33.0	16.0	19.9
1996	48.5	41.3	42.4	33.4	20.5	6.5
1998	48.3	45.7	41.7	36.5	24.0	25.6
1999	52.5	46.6	47.2	27.3	23.0	23.8

* Vote share received by the Swatantra Party. Under an electoral arrangement, the BJP stood no candidates in Gujarat in 1967 and lent its support to SP candidates.
Sources: Butler, Lahiri and Roy, *India Decides*, pp. 98–9; Nandy *et al.*, *Fear of the Self*, pp. 73, 75; Malik and Singh, *Hindu Nationalism*, pp. 186–7; *Economic and Political Weekly*; *Frontline*; *Hindustan Times*; *India Today*; Election Commission of India website, http://eci.gov.in, accessed 21 February 2003.

(VHP) to build a Hindu temple on the site of the Babri Masjid at Ayodhya, a site sacred to Hindus as the birthplace of the god-king Rama. In the 1989 parliamentary elections, fought at the height of the VHP's 'Ram Shila Puja' campaign, in which bricks hand-crafted by devotees were carried in a series of much-publicised ceremonial processions to the Ayodhya site, the BJP's national vote went up by 4 per cent (7.4–11.5 per cent), enough to secure it 83 additional seats in the Lok Sabha.

The thesis that the upsurge of Hindu–Muslim communal riots in the late 1980s was closely bound up with the rise of the Hindu Right has a solid empirical foundation. Wherever the VHP–BJP 'Ramjanmabhumi' movement took hold in Rajasthan, riots broke out: in Beawar in 1986, in Mekrana and Tonk in 1988, in Kotah, Fathepur, Udaipur and Jaipur in 1989. The Jaipur outbreak, Shail Mayaram shows, was triggered specifically by a BJP victory procession following the general election.[9] Likewise, riots 'in many areas followed directly on the passage of the VHP's *rath yatra*'.[10] The evidence suggests that the manipulation of religious issues by the BJP has been—for the country if not for the party—a very costly electoral strategy.

Nevertheless, the links between the growth of communal violence and the rise of the Hindu Right may not be as straightforward as some commentators have proposed. For one thing, BJP rule at state level has not always led to an upsurge of rioting. In fact, rather the opposite is true. During the 20 months of V.P. Singh's Congress government in Uttar Pradesh, from 1980 to 1982, there were ten riots; during the 14-month tenure of the Kalyan Singh's BJP ministry, from 1991 to 1992, just one. During the lead-up to the 1998 elections, the editor of a prominent Urdu daily claimed that 'the fact that no riots had taken place in BJP-ruled states' was one reason why 'a section of Muslims' had indicated their intention to vote for the BJP rather than the Congress.[11] Conversely, communal riots do not necessarily translate into BJP seats. Against expectations, the BJP vote in Uttar Pradesh in 1993 went down, confirming exit polls that showed that the Ramjanmabhumi issue was not a top priority with most Uttar Pradesh voters. Moreover, communalism as an explanation of the BJP's success does not sit easily with what the electoral data reveals about the regional configuration of the party's support base. As Tables 1.2 and 1.3 make clear, the BJP, like its predecessor the BJS, has always struggled in Haryana and Bihar, while its vote share in other northern states has fluctuated. On the other hand, since 1951–52 the BJS and the BJP have scored consistently well in Rajasthan and Madhya Pradesh (MP), while since the 1990s the BJP has enjoyed quite spectacular success in Gujarat. For instance, at the 1991 Lok Sabha poll

Table 1.3   BJS/BJP vote share, Vidhan Sabha polls, 1957–98 (per cent)

Year	Gujarat	Madhya Pradesh	Rajasthan	Uttar Pradesh	Bihar	India
1957	–	9.8	5.4	9.8	1.2	3.1
1962	1.3	16.7	9.2	16.5	2.8	5.0
1967	1.9	28.3	11.7	21.7	16.4	9.1
1972/74	9.3	28.7	12.2	17.1	11.7	10.6
1980	14.0	30.7	18.6	10.8	8.4	10.0
1985	15.0	32.4	21.2	9.9	7.5	11.3
1990	27.7	39.2	25.2	11.6	11.0	15.1
1991/93	42.5	39.0	39.5	33.4	13.0	26.3
1996/98	44.8	39.3	33.2	32.5	13.0	23.6

Sources: Singh and Bose, *State Elections in India*; Nandy *et al.*, *Fear of the Self*, pp. 73–4; Malik and Singh, *Hindu Nationalism*, pp. 182–4, 209; *EPW*; *Frontline*; *Hindustan Times*; *India Today*; *Organiser*; Election Commission of India website, http://eci.gov.in, accessed 21 February 2003.

the BJP gained vote shares in these states of between 41 and 50 per cent, compared to an all-India average of 20 per cent. Likewise the BJS's best-ever result was achieved in MP—78 seats and 28.3 per cent of the vote in the 1967 Vidhan Sabha poll.

The problem here is that neither Rajasthan nor MP has a notable history of Hindu–Muslim conflict. Certainly Jaipur exploded in 1989; but this was exceptional. Figures on riot deaths published by the Home Ministry show Rajasthan ranks a low 11th among the states of the Union; while MP comes in a moderate seventh. Even Gujarat, which, on the face of it, particularly in the light of the holocaust of 2002, seems to have a very bad record in respect of communal violence, has suffered relatively few *incidents* of this nature since 1950. According to Ashutosh Varshney, for 25 of 46 years between 1950 and 1995, Gujarat had no riots or very few incidents of communal violence.[12] Gujarat's outbreaks have been severe—but infrequent. And most of that state's really big riots have occurred in just one location, Ahmedabad. Significantly, for the thesis being advanced in this book, communal riots have rarely afflicted the western part of the state—Saurashtra. Once we factor Ahmedabad out of the equation, we get a riot profile for Gujarat that bears a much closer approximation to those of Rajasthan and MP.

In current writing about Indian communalism the state is generally held to be an active force in the creation of communal conflict. Governments in India, the argument runs, being in the last resort dependent on the favour of the electorate, are compelled to compete fiercely and continuously for public support, and for a long time it has been accepted by politicians in South Asia that appeals to ethnic solidarities and prejudices are a fairly sure-fire way to marshal votes. Between times, it is said, Indian politicians find it convenient to keep the social pot simmering, for the more society is riven by violence, the easier it is for the politicians to argue the need for a strong governmental presence for the protection of the weak. But just as it is hard to prove a direct link between the recent upsurge of communal violence in India and the rise to power of the BJP, so the notion that the state in the abstract is necessarily and has always been a divisive factor in communal relationships is open to question. On the fact of it, the BJS/BJP would seem to have prospered in a region with a relatively benign communal history. If this is so, it would suggest, first, that even BJP-ruled states do not always actively promote communalism as a tool of governance, and secondly, and more importantly, that it may, in fact, be within the capacity of states, so minded, to actually ameliorate the intensity of communal conflict among their citizens: 'riots can be prevented and controlled', avers Brass, 'when the political will ... exists'.[13] Clearly this is an issue worth further investigation.

Early twentieth-century India represents an ideal testing ground. In the British Raj, India had a government that was avowedly secular in its aims and prided itself on its 'neutrality' in matters of religion. At the same time large areas of India—the 'princely states'—had rulers who were, by definition, practising Hindus and Muslims. The princely *darbārs* may have been, in many cases, even-handed, but they were certainly not secular governments in the sense that the Raj was. Moreover the 'two Indias' were markedly different polities. By the early twentieth century, representative institutions were well established in British India, particularly at the local and provincial levels. Until almost the end of the colonial period the majority of the states remained unrepentantly autocratic. An analysis that compared the communal record of the states and the provinces could help to settle the issue of whether elections make a difference. More broadly, it could tell us a lot about the roles that governments and governing systems play in the genesis of collective violence. So far, however, the communal life of the princely states has been scarcely studied. Dick Kooiman has done some interesting work on the South,[14] comparing Travancore's, Hyderabad's and Baroda's records in respect of communalism, but three states (albeit three of the biggest) among 600 is not a sufficient sample to sustain generalisations about princely India as a communal phenotype. There are also compelling reasons why the sample *should* include a large slice of the northern Indian states, which I shall revert to later.

Patterns of riots

As British official sources attest, Hindu–Muslim collective violence was clearly a fact of life in colonial India long before it became a 'problem' in the eyes of the colonial authorities.

But what of the situation before the British took over? Were the riots of the nineteenth century simply a continuation of an old feud, or something new, a *product* even of the colonial nexus? For a long time the latter view held sway. Among the post-independence generation of Indian historians, it was almost an article of faith that the British actively and consciously cultivated religious divisions and tensions (for example, by conceding separate electorates to Muslims) in order to justify keeping the reins of power firmly in their 'impartial' hands. Likewise, scholarly opinion in the 1970s and early 1980s, while more willing to acknowledge the contribution of Indian agency to the souring of Hindu–Muslim relations, did not, by and large, disagree with the proposition that communalism was fundamentally a modern phenomenon—a product of the ferocious elite competition unleashed by the open-market policies and administrative mechanisms of the colonial government. As Bipan Chandra puts it,

> communalism and its growth were products of the Indian social, economic and political developments and conditions during the nineteenth and twentieth centuries. Economic backwardness, interests of the semi-feudal jagirdari classes and strata, the precarious economic condition of the middle classes, social cleavages within Indian society . . . and the ideological-political weaknesses of the nationalist forces – all combined to promote communalism or to weaken the struggle against it. . . . But, above all, the social framework for the growth of communalism was provided by the colonial economy and polity. Colonialism was the foundation of the social structure which generated and then propelled forward communal ideology and politics.[15]

More recently, however, some scholars have sought to change the parameters of the debate by suggesting that Hindu–Muslim conflict was already endemic in South Asia by the time the British arrived on the scene. Addressing himself to what he terms the 'pre-history' of communalism, Christopher Bayly argues convincingly that the numerous Hindu–Muslim–Sikh conflicts of the eighteenth century, conventionally portrayed by Indian historians as 'wars', 'bear a very close resemblance to the riots of the later colonial period' and can justifiably be regarded as communal encounters.[16] But whereas Bayly is concerned to understand how these outbreaks occurred 'in a predominantly syncretic culture',[17] other revisionists have rejected even this long-held assumption. Cynthia Keppley-Mahmood asserts: 'Recognition... of the very important ways in which politics shape community affiliation... need not lead us to the rote claim that without modern politics there would be no... communal conflict.'[18] Achin Vanaik agrees. Drawing a sharp distinction between religious pluralism, which he equates with the mere co-existence of variant beliefs, and true tolerance, which for him depends on an active dialogue between them, Vanaik suggests that Hinduism has always been arrogantly essentialist, uninterested in dialogue except to assert the primacy of its own mystical insights.[19] Similarly, while acknowledging, with Vanaik, the pluralist tendencies in South Asian religious life, Peter van der Veer takes pains to emphasise the very defined limits to that syncretic tradition. Hindus, he notes, can and do participate in the rite of '*urs* at the tombs of Sufi saints, 'but the participation of Hindus in the celebration is restricted'. Conversely, 'Muslims can and do participate in Hindu festivals. They can and do seek the blessings of powerful gurus... but they cannot go into a temple or worship an image without losing their identity as Muslims.'[20]

In the light of this new work it is clear that communalism in India arose not, as Chandra claims, 'in the last quarter of the nineteenth century',[21] but very much earlier. Secondly, the revisionists have effectively demolished the romantic notion that, prior to the coming of the British, the prevalence of tolerant attitudes towards variant beliefs ensured complete harmony between Hindus and Muslims. Nevertheless there is a danger in this revisionist enterprise of *over*-correction, of pushing the pendulum too far the other way. Although we now know that communal riots were a regular occurrence throughout the nineteenth century, the official record indicates that they remained, until late in the piece, relatively unusual events. Thereafter, they became much more commonplace. From 1870 to 1921 there were 34 serious disturbances—an average of about one every two years. From 1923 to 1928 there were 112 major riots—an average of about 20 per year. Even allowing for an element of bias in these figures due to changing reportage protocols on the part of British officials, they bespeak a revolution in Indian social and religious life. By the second decade of the twentieth century the country clearly had an epidemic on its hands.

That said, though, we need to remember that epidemics are by nature selective in their virulence. Communalism's progress in India was chronologically steady but spatially uneven. Broadly speaking, it took root first in the coastal cities (like Calcutta) and the big riverine towns (like Benares). Thereafter, it spread up-country to the smaller market towns and urban villages and (at a still later stage) to the countryside. However, not all parts of the hinterland were equally affected. Some areas succumbed quickly; others—including inexplicably some towns with considerable Muslim minorities—appear to have remained virtually riot-free throughout the entire colonial period and beyond. Bijnor, for example, unpromisingly situated in the heart of riot-torn western UP, managed to buck the odds until October 1990.[22] What is more, riots, when they occurred, remained for the most part localised. Neighbouring *mohullas* might erupt, but almost never whole towns. Looking back on his childhood years in Bihar, the eminent Congressman Rajendra Prasad recalls: 'there was perfect harmony between Hindus and Muslims. Muslims would join Hindus in the boisterous festival of Holi. On the occasion of Dasahra, Diwali and Holi, the Maulavi would compose special verses.'[23] 'In my home town in the Punjab', writes historian Bipan Chandra, 'it was usual for the Hindu middle class families to send Diwali sweets to their middle class Muslim friends. The latter in turn sent Id sweets.'[24] If these and other similar stories are to be believed, there were still pockets of Hindu–Muslim amity to be found in India even in the strife-filled decades of the 1920s and 1930s.

But were they few and concentrated in just a couple of spots, or many and geographically dispersed? Important as this question is, one can only conjecture an answer. My guess is that overt antagonism between Hindus and Muslims during the colonial period was, indeed, far more the exception than the rule. But a definitive assessment will not be possible until more systematic work is done in the archives. So far, nearly all the work that has been done on the 'rise' of communalism has been area-specific; and that too has been concerned more with finding reasons (or apportioning blame) than in analysing the process by which communalism was reproduced/transmitted. Moreover, these histories are limited in their geographical compass. As noted above,[25] they are all, explicitly or implicitly, studies of the communal situation in British India. The neglect of the princely states means that about a third of the subcontinent has been left out of account. This constitutes a very substantial *lacuna*, not simply because of the size of the area involved, but because, as indicated above, the states and the provinces were vastly different types of political arenas.

The problem

When I ask people about the antecedents of Hindu–Muslim communal conflict in their neighbourhood, a common response is 'there was none'. As an old Bikaner retainer informed me, with some vehemence, 'There was no Hindu–Muslim trouble here [before 1947]—nothing. Everybody lived in peace.'[26] One finds the same line, too, in press reports, an article on a riot at Ajmer in February 1998 expressing surprise that this had occurred in a town 'known for its communal peace'.[27] Not surprisingly, these folksy recollections are often at variance with the information contained in the written record. But even where the archives are silent, we tend to remain sceptical of assessments that seem so obviously utilitarian, so obviously tied to the construction of a 'usable' past that people today can live with. Like the Jeffreys, who were 'repeatedly told that Bijnor had never suffered from communal violence' prior to 1990,[28] we are tempted to dismiss such reports as mythological. There 'has never been a period in modern Indian history, most especially in the north, when Hindu–Muslim riots have not occurred', Brass asserts confidently.[29] However, in respect of princely north India, the 'myth' appears to have a solid kernel of truth.

Certainly, the claim was widely asserted, at the time, by people who were in a position to know. 'As in this State, so in the States generally', opined Bikaner's Maharaja Ganga Singh in an address to mark the 1932 New Year, 'the communal question does not really exist; and I cannot conceive of any Prince—Hindu or Moslem—who would like to see this evil brought into ... the States.'[30] Testifying a few weeks later before the Round Table Consultative Committee, veteran Baroda Chief Minister Sir Manubhai Mehta declared: 'this communal question has never entered into the arena of State politics ... They are altogether innocent of these differences.'[31] 'There is no boast', averred Maharaja Bhom Pal of Karauli, 'when I say that my state has never witnessed ugly scenes of communal trouble.'[32] Of course the princes were partial witnesses. But many princely subjects privately voiced similar sentiments. 'Uptill [*sic*] recently', a Barwani man informed Congress supremo M.K. Gandhi in 1947, 'no one [in the state] knew what the communal problem was. The Hindus and Muslims [here] were living like brothers.'[33] And the Mahatma got a similar message from Patiala journalist R.S. Azad: 'Before the [recent] [in]flow of outsiders to Patiala State there existed no communalism. The Hindus, the Sikhs, the Muslims and the Christians all used to live as one happy family.'[34] Last but not least, the *darbāri* claim was widely accepted by contemporary British observers, including Sir John Simon's Statutory Commission of 1927.

'Communalism', as the suffix suggests, is a mental construct—a way of looking at the world. In the sense that it is commonly understood in South Asia, the term describes a mode of thinking that holds religious affiliation to be the primary marker of identity. Tracing the growth of mentalities, as such, is difficult; however, their manifestations in action are, to some extent, amenable to empirical inquiry. In its most virulent form, communalism in India manifests itself in episodes of collective violence—'riots' in official parlance—and these—in theory—can be tracked and quantified. To be sure, the evidence currently to hand on communal riots in South Asia is rather fragmentary. There is not, for example, as one might have expected, any single official report that summarises the death and injury toll from communal violence for British India—not even for the late colonial period when the problem weighed heavily on the official mind. There are good data for the 1920s in the files of the Home Department and in the volumes of the Statutory Commission *Report* (*SCR*), and some useful figures for the late 1930s in Coupland's *Indian Politics*, but nothing approaching a full accounting. By comparison, statistical information for the princely states is still patchier. Consequently, the findings summarised in Table 1.4 and Figures 1.1 and 1.2 had to be constructed pretty much from the ground up, by way, mainly, of English-language press reports. As a number of people have reminded me, this is not by any means a foolproof method.[35]

But then, even the official records cannot be trusted in this matter. As the Government of Bengal pointed out in defence of an incomplete return of riots from 1924 to 1926, many small affrays simply do not get reported;[36] people injured in riots are sometimes not hospitalised, and therefore not counted; and the police have a vested interest in minimising casualty figures. Conversely, some reported incidents are wholly fictitious, trumped up to show the other community in a bad light. As the chief police in Jodhpur noted of one such report, involving broken idols, 'there is no evidence whatsoever to show all this was done by Mohamedans'.[37]

Even if one allows a wide margin for error, however, the thrust of the statistical evidence seems incontrovertible: it lends solid support to the claim that communal violence was less endemic in the territories of the princes. According to the 1941 Indian census, the population of princely India was 93.2 millions and that of British India 258.8 millions. On that basis, one would expect the provinces to have suffered approximately two and three-quarters more carnage from communal conflict than the states. In fact, depending on whether one is counting injuries or deaths, they suffered between 12 and 13 times more! Further, in so far as the two sets of figures are closer together in respect of incidents than casualties, we may conclude that communal conflict was not only more widespread in the provinces than in the states, but on

Table 1.4   Major Hindu–Muslim communal clashes in India, 1920–40

Year	Incidents		Killed		Injured	
	P	S	P	S	P	S
1920	1	–	–	–	–	1
1921	4	2	8	1	29	6
1922	4	–	15	–	172	–
1923	13	2	21	6	518	7
1924	23	3	88	5	849	32
1925	20	–	25	–	987	–
1926	33	8	292	3	1878	80
1927	41	3	199	9	1510	35
1928	14	3	167	1	975	163
1929	12	3	186	6	1020	66
1930	14	2	66	–	347	3
1931	27	4	360	12	2645	20
1932	6	9	235	28	2726	363
1933	6	7	10	16	59	52
1934	6	5	16	21	80	71
1935	8	5	71	14	223	110
1936	6	1	99	–	791	–
1937	22	5	30	19	180	115
1938	24	3	59	7	540	203
1939	39	8	306	18	1331	78
1940	5	5	10	6	31	42
Total	322	79	2273	172	16891	1447

P = provinces; S = states
Sources: Coupland, *Indian Politics*, pp. 11, 35, 47n, 48–9, 69–70, 130–1, 131n; *SCR*, Vol. 1, pp. 27–8, 253, Vol. 4, pp. 108–20, Vol. 6, pp. 586–99, and Vol. 7, pp. 233–8; Home (Pol.) file 249/XI of 1924; IOR R/1/1/1404, R/1/1/1448, R/1/1/1570, R/1/1/2035 (1); PSA, Patiala, Ijlas-i-Khas, file 2051; RSAB, Bikaner, Home Dept, file 67/1932; RSAB, Jodhpur, Social, C 2/21 of 1928–46; *The New York Times* 1920–40; *The Times* (London) 1920–40; *The Times of India (TOI)* (Bombay) 1920–40.

balance more severe. This dichotomy has yet to register with most scholars of communalism in South Asia, yet it demands an explanation. This book seeks to offer one.

Yet the statistics also point up another problem. Note that after 1929, the difference between the columns in Table 1.4 begins to narrow.[38] As we shall discover in Chapter 4, the 'gap' between princely and British India in respect of their exposure to communal violence continued to shrink during the early 1940s. By 1947, at the time of partition, the scale of Hindu–Muslim mayhem in some parts of princely north India would rival and even exceed that experienced by the northern provinces. It

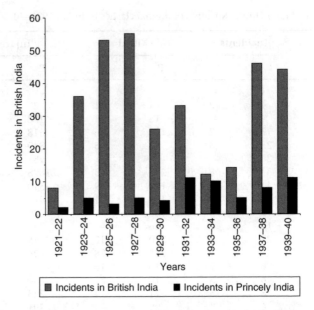

Figure 1.1 Major Hindu–Muslim communal incidents in India, 1921/22–1939/40.

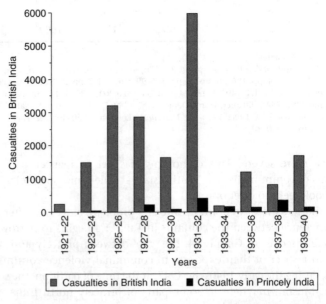

Figure 1.2 Casualties in major Hindu–Muslim communal incidents in India, 1921/22–1939/40.

would appear that, in so far as the states at large enjoyed a relative 'immunity' from communal conflict during the late colonial period, this immunity was a depreciating asset. As well as looking to understand what protected the states, in the early decades of the twentieth century, from outbreaks of communal violence, we will also need to discover why the magic gradually lost its potency.

The argument

It is not that princely India lacked sites and occasions for religious contestation between Hindus (or Sikhs) and Muslims. In Dera Bassi, Kalsia, for example, the Muslim festival of Mohurrum, in which participants mourn the martyrdom of Imam Hussain, son of the fourth Khalif, was a perennial source of trouble. Mohurrum culminates with a procession in which 'mourners' carry elaborate wood and paper *tazias* modelled after the tombs of the Imam and his family, and for the most part Hindus are content to look on and delight in the holiday spectacle. However, in Dera Bassi the route traditionally followed by the procession took it along a street bordered by three trees sacred to the local Hindus. Each year some Muslims would try to lop the overhanging branches of one of these trees, a *pipal*, to facilitate the passage of their *tazias*, and each year some Hindus would band together to stop them. Sometimes the standoff would escalate into a scuffle requiring police intervention.[39] Mohurrum regularly posed problems, too, for the authorities in Sawai Madhopur in Jaipur. In this case the traditional processional route passed within a few feet of an image of the god Balaji, and it became the habit of local Hindus to display a large saffron flag on top of the Balaji when the *tazias* went by. The Muslims interpreted this action—correctly—as a symbolic challenge.[40]

Another issue that frequently triggered altercations between Hindus and Muslims in the states was the playing of music and the singing of bawdy songs (as often happened during the celebration of the Hindu Holi festival). Thus in May 1935, early evening prayers at the Lohar's mosque in Malerkotla were interrupted by the sounds of a *katha*, or musical recitation of the *Rāmāyana*, being staged for the benefit of a sick Hindu woman in the upper storey of a nearby shop; and in July 1935 Magrib (sunset) prayers at the Weavers' Mosque in the same town were disturbed by a noisy sunset Arti being performed by Brahmins in the Chaudhri's Temple down the road.[41] And cow killing by Muslims was yet a further source of trouble. Sometimes just the perception that an animal was slated to become meat at a Muslim's table was enough to spark trouble. Last but not least, the official files of the states are replete with cases involving disputes between Hindus and Muslims about rights over ritual objects and spaces. In Lalsot, Jaipur, the two communities jostled for access to a *chhabutra* or platform which, though located within the precincts of a Hindu temple, was coveted by local Muslims as a site for *namaz*;[42] while in Sarwar, Kishengarh, Hindus connected to the Sithala temple and the Muslim custodians of the Dargah of Khwaja Fakruddin Chishti fought to exclude each other's constituents from using a communal well located in the middle of their shared compound.[43] It would appear, on this reckoning, that there was every bit as much potential for overt Hindu–Muslim conflict in the states as there was in the provinces.

Nevertheless *The Times* read the signs wrongly when it opined smugly in 1924 that 'expressions of fanaticism' were as 'possible in any of the cities of the feudatory princes as they are in Agra or Multan'.[44] Although religious differences *per se* may have been no less acute in princely than in British India, the evidence of the statistics summarised in Table 1.4 is that they rarely resulted, before the 1930s, in displays of communal aggression serious enough to cause personal injury. Were princely subjects, then, more tolerant of communal differences?

[margin note: IMPOR - TANT.]

I have heard much personal testimony to this effect. A former Hindu subject of Patiala assured me: 'Yes, I had Muslim friends, lots of them.'[45] In Kota several informants told me that in the old days Muslims would greet Hindus in the street with clasped hands and the cry of 'Jai Ram!' as a gesture of respect.[46] Another Patiala man that I talked to, a Sikh this time, recalled with great warmth his adolescent friendship in Nabha with a Muslim boy from a neighbouring family, adding that on Fridays he would often give the lad a lift to the local mosque on his bicycle.[47] And one finds similar sentiments expressed in letters and memoirs. 'There is no bitterness in this ilaqa', affirmed Chaudhury Abdul Aziz of Begowal, Kapurthala, in 1936. 'Our relations with the Sikhs are [as those] of brethren.'[48] However, there is a limit to how far one can push such idiosyncratic data. There is a tendency in interviews for people to tell you what they think you want to hear. Besides, as we saw earlier, nostalgic stories of toleration are also commonplace in the literature of late colonial British India, supposedly by this time a cauldron of communalism.

More convincing is the evidence from the archives about the way Hindus and Muslims in the states handled communal problems when they arose. Overwhelmingly, local religious disputes were settled through negotiation. In 1935 some Muslims living in Annandpura Kalu village, Jodhpur, announced that they wanted to construct a mosque. The Hindus of the village objected to the chosen site, which abutted a

Hindu neighbourhood and was only a hundred metres from a cluster of temples. However, the leaders of the communities got together and after an amicable discussion, the Muslims agreed to construct the mosque at another site on land offered for the purpose by the Hindus.[49] Two years later, another potentially explosive wrangle about sacred space in Jodhpur, this time involving a temple in the town of Mekrana, was resolved when the Hindu management committee agreed 'not to place an idol at the place in dispute or to play any kind of musical instrument there'.[50] Again, the archival record indicates that princely subjects thrust into situations of confrontation over matters of religious belief or ritual generally exercised restraint. Not only was there widespread acknowledgement among Hindus in the princely states that 'Mussalmans need absolute silence when they offer their prayers',[51] but most showed themselves willing to accommodate Muslim objections by diverting their religious and marriage processions away from mosques and regulating their hours of religious worship so as not to coincide with Islamic prayer times. In July 1928 Muslim worship at a mosque in Bawal town, Nabha, was interrupted by band music from two passing Hindu marriage parties. But the Muslims, although annoyed, did not react violently; they merely requested the Hindus to stop. The latter in the same spirit 'quietly consented to their request', and afterwards tendered a formal apology for their rudeness to the town's Muslim leaders, who in reply assured them 'that there was not the least chance of any fracas'.[52] Similarly, Hindus and Muslims in the states appear to have made a genuine effort to accommodate one another's prejudices in the matter of animal slaughter. For decades cows were routinely killed in Mangrol, and until the 1930s no objection was raised. According to the local Muslims, this was because their Hindu neighbours understood and accepted that beef represented the only kind of meat many poor Muslims could afford to buy.[53] Conversely, Muslim butchers in Malerkotla did not object to closing their shops during the annual Samatsari festival of the Jains, to whom all killing is repugnant.[54]

Moreover when religious disputes did spill over into violence, the mayhem was usually short-lived and rarely resulted in a lasting falling out between the communities. In September 1926 an argument broke out in the *bazaar* at Nathdwara, Udaipur, between a Bohra Muslim shopkeeper and some Hindus who believed they had been given short weights. As other Bohra merchants rushed to the assistance of their co-religionist, nearby Hindus came to the aid of the aggrieved customers. In no time at all the two groups were hard at it, kicking and punching. By the time the police arrived some 40 people were nursing bruised heads and broken limbs and about Rs 6000 damage had been done to the Bohras' shops. Nevertheless, after a few days the two sides agreed to bury the hatchet with an exchange of apologies.[55] Similarly, a potentially serious situation loomed at Sultanpur Lodi, Kapurthala in 1932 when someone, presumed to be a Sikh, set fire to the door of the village mosque, but trouble was averted when the elders of the Sikh community in Sultanpur publicly apologised for the incident and collected money to repair the damage.[56]

Interviewing people from disadvantaged urban neighbourhoods in Australia in the early 1990s, Mark Peel found many of them to be deeply intolerant of other ethnic groups, and especially of 'immigrants'. This was not unexpected. What surprised him was that this 'abstract intolerance' did not inhibit community members of different backgrounds from working and even socialising together. In the end, Peel concludes, it is peoples' innate capacity for 'concrete tolerance' which holds community life together.[57] Something similar seems to have obtained in the villages and *mohullas* of princely India. Hindus and Muslims in these communities did not fraternise much, and sometimes made rude remarks about one another; but they were able, for the most part, to put aside their differences at least to the point of avoiding open conflict.

But if that is so, why were princely Indians apparently more willing to exercise restraint than British Indians—people who in their biological and psychological makeup were essentially the same? Since it cannot have been a function of instinct, or human nature, it must have been a matter of culture and political economy. How—if indeed at all—did the princely states and the provinces of British India differ in respect of each of these variables?

The ur-question that analysts of communal riots in South Asia need to ask of their data is, why here and not there? As Table 1.4 shows, even in the halcyon 1920s the princely states of north India were not entirely free from communal violence. Several riots punctuated the peace of the 1920s, of which the biggest and most destructive was the 1927 outbreak in Indore, in Central India (CI). Why did Indore fall prey to violence even as other princely capitals in the region remained quiet? Examining this event in some detail will help us understand what made that city vulnerable. Once we know that, we should be ready to frame some working hypotheses about the states' relative freedom from communal violence in late colonial India: about the sources of this comparative immunity, and about the factors and processes that led to them becoming less effective in the 1930s and 1940s.

Indore City was simultaneously the political capital of the Holkar State of Indore and a major industrial centre. Hence while Indore was a Hindu kingdom populated predominately by Hindus, the capital had a significant leavening of Muslim artisans and textile factory workers. In total, about 21 per cent of the townspeople were Muslims (Table 2.6).

As a mill-town, Indore was accustomed to outbreaks of industrial unrest—but until 1927 these largely Muslim protests did not take on a communal complexion. Conversely, the town's Hindus seem not to have viewed the Muslims, before 1927, as a collectivity—certainly as one to be feared or resisted. In 1926, however, an event occurred that appears to have triggered a shift in this benign attitude—the murder in Delhi of the revered leader of the Arya Samaj, Swāmī Shraddhānanda, by a deranged Muslim. Luridly written up in the local Hindi press, the incident sent a shock wave through the state's Hindu community, and thousands of Hindus came from far and wide to pay their respects at a series of 'condolence' meetings organised by the Indore branch of the Samaj. At these meetings, they heard speeches accusing Muslims, as a group, of conspiring against the Hindu religion. Understandably local Muslims were deeply offended by these attacks, and when they showed no signs of slackening, a deputation of community leaders led by Maulvi Abdul Gani of the Jama Masjid approached the government to have the meetings stopped. To their dismay, however, the authorities refused to intervene on the disingenuous plea that the meetings were 'religious'. When news of this got around, Muslims in several quarters of the city vented their frustration in noisy anti-*darbāri* demonstrations. Much of this spleen was focussed on Thakur Balwant Singh, the Subah (governor) of the city of Indore, who had overall responsibility for licensing public gatherings. Earlier Singh had refused to prohibit the playing of music before the mosque in Nayapura, the district in which his residence was situated.[58]

This went on for several weeks. Then on 14 February 1927, some female relations of Thakur Balwant Singh, and their servants, went for *puja* to Juna Thopkhana. Around noon they set out for home in three open cars, singing lustily as they motored along. As the convoy passed the Nayapura mosque, around 40 Muslims ran out and began throwing stones and brickbats at the cars, before pursuing them to Balwant Singh's house, which was situated about 400 metres further down the road. Frightened for their lives, the Hindu women scurried inside. Outside, the Muslim mob torched the Thakur's outhouses and one member of the crowd fired a muzzle-loading gun at the house. However, the mob was kept at bay by the Thakur's retainers who kept up a steady returning fire. Meanwhile, news of the encounter was relayed 'by runners and by bicycle riders' to other parts of the city. When the news reached Abdul Gani at Hadni Chowki, he was heard to instruct several Muslims there to hasten to Nayapura 'and kill the Kafirs'.[59] Later the Maulvi was seen giving a sign to a mob of Muslims outside the City Hospital.[60] Soon the crowd at Nayapura had been swelled by the addition of over 2000 Muslim mill-hands. While some of them stood guard at the entrances to the *mohulla*, others launched indiscriminate attacks on its non-Muslim inhabitants, one of whom—an employee of the Fire Department—was stabbed and killed while eating a meal. By evening nine people (one Sikh, one Christian, three Hindus and four Muslims) had been killed and over 40 others (again, mostly Muslims) seriously wounded. For the next two days, 'wild rumours' circulated by 'mischief-mongers' intent on 'creating a panic' flooded the city; a further wave of stabbings ensued, resulting in four deaths and 30 injuries. However, there were no fresh outbreaks of mob violence, and by the evening of 15 February the authorities had regained control of the town. A sweep of the haunts of known troublemakers over the next few days resulted in 200 arrests and a haul of 'several hundreds' of knives and lathis. After questioning the accused, the police concluded that at least 3000 people had taken an active part in the riots.[61]

This short narrative brims with clues as to why Indore became a riot scene while other places in princely north India remained quiet. With a population of just under 100,000 in 1921, Indore was a large town by contemporary princely standards (in the North, only Jaipur was bigger), and relatively well connected to the metropolitan centres of Bombay, Agra, Delhi and Cawnpore by main-line rail. Its residents had access to several local newspapers and all the major north Indian dailies, although the latter sometimes took up to a week to arrive. It even had a branch of the Punjab-based Arya Samaj. Unlike the majority of north Indian states at this time, Indore was plugged into the sectarian politics of British India; thus the excitement over the death of Shraddhānanda. And it was an industrial town. It had a substantial proletariat—a pool of marginalised factory workers available (and in many cases probably eager) to be mobilised for action at the behest of people like Maulvi Abdul Gani. In short, Indore possessed many of the ingredients that scholars think are conducive to outbreaks of collective violence. In today's parlance we would say that it was a riot-prone environment. This being so, it seems reasonable to conclude that a lack or absence of these same incendiary ingredients—factories, newspapers, missionary organizations, a significant minority population of Muslims—could have been one of the major reasons why the other northern states mostly stayed free of communal conflict during this period.

But as Paul Brass and other scholars rightly insist, communal riots do not occur simply because a town or city happens to possess an abundance of combustible material.[62] They are to a large degree planned events, not spontaneous explosions. They unfold in ways dictated by the instructions of elite leaders—men whose motives are more often political than religious. Witness the machinations of Maulvi Abdul. Moreover they are, to an extent, events that happen or not at the bidding of the state. As we noted earlier, the BJP is widely accused of fomenting communal incidents for electoral advantage. But more insightful analysis points out that Congress also used communalism for electoral purposes, and that the common factor is not party ideology but the willingness of the governing bureaucracy, most especially the police, to maintain the peace in a non-partisan manner. Vigilant and fair-minded governments can help reduce communal tensions by following equitable policies and promoting toleration; they can also, by main force, prevent these tensions from spilling on to the streets. Or they can choose to play divide-and-rule politics by covertly licensing acts of mob violence. The Indore *darbār* in 1927 was caught napping—in part by the rapid march of events and in part because it was unprepared, the city having never before experienced a major communal riot—but once it had grasped what was happening in the streets it moved quickly to hose down the trouble. In two days peace was restored. Also, as the *dewan* hastened to point out, the mayhem had been confined to a small part of the town, and had 'not affected the old, respectable members of the two communities'.[63] The implication that the people of Indore, in the main, still subscribed to a culture of 'practical toleration' was borne out by subsequent history: Indore would not suffer a similar disturbance until 1948, and then under very unusual conditions. Arguably the princely states possessed a physical and/or cultural environment conducive to the proliferation of grass-roots tolerance; arguably this had something to do with the fact that they were autocratic monarchies wedded to the support of traditionalist (including religious) values.

To sum up, the Indore case study suggests that five main factors may have underpinned the princely states' good communal record in the early twentieth century, namely:

1. their generally small Muslim populations
2. their relative isolation from British India
3. their comparative backwardness
4. their greater adherence to traditional forms of 'community'
5. their monarchical polities.

Chapter 2 will explore the implications of each of these variables, and weigh up their impact. Chapter 3 will examine the reasons why, in every case, their effectiveness declined with the passage of time. Chapters 4 and 5 will show how that the process of erosion was greatly accelerated by the effects of partition and integration between 1947 and 1950.

Finally, a word about the coverage of this book: as a discussion of 'communal' conflict, it necessarily takes no account of other doubtless far

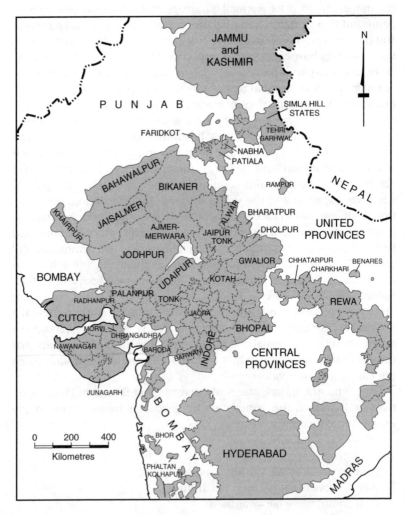

Map 1.1 Northern India showing location of major princely states referred to in the text.

more ubiquitous[64] forms of social violence, such as spousal assault, arson, street brawling and robbery; secondly, in focussing on just one category of community, namely the religious, it ignores many other markers of ethnic identity, which in some regions have played an even more important role than religion, as conventionally defined, in setting people against one another; thirdly, it makes no claim to comprehensiveness in its geographical coverage, even within the restricted compass of the Indian states. Broadly the focus is on north India. In princely terms this translates roughly as those regions which, in the colonial period, were designated as the Kashmir, Punjab states, Rajputana (modern Rajasthan), CI and Western India States Agencies (Map 1.1). I make only passing reference to the Eastern (Orissa) states, and to the states of the Bombay Deccan, and I have deliberately left out of account the three great southern kingdoms of Hyderabad, Travancore and Mysore, the first two of which have been extensively studied by Kooiman.

Amongst many possibilities, I chose to focus on the Muslim–Hindu (and in the Punjab the Muslim–Sikh) conflicts because they were the ones that had far and away the greatest political impact. Other communal clashes also left their legions of dead; but only one resulted in the creation of a new nation-state. Once I had made that initial decision, it seemed sensible to concentrate on north India since the vast majority of India's Muslims and Sikhs live north of the Vindhya–Narbada divide. As for the choice of states, this was dictated partly by considerations of manageability and partly by the fact that with the exception of a few outliers such as Rampur, and of course Kashmir, the northern states were mostly contiguous. Their contiguity provides an over-arching framework for our inquiry; it means we can focus, not just on a scattered array of separate states, but on a specific territorial region.

The subject, then, is Hindu–Muslim/Sikh–Muslim communal conflict in the erstwhile princely states of north India; my point of departure is the extraordinary statistic that the scale of Hindu–Muslim/Sikh–Muslim communal violence was lower, by many orders of magnitude, in these princely states than in the neighbouring provinces of British India. Why were the states so different in this respect? Why, nevertheless, did the degree of difference lessen with the passing of time?

2
Islands in the Storm

> I was very surprised to see our Mohammedan cook taking part in this idolatry [worship of Hanuman]...Narayan said it was not at all an uncommon sight; many of the Mohammedans resident in the State had adopted the Hindu customs...
>
> J.R. Ackerley, recalling his time as private secretary to the maharaja of Chhatarpur during the 1920s

A question of numbers?

In the early twentieth century, communal riots between Hindus and Muslims were far less frequent and far less sanguinary, *per capita*, in princely than in British India. Indeed the difference was so marked that it led some commentators to claim, somewhat excessively, that the states were 'free' from communalism. What magic or artifice allowed the major religious communities in the states to co-exist more or less peacefully at a time when collective violence between Hindus and Muslims was fast becoming the scourge of the provinces?

Let us begin with a trite but nonetheless important observation. Communal riots are, by definition, collective episodes—public encounters between antagonistic groups of religious affiliates. Accordingly, the first precondition for a communal riot is the proximate presence of such collectivities. A neighbourhood peopled entirely by Hindus or Muslims might contain more than its fair share of religious bigots, but it is unlikely to become a site for religious contestation. Similarly, communal violence is unlikely to occur where the numbers on either side are very small. A couple of Muslim families living in a dominantly Hindu locality cannot do much mischief; and if they are sensible they will not attempt to. Conversely, small, obviously vulnerable minorities are much harder to demonise than large, powerful ones, especially if they consciously eschew extravagant displays of communal allegiance. Thus the real danger areas are likely to be neighbourhoods inhabited by mixed populations of more or less equal strength. Nevertheless, if the optimum demography for communal confrontation is one of parity, it is also a fact that communal riots can and do occur in less 'favourable' environments, a circumstance which has led some social scientists to suggest that the population threshold beyond which minorities stop being acquiescent and respond with aggression, may be as low as 15 per cent.[1] In fact, this insight is not new. As early as 1930, Sir John Simon's Statutory Commission noted that riots typically occurred in areas where the Muslim population was 'not sufficiently small to be disregarded, and not sufficiently large to claim the mastery of numbers'.[2]

Applying these rudimentary principles to the princely states, what do we find? In 1921 British India had a population of approximately 247 million, of whom about 163 million were Hindus and 59.5 million Muslims. Princely India by 1921 had a population of just under 72 million, of whom 53.5 million were Hindus and 9.25 million Muslims. These numbers equate to a Muslim population share of 24 per cent in the case of the provinces and about 13 per cent in the case of the states. Clearly, Muslims were far less ubiquitous in princely than in British India. Moreover, as Table 2.1 shows, in most states their numbers fell well short of what we might regard as the danger zone for conflict. In CI, Muslims comprised only 5.5 per cent of the population, in Rajputana barely 9 per cent, in western India (the Kathiawar states) just on 13. Although, as we shall see, there were some important exceptions, the overall trend was so dominantly one-sided that the states were popularly thought of as a Hindu stronghold—which is principally why, in the 1930s, the Indian Muslim League set its face against the British Government's scheme for an all-India federation even as the Hindu Mahasabha warmly embraced it.

The actual position, though, was more complex than these global figures would suggest. For one thing, there was considerable regional variation, across princely India, in the density of the Muslim population. Muslims were an overwhelming majority in Kashmir and Bahawalpur, and the dominant group in Faridkot, Kapurthala, Malerkotla and Tripura in east Bengal. Elsewhere—as in Bharatpur, Alwar, Jodhpur and Junagadh—their numbers were well in excess of the 15 per cent share that we have identified as probably the minimal precondition for open conflict. Indeed in parts of rural Alwar, where the Muslim Meos were

Table 2.1 Distribution of population by religion, India and selected states, 1921

Territorial unit	Population	Hindus	Per cent	Muslims	Per cent
India	318,942,000	218,500,000	63.41	68,750,000	21.74
British India	247,000,000	163,000,000	65.89	59,500,000	24.07
Provincial states	71,900,000	53,500,000	74.40	9,250,000	12.86
Kashmir	3,672,000	740,335	20.16	2,818,489	76.75
Punjab states	4,008,078	2,004,439	50.01	1,242,504	31.00
Jind	308,183	234,712	76.16	34,023	11.04
Patiala	1,499,739	632,590	42.18	330,393	22.03
Kapurthala	284,275	58,419	20.55	160,455	56.44
Bahawalpur	781,191	114,601	14.67	647,217	82.85
Rampur	453,607	236,284	52.09	213,785	47.13
Central India	5,997,023	5,210,120	86.87	331,550	5.52
Gwalior	3,195,475	2,813,958	88.07	177,417	5.55
Indore	1,151,578	996,257	86.51	91,072	7.09
Bhopal	682,448	522,866	75.50	91,711	13.15
Baroda	2,126,522	1,742,259	81.93	162,254	7.63
Western states	2,538,497	3,099,730	82.71	332,564	13.10
Bhavnagar	426,404	368,975	90.75	36,062	8.66
Nawanagar	345,353	275,550	79.78	56,349	16.31
Gondal	167,071	129,455	77.48	31,263	18.71
Junagadh	465,493	368,053	79.05	90,091	19.35
Rajputana states	9,844,384	8,166,501	82.95	900,341	9.14
Udaipur	1,380,063	1,069,056	77.46	48,295	3.49
Dholpur	230,188	213,200	92.62	14,962	6.50
Jaipur	2,238,802	2,216,667	90.93	179,620	7.68
Bikaner	659,985	552,156	83.70	73,423	11.13
Bharatpur	496,437	398,652	80.30	94,124	18.95
Alwar	701,154	518,845	73.99	178,809	25.50
Jodhpur	1,848,825	1,577,580	85.32	497,780	26.92

Sources: Census of India, 1921, Vol. 7, Pt 2, pp. 58–61, Vol. 15, Pt 1, p. 191, Vol. 16, Pt 1, p. 60, Vol. 18, Pt 2, p. 120, Vol. 20, Pt 2, pp. 14–15, Vol. 24, Pt 1, pp. 89, 105–6 and Pt 2, pp. 20, 23–7; *Memoranda on the Indian States* (Calcutta, 1930).

thickly clustered, the figure was closer to 45 per cent (Table 2.2). For another thing, the global figures conceal the extent to which Muslims were represented in the towns of princely India. While Muslims comprised just 6 per cent of the population of Kotah state, they made up 15 per cent of the population of Kotah City. In Gwalior, Muslims were only 4 per cent of rural-dwellers but a substantial 23 per cent of urban-dwellers. In the Patiala town of Narnaul, Muslims numbered 11,000 out of 24,000, or

Table 2.2 Distribution of the Muslim population in Alwar, selected Nizamats, 1931

District	Meo population	Total population	Per cent
Tapukrah	12,411	27,058	45.8
Ramgarh	15,089	33,036	45.7
Alwar	18,937	43,705	43.4
Govindgarh	11,877	28,176	42.2
Kishangarh	7,713	31,083	24.8
Khairtal	7,027	31,374	22.4
Malakhera	5,722	35,017	16.5
Lackmangarh	8,140	49,472	16.4
Mandawar	3,580	31,079	11.5
Tijara	13,243	39,620	33.4

Source: *Census of India*, 1931, Vol. 27, Provincial Tables I and III.

nearly half. The capital of Muslim-ruled Rampur was 80 per cent Muslim (Tables 2.3 and 2.4). Only a small minority in the states overall, Muslims constituted a numerous and visible element in the princely centres of industry, commerce and government. Significantly, these were the places most given to communal riots.

Moreover, numbers do not tell the whole story. Although the Muslims generally were less well off than the Hindus, there were some important exceptions—as in Rampur and Bhopal where they constituted the core of the bureaucratic elite. Conversely in Muslim-majority states such as Khairpur and Bahawalpur, Hindu (and Jain) merchants wielded considerable power in consequence of their wealth and strategic control over the economy. For instance, when a Muslim mob, conspicuously

Table 2.3 Distribution of the urban population by religion, selected political agencies, 1921

Unit	Urban population	Hindus	Per cent	Muslims	Per cent
Kashmir	291,693	85,612	92.35	200,057	63.58
Punjab	384,487	169,784	44.15	171,844	44.64
Gwalior	308,383	225,045	72.97	70,910	22.99
Central India	550,474	382,794	69.53	142,675	25.19
Rajputana	1,317,642	907,218	68.85	319,315	24.14
Baroda	440,823	340,817	77.31	69,166	15.59
Kathiawar	613,380	390,784	63.70	166,777	27.18

Sources: *Census of India*, 1921, Vol. 1, Pt 2, pp. 34–6, Vol. 8, Pt 2, pp. 48–9, Vol. 18, Pt 2, pp. 14–15, Vol. 20, Pt 2, pp. 10–11, Vol. 24, Pt 1, p. 91.

Table 2.4   Distribution of the urban population by religion, selected towns, 1921

Town	Population	Hindus	Per cent	Muslims	Per cent
Bhavnagar	59,392	43,941	73.98	9,958	16.76
Bikaner	69,410	50,648	72.96	13,238	19.07
Indore	93,091	69,872	75.05	19,738	21.18
Cambay	27,251	18,336	67.28	6,257	22.96
Lashkar	80,397	60,307	75.02	18,531	23.05
Jodhpur	73,480	50,410	68.60	18,125	24.66
Ujjain	43,898	31,159	70.98	11,432	26.04
Jammu	31,506	20,797	66.00	9,001	28.56
Jaipur	120,207	78,458	65.26	35,177	29.26
Dholpur	16,220	11,151	68.74	4,911	30.27
Fatehpur	17,315	11,476	99.27	5,275	30.47
Jamnagar	42,495	24,949	58.47	14,111	33.20
Junagadh	33,221	18,737	56.40	13,137	39.53
Ajmer	113,482	52,088	45.89	53,407	47.11
Bhopal	45,094	16,616	36.84	27,515	61.01
Malerkotla	24,564	6,701	27.27	16,599	67.57
Rampur	73,156	14,047	19.20	58,808	80.38

Sources: Census of India, 1921, Vol. 1, Pt 2, pp. 34–6, Vol. 8, Pt 2, pp. 48–50, Vol. 18, Pt 2, pp. 114–17, Vol. 20, Pt 2, pp. 10–11, Vol. 24, Pt 1, p. 91 and Vol. 24, Pt 2, pp. 18–21.

unrestrained by the police, went on the rampage through the town of Minchnabad, Bahawalpur, in 1935, stoning shops and houses and desecrating shrines, Seth Nagarmal 'took the management of the city into his own hands by deputing 500 labourers on guard duty for the safety of the lives and property of the Hindus'. At the same time the Hindu *seths* effectively shut down the economy of the town by imposing a blanket *hartal*, which led to a sharp reduction in the *darbār*'s revenue from sales taxes. The *hartal* was not lifted until the Bahawalpur *darbār* had agreed to receive a Hindu deputation and hold an inquiry into the incident.[3]

To sum up, majorities are not usually disturbed by the presence on their patch of insignificant minorities but they may well be bothered by substantial minorities or minorities that are powerful or concentrated in strategic places. As the Central Provinces Hindu politician B.S. Moonje confessed revealingly in 1923, 'Out of a 1.5 lakh population of Nagpur, Muslims are only 20 thousand. But still we feel insecure.'[4] Generally in princely India, Muslims were too few to openly challenge the prevailing religious hegemony. Yet this general picture was not everywhere true, at least to an equal extent. In the Punjab states and in eastern Rajputana there were significant princely pockets of Muslim settlement. Elsewhere, especially in urban areas, Muslims, although ordinarily a minority, were sufficiently numerous to represent a potential source of trouble—as were, conversely, the Hindus and Sikhs in states such as Bahawalpur and Kashmir. This begs the question of why, nonetheless, even in these places, Hindu–Muslim relations in the early twentieth century rarely became violent.

The states as backwaters

The urban bias of communal outbreaks (as much in evidence today as it was in the late colonial period) has often been remarked on, and it is not difficult to find reasons to account for the phenomenon. First, and most obviously, towns are places that, by definition, contain concentrated supplies of the essential raw material needed for riots—that is to say, people. Secondly, towns house economic activities such as merchandising and manufacturing which require, and attract, large populations of artisans, labourers and factory workers. In South Asia these occupations are generally gruelling and poorly paid, and the people in them are frequently subjected to physical and verbal abuse. Typically many of them will be recent immigrants from the countryside, single males cut off from families and childhood friends. Such groups, it can be argued, have a predisposition to collective violence. Not only have they little to lose, but potentially also much to gain. Aside from the (always welcome) prospect of loot, violence provides the oppressed with an outlet for their humiliations; it offers them a way to get even with their tormentors. And the act of merging with the mob may, in itself, assist in this respect by creating a temporary illusion of levelling. In crowds, individuals surrender their identity and become part of a homogenised mass. They 'become equal'.[5] Likewise, one can readily understand how collective action around the banner of 'community' might have a strong appeal to rootless, deracinated men gripped by alienation and anomie. Significantly, recent data suggests that Indian towns where the migration flow is heavily outwards are consistently less prone to communal violence than towns with a net inflow of migrants.[6] Thirdly, the crowded nature of Indian cities and towns is conducive to the rapid spread of information and rumour, and allows for the rapid mobilisation of retainers. Fourthly, because urbanites until recently have tended to enjoy better access than their rural cousins to the press and other media of mass communication, they have been, over the long term, more heavily exposed to orchestrated communal propaganda.

On the other hand it could plausibly be contended that the pathologies of urban life are merely a highly developed form of that much broader social phenomenon, modernity. As we noted in Chapter 1, the 'communities' fashioned by Indian communalists over the past 100 years, the communities of 'Hinduism' and 'Islam', are in many ways quite artificial constructs, products of imagination rather than of biology. From this point of view they are quintessentially *modern* artefacts, expressions of that 'great shift, in the modern era, from an emphasis on relationships that are primarily face-to-face, based in geographically small communities, to ones that encompass groups whose members can never be known to each other'.[7] Moreover the creation of these impersonal macro-communities would not have been possible without the panoply of technologies that have come to be associated with modernisation—electricity and machine-power, railways and telephones, printed books and newspapers. Without the first two there could have been no industrialisation and no massified urban proletariats; without the last four, the urban masses could never have been mobilised effectively.

But modernity is not simply about technology; it is also about ideas (democracy, equality, secularism) and institutions (elections, the public society, the public school). Is there a link here too? Many believe so. Although a conjunction of religion and secularism might seem paradoxical, it has been suggested that the gathering perception among Indian elites that the secular sphere was expanding at the expense of the sacred may have been one of the things that spurred them to organise politically. Likewise, the British colonial government's express philosophical commitment to the ideal of social improvement encouraged Muslims—generally, in South Asia, an economically disadvantaged group—to organise communally to press for assistance from the state. As for democracy, the mushroom growth of communalism during the 1920s and 1930s, a period in which the Indian constitution was being progressively liberalised in the direction of responsible government, seemed to British officials of the time a fairly obvious case of communal competition for the fruits of political power. 'The Reforms as they were bound to do have created the belief that the old strong hand is going and that those communities who fail to assert themselves will be left in the lurch', noted the Government of India's (GOI's) Home Member Sir Alexander Muddiman in 1924.[8] More recently, scholars have pointed to the way electioneering in South Asia has served variously to polarise public opinion, buttress putative group identities and excite bursts of 'ecstatic religious activity' among constituents frustrated by the persistent failure of the politicians to translate their unrealistically utopian vote-catching promises into action.[9]

Last but not least, communalism can be seen as a substitute for more traditional forms of social bonding lost in the transition to modernity, a view eloquently put for South Asia recently by American anthropologist Richard G. Fox. With modernisation, Fox points out, the mythical, supernatural, familial and tribal realms that once sustained people and helped them make sense of their place in the world were largely swept away. As a result, they were cast adrift from their moorings, left to fend for themselves as individuals in a functionally rational but ultimately bleak universe of private religion, contracts and impersonal relationships. Thus, Fox argues, modernity 'created its own conditions for [the formation of] new enchanted identities, that is, new loyalties based on sect, tribe or race'. Collectivities organised around real or imagined ties of religion are manifestations of the process of 'hyperenchantment' that inevitably 'comes in the wake of modernity to fill the vacuums it creates'.[10]

If the modernisation theory of communalism is valid, we would expect to find, in any society, a broad correlation between the incidence of ethno-nationalist violence and the spread of urbanisation, industrialisation, politicisation and literacy. We do. 'Empirical data...', affirms Ashis Nandy, 'suggests that communalism in India has increased *pari passu* with modernization and secularization ... [Moreover] it tends to be concentrated in cities, and within cities, in industrial areas where modern values are conspicuous and dominant.'[11] If Nandy is correct it would be reasonable to suppose that societies in which these variables are absent or weak (for example, pre-modern or 'under-developed' societies) would register a comparatively low level of ethno-communal violence. Most of the early twentieth-century princely states, particularly in north India, could be characterised as pre-modern societies.

Even at this relatively late phase of the colonial period it is difficult, if not impossible, to generalise meaningfully about the level of economic and institutional development of the entire body of Indian princely states. Separated by large distances, situated in different geographical environments and presided over by administrations of varying competence and political inclination, the states were not so much at one socio-economic level as several, simultaneously. Indeed the most advanced ones, such as Mysore, Travancore, Baroda, Gondal and Bhavnagar, were in some ways ahead of any of the British-administered provinces, especially in education and social reform. Likewise, local variations make statistical comparisons with British India, even at the provincial level, of doubtful value. For what it is worth the statistical picture (Table 2.5), does, in fact, support the contention that the states were more backward than the provinces; however, the differences revealed are not great, and certainly not sufficient to account for the large variations we have identified in the incidence of communal violence between the 'two Indias'.

A much starker picture emerges, however, when one begins to look at specific cases—in particular at the legions of small- to medium-sized states scattered across the breadth of middle India from the Punjab to Orissa. These states were backward by any measure. In Malerkotla, which was by no means the worst of them, many primary schools and even some hospitals were 'without buildings'.[12] In Baoni there were 'no roads'.[13] The capital city of Kishengarh had no proper system of sanitation. Half of the sub-inspectors of police in Dholpur were untrained. Balasinor had just 15 schools, Jaisalmer a dozen. Lacking amenities, these backwoods states were also underdeveloped economically, most production therein being rural-based, agricultural and designed for subsistence or for local markets; aside from some food-processing and textile-weaving in the bigger towns, there was little activity of the type one associates with modern 'industrial' economies. Again, such statistical evidence, as exists, points to a significant difference in these

Table 2.5   Percentage of the population in selected states and provinces, 1921

Unit	Criteria		
	Literate	Living in towns	Working in manufacturing
Baroda	14.7	17.3	11.9
Gwalior and Central India	3.7	9.4	10.7
Kashmir	2.6	8.8	7.4
Rajputana	4.2	14.3	13.9
Hyderabad	3.3	9.8	13.7
Average	5.7	11.9	11.3
Bombay	9.5	22.9	12.1
UP	4.2	10.6	11.0
Bengal	10.4	6.7	7.6
Punjab	4.6	11.3	19.3
CP and Berar	4.9	9.0	9.2
Average	5.8	12.1	11.8

Source: *Census of India*, 1921, Vol. 1, Pt 1, pp. 65, 177, 280–1.

'developmental' aspects as between comparable states and British Indian districts.[14]

Nor is this dichotomy accidental. A number of states were situated in less favoured parts of the subcontinent (the British having annexed the parts which promised the best economic returns) where agricultural productivity was limited by drought, poor soils and natural barriers to communication. As a result, many of the states simply did not have the funds, and could not afford the specialists needed 'to give their subjects the...amenities', which, by the twentieth century, had come to be associated with a 'modern administration'.[15] Besides—shining exceptions such as Sayaji Rao of Baroda apart—the princes as an order showed little interest in state-sponsored modernisation, preferring to spend such tax surpluses as came their way on themselves, their families and their feudal clients and retainers rather than on development. In Limbdi and Palanpur, the expenses of the ruling families absorbed around 20 per cent of the revenue surplus; in Baoni the equivalent figure was 30 per cent, in Jaora 50 per cent. The ruler of Alirajpur spent twice as much on himself as he did on education. Bharatpur at the end of the 1920s had a debt of a crore of rupees, most of it due to Maharaja Kishen Singh's extravagance 'in the matter of motor cars'.[16] By the end of his reign in 1945, Maharaja Gulab Singh of Rewa had salted away at least seven crores from the treasury into private accounts in Indian and overseas banks, one of which he disarmingly referred to as his 'Old Broad Street nest egg'.[17] Although the evidence is patchy and perhaps not very reliable, it seems safe to say that the states typically taxed their subjects more heavily than the governments of the provinces and spent significantly less *per capita* on infrastructure and social welfare.

Similarly, monarchical self-interest conspired to rule out any comprehensive programme of political modernisation in the states. While a number of states, by the early twentieth century, were beginning to move away from absolutism pure and simple towards a more bureaucratic mode of governance articulated through specialised departments manned by paid officials, virtually none were yet prepared to share power with popular representatives chosen by means of election. To be sure, about a score of northern states, by the 1920s, had established some form of 'council' government. Yet only a handful of these bodies were even partially elected (in every case on a very narrow franchise), and none had real power. The eighteen-member Baroda Legislative Council, for example, was dominated by officials and government nominees, and was restricted to offering advice. Likewise the Bikaner Council, although given a notional non-official majority in 1927, remained, as it had been since its inception in 1913, a piece of elaborate royal window dressing. It rarely met; and when it did, its discussions were limited to rubber-stamping the edicts of the maharaja. As the Council's own minutes noted deferentially, 'all matters of policy or matters of importance are submitted to H.H. [for decision]'.[18] Even Rajkot's unusually representative assembly, elected on an adult franchise, lacked any real legislative or inquisitorial power. Thus, while the princely polity of north India in the early twentieth century was no longer, for practical purposes, a purely autocratic one, it was by no means a democratic or even representative polity, such as British India was gradually becoming as a result of imperial policies of devolution. Except to a limited extent in the South, and at the municipal level, princely India in the 1920s and 1930s was a region devoid of elections. Consequently people in the states had less incentive to organise communally for political ends.   EXACTLY.

Communitas

However, the Indian princely states in the early twentieth century were not simply *un*-modern, in the sense of lacking certain technologies and institutions. They were also, to some extent, *pre*-modern, in the sense that their rulers and peoples still held on firmly to important vestiges of pre-modern culture. One of these, which we shall examine in the next section, was their monarchical polity. Another was the prevalence in the states of long-established parochial communities that were at once coherent, tightly knit and demographically stable. Arguably, the spirit of *communitas* that flourished in these village and neighbourhood localities was yet a further reason why the states were able to resist, for a time, the surging tide of Hindu–Muslim communal violence.[19]

Parochial neighbourhood life encouraged 'communitas'—social bonding—in a number of ways. The most basic was through public space. Being smallish, confined places, villages and *mohullas* lend themselves to face-to-face contact; as a result, the inhabitants are usually known to one another by sight or reputation. This, in itself, probably inhibited outbreaks of communal violence since it is potentially easier to strike a stranger one will never see again than to trade blows with a person one is likely to run into next day in the street or at the bazaar. 'We have to live here,' a former Kotah subject told me, 'so hatred will not do.'[20] Similarly, the fact that villages and neighbourhoods in India were usually self-sufficient as regards household essentials meant that their inhabitants were dependent upon one another for the things they needed in order to survive. Virtually everyone was a producer, a worker, a seller or a buyer. What is more, these economic relationships routinely transcended the boundaries of religion since many trades traditionally have been the province of Muslims. In Jaipur the gem-cutting trade was, and is, largely a Muslim affair. In Kotah the dyeing of cloth fell to Muslims called *neelgars*; and Muslim women dominated the profession of midwifery. In Patiala, Muslims ran the cycle-repair, carpentry, brick-laying and dyeing trades. Indeed this dependancy on Muslim artisans carried over even into the arena of Hindu ritual, for, as Shail Mayaram explains with reference to modern-day Jaipur:

> The Manihar women make the mandatory lac bangles for Hindu married women, and stands of the *katāvā* (Hindu sacred thread required for Yajna) can be found hanging from the balconies in the Nilgaron ka Mohulla behind Ramganj. *Sankrānt*, a major festival in Jaipur, when kites literally crowd the city's skies, is inconceivable without Muslim kite-makers, exactly as Diwali is unthinkable without Muslim firework manufacturers.[21]

Religious minorities were not merely an integral part of the social makeup of the territorial community—they were necessary to its economic—and religious—well-being.

However, while rooted in the necessities of day-to-day living, co-existence at the local level in early twentieth-century princely India was not just a concession to practicality; on the contrary, it seems to have embodied a strong consensual element which may be likened to the normative principles which social historians such as E.P. Thompson and George Rudé have identified as operating in the working-class neighbourhoods of pre-modern Europe. Researching English crowd violence in the eighteenth century, Thompson observed that while the endemic grain riots of the period were clearly

> triggered off by soaring prices, by malpractices among dealers, or by hunger . . ., these grievances operated within a popular consensus as to what were legitimate and what were illegitimate practices in mar-keting, milling, baking etc. This in turn was grounded upon a consistent traditional view of social norms and obligations, of the proper func-tioning of [the] several parties within the community . . .[22]

Thompson called this communal consensus the 'moral economy of the poor'. Significantly for our purposes the moral economy concept has since been convincingly applied by James C. Scott and others to the Asian countryside, specifically to the analysis of rural revolts in Burma and Vietnam during the late colonial period.[23]

Of course, the analogy is not exact. Thompson's labourers and Scott's peasants are concerned primarily with establishing a right to subsistence, which is a rather different moral equation than the one I have in mind for the Indian states. Nevertheless, I would argue that the basic thesis of the moral economists—that parochial, face-to-face communities in the pre-modern world had a robust sense of what constituted appropriate 'social norms and obligations', and that this shared moral code defined 'the proper functioning' of relations between the 'several parties' which comprised the community—is in principle equally applicable to the issue of religious difference. What is more, it fits the evidence. Like the English town labourers and craftsmen studied by Thompson, the villagers and *mohulla*-dwellers of the states appear to have had a highly developed sense of what was right and proper. Among the petitions that lie in the princely archives, one finds a number that refer to and sometimes quote written agreements about permissible religious behaviour—ostensibly arrived at by means of patient negotiation and therefore products of consensus. Moreover, people living in these grass-roots communities were quick to respond if they felt the established moral code had been infringed. In Phalodi town, Jodhpur, convention decreed that goats not be slaughtered during the month of Kartik. This was formalised in 1903 with a written agreement between the *panches* of the Pushkarna Brahmins and the butchers. But in 1931 some of the butchers reneged. At once the Pushkarnas placed a picket around the offending butchers' shops and stopped all dealings with them. Most people in the town—including most Muslims—thought the boycott justified.[24] Similarly, a decade later, when a bier carrying the body of a Hindu Chhipa to the cremation ground in the Jodhpur town of Pali was prevented from entering a street near the mosque by a crowd of Muslims, the action was protested on the grounds that the same route had been used by the caste 'from the times nobody knows'—always before without restriction.[25] Again one gets the sense that the issue was at heart a legal and moral one—the defence of a long-established customary right acknowledged by the community.

Thirdly, if paradoxically, neighbourhood life also helped to reduce the potential for disputation between Hindus and Muslims by virtue of its social diversity. For one thing, Indian localities are not solely or even mainly zones of interaction between 'Hindus' and 'Muslims'. At the functional level they are primarily a meeting ground for 'castes'—or more accurately *jatis* or 'sub-castes'. And *jati* membership is highly exclusive. Not only do members of different castes rarely eat together, and almost never intermarry, they also tend to look down on those they consider to be of inferior status to themselves. Throughout his long and busy life, Jaipur *jagirdar* and *tazeemi sardār* Amar Singh Kanota kept a personal diary in which he recorded faithfully the large and small events of his life and his opinions of the people he met along the way. Often, these opinions were not flattering. As a martial Rajput, he had little time for the pen-pushing merchant castes of Gujarat, whom he thought 'degenerated in mind and vigour', nor for priestly Brahmins who struck him as 'human blood suckers'. He did not even care much for some Rajputs, including some branches of his own Rathore clan. As for Muslims, who, as we shall see, were strongly represented during the early twentieth century in the armies and police services of many princely *darbārs*: 'I would not employ them. I would take Rajpoots every time. [But] I would not take Jats, Goojars or Meenas either.'[26] Framed in this context, we can see that Amar Singh's prejudice against Muslims was nothing special, neither greater nor lesser than his other myriad prejudices. And so it was with most other Hindus. At the grass roots, Muslims were merely another deviant social group among many, and not, by any means, necessarily the most despised. In Dhrangadhra, Muslims were permitted to enter temples (and often did so) whereas until very late in the piece Hindu untouchables were barred.[27]

Caste though was not the only thing that separated people within territorial communities; particularly on the Muslim side, sectarian differences too were important, notably as between Sunnis and Sh'ias but also, in certain regions, between rival coteries of Sunni worshippers. For instance by 1910, relations between the hereditary preachers of Srinagar's two major religious shrines, the Jama and Hamdaami mosques, had become so bitter that the Kashmir government ordered the city divided into two separate religious jurisdictions.

Again, social differences between the major religious groups tend to be narrower and much less obvious at the grass roots than at the elite level. At the elite level, Muslims and Hindus dress differently, eat different foods, write in different scripts and of course follow very different rituals; but at the local level, the boundaries are much less clear-cut. On the one hand many Muslims still cling to vestiges of the customs of their Hindu convert ancestors. In Patiala, Hindu women sometimes take their ailing children to the local mosque, it being widely believed that the touch of a Muslim who has recently offered *namaz* has the power to heal. At Pandiayat in Kota district, Muslim villagers join with their Hindu neighbours in celebrating the coming of the rains with a procession of deities. In Bikaner, Muslim males guard the shrine of the region's patron goddess Karni Mata, whilst Muslim women lustily sing her praises during the festival of Navaratras. In the neighbouring Shekhawati region of Jodhpur, 'Muslim Rajputs' known locally as 'Kyamkhanis' incorporate both the Rajput *bhaanwar* and the Muslim *nikah* in their marriage ceremonies, keep Holi and Diwali, gift cows to Brahmins and commonly greet one another with the phrase 'Ram-Ram'. In Jaora, Muslim cultivators follow Hindu marriage customs and propitiate the goddess of smallpox. Amongst the Meos of Alwar and Bharatpur it is prohibited for women to divorce or inherit property. And Little Tradition syncretism is not only found amongst Muslims; Hindus borrow Islamic practices too. In Kashmir, Hindu Pandits—though Brahmins—eat mutton prepared in the *halal* style and use the services of Muslim foster-mothers. In Jhalawar, Hindus join enthusiastically in the annual cele-bration the *'urs* of the Chishti saint Ham'muddin, locally known as Mathe Mahabali; and songs in praise of the saint are still sung locally during Hindu marriage festivities. As a Jaipuri woman told Shail Mayaram in 1990: 'I follow all Hindu *devatas* and I also believe in Muslim gods. I believe in Ajmer's Khwaja saheb and Sayyad baba...All people who do good work must be worshipped.'[28] Similarly, Meos have been heard to declare that they are 'not Muslims' although they have always been so recorded in the census. Still evident today, this local tradition of syncretism was even more entrenched and widespread a century ago, especially in those areas far distant from the metropolitan centres of elite culture.

Last but not least, small territorial communities are renowned for being inward looking, wary of strangers and suspicious of novel ideas originating from outside. Faced with an unwanted intrusion, their immediate visceral reaction is to close ranks against it. So it was with the heady new ideology of 'communalism'. Although by the early 1920s communal ways of thinking were already well entrenched in the provinces, particularly among the urban middle classes, initial attempts to export them into the hinterlands of princely India generally foun-dered on the rock of parochialism. As the Akali Dal threatened to swamp Jind with *jathas* as part of its campaign to wrest control of the state's Sikh *gurudwaras* from the state government, a meeting of the Jind Parja Mandal attended by a thousand local Sikhs warned the Akalis that 'outsiders have no right to take possession of any of our buildings without...permission...we advise outsiders to look after their own affairs first'.[29] And Muslim communalists from Delhi received an equally cold welcome when they landed in Bharatpur in 1924 bent on assisting the State Anjuman-i-Islam to resolve a dispute over a local mosque. 'We know how to manage our affairs more efficiently than outsiders', they were peremptorily informed.[30]

To be sure, none of these elements was wholly peculiar to the princely states. Parochial communities criss-crossed by caste-ties yet yoked together by a mutual interest in peaceful co-existence, economic interdependence and a shared suspicion of outsiders still flourished, at this time, in many parts of British India too, especially in the provincial countryside; which is why, as noted earlier, communalism at this time was not yet wholly endemic there either—even in provinces such as Bengal and UP. No simple black and white contrast can be drawn between the provinces and the princely states on these grounds, and it is certainly not my intention here to imply otherwise.

Nevertheless, if we accept the conventional wisdom that modernity—with its insatiable appetite for integration and homogenisation—is inherently destructive of local parochialism, it follows that parochial communities had a greater chance of survival—and survived longer—in the relatively backward region of princely India than in the relatively more developed region of British-administered India. The historical evidence seems to confirm this contention. Not only were the villages and *mohullas* of the states mostly peaceful in the early twentieth century, but as we shall see they became—significantly—less so with the passage of time, as modernity began to make inroads into the more rustic parts of the interior.

But in the meantime the states were to some extent 'protected' from these intrusions of modernity, both by the selfish, self-serving policies of many of the princely *darbārs* and by their distance, absolutely and relatively, in terms of travelling time, from the provincial eye of the communal storm. This brings us, finally, to the factor of geography.

Just how important was the geographical variable in the equation can be gauged from the map (Map 2.1) summarising the distribution of major Hindu–Muslim communal riots in the states between 1920 and 1940. It shows that riots were more frequent and severe in Mysore than in the Deccan states, in princely Punjab than in Gujarat and in Rajputana than in CI. More specifically, it shows that the eastern half of Rajputana was significantly more riot-prone than the western half of the Agency. In part, these regional variations can be accounted for by the factors of urbanisation and modernisation discussed earlier. Most of the places listed are big towns and a number of them (Bangalore, Gulbarga and Indore) were already, in the early twentieth century, considerable centres of commerce and industry. Nevertheless the real key to the map

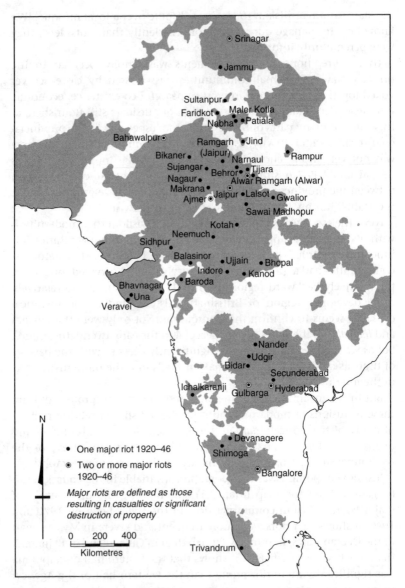

Map 2.1 Distribution of major Hindu–Muslim communal riots in princely India, 1920–46.

is distance—how far each of these places was from the then provincial epicentres of communal conflict (Punjab, Delhi, western UP, Bombay and Calcutta). Although prosperous and rapidly developing, the maritime states of Kathiawar were a long way from Bombay and even further from the communal cockpit of northern India. Conversely the Punjab states, surrounded by and thoroughly intermingled with British territory, all lay within 300 kilometres radius of Lahore and Amritsar; while Dholpur, Alwar and Bharatpur on the eastern fringe of Rajputana were but 200 kilometres shy of Delhi.

Yet it was not so much distance *per se* that conferred a protective mantle on the states, during this period, as their relative inaccessibility. No railway line connected Cutch with the rest of Kathiawar, and the desert kingdom of Jaisalmer could be reached only by camel-train. The nearest railway station to Radhanpur was five miles across the state border, in Baroda. Tripura was linked to the outside world by one phone line, which was often down. To get to Loharu, visitors from south-east Punjab had to negotiate a 42-mile 'sandy track' impassable during the wet and tortuous in the dry; while Baoni was six hours arduous drive by motor car from the nearest railway station at Nowgong. Indeed, communications over much of princely north India were so poor that one suspects more was involved here than mere royal parsimony—that the region's rulers had deliberately cultivated a strategy of isolation as a way of protecting their patrimony.

But whether it came about through design or simply neglect, there is no doubt that the physical isolation of the states was an asset in respect of the maintenance of social harmony. By the early twentieth century, provincial north India was awash with virulent communal literature. However, until the 1930s very little of this corrosive propaganda managed to penetrate the states' natural defences. As a British political agent (PA) observed smugly, but perceptively, of rural Udaipur: 'the truth is that agitators do not much like to get away from bus routes'.[31] As it was, the places in princely north India most affected in this period by outside communal propaganda were—significantly in this context—railway junctions having direct main-line connections to Delhi and UP, such as Ajmer. Ajmer was the site of Rajputana's first substantial riot, in July 1923. Triggered by the refusal of a coterie of hard-line Muslims to let a Jagdish procession pass by a hallowed Islamic shrine, the Dargah Sharif Khwaja Sahib, the 1923 affray cost four lives. The city would erupt again in 1928, 1936 and 1948.

Ajmer, though, was not just an important railway junction; it was (and is) also a famous religious centre. Notably, Ajmer is home to the tomb of the Sufi saint Mu'in al-din Chishti who died in 1233. (This is the *dargah* that featured prominently in the 1923 riots.) So affectionately is this shrine regarded, that some Muslims now reckon it more important to the Islamic life of the country than either the Jama Masjid or the Fatepuri Mosque in Delhi. As well, Ajmer is near to the Pushkar Lake, which is holy to Hindus. Consequently the city has become a magnet for religious pilgrims, particularly Muslims. From this point of view, it is interesting to note that the man who in 1923 actually 'gave the order to fire' on the Hindu procession as it passed by the Dargah—Sahibzada Abdul Rashid Khan—was from the royal family of Tonk, a nearby Muslim state.[32]

And Ajmer was distinctive in another way too. The city and its environs were an island of British territory, one of several such imperial enclaves within the Rajputana and Central and Western India Agencies. If we allow that this, too, contributed in some way to Ajmer's bleak record of communal violence, then it follows that princely governance *itself* must have been a factor in the communal equation. But if so, what precisely was the nature of its contribution? Did it lie in the special prerogatives and responsibilities associated with Indian kingship, or in the system of *darbāri* administration, or in the governing ethos of particular states and rulers?

Rājadharma

Although some important exceptions jump to mind, generally governments do their best to maintain law and order. Civil strife is trouble and in the last resort fatal to the authority of the state. For the most part of the late colonial period, the Indian kingdoms conformed to this paradigm—particularly in respect of ethno-communal violence. Apart from the fact that 'religious' riots tended to be very bitter and bloody affairs, severely draining of police and other resources, they invited Political Department intervention, which usually brooked trouble for the ruler. Despite the superficial attraction of divide-and-rule (of which we shall have more to say later), the majority of princes preferred to let the sleeping dog of communalism lie.

But then, so too did the harassed governments of the imperial provinces—which begs the question: How did the princely governments apparently manage religious difference and conflict better than their British counterparts?

In part, the answer lies in the nature of the *darbāri* polity. Strictly speaking, the states were something less than pure autocracies. To be sure, many princes were deeply committed to the idea of hereditary personal rule, and some struggled hard to play the part of absolute kings. Maharaja Udaibhan Singh ruled Dholpur for nearly 40 years. He did so, by his own admission, 'in a real Hindu cultural way of absolute fatherly despotism', issuing edicts and spending money pretty much as he pleased.[33] About Brijendra Singh, Maharaja of Bharatpur, the Political Department's K.P.S. Menon wrote: 'this child of impulse has only one fixed notion—that he was born to be a Maharaja, and that as a Maharaja he is above all law and procedures'.[34] Yet another would-be Rajput autocrat, Maharaja Ganga Singh of Bikaner, took his fatherly responsibilities so seriously that he sometimes felt obliged to slap the faces of courtiers who displeased him; while Mohammad Ibrahim Ali Khan of Tonk (r.1884–1930) was described as 'a perfect example of "L'etat C'est Moi" '.[35] But while absolute in theory, princely power was in practice hedged about with numerous checks and balances. Since the workload entailed in administering even a small principality was much greater than any one man could handle, all rulers were compelled to delegate; and even the most able were dependent upon officials for specialist advice. For instance, the nawab of Cambay passed orders on broad policy issues only 'after consulting the Dewan'.[36] Indeed, as noted above, by early the twentieth century some of the *darbārs* had started to solicit non-official advice more extensively through the agency of formally constituted 'legislative' councils. Secondly, all sensible princes kept a weather eye on the views and interests of influential groups of stakeholders among their subjects, such as the feudal nobility, the priesthood and the merchant castes (who appear to have been past masters at pre-modern forms of civil disobedience such as mass emigration or striking).[37] Thirdly, all rulers were supposed to take advice from their residents or PAs, and many, for pragmatic reasons, did so. Fourthly, the 'paramountcy' powers of the government, which included in the last resort the sanctions of deposition and externment, represented an ultimate external check on Indian princely authority.

That said, it is also true that the ruling authorities in the states were much less hampered, in the exercise of administrative discretion, than their counterparts in the provinces who had to contend with substantial and increasingly legislative and judicial interference. As we have seen, only a handful of states in the early twentieth century possessed proper legislatures and in virtually all cases these bodies lacked the power to second-guess executive decisions. Likewise, superior courts in the princely states tended to be servants of royal power, rather than the separate and substantially independent bodies they were in British India. In many small states the ruler was himself the chief judicial officer; in others he sat as a court of appeal; in others again that responsibility fell to the *karbhari* or chief minister. Only in a few of the most progressive states, such as Baroda, was the judiciary both separate from the executive and irremovable.

Compared to provincial governments, therefore, the princely *darbārs* enjoyed much more freedom of action. They could act more swiftly; also, when necessary, they could act more punitively, since they were much less accountable for their actions. This ability to repress with relative impunity gave the *darbārs* a significant advantage with respect to the prevention and containment of communal violence.

For instance, when communal politicians from British India came to Indore, the Holkar government had ready to hand a 1921 notification which directed that 'no outsider should on any account...deliver lectures...without the express permission of the Chief Minister';[38] while Bikaner, in similar circumstances, could invoke the provisions of its draconian Aliens Law, which required every visitor 'to report himself to the Magistrate of the District' within 48 hours of his arrival, on pain of summary deportation.[39] Most *darbārs*, however, simply acted, when need arose, on the strength of royal prerogative. In November 1926, Nabha banned six seditious Akali Dal newspapers and ordered copies of the papers circulating in the state to be destroyed. Bundi, in October 1929, summarily banished a Jodhpur man who had been working in the state as a junior official on the grounds that his continued residence was 'not desirable'.[40] In 1941 the Sirohi *darbār* authorised the arrest without warrant of anyone overheard spreading rumours designed to inflame communal passions.

And the more autocratic style of governance in princely India also reduced the incidence of communally inspired litigation. In the provinces, communal groups regularly went to court in the hope of obtaining judgements unfavourable to their adversaries or officialdom, or both. But successful suits were invariably contested on appeal or protested violently in the streets, further embittering relations between the groups. Matters were not helped, either, by the tendency of the provincial courts to reverse each other's decisions. In the states, by contrast, litigation was less favoured as a means of disputation since it was known that the princely courts rarely contested executive orders. Significantly, one of the few serious riots in the states whose origins can be traced to a judicial dispute occurred in Junagadh, where a right of appeal in capital cases lay with the judicial assistant to the resident, Western India States—a British official.[41]

'In the Hindu States', opined nationalist MLA C.S. Ranga Iyer, in a book published in 1928, 'the Maharaja sees to it that no [communal] riot takes place.'[42] Autocracy in the states did not work quite as simply or effectively as that, but it did keep the lid on things in a way the more liberal provincial system did not. On the one hand, autocracy facilitated the taking of pre-emptive action against likely offenders. On the other, it discouraged breaches of the communal peace because people were left in no doubt about what would happen to them if they crossed the prescribed communal boundaries.

However, the princely *darbārs* did not limit themselves just to restricting opportunities for communal assertion; they also strove in various ways to conserve and promote the popular tendency towards inter-communal harmony and to entrench the principle of universal religious toleration within their bureaucracies. For example, the message of co-existence was hammered constantly in pronouncements from the throne. In an address to the Bhopal legislative council in 1930, Nawab Hamidullah Khan urged his Muslim co-religionists 'to be extra-magnanimous, large-hearted, tolerant, and sympathetic towards...other communities'.[43] Appearing before the convocation of Benares University in 1935, Ganga Singh of Bikaner observed, 'We must live in peace with our fellow subjects—our Muslim brethren—for pray do not forget that...we are Indians first and foremost and Hindus and Muslims and everything else only afterwards.'[44] In his birthday *darbār* speech of 1939, Man Singh of Jaipur protested his 'uniform regard for all Religions'; while in 1942 Yeshwant Rao Holkar of Indore declared himself to be 'impervious to religious or communal differences'.[45] Widely reported in the press, these remarks proclaimed that the order of princes stood for pluralism and peaceful co-existence.

On another level, the princely governments put the same message into the public domain via proclamations enshrining their subjects' right to freedom of worship within the boundaries of the law. According to Gwalior's 'fundamental rights' edict of 1941,

All Our subjects and all persons residing within Our territories, of whatever religious persuasion, caste or creed, will have the fullest liberty to entertain their beliefs and to perform their worship and other religious rites in any manner enjoined by their Religion and Our Government will, consistently with its immemorial traditions, refrain from interfering with the due and lawful performance of such worship and religious rites. But noone will in the exercise of this right do anything which may be opposed to any law in force in the State.[46]

Again, most princely governments endeavoured to ensure that their public servants dealt evenhandedly with all groups of subjects by fining, transferring or demoting those found guilty of religious insensitivity or partisanship. As Jodhpur's Revenue Minister declared, 'it cannot be too emphatically emphasised that it is the duty of all public servants to abstain from any act which will give rise to the suspicion that... [they are] in favour of any communal matter'.[47] So keen, indeed, was the Bharatpur government to do the right thing on this score that it issued an order making it compulsory for Muslims in the state forces to perform daily prayers.

Finally, the message of pluralism was reinforced in the northern states by their proudly syncretic style of administration. Historically Urdu, not Hindi, was the regional court language and it remained so in some parts down to the 1950s. Gwalior, Indore and other states conferred Mughlai titles and decorations on their officials and employed Persian technical terms to describe administrative units and functions. In Jaipur the ceremony of changing the colours, the most important event in the state's military calendar, was 'performed on Mahomedan lines'.[48]

Nevertheless the question posed earlier remains pertinent: Why did people in the states apparently pay more heed to moral injunctions issued by their rulers than people in the British provinces? First, it should be observed that princely efforts to wring compliance from their subjects in the matter of toleration were more thoroughgoing than their provincial equivalents. For instance, no British Indian government ever ventured to introduce anything equivalent to Bikaner's Freedom of Religion Act of 1927, which contained draconian penalties for religious vilification, desecration of sacred sites and forcible conversions. Secondly, it could be argued that the princely *darbārs* were better positioned, from the viewpoint of legitimacy, to sell the pluralist message.

Among the guiding tenets of British colonial policy, as it evolved in South Asia, was the belief that religion was essentially a private matter and therefore not within the legitimate political domain of the state. Acting on this belief, the government of British India endeavoured as far as possible to keep out of religious controversies, and where this proved impossible to do, it strove to act evenhandedly, or 'neutrally', as between competing sectarian groups. At an abstract level, this policy reflected the secularist thought of the Western Enlightenment; but at a more prosaic level, it reflected the hard-learned lesson that religion tended to ignite unruly passions among the subject populace. As an official resolution of 1920 opined:

The caution... which has characterised the policy of the Government of India in this respect was dictated by the difficulties which naturally presented themselves to a foreign power which found itself in a position of isolation, confronted by a vast population divided in faith,... and each sect imbued with a strong sense of its own tenets.[49]

This was not, however, the traditional Indian way of doing things in respect of the management of religious difference. As Sandria Freitag has shown in the case of Benares, it marked a decisive break with former practice: 'where earlier the ruler had fully participated in the public arena to establish his legitimacy, the imperial state had now withdrawn. In its place it had deputed certain local power-holders to act as its intermediaries.'[50] Likewise, Arjun Appadorai's study of colonial temple management in Madras is essentially the story of the severance of a close functional relationship and its eventual replacement in the early twentieth century by one of decentralised supervision through elected boards of management.[51]

By contrast, the 'church–state relationship' remained direct and intimate in the princely states. In 1932, for example, orthodox Vaishnavas in Udaipur were scandalised by the news that Damudarlalji, son and heir of the titular head of the chief temple at Nathudwara, had married a singer from Delhi. Indeed, public wrath was so great that when the couple returned from their honeymoon to Nathudwara there was a riot. Fearful of the consequences and burdened by a sense of shame for Damudarlalji's conduct, the boy's father begged him to give the girl up, but he refused. At this juncture, anxious about a possible disruption to the lucrative pilgrim trade, the maharana took a hand and told the boy through his *dewan*, Sukdeo Prasad, that he was removing him by royal authority from the line of succession to the Nathudwara *gaddi* and that this exclusion would remain in force for such time as the 'illicit' liaison continued. Chastened, Damudarlalji agreed to separate from his wife.[52] Likewise, the *darbārs* paid close bureaucratic attention to the upkeep of places of religious worship and the performance of their incumbent religious professionals, and did not hesitate to intervene directly if occasion warranted. When a fire broke out at Gurudwara Gangsar at Jaito, Nabha, the government held an investigation, which found that the *granthi*, Nihal Singh, had improperly left the gurudwara in charge of a young boy while he visited friends. His appointment was abruptly terminated.[53] Likewise, the Patiala authorities displayed no mercy when they discovered that the *pujari* of the Badri Narain temple near Bahadurgarh had been having an affair with the wife of the temple *mahant*.[54] Again, princely governments did not shrink from trampling on the religious susceptibilities of sectarian groups of subjects where these appeared to run counter to the larger interests of the state. Jey Singh of Alwar, for example, boasted that he often 'removed mosques and temples [to allow] for [the] construction of roads'; while the Jaipur and Jodhpur authorities at various times bulldozed Hindu shrines and even dug up whole Muslim graveyards in the cause of civic improvement. No British-controlled provincial government, it need hardly be said, would have dared to act so cavalierly.[55] By assuming direct responsibility for the protection and efficient management of religious institutions, the *darbārs* normalised the notion of public intervention in the 'private' domain of religion and accustomed their subjects to its exercise. As active religious brokers, they acquired a claim to speak out on issues like tolerance, which the 'secular' British could not aspire to.

However, the greatest advantage possessed by the *darbārs*, compared to the provincial governments, in this arena, was arguably the great moral authority possessed by the princes as hereditary monarchs, practising Hindus, Muslims and Sikhs, communal leaders and key ritual facilitators.

As foreigners and nominal Christians, the British could claim, with some justification, to be disinterested observers of Indian religious life, whereas the princes, as practising Hindus, Muslims and Sikhs, had a personal and vested interest in the welfare of their respective faiths. Moreover, even those whose personal beliefs edged towards the agnostic could not stand aside from performing the public religious duties that went with the office. Seated on the *gaddi*, a Hindu prince was not simply a ruler holding court, but also a conduit for ritual interactions and exchanges, an intermediary between men and gods. 'The raja was displayed in order to allow his subjects to take *darśan*—a term usually used in connection with the ornamented images of deities displayed in the sanctum of a temple...He was an icon.'[56] Similarly, Hindu rulers were required by convention to preside over major public ritual events, such as festivals, and most particularly over the autumnal festival of *Dasehra* (which, commemorating as it does the start of Rama's successful war of revenge against Ravana, is the one most sacred to *khshatriyas* and was therefore counted 'the most important function' of the year in most northern princely states).[57] For instance at Jaipur, it was the custom on the final day of *Dasehra* for the maharaja, 'with his own hands',

> to perform *puja* to the arms and throne in the Chandra Mahal Palace, while one vassal noble stands behind the throne holding in his hand the feather of a *huma* (a most auspicious bird which has been an

heirloom of the Kachhwa Dynasty for many centuries)...Afterwards, a public darbar is held, usually in the pillared Hall of Public Audience (Diwan-i-Am). The Maharaja sits in a chair of gold and silver; dancing girls sing songs specially composed for the occasion; bards and *brahmans* chant their odes in glorification of the dynasty and to invoke Heaven's blessing on the ruling prince; the nobles, officers of state and the leading merchants present *nazar* in gold or silver coins according to their status.

Then the Maharaja...does *puja* to the paraphernalia of State (palan-quins, elephants, throne etc.) Next, at sunset,...His Highness rides in procession through his capital and as he reaches the Jai-pol gate the auspicious bird *nilkanth* (blue throat) is let loose...[while] the Maharaja adores a *kheri* tree and presents one gold *mohur* and one coconut to the mahant of Balandji's temple.[58]

Lastly, both in the Hindu and Muslim traditions, rulers were enjoined to conserve and nourish established religion by affording it the protection of the state and by extending patronage to men of piety and religious learning. Indeed, in some cases, this obligation was expressly stated in royal titles. Amongst other laurels, the rulers of Bikaner bore the title *Gau Brahmin Pratipalak*—'Defender of Cows and Brahmins'; whilst one of the dynastic titles of the Dhrangadhra royal house was *Dharma-Dhurandhar*—'Yoked to *Dharma* (religion)'. But always it was implicit, and expected. Rulers were supposed, in matters of religion, to set a salutary example. As a former princely high court judge put it in an open letter published in the early 1900s: 'Your subjects...have a claim to some-thing more than mere secular good government at your hands.'[59] For all these reasons, secularism in the sense that it was defined in British India was never an option in the princely states.

Another important prop to princely authority in matters of religion was the nature of the office. Kings typically exercise what Max Weber calls 'traditional' authority, which has its roots in the reverence that society accords 'the sanctity of immemorial traditions'.[60] In India, at least, kingship is undeniably a venerable institution, 'stretching back', as Maharaja Ganga Singh of Bikaner proudly informed the members of the Carlton Club of London, 'through unbroken centuries to the dawn of history'.[61] Moreover, it was legitimated by religion. 'Whatever a king does is right, that is a settled rule; because the protection of the world is entrusted to him', opines the sage Narada. 'If the king does not properly protect us', observes the *Mahābhārata*, 'we fare very ill; we cannot perform our religious rites according to our desire.'[62] In the Indian political tradition even despotic and arbitrary rule was considered preferable to anarchy.

Indeed many Hindu scriptures hold the institution of kingship to be an integral part of the divine cosmic order, which has led to the perception in some quarters that Hindu kings are themselves divine—at least while they are enthroned on the *gaddi* and in touch with its *shakti* (power).[63] Not surprisingly many princes of the colonial era (whatever their private thoughts on the matter might have been) were quite happy in public to go along with this dogma, even to the extent of having pedigrees produced and vouchsafed by Brahmins that explicitly linked them with the ancient god-kings of the epics.

What is more, this perception of the princes as divine or semi-divine beings seems to have been widely shared by, at least, the unlettered sections of the Indian population, including interestingly that part of it resident in the provinces—which helps to explain why this group, as well as many in the middle class, for a long time envisioned the states as providing a template for future 'home rule'. Before visiting Benares in 1948, Congressman Rajendra Prasad discreetly inquired how the maharaja was regarded by his subjects and was told that he was 'venerated as the representative of Vishwanath', and greeted with ecstatic cries of 'Har Har Mahadeva' whenever he passed through the town.[64] Likewise, when the maharajas of the northern hill state of Tehri Garhwal appeared in public, they were greeted as embodiments of the deity of the shrine of Badrinath, an association celebrated too in the popular name for the Tehri rulers: 'Bolanda Badrinath', meaning 'Speaking [for] Badrinath'.[65] To be sure, nothing like the same spiritual sanction attached to rulers in the Islamic tradition, and some north Indian Muslim rulers, like Hamidullah of Bhopal, were discomforted by the uncritical adulation they received from the superstitious masses. 'I am not the incarnation of God', Hamidullah told an American reporter,

> and my Moslem subjects do not worship me. However my Hindu subjects persist in doing so, even though I am a Moslem. According to our teachings, a ruler is blessed by God and should be obeyed; that is all. If I accept worship, I am committing a sin. So, when a Hindu prostrates himself to me, I make him get up.[66]

Most South Asian Muslim rulers, though, were happy to play along with the deception. At any rate, the evidence is pretty clear that many, if not most, princely subjects believed that royal commands carried 'supernatural sanction'.[67]

But while this sanction applied generically to all Indian rulers, including Muslims, by virtue of their office, it could be strengthened (as in Hamidullah's case) by personal reputation, rulers known for their religious learning and piety being held in particular esteem. And many north Indian princes fell into this category. One was Ganga Singh of Bikaner, of whom it was recorded: 'Not a single day passed without the ardent worship of God' by the ruler.[68] Another was Tukoji Rao Puar, ruler of Dewas Senior. Somewhat against his better judgement, touring English writer E.M. Forster, who had taken up a temporary position as the maharaja's private secretary (PS), found himself moved by the fervour of his employer during the Gokul Astami festival:

> I have never seen religious ecstasy before and I didn't take to it more than I expected I should, but he managed not to be absurd...He is dancing all the time...jigging up and down with a happy expression on his face and twanging a stringed instrument that hangs by a scarf around his neck. At the end of two hours he gets wound up and begins composing poetry...and yesterday he flung himself flat on his face on the carpet...His Highness has what one understands by the religious sense and it comes out all through his life. He is always thinking of others and refusing to take advantage of his position in his dealings with them; and believing that his God acts similarly towards him.

More than once, Forster adds, the maharaja had contemplated abdicating and 'retiring from the world' to concentrate on his devotions.[69] Similarly, Maharaja Pratap Singh of Kashmir took the precepts of his Hindu faith so seriously that he kept a dozen cows tethered in the garden outside his bedroom window so he would be sure to see one first thing upon waking up every morning; while others, like Jey Singh of Alwar and Sawai Madho Singh of Jaipur in his later years, spent months and even years on pilgrimages to Hindu holy places. However of all the Hindu rulers, Jey Singh was probably the most extreme in his orthodoxy. Terrified of ritual pollution, he wore cotton gloves as an insurance against bodily contact and would not abide a single piece of leather furniture in his palace. And his public outbursts of religious fervour were legendary. On one occasion, in 1933, returning from one of his periodic visits to Benares, Jey Singh stepped off the train clad only in a coarse white *dhoti* and saffron *pugree*, and proceeded to walk barefooted all the way from the station to his palace, clutching a *lota* filled with holy water from the Ganges. Some time later, the British resident found him wandering the palace 'in an ecstasy of religious emotionalism', frequently shedding tears and talking of becoming a *sanyasi*.[70] Both Jey Singh and Udaibhan Singh of Dholpur were leading figures in the Sanatan Dharma Sabha, the premier vehicle of orthodox Hinduism. But conspicuous piety was not confined to the ranks of the Hindu rulers; the nawab of Rampur, Mohammad Hamid Ali Khan, was so dedicated to his Shi'a faith that he insisted on being buried at the holy shrine of Najaf in Iraq.

Not all rulers were religious fanatics, by any means, but almost all saw the benefit of conforming to the public religious roles expected of them. As a Cambridge-educated student of anthropology, Mayurdhwaj Sinhji's personal approach to religion was tinged with scepticism; but he never for a moment neglected his public religious duties or his private ritual obligations as a Hindu: 'if I was thought not to be a religious person,' he recalls, 'what I said would have carried less weight'.[71]

In some cases, too, princely authority in matters of religious behaviour was buttressed by the dynasty's ownership of valuable totemic objects, such as sacred images or personal relics associated with legendary teachers and saints, or by virtue of their custodianship of important sacred sites. Part of the symbolic capital of the Nabha house included personal items bequeathed to its founder by the tenth and last Sikh Guru Gobind Singh, notably his *kirpan* or dagger, and his *saropa* or cloak;[72] that of the Danta dynasty, their lordship of the shrine of Amba Bhawani Mata, revered by Hindus as the 'Divine Mother of the Universe'.[73]

Finally, Indian princes gained influence over the religious hierarchy through patronage. Religious charities and institutions all over India, and some even much further afield (such as the hospices maintained for *haj* pilgrims at Mecca), benefited from their largesse. Recipients included schools, universities, temples and shrines. The Sikh rulers, for instance, gave lavishly to Sikh educational institutions in the Punjab, bankrolled conservation work at Sikh sacred sites, subsidised several regional newspapers and to a large extent met the running expenses of the Khalsa College at Amritsar. The latter outlay, though costly, brought especially useful dividends for it gave the Sikh rulers considerable leverage (albeit at one remove) over the curriculum and thereby over the developing minds of the sons of the Punjabi Sikh elite.

So when the princes spoke on matters of religion and appealed to their subjects to put aside their differences in a spirit of fruitful co-existence— for the most part they were listened to. Just as important in this regard, though, was the way the rulers, by and large, enthusiastically embraced pluralism in their own lives, thereby creating positive role models for the population. Thus the Muslim ruling families of Junagadh and Mangrol underlined their identification with 'the culture and royal traditions of Kathiawar' by designating their sons and daughters '*kumar shri*' and '*kumari shri*'—Hindu titles—and by offering public worship at a renowned local shrine dedicated to the goddess.[74] Similarly the Kotah *darbār* every year acknowledged the '*urs* of the Muslim saint Mathe Mahabali by presenting a *chadar* (sheet) to the trustees of the saint's tomb at Gajron; while at Gwalior the maharaja and his *sardars* not only attended Mohurrum but contributed *tazias* to the procession.

This eclectic symbolism spoke volumes. So too did cross-communal royal marriages and friendships. Several Hindu rulers in the early twentieth century had Muslim or Christian wives and others were known to keep Muslim concubines. The courtesan Zubaida, for instance, became something of a celebrity at Jodhpur during the reign of Umaid Singh. Likewise, most rulers ignored religious differences when it came to choosing their friends. Ganga Singh of Bikaner counted Nizam Osman Ali of Hyderabad and Nawab Hamidullah of Bhopal 'amongst some of my closest...personal friends in this world',[75] and a similar closeness characterised the relationship between Hamidullah and the Maratha prince Yeshwant Rao Holkar. Even the ultra-orthodox Jey Singh, who, as we shall see shortly, scandalously discriminated against his own Muslims within Alwar state, was often seen at Mount Abu or Bombay relaxing in the company of eminent Muslim friends such as Muhammad and Shaukat Ali and the Aga Khan.

Finally, many rulers used patronage not only to buy influence, but also to demonstrate their impartiality on the score of religious affiliation. The maharaja of Kapurthala, a nominally Sikh ruler, not only contributed handsomely towards the cost of the city's jama masjid, but engaged an architect to produce a design that could compete with the finest mosques of Algeria or Morocco. Bhupinder Singh of Patiala, another Sikh ruler, financed the building of the Mata Kali Devi temple, the city's largest, and personally oversaw the installation there, in 1936, of an image of the goddess imported from Calcutta. In the same vein, the Gaekwar endowed at Baroda a 'Kirti Mandir' to serve as a 'meeting place for all religions and creeds';[76] while the raja of Lunawada donated land and money to the state's Sunni Muslim community for the construction of a *madrassah*. In 1942, Yadavindra Singh of Patiala gave 10,000 rupees out of his privy purse for repairs to the Idgaṭh. By means of these salutary examples, the Indian princes helped to educate subject and community perceptions about what constituted acceptable social behaviour towards members of minority groups.

The thesis developed above resonates at several points with arguments advanced over a number of years by Iqbal Narain and P.C. Mathur with respect to the polity of Rajasthan, most eloquently and cogently in their joint article 'The Thousand Year Raj'. According to Iqbal and Mathur, the millennial-long Rajput domination of Rajasthan led to the emergence there of a high culture built around the martial ideals of the warrior Rajputs rather than, as in other regions, the Brahminical values which were enshrined in the classic scriptures of Hinduism. As a result, they claim, Hinduism acquired, in Rajasthan, something of a heterodox flavour, of which one expression was the lesser importance placed in Rajasthani society on ritual purity and pollution. But for our purposes, the key passages in the article are those that tease out the implications of the Rajput *khsatriya* culture for Hindu–Muslim relations. They deal especially with the notion of *sharan* or protection:

> The Rajputs were interested in ruling: to them Brahminical purity-pollution rituals were secondary and, indeed, could be subordinated to political goals. Thus, even while engaging Muslims rulers on the battlefield, the Rajputs never subscribed to the orthodox Brahminical stereotype of Muslims as being *mllechas* not worth of social intercourse. Rajput princes' matrimonial alliances with the Mughals (and even pre-Mughal rulers) are, of course, well-known. [However] A much more powerful manifestation of secular outlook among the Rajputs is provided by their theory and practice of the *sharan* doctrine...

> This was the doctrine asserting that a ruler must give protection to anyone who seeks it, irrespective of any other consideration and totally unmindful of the consequences of providing such protection.... [Thus] Rajput princes provided shelter, security and even military support to potential Mughal emperors after their unsuccessful revolts against their...fathers...

> By itself *sharan* is not devoid of the Hindu religious ethos. But its continuous practice with regard to Muslim nobility imparted secular overtones to the political life in the princely states, which helps explain the widespread cultural norms of inter-religious harmony.[77]

It will be seen that this formulation goes somewhat further than the one I have ventured, particularly in its implicit critique of M.N. Srinivas' 'sanskritization' model and its claim that Hinduism wore a less Brahminical face in Rajasthan than in other places. However, with respect to the core matter of the mediatory social role played by the Rajput rulers, we are in complete accord. Indeed, I have only one real problem with the Narain–Mathur argument, and that is the use the authors make of the term 'secular' to describe the aforementioned princely culture.

Although one often sees the terms 'secular' and 'secularism' employed in India in the Narain and Mathur sense of religious toleration, this is an incorrect usage. 'Secular' properly means being 'not concerned with or related to religion', or, in a more restricted sense, 'having no particular religious affinities'.[78] The truly secular state, therefore—even if led by personally devout individuals—can have no institutionalised religious connections and certainly no sectarian ties with a particular faith. Obviously, this is not how things worked in the states ruled by the Indian princes, whose very *raison d'être* was to protect and nourish religious virtue in society. Yet, paradoxically, the very unsecular nature of these Indian kingdoms entitled them to engage with organised religion in ways not open to the colonial state in the provinces. This made it much easier for them to keep the lid on aggressive communal assertion.

Princes and publics

If not secular states in the proper sense, the Indian princely states were nevertheless places where members of different religious groups could confidently expect the support of their governments in guaranteeing them freedom to worship in the manner of their choice. Although Kashmir was ruled by a dynasty of Hindu Dogra Rajputs, the *azan* rang out freely every Friday from the state's mosques. *Darbāri* police flanked the route of the annual *Mohurrum* procession in Hindu-ruled Jaipur, and watched over Jain pilgrimage sites in Muslim-ruled Junagadh. When a communal riot broke out at Ujjain, Gwalior, in 1942, the government of this Hindu-ruled state paid out substantial compensation to Muslim Bohra victims of the rioting, but gave nothing to their Hindu assailants. In law, religious minorities in the states were free to worship pretty much as they pleased.

But the enjoyment of these rights and opportunities, important as they were, did not entirely equate with a situation of communal equality. For one thing, princely spending in areas of public welfare, such as education, generally favoured members of the ruler's community. In Patiala, there was a state scholarship scheme to send deserving students to Lyallpur Agricultural College. Four scholarships annually were awarded; of these two were always given to Sikhs, who comprised only

40 per cent of the population. Similarly Gwalior government scholarships for advanced study went overwhelmingly to members of the minority Maratha-Hindu community to which the ruling Scindia family belonged; Muslims, by contrast, though not a numerous group in Gwalior, rarely won a government grant and struggled to get admission to the state's elite Victoria College obtaining just one out of 70 places in 1943. But in Tonk and Palanpur states, where the Muslim population share was no greater, but where the rulers were Muslim, the position was dramatically reversed. Typically three out of every four Tonk state scholarships for higher study went to Muslims; while Palanpur's tiny Muslim population regularly secured a majority of free school places. And it was the same story with ecclesiastical patronage. *Gurudwaras* in Sikh-ruled Patiala received substantially more government funds *per capita* than did temples or mosques in the state, and the reverse applied, as we shall see, in Muslim-ruled Bhopal. Last but not least, preference was commonly given to co-religionists of the ruler in the allocation of government contracts and concessions as happened at Junagadh:

> Apparently there is a system [in Junagadh] of monopolies which gives great offence to them [the Hindus] as most of the concessionaires are Mohammedans. For example, there is a firm called 'The General Stores' in Junagadh, of which the Superintendent of the State Garage is a member, and the relatives of various servants of the nawab and the Dewan are also represented. Through this firm all stores of whatever kind and for whatever purpose bought for the State are purchased and the firm takes a percentage of everything. This naturally causes inconvenience to the ordinary Hindu trader.

Likewise, Muslim merchants in Junagadh got the lion's share of state loans.[79]

And a close examination of the protocols of princely governance reveals that a similar imbalance applied there too. At the higher levels, it is true, cross-communal bureaucratic hiring was quite commonplace in the states—a point the rulers made much of in their propaganda. In the early 1930s, Jhalawar in Rajputana, and Datia and Charkhari in CI—all of them Hindu states—had Muslim chief ministers. During Ganga Singh's reign, Bikaner had two Muslim prime ministers and a Muslim chief justice. In Patiala and Jaipur there was a tradition of employing Muslim revenue members. Even that paragon of Hindu orthodoxy, Maharaja Jey Singh, was happy to make use of the talents of the young Muslim radical K.M. Ashraf, appointing him in 1928 as his personal adviser. Yet these selections were not simply communal-based. Ability was naturally an important criterion. As the Household Minister at Kapurthala told Akali leader Tara Singh: 'His Highness always appoints his Chief Minister regardless of his religion, choosing the best man he can find whether he be an English-man, Sikh, Muslim or Hindu.'[80] Nepotism was another; the tradition of sons following fathers into *darbāri* service was deeply rooted in the political culture of the states, and family ties were considered a good indicator of suitability for government employment.[81]

More importantly, the policy in respect of other levels of public-service recruitment does not bear out the *darbārs'* claims of evenhandedness. Such scanty data, as can be readily obtained from published administration reports, shows that on a population-basis Muslims were generally grossly under-represented in Hindu- and Sikh-ruled states in all branches of government except the police and the military, although the imbalance was less, for some reason, in CI than in other regions. Conversely, the published data reveals that Muslims were significantly over-represented in the Muslim-ruled states although, again, one finds some regional variations (Table 2.6). There is evidence, too, that, at least in some states, public servants belonging to the same community as the ruler were treated more generously in regard to promotion and more leniently when they erred or underperformed.[82]

Thirdly, and perhaps most revealingly, where Hindu and Islamic religious injunctions were mutually antagonistic, as they were, for example, in respect of cow-slaughter and music accompanying worship, it was almost always, in princely states, those of the ruler's faith that took precedence. In Muslim-ruled states, the playing of music in the vicinity of mosques was totally prohibited at prayer times and for the most part at other times as well. And restrictions were even tighter on Islamic holy days such as during Mohurrum and Ramadan. But music was not the only form of religious expression curtailed in Muslim states. In Bahawalpur, Sikh men faced arrest if they were caught carrying *kirpans*, which they were required to do by their faith; while in Bhopal, Hindus

Table 2.6 Muslim employment in gazetted posts, selected states, 1926 (per cent)

	Punjab	Rajputana	Central India	Western India
Hindu-ruled states (54)	–	2.22	14.29	1.35
Sikh-ruled states (4)	23.53	–	–	–
Muslim-ruled states (10)	50.00	16.66	50.00	15.79

Source: State administration reports, various, c.1925–26.

were discouraged from proselytising by special laws against apostasy and the enforcement of *Shari'a* laws disinheriting converts. Last but not least, cow-slaughter was permitted 'on a very liberal scale' in almost all Muslim-ruled states even though the practice was profoundly offensive to the moral susceptibilities of their non-Muslim subjects.[83]

On the other hand, the Hindu *darbārs* generally took a permissive line in the matter of music in the vicinity of mosques. In most Hindu states, the practice was to prohibit the playing of music only during Muslim prayer times, and then only upon the receipt of specific written complaints from Muslim worshippers. Again, all the governments of Hindu-ruled states went to great lengths to restrict the slaughter of domestic animals, even for food. Licenses for meat markets were kept to a minimum. Such markets as did receive government approval were confined to 'not easily accessible' places well away from the main *bazaars*. Animals destined for slaughter had to be taken to the abattoirs by roundabout routes, so as not to attract attention, and were not permitted to be 'paraded' or decorated. Slaughtering was restricted to set times (generally very early in the morning) and subject to the payment of a heavy fee.[84] And further restrictions applied on holy days. In Sirohi there was a standing order prohibiting the slaughter of goats during the Pachusan festival, and in Jodhpur 'no Mohammadan' was allowed to 'take out a goat in the Bazar [*sic*]' during any period of religious celebration.[85] As for cow-slaughter, it was totally prohibited, and heavy penalties were imposed on transgressors. Under the Patiala Penal Code, kine-killers were liable to seven years rigorous imprisonment and a heavy fine. A similar sanction applied in Kashmir. In Nabha, convicted offenders face six years jail followed by banishment from the state. In Bikaner, even the import of beef slaughtered in British India carried a hefty fine. It bears emphasising that nowhere in the British-ruled provinces was there anything equivalent to this blanket ban.[86]

Widespread across princely north India, structured inequalities between communities were greatest in Alwar, Kashmir and Bhopal. In Alwar—a state in which the Muslim population approached 40 per cent in some districts—public-service regulations forbad the wearing of beards, a requirement that was 'quite obviously designed [to work] against Muslims';[87] Islamic religious education was discouraged and for a period in the late 1920s and early 1930s, totally outlawed; state schools taught only in Hindi, which most local Muslims, especially those living in the rural areas, did not speak; and officials regularly put obstacles in the way of Muslims building or repairing mosques, or even, on occasions, prevented them from worshipping in the prescribed manner.

In Kashmir, although Muslims there comprised over 70 per cent of the population, their share of state scholarships and places in government schools was the smallest of the three major communities; while they held as of 1931 only 22 per cent of senior (gazetted) appointments in the Kashmir public service and only about 25 per cent of places in the Kashmir army, which was mainly filled by Hindu Dogras (the maharaja's community).[88] Additionally, Kashmiri Muslims were disadvantaged by discriminatory laws and regulations—such as those which prohibited apostates from inheriting ancestral property and made gun-licenses compulsory for people in the Kashmir Valley region, where most Muslims lived, but not for people residing in predominantly Hindu Jammu.

But quite the reverse applied in the nawabi raj of Bhopal. Although they comprised only a small fraction of the Bhopal population, Muslims filled over 90 per cent of all gazetted public service positions, all the top jobs in the police force, and all but one cabinet post. In 1931 just 97.8 per cent of the state budgetary allocation of 2.7 lakhs for religious charities went to Islamic institutions, mainly to pay the salaries of some 300 *imams* and *muezzins* attached to the state-owned mosques. As well, Bhopali Muslims benefited from laws that banned 'processions, religious or otherwise' from using roads near mosques and allowed converts to Islam to inherit ancestral property, and from the ascendancy of Urdu, which was the sole medium of instruction in schools.[89] It says a great deal of the sagacity and flair for public relations of the Bhopal government under Nawab Hamidullah that, notwithstanding these palpable inequalities, the state was generally regarded in British India, especially in imperial circles, as a well-managed one in which there was no preferential treatment 'of one community at the expense of the other'.[90]

The notion that any one religious group should occupy an entrenched position in the state was from the first strongly repudiated in British India. There, as we have seen, the official policy was one of *laissez-faire* neutrality (although it would be qualified, from the late nineteenth century on, by initiatives in favour of allegedly 'backward' groups such as Muslims and non-Brahmins). In the states, though, where the rulers were regarded as religious icons and where, for the most part, the ruling elites had established themselves by means of conquest, members of the ruler's community expected to be favoured above all others. Amongst Jats, there was a firmly held perception that Bharatpur was a 'Jat State', wherein members of the community were entitled to hold superior rights. A similar view—Robert Stern informs us—was held about Jaipur by Rajputs.[91] Amongst the Sikhs, the five

Sikh-ruled kingdoms were regarded almost as communal property, and Sikhs expected to occupy 'a dominating position' there. Significantly, census figures show that, all other things being equal, Sikhs preferred to live in Sikh-ruled states and Muslims in Muslim-ruled states, rather than in other states or in British India.[92] As well, these dominant communities looked to their co-religionist rulers for religious leadership. They expected them not only to be pious and scrupulous in the observance of their own ritual obligations, but to take an active role in the protection and propagation of the 'state' religion at large. 'Your Highness is the protector of our religion', a petition from the Hindu *chaudhuries* of Ladnun, Jodhpur, began.[93] 'It is indeed the Rajadharma ... revealed to Yudisthir in the Mahabharata which should be Your Highness's guide as a true Hindu', a well-wisher advised the maharaja of Tehri-Garhwal on his investiture.[94] When Muslims in Tijara, Alwar, rioted in 1933, Hindus in the affected area expected the maharaja, 'our Shri Pabhu Dev', to come to their rescue.[95]

Moreover, dominant communities in the states did not hesitate to rebuke their princely patrons if they thought they were failing in their communal 'duty'. Akali Sikhs, for example, were critical of the allegedly loose habits of the Phulkian maharajas, who were said, amongst other things, to smoke cigarettes 'against the order of the Guru'.[96] As Punjab MLA Giani Kartar Singh explained, the Akali goal was to bring about 'the re-establishment of the Sikh character of the State[s] ... In Kapurthala things have come to such a pass that some people have publicly begun to claim it as a Hindu State.'[97] Similarly, Hindus were critical of the maharajas of Karauli and Sirohi for keeping Muslim mistresses, partly on moral grounds but mainly because the ladies in question were suspected of acting as a conduit for backstairs 'Muhammadan' influence at court. Indeed some critics went so far as to suggest that Sarup Singh of Sirohi had been persuaded by his paramour to become a secret convert to Islam.[98] Again, some Hindus found the institutionalised pluralism of Bikaner discomforting. As one put it in a letter to the Hindu Mahasabha's B.S. Moonje, 'the Hindoo population in this Hindoo State is not so much respected as one ought to expect'.[99] Public opinion—both local and all-Indian—put a lot of pressure on the *darbārs* to privilege the dominant communal group among their subjects and to restrict the rights of minorities.

To be sure, the rulers were not obliged, constitutionally, to listen to these pushy lobbyists. They were autocrats, legally answerable to nobody. But as we noted earlier, the absence of constitutional forms in the states did not mean that princely subjects were without influence. At one level, the polity of the states was a very open one in that even the poorest subject had a right of access to the prince, and what is more, most rulers seem to have been willing to hear their petitions. The maharawal of Dungapur 'saw anyone and everyone who came'; in Dhrangandhra, it was the custom for the ruler to hear petitions at 'the hour when the lamps are lit', that is to say, daily at sunset; when Maharaja Umed Singh of Jodhpur toured, complaints were heard and 'investigated on the spot with the aid of local officials'.[100] At another level, and more importantly, rulers could ill afford to alienate powerful castes or individuals or even large numbers of the populace on whom they depended for the generation of wealth, and therefore revenue, and who in the last resort had the capacity, through rebellion or mass emigration, to bring down on the state the ire of the imperial authorities. The Political Department might have been wedded in the early twentieth century to a policy of *laissez-faire*, but when they did act it was usually with ruthless effect. Thus, when dominant communities made demands or offered criticisms, rulers tended to listen attentively and, more often than not, make an effort to accommodate their concerns. In 1926 the Jain custodians of the Shatrunjaya Hill shrine in Palitana, faced with an attempt by the *darbār* to impose an additional tax on pilgrims visiting the shrine, closed it, and kept it closed until the government backed down. In the same year the Nabha *darbār*, bowing to Sunni pressure, refused the minority Shi'a community permission to take out a separate *tazia* procession during Mohurrum. And in 1932 the leaders of Junagadh's Memon community pressured the nawab into sacking his moderate PM, Sheikh Muhammadbhai, whom they regarded as too partial towards Hindus.[101] But even the more efficient governments of the bigger Indian states were not immune from communal lobbying, as the example of Indore, effectively run during the 1920s and 1930s by a cabal of wealthy Hindu mill owners, shows.

Moreover, where state rulers found themselves obliged, under pressure from dominant communal groups, to give preference to their co-religionists in recruitment, the administrative services of such states inevitably acquired a communal outlook to match their communal complexion. In Jhalawar, the majority of primary- and middle-school teachers were said to be people given to 'sectarian and hurtful prejudices'.[102] Likewise the lower echelons of public service of Jodhpur contained many Hindus who, like the Manager of the Kuchaman Thikana, feared and despised the Muslim 'mentality'.[103]

Discrimination in favour of dominant religious groups was not only widely practised in the Indian states; it was structurally enshrined in the princely polity. Nevertheless the subordinated communities did not usually question or try to challenge the system. Muslims living in Hindu- or Sikh-ruled states, for example, almost never killed cows even for food.[104] Why such compliance? In part it was an acknowledgement that harsh retribution awaited them if they stepped out of line. Defending his suggestion that his co-religionists should 'respect' their 'elder brothers', the Hindus, a Bikaner Muslim observed sagely: 'they are large in number'.[105] And there was probably an element, too, of weary resignation. With enough practice, deference can become habitual. But mostly it seems that the subordinated communities went along with the system because they did not think it particularly wrong or unjust. On the face of it, Hindus in Muslim-ruled Bahawalpur suffered considerable discrimination. Their share of educational scholarships and public-service positions was tiny, they could not take out religious processions near mosques and they had to suffer the sight of cows being butchered in the bazaars. Yet when accusations of a 'lack of religious freedom' in the state were mounted in the provincial Hindu press, leaders of the Bahawalpur Hindu community leapt to the *darbār*'s defence:

> Government has never interfered in the celebration of national [i.e. Hindu] fairs. It has been on the contrary rendering every facility and even pecuniary assistance ... [The] Order regarding Beef Shops is based on a time-honoured custom. This question can be decided by the two communities amicably ... A Hindu–Muslim Committee might consider it anew ... There is no Hindu Minister in the Cabinet. [But] considering the population [of] the Hindus ... the objection does not stand to reason.[106]

Outsiders regarded the 'minorities' in the states as 'oppressed'. Perhaps they were, objectively. But it was a condition to which the victims were resigned. As a Rampuri Hindu Congress worker lamented in 1948: 'every Muslim in the State still today regards himself as the ruler while every Hindu thinks [that] it [is] his fate to be suppressed'.[107]

In a dispatch to the secretary of state in 1893, the then viceroy Lord Lansdowne drew a sharp contrast between religious life in the provinces and the princely states:

> The ordinary course of things in a Native State is that one or the other religion is dominant in the administration, and that the party professing the creed which is not that of the ruling party has to submit to the loss of the privileges which it would enjoy if it were in the

ascendant or free to carry out its rights as it pleased. This was the case in the Punjab before [British] annexation, and it is still the case in most Native States, whether Hindu or Mohamedan.[108]

Thirty years on, this hierarchic arrangement still, for the most part, held good. Heirs to a pluralistic culture of governance, the princes were generally fine exemplars of tolerance; likewise, their *darbārs* were in the main strongly committed to the promotion of civic harmony and the elimination of religious discord. But the civil society of the princely states was not one in which all communities were of equal standing. Almost everywhere in princely India the community of the ruler was privileged—privileged in its access to education and the public service, privileged in the distribution of government patronage, privileged in legislation that decreed what was permissible social behaviour, and privileged in respect of the right to take out religious processions. What is more, this hierarchical system was to a large extent accepted by those against whom it told—not gladly, perhaps, but on the whole uncomplainingly. More than anything else, it was the willingness of disadvantaged religious groups in the states to sacrifice peripheral rights of religious expression in return for broad community tolerance of their basic right to worship that kept princely India largely free from the scourge of Hindu–Muslim communal violence in the early twentieth century.

3
Metamorphosis

> The time has come when the communal holocaust must be confined to the Indian States... There was a time when our politicians like Gokhale rightly used to take pride in Indian States being free from communalism, which was a vice in British India... But the table appears to have been turned.
>
> C.S. Ranga Iyer MLA, 1934

Cracks in the façade

Communalism is often characterised as a 'virus' eating away at society. The metaphor is arresting but inaccurate. Like all social phenomena, communalism is a product of human action and decision. Riots happen because people for a variety of reasons choose to take part in them. Conversely, a riot cannot occur if no one turns up. As we have seen, non-action or reaction undertaken in a spirit of communal compromise was much more the behavioural norm in early twentieth-century princely India than aggressive communal assertion—and perhaps continued to be so, on balance, down to the end of the monarchical period. Nevertheless, there are clear signs from the early 1930s that the established communal consensus in the princely states was starting to wear thin. This chapter looks first at the evidence for this proposition and then goes on to examine the factors and processes that changed irreversibly the communal climate of princely India during the late colonial period.

We have already charted the broad outlines of this narrative of growing communal assertion statistically.

But aggregate casualty figures do not tell the whole story. Not only did the number of communal incidents rise steeply after 1930, the character of these episodes also underwent a transformation. They became larger in scope and more intense; they grew increasingly political and politicised; they had longer-lasting and more far-reaching consequences. What is more, communalism now began to impact on regions and populations that had never been affected. In short, we can say that the 1930s saw an *enlargement of scale* as regards communal violence in princely north India. The implication is that the structures and belief systems we have identified as supporting communal co-existence in the states were starting to break down. Let us now examine these features in more detail.

The first of the new arenas of Hindu–Muslim confrontation to erupt was Kashmir. In July 1931 a Srinagar activist named Abdul Qadir was arrested for taking part in a prohibited political meeting called by the Muhammadan Youngmen's Association (MYA) of Kashmir to press its case for an official inquiry into Muslim grievances. The following day, a crowd gathered outside the gates of Srinagar Jail to show their solidarity with Qadir. Fearing that the demonstrators intended to force an entry, the jail guards opened fire, killing at least nine people and wounding a score of others. The mob dispersed, but regrouped in Maharajganj Bazaar in the predominantly Hindu quarter of Vicharnag, where it proceeded to wreak vengeance on local shopkeepers and their property. The Hindus retaliated, setting off a chain of communal riots that paralysed the Kashmir capital for a week.

Initially the *darbār* reacted moderately and sensibly. It imposed a curfew and bound over the leaders of the communities to maintain the peace. But while this evenhanded stance had the backing of Kashmir's Dogra ruler, Hari Singh, it was bitterly resented by communal elements within the government headed by the Pandit brothers Hari and Daya Kishen Kaul. When, on 21 September, Aligarh University graduate and rising MYA leader Sheikh Mohammad Abdullah rose to address a crowd outside the Jama Masjid, the Kaul brothers seized their chance and had Abdullah arrested for breaking the undertaking to keep the peace. The following day a protest meeting was held at the same spot, after which a group of militant Youngmen attempted to process through a side street guarded by Sikh and Dogra police and troops; five were shot dead and a similar number wounded. When news of this affray reached Islamabad, 34 miles distant, another illegal procession was taken out and a further 22 Muslims were killed by police firing. Nearby Shopian was the next place to erupt. On the 25th, following Friday prayers, a Muslim mob beat up a posse of constables keeping watch on the mosque and stormed a police station before being overpowered by the military.

Kashmir continued to simmer until the mid-1930s. Meanwhile, the first Punjab outbreak took place in Patiala, a state with no previous history of communal rioting. In 1930 four Muslims belonging to the Patiala town of Narnaul were accused and convicted—perhaps unjustly— of breaking some idols in a Hindu temple. After this, communal relations in the locality soured; and in 1932 Muslims 'excited by outside agency' opposed for the first time the playing of music during the annual Holi-Dulhendi procession through the town centre, which resulted in a violent confrontation between Hindu festival-goers and about 6000 Muslims armed with swords, lathis and brickbats. In the event most of the ensuing casualties were due to misdirected police bullets; but at least one Hindu moneylender was stabbed to death.[1]

Alwar's descent into communal mayhem the following year followed a similar pattern. Prefigured by a confrontation in Alwar City in May 1932 between rival groups of religious processioners,[2] the situation became serious when the locally dominant Muslim peasantry of the region, the Meos, hard hit by the global fall in agricultural prices, were pushed over the edge by a rapacious *darbār*. In November 1932, following a ham-fisted attempt by Alwar officials to collect revenue arrears due from the village of Damokar, in the *nizamat* (district) of Kishengarh, Meos from some 70 villages in the eastern part of the state raised the standard of rebellion. They dug in, set up an early warning system consisting of watchmen on the hills equipped with drums, cut down trees and rolled boulders across the roads to slow the progress of the expected *darbāri* punitive force, sent their women and children across the border into Gurgaon District, and sought contributions for a war chest. When an advance party of troops and police arrived at Bhagar village on 3 January 1933, they were met with a fusillade of bullets and forced to retire. Shortly afterwards, another Meo band destroyed the octroi post at Mubarakpur, the first of several attacks on government offices. Then, on 7th, some 6000 Meos led by retired Indian Army *jemadar* Bakhtiwar Khan launched an overnight assault on soldiers guarding the revenue office at Govindgarh, killing and wounding about a dozen and forcing the rest to beat a hasty retreat to the capital.

The next Punjab state to succumb was Kapurthala. Despite its tradition of eclecticism in government, from 1931 onwards, the Kapurthala *darbār* was repeatedly targeted in the Punjabi Muslim communal press for showing a 'grudging' attitude towards the needs and aspirations of the majority Muslim population and for its alleged indifference to 'Sikh attacks on mosques';[3] meanwhile, inside the state, a campaign was started up to persuade Muslim peasants to withhold payment of interest on debts. Partly to appease this agitation, the state's Muslim Chief Minister Sir Abdul Hamid in 1933 introduced a Land Alienation Act on the Punjab pattern, designed to prevent indebted land passing into the hands of urban moneylenders. But this partisan measure drew flak from the Hindus (who comprised the bulk of the urban population). At the same time, Sikhs connected with the Akali Dal came out in opposition to what they construed as Hamid's pro-Muslim policy. By late 1933, communal tension was running high, fanned by false reports that several Hindu temples had been desecrated by Muslim *goondas*. In this charged atmosphere, Muslims celebrating Mohurrum attempted to force a passage for their *tazias* past a Sikh *gurudwara* and a *banyan* tree revered by both Sikhs and Hindus. Police (commanded, ironically, by the brother of the leading Muslim dissident) fired on the Muslim processioners, killing 22 and injuring more than 40 others. This atrocity triggered a second wave of Muslim agitation, which was summarily put down with the aid of 100 British police from Jullundur.

Then it was the turn of Jind. In deference to its substantial Muslim population, the Jind government since 1874 had permitted the slaughter of animals (other than cows) for food almost without restriction. The main exception was the ban imposed on Ikadshi day, when local Hindus remembered the fallen heroes of the battle of Kurukshetra. Neverthless in 1933 Jind Muslims began to agitate for even this token ban to be removed. As Ikadshi day 1934 approached, they stepped up their campaign with a series of highly charged public meetings. With recent events in Kashmir and Kapurthala fresh in their minds, the local Hindus felt angry and affronted. Morever the situation in spring 1934 was complicated by the conjunction of Ikadshi and Holi, which involved raucous processions. On 26 March, Ikadshi day, Holi *ghair* revellers passing through the capital were greeted by jeering Muslim mobs. The Hindus retaliated in numbers, overwhelming their assailants. By the time the police had restored order, ten Muslims had been seriously injured. For several weeks afterwards, Muslims in the capital took out daily black-flag processions, some of which provoked further communal violence.

But it was not just the Sikh-ruled Punjab states that felt the lash of communal violence during the 1930s. On 18 July 1935, worshippers at evening prayer in the capital of Muslim-ruled Malerkotla were discomforted by a noisy *arti* being performed in a nearby temple. The Muslims spilled out on to the street where they were met by an exodus of Hindu devotees from the temple. A fight ensued, in which several Muslims were badly beaten and one, a young girl, stabbed to death. Later that evening a large crowd of Muslims gathered in the main bazaar, bent on revenge; and over the next few days, the Muslim mob was reinforced by *jathas* from neighbouring states, drawn into the fray by newspaper reports which suggested that Nawab Sir Ahmad Ali Khan's government had done a deal with its Hindu bankers to go easy on the girl's attackers. Now fearful for his personal safety, the nawab on 20 July ordered the streets to be cleared. The police unleashed a *lathi* charge scattering the rioters. Most then fled. Those who remained—about 450—were arrested. Again, what principally struck outside observers about these events was their singularity. As the British author of the official report on the riots glumly remarked: 'it is an admitted fact that there has been no Hindu–Muslim trouble in this State within living memory, until the present year'.[4]

Compared to those in Kashmir and the Punjab, the communal outbreaks in western India during the 1930s were relatively minor: two small affrays, resulting in minor injuries, at Kathor and Desar in the Gaekwar state of Baroda during the winter of 1932–33; a fatal encounter at the capital of Bhavnagar in May 1939; and a much more serious riot at Baroda City in January of 1939 that left one man dead and dozens injured. Even so, these episodes constituted further hard evidence that the communal contagion was spreading.

But the riots of the 1930s were not only more numerous and more widespread—they were also qualitatively different: generally bigger, more sustained and more destructive of life and property; more 'sophisticated' in the sense that while usually triggered by the traditional disputes over sacred space, they tended also to feed off economic and other grievances and, in many cases, specifically targeted the *darbārs* as agents of communal discrimination; and above all, more pre-meditated. 'They show[ered] colour deliberately in the direction of the mosque', a group of Bikaner Muslims complained after the 1934 Holi.[5] Likewise, officials investigating the causes of the Malerkotla disturbances of 1935 learned that the offending *katha* performance had been timed to coincide with evening prayers precisely in the expectation that it would 'give rise to objection from the worshippers in the mosque'.[6] Bent on causing trouble, communal *agents provocateurs* in the 1930s even went so far, sometimes, as to destroy their own religious relics and properties in the hope that the blame would fall on members of the other community—as when three mosques were set on fire in Jammu City in 1933 'by Muslims themselves, in order to create a suitable atmosphere' for the taking of revenge.[7]

Drawing on evidence mainly from the 1970s and 1980s, Stanley Tambiah has identified two interlinked processes in the production and dissemination of communal riots, which he calls *focalization* and *transvaluation*. The former he defines as 'the process of progressive denudation of local incidents and disputes of their particulars of context and their aggregation'; the latter as 'the parallel process of assimilating particulars to a larger, collective, more enduring, and therefore less context-bound, cause or interest'.[8] Clearly similar processes to those described by Tambiah were at work in princely India in the 1930s. For the most part, riots in the states remained micro-events in terms of their immediate spread and impact, but now the tendency was to view them as part of an interlocking tapestry of communal conflict. Thus when Alwar Muslims started to leave the state in the aftermath of the May 1932 riot, sympathisers in Lahore promised to send armed *jathas* and turn Alwar into a 'second Kashmir'.[9] Increasingly aware of the political leverage which could be got from the transvaluation of local squabbles, Muslim and Hindu communalists in the states began actively to solicit the support of their extended religious and ethnic kin by staging dramatic actions, such as mass *hijrats* and death-fasts,[10] which, of course, served to further raise the communal temperature locally.

Predictably, Hindu *darbārs* saw the growing communal violence as a problem mainly of Muslim making. The 'mentality of the Mohammadans...has changed considerably', opined Bikaner's inspector-general (IG) of police in 1938.[11] And that was also the view, more surprisingly, of most British observers. Events in Faridkot, the agent-to-the-governor-general (AGG) reported, were symptomatic of the 'new spirit actuating the Muslims of Northern India as evidenced recently in more than one of the Punjab States'.[12] However, the example of Bahawalpur shows that it was not just Muslims who were behaving uncharacteristically. Traditionally Bahawalpur's Hindus had never made much of a fuss over cow-slaughter; but in 1935 they demanded that the practice be made illegal. Underprivileged Hindus too were speaking out, as were underprivileged Sikhs. Minorities of all colours were asserting themselves, slowly but surely throwing off the yoke of self-imposed restraint.

Anxious to protect their reputation as honest religious brokers, the princes as a body roundly condemned the descent into violence and committed themselves anew to fighting and defeating communalism. Reza Ali Khan of Rampur issued press statements calling on interested parties to 'help restore a calm atmosphere'; while Ganga Singh of Bikaner took the unusual step of implicitly criticising another ruler—Hari Singh—for allowing Hindu–Muslim trouble to erupt in Kashmir.[13] Yet even as they reaffirmed their pluralist credentials, the princes sensed that a watershed had been crossed. 'We seem to have entered', Reza Ali opined sadly, 'upon a new and unfortunate phase.'

   What had gone wrong?

The price of progress

In Chapter 2, we examined several prominent sociological theories of communalism that postulate a connection between the growth of communal feelings and animosities in India over the past century, and the coming of modernity in its various guises: with urbanisation, with the advance of technology (including print technology) and industrial-isation, and not least with the spread of newspapers, political parties and elections—all features significantly lacking in the Indian states in the early twentieth century.

   But much as some of the rulers tried valiantly to stop the clock, in the end, they had to yield to the forces of progress. For such forces are irresistible. They may be delayed, but in the end they are unstoppable. Economic and political change came to the states late, and slowly, but in the 1930s and 1940s its pace accelerated, with devastating conse-quences for communal peace in the region. Let us now examine, in detail, how this socio-economic transformation occurred. During the 1930s some of the larger north Indian states in particular—acting partly in response to pressure from the Political Department and from nationalist opinion (of which more below), but chiefly with a view to expanding the size of their tax-base—began pouring more of their revenue surpluses back into rural development and putting in place measures to encourage private investment in industry. The Sutlej Valley irrigation project, completed in 1933, boosted the value of Bahawalpur's agricultural production eightfold and doubled its tax receipts; and the Ganga Canal scheme, opened in late 1927, brought similar benefits to Bikaner. On the industrial front, Baroda, between 1921 and 1941, more than trebled the size of its factory workforce; while Indore established itself in the same period as one of the subcontinent's major centres of silk textile production. All this, however, was but a dress rehearsal for the industrial revolution—the term is not excessive—that overtook the states during the early 1940s under the impact of hothouse wartime demand for munitions and manufactures. Jaipur, for example, by 1945 had 158 factories operating, compared to 57 in 1942. Industrialisation not only made the states richer, it created a massive demand for labour, which attracted more people into the towns (Table 3.1). By the 1940s condi-tions in, at any rate, the larger princely cities were beginning to take on

Table 3.1 Percentage of the population living in towns, selected states and agencies, 1921–51

Unit	1921	1931	1941	1951
Jammu and Kashmir	8.0	9.4	10.3	17.3
Punjab states/PEPSU	11.3	9.2	17.9	19.0
Rampur	21.0	19.6	25.3	29.3
Rajputana/Rajasthan	14.3	13.9	15.1	17.3
Bikaner	25.5	24.1	26.2	38.1
Jodhpur	17.7	13.3	13.8	18.0
Jaipur	16.2	17.0	17.2	28.3
Kathiawar/Saurashtra	31.2	22.1	23.5	33.7
Nawanagar	16.5	20.8	23.6	n/a
Baroda	17.3	21.0	23.6	n/a
Central India/Madhya Pradesh/ Madhya Bharat	9.2	10.2	11.7	13.5
Gwalior	9.4	11.1	13.7	36.7
Bhopal	10.3	12.7	17.7	16.3
Indore	17.0	17.6	21.6	n/a

Sources: Census of India, 1921, Vol. 1, Pt 1, p. 64, Vol. 10, Pt 1, p. 16 and Pt 2, p. 3, Vol. 8, Pt 2, p. 3, Vol. 24, Pt 2, p. 3; *Census of India,* 1931, Vol. 1, Pt 1, pp. 44–5, Vol. 10, Pt 1 and Pt 2, pp. 3, 96, Vol. 17, Pt 1, p. 89, Vol. 18, Pt 1, p. 153, Vol. 19, Pt 1, p. 67, Vol. 20, Pt 1, p. 50, Vol. 24, Pt 1, p. 90, Vol. 27, Pt 1, p. 26; *Census of India,* 1941, Vol. 3, pp. 3–5, 28, 34, Vol. 5, pp. 5, 17, Vol. 6, p. 3, Vol. 17, Pt 1, para. 56, Vol. 20, Pt 2, pp. 7, 13, 26, Vol. 22, Pt 2, pp. 72, 92, Vol. 24, Pt 2, p. 3; *Census of India,* 1951, Vol. 2, Pt 2-A, p. 2, Vol. 4, Pt 1, p. 31 and Pt 2-A, Pt 18, Vol. 7, Pt 1-A, p. 70, Vol. 8, Pt 1-B, p. 30 and Pt 2-A, p. 3, Vol. 10, Pt 2-A, pp. 4–5, and Vol. 15 Pt 2-A, p. 7.

the bleak proletarian characteristics that some scholars think are constitutive of communal violence. Importantly, too, a sizeable portion of this accelerated labour demand in the states was met by recruitment of outsiders, many of them from neighbouring provinces. As noted previously, in-migration has communal implications. Even migrants belonging to the same ethnic community, but drawn from a different region, are likely to seem strange. Almost certainly they will not at first grasp all the nuances of local custom or be so willing to share the locals' acceptance, born of long association, of alien Others residing in their neighbourhood. Although they might well have an inherited sense of the moral order of things—of what is acceptable and not acceptable—it will surely not be quite the same as the one that guides social behaviour in their new home. Thus it was often observed of the newcomers to the northern states that they did not show the customary respect for the dynasty. 'The [Bikaner] canal irrigated lands are prosperous', New Delhi's Director of Intelligence noted sadly, 'but are colonized by new-comers from outside...who neither know or care for the Ruler.'[14] Given that the princes generally set an admirable example of religious tolerance for their subjects to emulate, any weakening of the mystical tie between ruler and subject was bound to have an adverse effect on the local communal climate.

Moreover, the disruption caused by in-migration was exacerbated by the fact that while the northern states were predominantly Hindu, the migrants were mainly Muslim. During the decade 1921–31, Jaipur's Muslim population increased by nearly 20 per cent (and over 25 per cent in Jaipur City), Bikaner's in the same period 89 per cent. Whilst some of this growth is attributable to natural increase, most stemmed from immigration. In Bhopal's case this was a direct result of the *darbār*'s policy of recruiting Punjabi Muslims (about which we will have more to say below). In the case of Rajputana and CI the reason for the heavy influx of Muslims is harder to pinpoint, but chain-migration was probably a factor.

However, it is the effects of this Muslim migration that are of more immediate interest to us. First, the Muslim influx had the effect of altering the communal balance across the north Indian princely states. The shift was not, to be sure, a very large one but it was sufficient to cause a flurry of concern and dismay among some locally dominant Hindu communities when the full extent and rapidity of the change became known with the publication of the 1931 Indian census. Echoing a refrain first heard in Bengal during the 1920s, Bhopal's Thakur Lal Singh declaimed forlornly in 1938: 'the Hindus are dying out'![15] Secondly, the influx of Muslims into previously Hindu-dominant localities increased the local potential for religious conflict by pushing Muslim numbers there closer to, or beyond, the demographic threshold for violence as delineated in Chapter 2. Thirdly, these new arrivals came with cultural baggage. They expected to be able to eat meat and not to have to walk far to get it, and to be able to attend Friday congregational worship in a proper mosque; so there was unleashed a spurt of new mosque-construction, which did not always take account of local Hindu susceptibilities. Of course, not all Muslims came to the princely states bent on making trouble; many, looking only to better themselves, tried hard to adjust and fit in. But the large majority, it must be said, displayed a communal assertiveness that made them awkward neighbours. Officials in the states attributed this mainly to the fact that most of them hailed from UP and the Punjab, provinces which had long been boiling crucibles of Hindu–Muslim communal rivalry.

Political change came to the princely states late, like industrialisation, and was embraced even more reluctantly. 'I always look to the interests of the State', the maharaja of Kapurthala declared in 1922. 'I introduced some reforms into the State when their introduction in other States was not even dreamt of. In future, too, I will introduce reforms when I deem proper.'[16] But changing circumstances eventually brought even paternalists like Kapurthala to accept the necessity of real and far-reaching constitutional advance. In the wake of a 1938 Congress-led campaign designed to force the princes into conceding immediate responsible government (of which more below), the British Political Department, under pressure from Whitehall, abruptly reversed its long-standing *laissez-faire* policy towards the Indian kingdoms. With the backing of his departmental head, Sir Bertrand Glancy, the viceroy Lord Linlithgow in March 1939 announced a new policy of constructive engagement with the *darbārs*, designed to raise governmental standards throughout princely India, but especially in the smaller states. After 1939 the rulers consequently found themselves under fairly sustained pressure from New Delhi to modernise their administrations.

Yet in some ways the policy revolution of 1939 merely reinforced an existing tendency within the princely order. Although the princes were by and large conservative in their political outlook, they were not wholly blind to what was happening in the wider world. Specifically, after the Montagu Declaration of 1917, they realised that they might one day have to deal with a nationalist government in New Delhi without the backing of British military power. During the 1920s the Standing Committee of the newly created Chamber of Princes (COP) devised what I have called elsewhere the 'Mehta strategy', after its main author Baroda *dewan* Sir Manubhai Mehta, to meet this potential threat. To ensure their long-term survival, Mehta averred, the *darbārs* needed to undertake significant bureaucratic reforms to improve their capacity to deliver good governance, and introduce selective constitutional reforms (in the shape of representative institutions) to shore up the organic relationship between the rulers and their subjects by giving the professional and landed classes a limited access to the decision-making apparatus. In 1927 the COP gave its official imprimatur to this strategy, and from the early 1940s it was actively marketed to member states by Chancellor Hamidullah of Bhopal, himself a notably progressive ruler. Although a minority of rulers—like Udaibhan Singh of Dholpur—remained intransigent, apparently indifferent to the threats gathering on their borders, the majority took heed and began to make changes, particularly on the administrative side.

Table 3.2   Percentage of the population over five able to read and write, selected states and agencies, 1921–51

Unit	1921	1931	1941	1951
Jammu and Kashmir	2.6	4.1	7.0	n/a
Punjab states/PEPSU	3.4	4.2	n/a	8.8
Rampur	3.6	3.4	n/a	7.4
Rajputana/Rajasthan	3.9	4.3	5.0	8.4
Bikaner	4.2	5.0	8.9	11.0
Jodhpur	4.1	4.5	5.7	12.4
Jaipur	4.0	4.2	6.7	11.2
Kathiawar/Saurashtra	13.0	12.5	14.6	18.5
Nawanagar	12.2	14.0	n/a	n/a
Baroda	14.7	20.9	26.7	n/a
Central India/Madhya Pradesh/ Madhya Bharat	3.6	5.2	n/a	11.7
Gwalior	4.0	4.7	7.8	14.8
Bhopal	n/a	4.1	6.3	8.6
Indore	n/a	10.9	15.7	26.6

Sources: *Census of India*, 1921, Vol. 1, Pt 1, p. 177, Vol. 8, Pt 1, p. 135 and Pt 2, p. 113, Vol. 20, Pt 1, p. 65, Vol. 25, Pt 1, p. 293, Vol. 26, Pt 1, p. 178; *Census of India*, 1931, Vol. 1, Pt 1, pp. 324–6, Vol. 10, Pt 1, p. 106, Vol. 19, Pt 1, p. 315, Vol. 20, Pt 1, p. 153, Vol. 27, Pt 1 p. 101; *Census of India*, 1941, Vol. 17, p. 114, Vol. 18, pp. 48–52, Vol. 20, Pt 1, p. vii, Vol. 22, Pt 2, pp. 253–5, Vol. 24, Pt 2, pp. 142–5; *Census of India*, 1951, Vol. 4, Pt 1, p. 139, Vol. 7, Pt 2-C, p. 106, Vol. 8, Pt 2-A, p. 154, Vol. 10, Pt 2-A, pp. 170, 176, Vol. 15, Pt 2-A, pp. 168–70.

The results were quite impressive. By the 1940s free and compulsory primary schooling had become the norm everywhere across princely north India. Improved educational services led, in turn, to a slow but steady rise in the percentage of princely subjects equipped with the skills of reading and writing (Table 3.2); considering that in a large state even a one or two percentile increase could mean tens of thousands of additional readers and writers, this was a development of major social and political importance.[17] Again, many states during the late 1930s and early 1940s extended the elective principle to existing or new legislatures, some of which were given the power to introduce bills and vote on the state budget; while a few states were emboldened to experiment with dyarchical or other limited forms of responsible government.[18] According to the Chancellor, the changes introduced down to 1942 meant that

> 90.5 per cent of the population of our States possess local bodies with non-official majorities. States with 72 per cent of the population [of princely India] have got Legislative Assemblies, out of which

35.3 per cent have a majority of elected members and 5 per cent have equality of elected and nominated members. States representing more than half of the total population [of princely India, therefore,] have recently renewed and enlarged the scope of [the] association of their subjects with their administrations.[19]

By 1946 almost every state of a substantial size boasted some kind of representative body, if only at the municipal level.

To be sure, the princely reforms of the 1930s and 1940s stopped a long way short of implanting democracy in the states. Yet for all their limitations, the reforms marked a watershed in the political development of the states and one that would have significant communal ramifications. Although a number of early elections, especially at the municipal level, were poorly contested or even uncontested, gradually the enfranchised people of the states came to understand not only that they had been given an opportunity to participate in the political process, but that election to public office afforded them a real, if limited, access to political power and patronage and a chance to make their mark. Increasingly, especially in the towns, electoral contests acquired a competitive edge that was reflected in voter participation. Even in backward CI, upwards of 60 per cent of voters turned out for local elections in 1941, a figure that compares favourably with post-independence rates. Similarly, a report on the first local board elections in Mayurbhanj concluded: 'Hitherto party politics had no favour with the people. They were, however, captured in this year's election.'[20]

Candidates in these contests, however, often had difficulty making themselves known to the voters; as we shall see shortly, parties in princely India were generally, at this stage, small and embryonic in structure. Lacking other means of connecting with a 'natural' constituency, many resorted to the device of appealing to the members of their community, who could be relied on to share many of the same interests, prejudices and goals. Moreover, although the object in most cases was simply to rally support, rather than to set one community off against another, the mere fact that a candidate was standing on a communal platform coloured the politics of the contest. In Bhopal, this was so widely understood, and accepted, that Hindu and Muslim candidates were routinely issued with yellow and green electoral symbols respectively by the *darbār*'s electoral officials. Inevitably, therefore, these electoral contests became arenas for communal confrontation. Usually the exchanges remained verbal; but sometimes they got physical. On the eve of the Bhopal municipal elections of January 1946, 'goondas' armed with sticks and knives burst into the nationalist party election offices and seriously wounded a dozen party workers.[21] Later in the same year, local Congress workers in Jammu City complained of incidents of 'rowdyism and personal attacks' during state assembly elections in Kashmir.[22] A shrewd contemporary analyst, Oxford's Reginald Coupland, wrote in 1943: 'Communal passion is there to be utilised; and it needs no artificial stimulus when a struggle for power has begun. That, of course, is what . . . [has] happened in the States as it . . . happened a bit earlier in British India.'[23] The essential acuteness of Coupland's judgement would be repeatedly confirmed over the next seven years as parties in the states jockeyed for positions of advantage in the leadup to independence.

Behind the Mehta strategy lay the logic that the people of the princely states, while still politically quiescent compared to British Indians, would sooner or later join with the latter in demanding a share of power, and that it was better to head off this demand than wait until it had become irresistible. The logic was flawed, however, because it assumed that domestic struggles for power in the states could continue indefinitely to be kept separate from the larger nationalist struggle against British imperial domination. Baroda's stated policy, for example, was 'to see that organisations in the State work the reforms without affiliating themselves to, or coming under the influence of . . . Political bodies in British India'.[24] In the 1920s this goal might have been realistic, but by the 1940s it had become unattainable. By the 1940s the mainstream Indian political parties, including notably the INC, which had earlier ignored or shunned the states, were taking a fraternal interest in their affairs. Conversely, state peoples by the 1940s were starting to see themselves not simply as subjects of particular rulers but also, and increasingly, as 'Indians', potential citizens of an integrated subcontinental nation-state.

How did this 'mainstreaming' of the states come about? Basically it was a consequence of the whittling away of their protective physical isolation, which was, in turn, a direct, though perhaps unforseen, side effect of the *darbārs*' flirtation with modernisation. Of course the states had never been totally cut off from the rest of India, even during the heyday of the Raj's 'two Indias' policy, which was built on the confident assumption that the two could be kept separate by imperial fiat. While it was easy enough to regulate visitors arriving by train, it was almost impossible to prevent people entering the states literally by walking in across country. The states had borders, certainly, but they were lines on maps rather than physical barriers. Indeed, in places like the Punjab or Kathiawar it was often difficult for the traveller to know when he had crossed over from one political jurisdiction to another, so complex and irregular was the territorial map of princely north India. Not only, therefore, was there considerable intercourse between the states and the outside world, but there was little that the *darbārs* could do to control the flow of ideas and subversive knowledge that sometimes accompanied this human exchange. For instance, it was next to impossible for state police to prevent banned provincial newspapers from entering in the luggage of visitors and returning subjects and thereafter circulating freely. Although something of an interested party, Jamnalal Bajaj nevertheless summed up the situation accurately when he reminded Jaipur's prime minister that: 'India is by nature indivisible, and it is impossible to divide the country into watertight [political] compartments.'[25]

Thus even when it was still in a good state of repair, the 'dyke' between the 'two Indias' was never watertight. People and ideas could and did seep through. With the passage of time the cracks in the princely retaining wall steadily widened, to the point where, by the 1940s, little, if any, defence-in-depth was left to the *darbārs*. As noted above, the main agent of their undoing was the juggernaut of modernity.

Even by the 1900s the states of Rajputana, western India and Punjab were fairly well served in respect of communications by rail, although most lines were of the metre-gauge type, which inhibited fast travel. Over the following decades, the rail network was expanded and the road system utterly transformed. By the 1940s almost all states boasted at least a sprinkling of metalled roads, navigable all the year round, and a string of sturdy stone bridges spanning their major rivers. Travel to and through them became much faster and easier as a consequence. For instance, the completion in 1940 of a *pukka* bridge over the river Banas reduced the car journey between Jaipur and Tonk to 'a pleasant two hours drive instead of, at times, a rather hazardous adventure'.[26] More importantly perhaps, the same period saw a general upgrading of existing dirt roads and the building of hundreds of new tracks suitable for foot and cart traffic. By 1941 nearly 68 per cent of the population of Gwalior lived within five miles of some sort of road, compared with just 18 per cent 20 years previously.

Of course, these improvements did not happen by themselves; in almost all cases they were planned and paid for by the *darbārs*. To that extent the princely governments helped to undermine their own physical defences. Yet they did not do this in a spirit of careless abandon. Most Indian princes still believed, in the 1940s, that they could ride out the storm.

Others were more prescient. In 1942 veteran legal heavyweight and Liberal Federation politician Sir Tej Bahadur Sapru commented:

> If the Indian States think that they can for long maintain their sheltered existence, I think they are greatly mistaken—indeed their existence is no longer sheltered. Ideas travel much more swiftly than even the bombers of the present day.[27]

As Sapru's observation acknowledges, the princely states in 1942 were still 'sheltered' by the umbrella of British paramountcy. But they were no longer sheltered by distance and isolation. The sturdy walls of the mansion had fallen, and the thief was already inside.

The coming of the missionaries

In November 1931 a Shi'a *faqir* named Dina arrived unannounced in the Patiala town in Barnala. Subsequent inquiries revealed that he had come from Ludhiana, where he was well known to the police. After several days of itinerant preaching, Dina set up camp on a plot of apparently vacant land near a market—land which, however, was used daily by 'Hindu women of the Mandi...to answer their natural calls.' Discovering this, Dina tried to forbid the women from 'easing themselves' there, telling them that they were trespassing on a place of God. Needless to say, this demand excited the wrath of the local Hindus, and some of them tried to remove the *faqir* by force. But in the meantime, Dina had built up something of a cult following among the poor Muslim labourers and artisans of the *mohulla*. They rushed to his defence, and the Hindus backed off. Dina, however, viewed this, probably correctly, as constituting only a temporary reprieve; and in a bid to entrench his position he instructed his Muslim supporters to collect bricks for building a mosque. At this point the police became involved, and Dina was moved on, but not before a difficult 'communal question' had been created.[28]

The Dina incident—trivial enough of itself—illustrates the potential danger that itinerant religious professionals posed to the grass-roots communal peace. Men who, so far as the masses were concerned, spoke charismatically from the vantage point of an intimate association with the divine had a singular capacity to stir up trouble if that was their desire. Until the late nineteenth century, however, the religious message carried to the princely states by these wandering holy men—*faqirs*, *sadhus*, Sufis and the like—was typically mystical and syncretic. Even when more mainstream and textually centred religious brokers such as Brahmin pandits and Muslim ulema visited, their harshest denunciations tended to be reserved for other like-minded sects rather than other religions—as in the debates that raged between Shaivites and Vaishnavas within the Hindu tradition and between Sunnis and Ahmadiyyas within the Islamic tradition. Dina might have looked like a traditional ascetic but his abrasive and confrontationist style marked him out as belonging to a new, far more intolerant, religious culture—the culture of the missionary.

The roots of this new religious culture can be traced to a series of linked ideological developments within the major Indian religious traditions during the late nineteenth and early twentieth centuries. Depressed by the spread of Western-inspired materialism in society and alarmed at what they perceived to be a steady decline in the rigour and intensity of popular religious observance, various Indian thinkers, such as Dayānanda Sarasvatī (1824–83) and Swāmī Vivekānanda (1862–1902) within the Hindu tradition, Muhammad Qasim Nanautawi (1832–80), Ashraf Ali Thanvi (1863–1943) and Maulana Ilyas (1885–1944) within the Islamic tradition and Avtar Singh Vahiria (1848–c.1920) within the Sikh tradition, began pushing for a return to more orthodox ways. However, while often referred to as 'revivalists', they did not just look backward. Although its polemics were fiercely condemnatory of the evils, so-called, of Western modernity, revivalism in colonial India had no problem with adopting and utilising such of its aspects as it found useful; for example, the printing press and the public society. Indeed much of the social impact of revivalism stems from the fact that it did not draw simply upon the charismatic appeal of gifted individual preachers but also on the collective power of institutions. Dayānanda's vision was disseminated through the Arya Samaj; Nanautawi spoke as a distinguished member of the seminary at Deoband in UP; Ilyas headed the Tabligh Jama'at (Preaching Congregation) of Delhi; Avtar Singh was the moving force behind the Amritsar Singh Sabha. A more accurate label for these several movements would be 'fundamentalist', a term which also has the advantage of placing them in a wider historical context.

According to Martin Marty and Scott Appleby, 'fundamentalism' is an ideological strategy deployed by groups of believers to 'preserve their distinctive identity'.

> Feeling this identity to be at risk in the contemporary era, fundamentalists fortify it by a selective retrieval of doctrines, beliefs and practices from a sacred past. These retrieved 'fundamentals' are refined,

modified, and given new expression in institutions and political movements that often move beyond the confines and practices of a given religion in an effort to keep it alive as an authentic way of life for modern people.... [However], these fundamentals are accompanied in the new religious portfolio by unprecedented claims and doctrinal innovations.[29]

The point is worth emphasising. Fundamentalists do not merely reassert orthodoxy, but rework the tradition in novel ways. The latter becomes rigidified and homogenised. Belief is simplified and rationalised, while liminal traditions at the grass roots are disparaged and marginalised. As a result, the new/old religion becomes more sharply bounded and more clearly differentiated from its competitors. In all these respects, fundamentalism can be regarded as constituting a potentially powerful spur to religious intolerance.

Nevertheless this new way of thought would have had little impact if it had remained locked up in the rarified domain of the intelligentsia. What made revivalism truly lethal to social cohesion was its harnessing of the tools of modernity, such as print capitalism and the public society, to disseminate its message. Islam, of course, had always been a missionary religion; but Hinduism traditionally had never sought to make converts. With the advent of the Arya Samaj in the late nineteenth century, that changed. From its foundation in 1875, the Samaj actively proselytised. It opened schools and orphanages, distributed religious tracts and employed full-time missionaries who had specific instructions to denigrate and expose in their preaching the 'false' doctrines of other faiths. And from the 1890s it began to sponsor conversions to Hinduism through the Christian-like ritual of baptism (*shuddhi*). In turn, the challenge of the Arya Samaj prompted Muslim revivalists to launch a retaliatory strike in the shape of the *tablīgh* (preaching) programme. In April 1923 the Muslims of Aligarh formed the Tabligh-ul-Islam; and in 1924 Maulana Ilyas launched his Tablighi Jama'at.

Although Dayānanda was raised in Morvi and spent a good deal of his preaching career in Rajputana, and whilst the early Singh Sabha movement benefited greatly from the patronage and enthusiasm of the royal family of Kapurthala, the major provincial revivalist organisations were slow to establish a significant presence in the states. Nevertheless, by the early 1920s, the Arya Samaj had branches throughout the Punjab states and the Jammu region of Kashmir, and was starting to make inroads into the eastern Rajputana states. By 1931 there were some 94,000 Aryas in Kashmir, 44,000 in the Punjab states, over 11,000 in Rajputana and 3000 in CI. Meanwhile the Rāmanandīs were making converts in Bundelkhand and Chhattisgarh; the Sanatanists in Jaipur, Alwar and Benares; and the Ahmadiyyas in Bharatpur and Bhopal. Last but not least, in 1927 *tablighi* preachers descended on Mewat and Indore.

The impact of the burgeoning Arya Samaj movement on communal life in the states was considerable, and almost entirely deleterious. One major reason for this was the aforementioned Arya tactic of trying to 'reclaim' converted Sikhs and Muslims. In 1900 about 100 Ramdasias were 'purified' in Patiala and during 1913 some 9000 Vasisths were inducted into Hinduism in Jammu. Still more spectacular results attended the Arya *shuddhi* campaign among the Malkana Rajputs of eastern Rajputana between April and November 1923, which led, by the Aryas' own reckoning, to the reconversion of over 15,000 Malkanas. Significantly, in this latter campaign, extensive logistic and propagandist support was provided by members of three of the region's major princely families: Durga Narain Singh, brother of the maharaja of Rewa; long-standing Arya Samaj supporter Naharsingh of Shahpura; and Kishen Singh the Jat ruler of Bharatpur. Apparently many Bharatpur Malkanas accepted baptism under the impression that this step was required of them by their ruler.[30]

Nevertheless, fearful of a Muslim backlash, even most north Indian Hindu and Sikh rulers took a dim view of the Samaj's increasing investment in evangelism. Udaipur, which had initially supported the movement, abruptly withdrew its patronage after the death of Maharana Sajjan Singh; while in Morvi, Dayānanda's native place, the maharaja pointedly observed in an address on the occasion of the guru's birth-centenary in 1926 that he had a duty to see that all faiths were 'treated with equal consideration' by his *darbār*.[31] As for the region's Muslim rulers, they made it clear that the Samaj and its Shuddhi Sabha offshoot were not welcome in their dominions. When in June 1923 the Arya Samaj announced that it planned to extend its *shuddhi* campaign to Bahawalpur, the nawab warned the organisation that anyone attempting to persuade a Muslim subject of the state to embrace Hinduism would be arrested; while the female ruler of Bhopal, the staunch Khilafatist Jahan Begum, was so incensed by the *shuddhi* campaign that she enacted a law criminalising apostasy and issued a veiled ultimatum to the Shuddhi Sabha to the effect that if it persisted in its efforts to reclaim the Malkanas, the propagation of Islam would be 'taken up in earnest in the State'.

Their apprehension was not misplaced. As noted above, communal conflict in the states rose in the late 1920s—just as the Arya and tabligh missionaries were getting into their stride. This was no coincidence. Everywhere that the evangelists went, relations between the religious communities deteriorated. During the *shuddhi* campaign of 1923 in Bharatpur, Malkanas and visiting *maulvis* who tried to intercede were abused, socially boycotted and, in a few instances, beaten; and at Hasanpur village the houses of Muslims who had refused to recant were looted. Jaipur police attributed the communal outbreaks at Phulera, Bandikui and Lalsot in 1926 to 'the activities of the Arya Samajists' and the counter-propaganda of the Jamiat Tabligh-ul-Islam.[32] An Arya Samaj festival at Jodhpur in 1928 sparked an economic boycott of Muslim craftsmen. Named by officials as one of the main instigators of the Ramgarh (Jaipur) disturbances of 1932, tablighi activist Abdul Qasim Ansari was later investigated in Bundi for 'inciting Hindus and Muhammadans against each other'.[33] Last but not least, Maulana Ilyas' sustained campaign to change the Islamic orientation of the Meos of Alwar seems to have been at least a contributing factor to the 1933 rising there and contemporaneous agrarian troubles in Bharatpur.[34]

From a long-term perspective, though, probably the most consequential legacy of the new missionary societies was their creation of institutional links between British India and the states—a process that broke with and helped to undermine the long-standing convention that the princely states were out of bounds to provincial-based organisations. In June 1924 a delegation of clerics from Delhi, representing the Tabligh-i-Islam and the Jamiat-ul-Ulama, arrived in the capital city of Bharatpur; it turned out that they had come to protest the *darbar*'s demolition of a mosque. When the maharaja objected that this was a local matter he was told:

> The news... [has been a] cause [of] pain and restlessness to Muslims throughout India, irrespective of any particular place, because to a Musalman a mosque is a divine emblem.... the matter does not concern the Muslim public of Bharatpur alone, but, as a religious duty, every Muslim wheresoever he may reside, is bound to protect the Houses of God and the Divine Emblem. Therefore, even if the Musalmans of Bharatpur, for some reason, fail to discharge their religious duty, the said duty will devolve on the Muslims of other places.[35]

It was a clever argument, and a dangerous one—for if it held good for religious groups, why not for all organised bodies of opinion?

By the late 1920s provincial-based missionary societies, Hindu and Muslim, were well entrenched in the princely states of northern India.

Their presence was a sign of things to come, for now that the missionaries had shown the way, other kinds of roving evangelists were sure to follow.

The coming of the politicians

'The outlook of the people is quite insular', complained the *dewan* of Karauli in 1932, frustrated by the total failure of his efforts to remove local prejudice towards untouchables.[36] Backward Karauli *was*, perhaps, extreme in this respect, but it was far from unique in its insularity. Princely India at the beginning of the twentieth century was a parochial world of fiercely proud kingdoms, a world of rulers and subjects bound to one another by iron clad ties of duty, allegiance and affection. Household, locality, *jati* and state were the defining markers of their existence, not 'region' or 'country'—let alone 'nation'. Thus, whilst educated elites in the states by the 1920s were receiving a fairly good supply of news from the provinces, and, specifically, knew all about the rapid progress of the nationalist movement led by the Congress, they did not generally consider it a matter of relevance to themselves. 'In [the] states', seethed the nationalist Delhi weekly *Vijaya*, 'there is neither movement, nor independence, nor the fire of discontentment...the Rajahs are still looked upon as an incarnation of God and Virtue.'[37] Yet if the editor of the paper had been better informed he would have seen that even in the backwaters of princely India, time and tide had started to bring attitudinal change. Indeed the first clear signs of this emerged, ironically, about the same time that the *Vijaya* chose to denounce the subjects of the states for their unpatriotic insularity. Inspired by what they had heard about the new Congress leader, Mohandas Gandhi, a number of young princely subjects, especially from western India, Gandhi's birthplace, journeyed to British India and joined his Non-Cooperation Movement against the Raj. Meanwhile others followed the Congress example and founded organisations to press for domestic political change. The first of these—the Indore State Subjects' Conference—had been established in 1911. But the Non-Cooperation period saw a rash of imitations: the Praja Pratinidhi Sabha of Kotah (1918), the Rajasthan Sevak Sangh (1919), the Rajputana and Madhya Bharat Sabha (1920), the Kathiawad Political Conference (1921) and the Bhor State Subjects' Conference (1922). They were closely followed by the Haraoti and Tonk Praja Mandal (1926), the Punjab Riyasti Praja Mandal and the Jodhpur State Peoples' Conference (SPC) (both 1928) and the Wadhwan State People's Conference (1929). In April 1927 a peak body, the All-India

States Peoples' Conference (AISPC), was established, with a permanent secretariat at Bombay.

Nevertheless, for a long time the popular oppositional movement in the princely states of northern India remained embryonic. In the 1920s the *darbārs* were still, for the most part, autocratic in spirit; they took a very dim view of subjects challenging their authority. When, at the height of the Non-Cooperation Movement, attempts were made—chiefly in Kathiawar—to hold public meetings and stage flag marches in support of the Congress and Khilafat causes, they were vigorously suppressed. Likewise, few of the early people's forums lasted more than a few months as lawful bodies. One after another they were closed down and banned. Some survived after a fashion by relocating to British territory— for example, the Rajasthan Seva Sangh, in 1920, shifted its headquarters to the Chief Commissionership of Ajmer—but this expatriate existence naturally limited their effectiveness. As for the rest, they were plagued by limited membership, chronic funding shortages, weak organisational structures and factional rivalries. Typically the *praja mandals* of the 1920s and 1930s were town-based bodies made up of high-caste merchant and professional men with a sprinkling of students. And even within this narrow social spectrum, participation rates were low. In 1939 Alwar's Praja Mandal boasted just 50 members; and the main popular organisation in Bahawalpur, '364 pledged members' as of 1940.[38] Even the Jaipur mandal, perhaps the region's biggest, struggled for lack of funds and dedicated workers to make its voice felt. Hiralal Shastri, the organisation's foundation secretary, was initially 'responsible for everything'.[39]

But that was not all. Notwithstanding the generally sterling secularist credentials of the senior Congress-affiliated *praja mandal* leaders—such as Shastri—the oppositional movement in the states increasingly took on something of a communal complexion. One reason for this was its singular failure to attract members of minority groups and particularly Muslims. Peer group pressure deterred some Muslims; others were put off by the *mandals'* putative links with the Congress; but most stayed away out of fear. Lacking other alternatives, Muslims, along with other minorities, trusted in their *darbārs* to protect them from exploitation by majority groups just as in the late nineteenth century, elite British Indian Muslims had put their faith in the benevolence of the Raj. Associating with anti-government elements could put that vital protection at risk. Although generally a wealthy group, Hindus in Bahawalpur stubbornly resisted overtures in the 1930s from the AISPC-affiliated Jamiatul Muslimin because they knew, from experience, that subjects of Bahawalpur who associated with dissidents invariably suffered persecution.[40] Thus Muslims had good reason to be chary of nationalists. Yet by keeping their distance, they made the popular movement in the states look superficially like a movement of Hindus.

For another thing, the very nature of the political struggle in princely India conspired to produce communal outcomes. Indian nationalists could claim, with the Congress, that they were fighting a common fight against foreign rule. But in the princely states, this perhaps fragile distinction did not apply. Sovereignty resided in the person of the monarch. In states where the monarch and the politically articulate section of the population belonged to different religious communities, any struggle waged against the 'state' was liable to be construed and branded as communal. Thus the perennial response of the government of Bhopal to any sign of organised dissent was to suggest that Hindu communal elements lay behind it—which was not too far from the truth, given the largely Hindu nature of the popular opposition in the state. Similarly, the Muslim *dewan* of Charkari was able to deflect much of the criticism directed at his somewhat autocratic style of administration by 'getting it nicknamed a religious movement' of Hindus.[41] By the same token it was hard for the *praja mandals* to press for administrative reform without appearing to take the side of one community or another, since, as we observed in Chapter 2, the majority of *darbāri* bureaucracies tended to be heavily lopsided in their ethnic composition.

Again, given how hard it was for oppositional parties in the princely states, with the limited resources at their command, to reach out to the unlettered masses, and given the visceral reluctance of the bourgeois politicians who controlled them to stir the pot of class conflict by taking up the cause of the poor and underprivileged, tailoring appeals to religious communities made certain logistic sense. Such constituencies were known, were more readily accessible and had discernable interests that were easily translated into cheap but effective populist slogans.

For these reasons, and also because there was no nationalist organisation in the states with sufficient moral authority to restrain them, community-based parties became, early on, a feature of the political landscape of princely India. As early as 1921 a Rajputana Provincial Hindu Sabha was set up with branches in Jaipur and Kishengarh. There followed a Bhopal Hindu Sabha (1923), a Jodhpur Hindu Sabha (1926), an Indore Hindu Sabha in 1927, and others of the same ilk during the 1930s. Often, these bodies began by doing what the Gandhians called 'constructive' work—agitating for low-caste uplift and prohibition, for example—and several insisted they were supporters of the Congress. Yet as time went by, the activities of these *sabhas* became more stridently communal in nature.

The Bhopal Sabha admitted in 1938 to be engaged in the 'protection of abducted and kidnapped Hindu girls, . . . protection of the Hindu orphans and [Hindu] Sangathan [strengthening]'; while the Rajputana Hindu Sabha reported in 1945 that it was helping to rehabilitate Hindus injured in 'riots committed by the Muslims', and was vigorously pursuing with the authorities 'the rights of the Hindus in the question of music before mosques'.[42] Similarly, in some states Muslims began in the 1930s to organise themselves communally under the banner of the *anjuman* movement. Initially these *anjumans* functioned mainly as forums for local Muslims to meet and exchange views, but as the communal climate deteriorated they, too, started to operate proactively on behalf of their members.

Finally, the emergence of multiple parties all vying for popular support, some of them drawn from particular religious communities, gave the *darbārs* a fertile field for Machiavellian manipulation. Learning in 1927 that his chief minister had rashly given the local Praja Parishad permission to hold a public meeting, Maharaja Daulatsinghji of Idar arranged secretly for Muslim *goondas* to obstruct the proceedings by beating drums and pelting the *pandal* with stones and the flesh of goats. The delegates retaliated, triggering a lively brawl. Eventually the maharaja himself arrived on the scene, 'sword in hand' and full of sham indignation, at the head of a detachment of police; but by then the meeting had dissolved into a shambles.[43] More subtle, but no less devious, was the Indore government's response to the rise of popular dissent. Worried by signs in the late 1920s that nationalism was starting to get a foothold in the state, the *darbār* skilfully drove a wedge between the established leaders of the Hindu Sabha and younger elements in the party who wanted to move it ideologically closer to the Congress. Then, hoping 'to widen the gulf further', it agreed, seemingly in a spirit of generosity, to permit some of the latter to undertake political activity on behalf of *swadeshi* and *khaddar*—Gandhian activities which posed little threat to its power but which were anathema to the more conservative Hindu Sabhites.[44]

Naturally, the princes never admitted to encouraging or using communalism for political ends. Nationalist accusations that they were—in Jawaharlal Nehru's words—'utilising communal differences to check popular movements',[45] were shrugged off as biassed and self-serving, or rebutted with the rationalisation that communal differences were a regrettable but imponderable fact of political life. But the evidence of the *darbāri* records is that the rulers and their officials knew exactly what they were doing. Ordered to inquire into the circumstances of a communal clash in Narnaul town arising out of an unauthorised *praja mandal* procession, the Chief Justice of Patiala wrote disingenuously:

> I would like to meet one allegation made by the Praja Mandalists to the effect that they were made [induced?] by the authorities to raise a clash between Hindus and Muslims ... What [actually] happened was that a certain number of Special Police Constables were enlisted after the promulgation of ... sec[tion] 144 ... Practically all of those ... belonged to the Mohammadan community ... I am very doubtful if any Hindus were willing to come forward to enlist themselves as Special Police Constables because the Praja Mandalists generally belong to that community, and secondly, when the authorities had to meet with a mob consisting mostly of the Hindu community, it is but natural that they should place more reliance on Constables enlisted from the other community.[46]

Religious tension in the states was not a creation of the *darbars*; it had other causes. But from time to time they sought to turn it to their advantage.

The institutional weakness of the *praja mandal* movement has already been noted. Add to that the opportunities that the communal divide provided for political manipulation and it is easy to see why most of the *darbars*, in the 1930s, felt confident of their ability to contain any small show of opposition to their rule. Yet the equilibrium of the 1930s was basically unstable, for it depended upon the continued willingness of the British Indian political parties to observe the convention that they were provincial organisations pure and simple, and that they had no business meddling in the territories of the ruling princes—a view that, ironically, mirrored the *laissez-faire* position of the Political Department, after 1909, with respect to the exercise of paramountcy. Even the Congress—an organisation in most other ways uncompromisingly anti-British—was party to this self-denying ordinance.

Alone among the numerous nationalist groupings of that time, the Congress could have made life difficult for the princes. Yet it chose not to use its power against them. Publicly, the party's high command defended its stance on the grounds that its resources were insufficient to mount a campaign on two fronts, and that it had its hands full with the challenge of confronting the British Raj in the provinces. 'It is not our want of appreciation or will that compels non-interference,' explained Gandhi, 'it is our helplessness.'[47] Yet this seemingly frank admission concealed a raft of other motives that were not admitted to so publicly. One was the party's scepticism towards the AISPC and its local affiliates. 'What does the policy of the States Peoples Conference amount to?' Jawaharlal Nehru asked himself in 1936. 'It seems to be very feeble and sometimes even reactionary.'[48] Knowing how weak the *praja mandal* movement was, the Congress leaders feared to risk party resources and prestige in a venture that could easily fail for want of grass-roots support. Another reason was supreme leader M.K. Gandhi's personal princely connections and sympathies. Porbandar-born, Gandhi hailed from an old *darbāri* family. The self-confessed main author of the non-interference policy, he wanted to give the monarchical system a chance to reform. 'I am the only true friend among public men of the Princes', he averred in a private letter to Sir Mirza Ismail.[49]

The INC would maintain this *laissez-faire* line until late 1938; but in the meantime other provincial groups saw, in the absence of Congress from the states, a golden opportunity to stake out a claim there. The initial contenders were, significantly, both communal parties—the Majlis-i-Ahrar of the Punjab and the All-India Hindu Mahasabha.

The Ahrar leadership, which included Habib-ur-Rahman, Maulana Daud Ghaznavi and Maulana Mazhar Ali, was mainly composed of Lahore-based journalists and lawyers. This gave the party an urban, middle-class character that set it apart from the other Punjabi parties of the day such as the Unionist Party and the Muslim League. Nonetheless, the political future of the Ahrar Party lay in its ability to make inroads into the power-base of the locally dominant Unionists. To do this, it needed to win a share of the rural Muslim vote, which in the Punjab tended to answer to the dictates of parochial religious leaders such as the *sajjada nashins*, who watched over the tombs of Sufi saints. Accordingly, the Ahrars looked around for an issue that could win credit for the party in the eyes of the local Islamic elite. The outbreak of July 1931 in neighbouring Kashmir seemed tailor-made to their needs.

Secondly, the Sunni Ahrars were driven to intervene in Kashmir by their hatred for the Ahmadiyyas, the heterodox Islamic sect based at Qadian in northeastern Punjab. Committed to thwarting the expansion of the 'heretical' Qadiani sect by any means, the Ahrars became deeply concerned during the late 1920s by reports that the Ahmadiyya missionaries had started to make 'mass' conversions in Kashmir, and that both Jamal-ud-din, the Kashmir *darbār*'s Director of Public Instruction, and Sheikh Abdullah, the popular leader of the MYA, had fallen prey to their propaganda. When, following the July agitation led by Abdullah, the Ahrars learned that an All-India Kashmir Committee (AIKC) was being set up to pressure the GOI on behalf of the oppressed Kashmiri

Muslims, and that the Ahmadiyya Khalifa, Mirza Bashir-ud-din Mahmud Ahmad, had managed to get himself 'elected' president of the AIKC, and his personal assistant, A.R. Dard, appointed its secretary, the Ahrars felt that the point of no return had been reached; seeing no other way to arrest Kashmir's slide into heresy, they resolved upon a strategy of direct action in the state.

The Mahasabha's motives were no less compelling. Founded in 1915 and re-constituted by M.M. Malaviya in 1922, the Hindu Mahasabha initially considered itself more of a cultural lobby group than a proper political party and was content to operate as an adjunct of Congress. The dominant consensus, as articulated by Malaviya in his 1924 presidential address, was that 'it would be a shame' for any Hindu to oppose the Congress.[50] But the murder of Arya leader Swami Shraddhānanda in Delhi in 1926 caused Malaviya to harden his communal stance; and during the late 1920s the party moved steadily closer to the position of the Arya Samaj on the controversial issue of inducting untouchables into Hindu society through the mechanism of *shuddhi*. Malaviya's replacement as president by Central Provinces Maratha Brahmin B.S. Moonje further accelerated this trend. Nevertheless, the party remained, at least nominally, allied to the INC, and the Malaviya faction was happy for that relationship to continue. Not so the party's Punjab branch led by Bhai Parmanand. Coming from a province where the Congress had always been weak, Parmanand shared little of Malaviya's deference for that organisation, and he resented operating in its shadow. He wanted the Hindu Mahasabha's 'activities extended to the field of politics', for the Sabha to develop a programme and policy that emphasised above everything else its commitment to Hindu *sangathan*.[51] In particular he wanted it to contest elections as a separate party, with its own Hindu *sangathanist* candidates. 'I think', he mused, '[that] the most important weapon which could be of service to us in this work is the capturing of [the Central] Legislative Assembly and [the provincial] Councils.'[52] Parmanand succeeded Moonje as leader in 1933. One of his first presidential initiatives was to authorise the construction of a permanent party headquarters at Reading Road, New Delhi, and the launching of two party newspapers—the *Hindu* in Hindi and the *Hindu Outlook* in English.

Bhai Parmanand was not oblivious, however, to the immensity of the challenge that lay ahead. In the early 1930s the Mahasabha remained a party without an organisational base or a national constituency. Its paid-up membership numbered under 6000, and the vast majority of its supporters hailed from towns in three provinces: Punjab, the United

Provinces (UP) and Bihar. Like the Ahrars, the Mahasabha leaders saw, in the northern princely states, a largely untapped constituency. More immediately, they saw in the evolving Kashmir crisis, and the provocative actions towards the state of the Ahrars and other provincial Muslims, a way of capturing some hearts and minds among the Hindu public of British India.

They did not have long to wait. In mid-August 1931 Mazhar Ali was sent to Sialkot by the Ahrar leadership to recruit volunteers for a non-violent flag-march into Kashmir. By early October a large contingent of *jathadars*, red-shirted in imitation of Abdul Ghaffar Khan's cadres in neighbouring North-West Frontier Province (NWFP), were camped at Sialkot. On the 6th the first *jatha* entered Kashmir. By the beginning of November, 2376 Ahrars had crossed the border.[53]

The Mahasabha began its campaign to counter the 'depredations' of the Ahrars rather sedately by expressing its 'alarm and indignation' at the 'violent agitation [being waged] against the Kashmir State' in a resolution of November 1931.[54] Moonje's faction, it seems, were chary about direct intervention.[55] Early in December 1931, however, Parmanand outmanoeuvred his old rival by persuading the party's Working Committee (WC) to fund an investigation into the grievances of Hindus in Muslim-ruled states across north India.[56] By this means the Mahasabha president hoped to take some of the heat off the beleaguered Hindu government of Kashmir. By the end of the month, the party's inquiry committee had visited Junagadh, Tonk and Bhopal, and collected a dossier on 'Muslim *zulum*', sufficient for a 'big book'. In addition, the committee used its time in Bhopal to forge links with local Hindus who might be relied on to come to the party should the Mahasabha decide to launch a fully-fledged agitation against that state—which was the course favoured by the irrepressible Parmanand.[57] Further muscle flexing took place at the end of December, when the Hindu Riyasti Sammelan of Lahore, a Mahasabha affiliate, issued a veiled summons to Hindus across the country to resist the Muslim 'rising' in Kashmir with their blood.[58]

But before the question of a move against Bhopal could be settled, news arrived of the Meo outbreak in Alwar. A second 'Hindu' state, it appeared, had a Muslim revolt on its hands. Moreover the Mahasabha saw other disturbing parallels with Kashmir, notably the eagerness of provincial Muslim organisations and politicians in New Delhi and the Punjab to rally to the side of their co-religionists. In July 1932 the Central Jamiat-i-Tabligh-ul-Islam of Ambala took up the Alwar issue; in October the president of the Muslim Conference Sir Muhammad Iqbal tried to involve the viceroy Lord Willingdon; in December an 'all-India Alwar

Conference' held at Ferozepur Jirkha in the Punjab passed resolutions condemning the Alwar government's 'anti-Muslim' policies; and last but not least the ever-opportunistic Ahrars began making noises about *jathabandi*. According to the Imam of the Delhi Jama Masjid, the Ahrars were determined to turn Alwar into a 'second Kashmir'.[59]

Inundated by telegrams from frightened Alwari Hindus, and assailed by ominous press reports of Ahrars massing in Gurgaon, just across the Punjab border, the Mahasabha needed no further incentive. Party general secretary Ganpat Rai hastened to the disturbed areas of the state; while Moonje called on Jey Singh at his palace and placed the entire resources of the Sabha at his disposal. Over the following months, the party organised an 'Alwar Day', staged a solidarity conference at Rewari, collected money for the relief of 'Hindu sufferers' of the state; and fired off propaganda broadsides characterising the Meo uprising as a political movement launched 'in furtherance of the Pan-Islamic designs of the Muslims of India'.[60] Even after the maharaja had had been forced by the British to step down from the *gaddi* and go into exile, the Mahasabha continued, quixotically, to champion his cause, the party maintaining close covert contact with the exiled ruler until his death in 1936.

By the time Jey Singh departed Alwar, a precedent of intervention in the internal affairs of the states by provincial-based political parties had been firmly established. Thereafter, cross-border interventions multiplied. In June 1933 Bahawalpur Hindu Sabha leader Darya Baksh led a march through the streets of the state capital in protest at the *darbār*'s decision to impose an income tax (which was calculated to fall predominantly on the mainly Hindu commercial class). Bahawalpur officials had little doubt that they were seeing the start of a campaign by the Hindu Mahasabha to 'create chaos in Muslim States—especially in northern India—as a counterblast to the events in Kashmir in 1931'.[61] And they were right. Sabhite cadres targeted Malerkotla in 1935, Bhopal in 1937 and Rampur in 1939. Meanwhile the Majlis-i-Ahrar showed that it was far from a spent force by sending *jathas* into Kapurthala in the wake of the aforementioned police firing of June 1934; while in 1936 Punjabi Muslim League MLA Ahsan Ali Khan, a disaffected relation of the Nawab of Malerkotla, got up a campaign to pressure his kinsman into cracking down on the state's Hindus, and at the height of the agitation persuaded Saharanpur *mufti* Mohammad Shafiq to organise a dramatic *hijrat* of about 2000 Malerkotla Muslims to Lahore via Ludhiana.

'These "leaders" from outside are a great nuisance', reflected Alwar's prime minister. '[In fact] ... without them we should have practically no trouble at all.'[62] Although too simplistic by far, this assessment nonetheless contains a core of truth. The increasing involvement of the provincial communal parties in the internal politics of the princely states had important domestic repercussions. Specifically, their inputs of money, advice and loaned expertise, and the added legitimation which their all-India status gave to political activity, encouraged local people who might otherwise have continued to keep their grievances to themselves to go public with them by joining or forming popular associations. Not surprisingly though, given which parties were making the running in this respect, most of this new political activism took a communal form. Hard on Ganpat Rai's visit to Alwar in 1933, the state's first Hindu Sabha opened its doors; and shortly after the troubles in Malerkotla in 1935, the City's Pathans took the advice of the Ahrars and established an *anjuman* to represent the views of the community to the government. By the mid-1930s the Ahrar Party and the Mahasabha had managed, between them, to substantially reorder the political landscape of the princely states.

Nevertheless, an even bigger transformation waited. In 1938 the INC decided, with the blessing of the Mahatma, to drop its long-standing *laissez-faire* policy towards the states. In an editorial in *Harijan* on 3 December, Gandhi wrote:

> I am responsible for [the] policy of non-interference hitherto followed by Congress. But with [the] growing influence of Congress it is impossible for me to defend it in the face of injustices perpetrated in the States. If [the] Congress feels that it has [the] power to offer effective interference it will be bound to do so when the time comes.[63]

A fortnight later, the Congress Working Committee (CWC) authorised such of its workers who so desired to directly assist the people of the states in their struggle for responsible government.

I have written at length elsewhere about the reasons for the reversal of policy towards the states.[64] They are complex, and need not detain us here. The consequences of this policy-shift, however, are another matter. They go to the heart of our inquiry.

The CWC's dramatic announcement of December 1938 was received in the states with perhaps understandable scepticism, given the party's track record. But when Vallabhbhai Patel took himself off to Rajkot to help local workers revive the Kathiawar Political Conference, and then headed to Sangli to chair the annual session of the Deccan States Peoples' Association, and Gandhi's offsider Jamnalal Bajaj offered to broker a solution to the simmering dispute between the Rao Raja of Sikar and his overlord the maharaja of Jaipur; and when Jawaharlal Nehru took up the presidency of the AISPC and Gandhi himself entered the lists against the ruler of Rajkot, the scepticism turned to jubilation. With the power and prestige of the mighty Congress at their backs, the states' peoples reasoned, their success was assured. Sooner or later the princes would be compelled to meet their demands! Overnight popular support for the *praja mandals* surged. The Alwar Mandal went from 50 members in 1938 to 400 by late 1939; by March 1940 the Jodhpur Lok Parishad had opened 30 new branches; while the Kotah Praja Mandal started to reach out for the first time into the 'rural areas'; in far off Orissa 10,000 subjects of Dhenkenal flocked to the state's inaugural political conference.

To a large extent the promise of 1938 was not fulfiled. Despite early signs of what the Political Department sneeringly described as a collapse of nerve on the part of the *darbārs*, the entry of the Congress into the freedom struggle in princely India proved something of a fizzer; except famously in Aundh, a small state in the western Deccan, the agitations waged across the states over the winter and spring of 1939 failed to bring about responsible government. And the cost for many of the participants was high. Hundreds of *praja mandalis* were thrown in jail; others felt the sting of police *lathis*; a handful, if AISPC documents are to be believed, suffered torture. In a notorious incident in Limbdi, in January 1939, perhaps 600 unarmed demonstrators were killed or injured by police firing.[65] Still, an important watershed had been crossed. Short-lived and outwardly unsuccessful though it may have been, the *satyagraha* of 1938–39 radicalised thousands of hitherto docile princely subjects. Never again would these people meekly acquiesce in a system of governance that formally excluded them from power.

Moreover, despite Gandhi's mounting conviction that the *satyagraha* had been another 'Himalayan blunder',[66] its political results were by no means negligible. It did have an impact in the corridors of power. As we have seen, it caused the Political Department to ditch its *laissez-faire* stance towards internal developments in the states; no less importantly, it swept away what was left of the rulers' complacency about the need for change. Together, these two consequences generated, during the early 1940s, a spate of constitutional reforms which, while stopping well short, except in tiny Aundh, of responsible government, added substantially to the number and powers of representative bodies in the states, and the size of the princely voting population. By means of these initiatives, the *darbārs* sought to refurbish the organic link between the rulers and their subjects, and in particular to build bridges to those amongst the professional middle classes who were pushing for political change. 'For several months now', Bharatpur's Prime Minister Sir Richard Tottenham explained,

> I have been pursuing a...policy...based on the idea that it is worth while giving our 'politicians' a...chance to prove the sincerity of their professed desire to cooperate on constitutional lines, so that, even if we *have* to take action against them again, we shall be able to do so...more effectively and with greater popular support than was the case last year.[67]

This bridge building had been, of course, a key prong of the aforementioned Mehta Strategy of the 1920s.

But had not the time for building bridges already passed? Had not the possibility of a lasting *rapprochement* with the middle class been expunged by the ruthless crushing of the agitation of 1938–39? On the face of it one would have thought so. However, to the surprise and somewhat to the dismay of the Congress leadership, most of the *praja mandals* grasped the olive branches proffered to them by the *darbārs* with considerable alacrity. The Baroda Mandal, although publicly critical of the limitations of the legislative assembly established by the Government of Baroda Act of 1940, duly contested the polls in May and June 1940 and carried 24 out of 27 elective seats, enough for the party to claim that it had a popular mandate but not enough, thanks to the checks woven into the constitution, to give the party a majority—a result which, for different reasons, also satisfied the Baroda government; similarly, the Indore Rajya Praja Mandal (RPM), against the advice of the Congress, endorsed 30 candidates to stand in the state's first general election in 1944. Welcoming Jodhpur's decision in 1940 to register the Praja Parishad as a legal organisation, its President Jai Narain Vyas proclaimed: 'every Marwari is loyal...to the person and throne of His Highness'.[68] In Kashmir, Sheikh Abdullah's National Conference party (NC) agreed to nominate representatives to government boards charged with issuing ration permits, and upon the maharaja approving the establishment of a limited dyarchical system in 1944, the NC's Mirza Afzal Beg was inducted into the cabinet as the Minister for Public Works. Against the odds, rulers and subjects started—hesitatingly—to mend their differences. Jaipur's *dewan* Sir Mirza Ismail summed up this new spirit of accord when he informed state Praja Mandal President Shastri:

I am deeply grateful for all you have done so far. I have informed His Highness of the invaluable services you have rendered to him and his State at this crucial juncture. He, too, is grateful to you![69]

But if the building of bridges between the *darbārs* and their erstwhile nationalist enemies was a cause for celebration in the corridors of power, amongst the princes' Muslim subjects it was a further cause for lament.

As noted above, minority populations in the states had traditionally relied on their rulers to shield them from majoritarian bullying. Thus they had kept aloof from popular movements, fearing to alienate their protectors. What they wanted was for the political system of the states to remain the same—autocratic, pluralistic and upholding of religious freedom and toleration. The political changes that followed upon the 1938–39 *satyagraha* were calculated to upset that fragile equilibrium; accordingly, they came as a nasty surprise to the minorities, and especially to the Muslims living in the Hindu-ruled states.

The move towards a representative system of governance worried the minorities because any system dependent on the counting of heads seemed geared to exclude them perpetually from a realistic share of power. In any sort of democracy, the Muslims protested, they would always be in opposition. Thus, as in the provinces earlier, the almost universal response of the Muslim leaders in the princely states, when proposals for constitutional advance were announced, was to call for reserved seats backed by separate electorates. Even the Kashmiri Muslims, although not a minority, joined in this demand. But whilst many important states agreed to set aside seats for minorities, all except Kashmir refused to depart from the principle of territorial electorates. The Muslims felt betrayed. When the first princely state elections were held, many Muslims eligible to vote stayed away in protest. As it was, the few Muslim candidates who did venture to contest these early polls were nearly all soundly beaten—a result that officials attributed to their political inexperience, rather than to any communal considerations *per se*, but which confirmed all the Muslims' worst fears.[70]

Likewise, the growing cordiality between the *darbārs*, on which they relied for protection, and the largely Hindu-controlled *praja mandals* left the Muslims of the princely states feeling uneasy and insecure. Had the Hindu states lost their zeal for impartiality? Worse still, were they looking to mend fences with the Congress—join the nationalists in a common fight to free India from British overlordship? A few years earlier, the latter idea would have been unthinkable, but by 1942 there were signs of a thaw in that direction too. When, in March, the Cripps

Mission was announced, the Standing Committee of the COP welcomed London's offer of negotiations and Cripp's enigmatic proposal for an early transfer of power on the basis of Dominion Status after the cessation of hostilities; and after the negotiations collapsed, several *darbārs* including Indore and, particularly, Kotah gave tacit support to the August Congress 'Quit India' demand and the ensuing, often violent, agitation.[71] In the light of these developments some Indian states' Muslims began to suspect that their ultimate sheet anchor—the 'unshakeable' alliance between the rulers and the Crown—was about to be cut adrift.

Given these Muslim anxieties, it is rather ironic that the one mainstream provincial political party yet to establish an organisational presence in the states was the All-India Muslim League (AIML). Even after its great rival the INC entered the lists in 1938, the League still held back. Its reasons were pragmatic. First, the princely states had little obvious attraction as a zone of expansion because of the relative paucity of Muslims there, and because the largest Muslim-majority state, Kashmir, had a Hindu ruler. Secondly, the party feared that if it started meddling on behalf of Muslims in places like Kashmir, such propaganda might rebound against the Muslim rulers of Hindu majority states like Tonk, Bhopal and Bahawalpur, which the League rightly saw as important pillars of Islamic power in the subcontinent. Not until 1940 did the League Council agree, very reluctantly, to sanction the establishment of an All-India States Muslim League (AISML) to lobby on behalf of the interests of the states' Muslims and attempt to secure for them, as the AISML's constitution rather ambiguously put it, an 'honourable political future'.[72] And this token commitment was robbed of much of its force by the Lahore resolution of March 1940, which harnessed the party to the chariot of 'Pakistan'. Although the resolution was—perhaps deliberately—quite vague, in calling for the setting-up of a 'Muslim homeland', about its nature and even extent, it was clear for all to see that a Muslim homeland limited to 'the areas in which the Muslims are numerically in a majority' was not going to include many princely states.[73] The League's life President, Muhammad Ali Jinnah, underscored this limitation when he declared that the reach of the Lahore scheme was 'confined to British India'.[74]

Interestingly, this narrow view was contested, from the start, by several states' Muslim leaders. 'You cannot ignore your brothers in Indian States', admonished S.M. Zauqi of Ajmer. 'Pakistan will never be happy if so many [Muslim] brothers in [the] Indian States...are left in the lurch.'[75] Yet to judge from published reactions, the overwhelming majority of the Muslims of the northern states do not appear to have been even slightly discomforted by the possibility that Pakistan might be established somewhere else. On the contrary, the Lahore announcement seems to have lifted the flagging spirits of Muslims right across the region—and, what is more, sensitised them to their communal identity. One expression of this was the provocative decision of many of Baroda's urban Muslims to return their language as Urdu instead of Gujarati in the 1941 census. Another was the post-1940 proliferation of new local Muslim organisations and the re-activation of moribund ones such as the Muslim Conference (MC) of Kashmir, which was revived in February 1942 by Sheikh Abdullah's disaffected Lieutenant Ghulam Abbas.

Hints of a more aggressive communal stance on the part of the states' Muslims started to surface during the Congress-led *satyagraha*. For instance, a visit to Bhavnagar in May 1939 by Congress leader Vallabhbhai Patel was marred by a violent attack by local Muslims on parading Hindu *praja mandalis*. But this orientation grew much more pronounced in the aftermath of the League's historic Lahore session. Only days later, Muslims in Charkhari 'ceremoniously brought a cow into the street and killed it'.[76] In August 1940 Muslim butchers desecrated an idol in a Jodhpur village. In September, stone-throwing Muslims attacked Bhaironji's temple in Ramgarh. In April 1941 a vicious fight erupted between Hindu and Muslim schoolboys in Gwalior City; according to the resident 'the Muhammadan boys were largely to blame'.[77] And in March 1942 Muslims in Pali town in Jodhpur, for the first time that anyone could recall, barred a Holi *ghair* party from passing the jama masjid.

It is hard not to read significance into the timing of these outbreaks. Yet if more direct evidence is needed for the hypothesis that this uncharacteristic behaviour on the part of the states' Muslims was connected to the passage of the Lahore Resolution and the genesis of the 'Pakistan demand', one has only to look at what happened a bit later that year in Ujjain, the second city of Gwalior—a state hitherto riot-free.

The first link in the chain of causes and effects that culminated in the Ujjain riot of 1942 was the arrival, in August, of a prominent Bohra from Cambay named Mullaji. To celebrate his coming, local Bohras took out a procession, which was punctuated by loud cries of 'Pakistan Zindabad' and 'Quaid-e-Azam Zindabad' (Quaid-i-Azam, or 'Great Leader', being a reference to Jinnah). Ujjain Hindus later claimed that this was the first time these highly charged slogans had been heard in the town. Shortly afterwards, came news of the passage of the All-India Congress Committee's (AICC's) 'Quit India' resolution on 8 August, and the arrest of its members the following morning. A number of mostly Hindu shopkeepers at once closed their premises in sympathy and the same evening the Gwalior Praja Mandal called a mass meeting to discuss what if anything could be done locally by way of support for the Quit India movement.

The meeting opened in an atmosphere of tension and excitement but there was no hint of violence in the air. Then, just as the president of the Mandal rose to speak, a group of Bohra 'youngmen' burst in 'and demanded that the... meeting be postponed, as it was the time of Namaz'. This was agreed to—but it was done grudgingly. The demand had no precedent. And many left the meeting mouthing curses at the Muslims for their lack of national spirit. On the 13th, some of the latter, mainly students, marched through the City's central commercial district, remonstrating with proprietors, mainly Muslims, whose businesses were still open. 'It is said that [when] these students [reached the vegetable market they] began to compel Boheras [*sic*] to close their shops.' Forewarned and perhaps forearmed, the Bohras poured out on to the street and attacked the students with sticks. Although 500 strong, the student militia fled. But they soon returned with reinforcements in the shape of some 'Hindu strongmen' from the nearby Patni Bazaar—and on this occasion the Bohras found themselves on the receiving end. By the time the police arrived on the scene, two had been killed, dozens wounded and scores of Bohra shops looted.

Outwardly peace was soon restored. Another small affray erupted on the 15th, but it did not result in any casualties. However, the incident left a bitter legacy. A couple of days after the second riot, Muslims held a mass meeting at which allegations of atrocities were levelled at the Hindus; and every 13 August thereafter, down to 1947, the Bohras of Ujjain observed *hartal* in memory of the event. For their part, the Gwalior Praja Mandal leaders concluded that the whole thing had been a set-up: 'these riots were intentionally devised by Muslim Leaguers to disrupt [the] August Movement'.[78] And the *darbār* privately concurred. 'Our Muslim subjects' seem to have been 'taken for a ride' by Islamic 'groups from outside', they lamented.[79]

One of the tragic aspects of tumultuous and bloody communal riots is that the memory of them is very difficult for the participants, and especially the relatives of the victims, to expunge—even when it is not kept alive artificially as it was among the Ujjain Bohras. Once the communal peace of a town or region has been broken by a major riot, the odds are that further outbreaks will occur. Gwalior would be no exception. But the Ujjain riot of 1942 need never have happened—would probably never have happened—if the provincial politicians, with their rousing communal slogans, had stayed at home.

Unholy alliances

As has already been discussed at some length, perhaps the main political strategy by which the princely order, in the 1930s and 1940s, attempted to secure its future was that of using reform to purchase—or perhaps more accurately to rekindle—the loyalty and cooperation of important sections of their subjects. However the rulers understood—or their more astute advisers did, at any rate—that more than this would be needed to ensure the survival of themselves and their states in the event of a British exit from the subcontinent. They would need friends at court in New Delhi. Therefore in the early 1940s the princes began to explore the possibility of reaching an understanding with the provincial-based nationalist parties while the Raj still lasted.

Ideally they would have liked to come to an arrangement with the Congress. This might have been possible had Gandhi still controlled Congress policy. By the mid-1940s, however, it was Jawaharlal Nehru who increasingly spoke for the Congress on the states—and as a Marxist fellow traveller, Nehru found the whole monarchical system unsupportably anachronistic. He told the AISPC's annual conference at Ludhiana in 1939:

> They differ greatly among themselves and some have advanced industrially and educationally, and some have had competent Rulers and Ministers. The majority of them, however, are sinks of reaction and incompetence and unrestrained autocratic power sometimes exercised by vicious and degraded individuals. But whether the Ruler happens to be good or bad, or his Ministers competent or incompetent, the evil lies in the system. This system has vanished from the rest of the world, and, left to itself, it would have vanished from India also long ago. But in spite of its manifest decay and stagnation, it has been propped up and artificially maintained by British Imperialism.[80]

Although this fiery Nehruvian rhetoric was intended mainly for public consumption, it severely frightened the rulers and convinced even their more nationalistically inclined advisers, such as K.M. Panikkar, that Congress under Nehru's leadership would probably repudiate any deal they tried to make. Thus the *darbārs* settled for trying to come to terms with some of Congress' less-radical rivals. One option was the

AIML, which was publicly friendly towards the states and would have welcomed an alliance targeted at the Congress. But for many of the Hindu princes the prospect of joining forces with a Muslim party was anathema. This narrowed the field considerably. It left only one viable all-India candidate—the Hindu Mahasabha—plus a handful of regional parties such as the Punjab Unionist Party and the Akali Dal. Moreover, there was no guarantee that they would play.

While the landlord-dominated Punjab Unionist Party seemed a natural ally, on the face of it neither the populist Mahasabha nor the militant Dal looked likely bedfellows. To be sure, the Mahasabha had shown itself willing, as we have seen, to help Hindu princes under seige, as in Kashmir and Alwar. Yet it had always represented itself as a genuine party of the people and as a staunch fighter for freedom. And with the accession to the presidency of the party in 1937 of the legendary revolutionary 'Veer' Vinayak Damodar Savarkar, a man once sentenced to two life terms in the Andaman Islands, it began finally to live up to that claim. As for the Akali Dal, its first five years were spent in sustained, and at times violent, mass struggle on behalf of the Shiromani Gurdwara Parbandhak Committee (SGPC) for the 'liberation' of Sikh shrines and places of worship from the hereditary control of heterodox Udasi priests. Although by the late 1920s the Dal had become a political organisation and had to some extent allowed itself to be incorporated into the system of imperial control (in 1926 several Akalis contested elections to the Punjab legislative assembly), its posture remained militant and for that matter fairly hostile to the Sikh princes, whom the Akalis saw as rivals for the leadership of the Panth. As well, SGPC president and *de facto* boss of the Dal, 'Master' Tara Singh (1885–1967), a devout, puritanical Khatri from Rawalpindi district, nursed a personal grudge against the maharaja of Patiala.

Nevertheless, for a variety of reasons, both parties gradually warmed to the idea of an association with the Indian princes. For its part, the Mahasabha by 1937 was in desperate need of powerful friends. As we have seen, Bhai Parmanand had dreamed of building the Sabha into a great national party that would eventually compete with—and perhaps even displace—the Congress in the affections of the Hindu masses. However, the beefed-up party structure created under his presidency failed at its first hurdle, when Mahasabha candidates were decimated at the 1937 elections, the party winning just 17 seats in its own right (Table 3.3).[81] Publicly the party's leaders tried to pass off its poor showing as the product of a conspiracy between the voters and the Congress. Privately, however, they saw no realistic prospect of the party, in the immediate

Table 3.3 Provincial election results, 1937

Province	Total seats	Number of seats won (Major parties and groupings)				
		INC	AIML	Hindu Sabha	Hindu Nat./DSP	Other majors
Assam	108	35	10	0	0	38
Bengal	250	60	39	2	3	39
Bihar	152	95	0	0	0	22
Bombay	175	86	20	0	6	32
CP	112	70	14	0	4	21
Madras	215	159	10	0	0	23
NWFP	50	19	0	0	0	3
Orissa	60	36	0	0	0	10
Punjab	175	18	2	11	0	119
Sind	60	7	3	4	8	34
UP	228	134	28	0	0	14

Sources: House of Commons, Command Paper 5589 of 1937; *IAR*, Pt I, pp. 168a–168p; Christopher Baker *The Politics of South India 1920–1937* (Cambridge: CUP, 1976), p. 311; D.E.U. Baker *Changing Political Leadership in an Indian Province: The Central Provinces and Berar 1919–1939* (Delhi: OUP, 1979), p. 175; P.D. Reeves *et al.* (eds), *A Handbook to Elections in Uttar Pradesh 1920–1951* (New Delhi: Manohar Book Services, 1975), pp. 246–7.

future, securing a parliamentary majority through the ballot box. This meant finding other avenues to power. It seemed to the Sabha's leaders that their best hope lay in a strategic alliance with some like-minded group. The party needed money; it had little influence with officialdom. Powerful, well-placed connections—like the princes—could provide both.

Besides, there was much about the princes and their rule that reson-ated with the Mahasabha's ideology. First, they fitted neatly into the Mahasabha's masculinist vision of Indian nationhood. Like their contem-poraries and putative protégés, Dr Hedgewar and M.S. Golwalkar of the Rashtriya Swayamsevak Sangh (RSS), the Sabha's leaders believed that the 'true Hindu' *dharma* was the *kshatriya*—or warrior—*dharma*. They admired physical strength and manly courage. The Hindu princes were drawn overwhelmingly from the martial Rajput caste. The blood of ancient warriors reputedly flowed in their veins. As B.S. Moonje lyrically put it, the Hindu ruler was 'a representative of the Hindu Raj of the past' who incorporated 'in himself all [the old, hallowed] traditions of dignity, suffering, and fighting [to protect]...the Hindu Raj against foreign aggressors'.[82] Here, the Mahasabha leaders felt, were a set of real leaders, fit and tried.

Secondly, even as they stood as congeries of individual administrative units under the umbrella of British paramountcy—the Hindu states were significant bastions of Hindu power. They had military and police forces; they commanded in some cases quite substantial revenues; and perhaps most importantly, their *darbārs* controlled territories and populations. Such features made them potential bridgeheads for 'the establishment of Hindu Raj in Hindustan'.[83]

> If the Hindu Sangathanists possess an insight into political realities they would soon find that the Hindu States are, in fact, really the only centres of... organized military, administrative and political Hindu strength and are bound to play a more active and more decisive part in [the] near future in moulding the destiny of the Hindu Nation than any other factor within our present reach... Of all the factors that are likely, under the present circumstances, to contribute to the resurgence of a consolidated Hindu Nation, the Hindu States constitute the most efficient one... we Hindus have never taken it into our heads what powerful resources we have in the existence of some fifty Hindu States with armies, organized police forces, treasuries, governmental machineries all relatively... efficient... and some of them as large as independent countries in Europe.[84]

Savarkar nurtured particular hopes, in this respect, for Nepal, which, unlike the princely states within India, already enjoyed the status of an 'Independent Hindu Kingdom'.

Finally, and crucially for the argument being mounted in this book, the Mahasabha saw in the princely states something of the condition of established Hinduness of which Savarkar had written in his 1923 essay, *Hindutva*. As we have seen, non-Hindus were much thinner on the ground in princely than in British India. That of itself was a plus for the Mahasabha. So was the fact, also noted earlier, that the administration in many of the Hindu states was said to be based on the hallowed principles of *rājadharma* enshrined in the Hindu scriptures. But what really excited the Mahasabhites was the way the princely polity appeared to include, yet subordinate, minorities. Although none of the Mahasabha's leaders, so far as I know, ever specifically used the term 'Hindutva' with reference to the princely states, it is clear from their writings and correspondence that they understood and thoroughly approved of the majoritarian polity that flourished there. Indeed, when Savarkar expounded his vision for the post-colonial Hindu *rashtra* to come at the party's annual conference at Calcutta in

December 1939, he could have been talking about any one of the existing Hindu kingdoms:

> all that an Indian National State can mean is that the Moslem minority in India will have the right to be treated as equal citizens, enjoying equal protection and civic rights in proportion to their population. The Hindu majority will not encroach on the legitimate rights of any non-Hindu minority. But in no case can the Hindu majority resign its right, which as a majority it is entitled to exercise under a Democratic and legitimate constitution.... [The Muslims] must remain satisfied with the status they occupy and with the legitimate share of civic and political rights that is their proportionate due.... The Hindus want henceforth to be masters themselves in their own house, in their own land.[85]

In this, it seems to me, lay the ultimate attraction of the Hindu states for the Mahasabha. They made the idea of Hindutva real; they showed that it was possible for governments in India not only to relegate non-Hindus to a secondary position in society, but to reconcile them to the necessity of Hindu hegemony.

And the *rapprochement* between the Akali Dal and the Punjab princes was rooted in a similar mixture of vision and pragmatism. For over three hundred years the Sikhs have held fast to Guru Gobind Singh's promise that they are marked out for a special destiny. The Guru had told them, on Baisakhi Day 1699: 'the Khalsa shall rule'. Since then, community aspirations have centred on acquiring the means to fulfil that destiny—in a word, political power. In fact it has become an axiom amongst Sikhs that 'religion is not safe without political power'.[86] Master Tara Singh made much the same point when he wrote, in an SGPC manifesto in January 1945: 'there is not the least doubt that the Sikh religion can live only as long as the Panth [community] exists as an organized entity'.[87] No less than their forebears, Sikhs in the early twentieth century nurtured the dream of statehood. More specifically they dreamed of one day restoring the Sikh Kingdom of Lahore, which for a brief half century had embodied Gobind Singh's communal vision. As one Sikh polemicist wrote in 1946, 'in asking for a Sikh State, we don't make a new demand. We only ask for the *return* of our homeland.'[88]

But how would this restoration be accomplished? Until the 1940s, many Sikhs hoped that the British upon their departure would simply hand over the Punjab by way of a reward to the community for its loyal service to the Raj. 'We thought we would be given the whole of the

Punjab as it was taken by the British for *safe-keeping'*, wrote a bemused Sikh officer of the Indian Army, 'without any [need for] conquest at all.'[89] In March 1940, however, this rather naïve expectation was rudely challenged by the League's resolution at Lahore calling for the establishment of a Muslim homeland, which rapidly turned into a demand for the cession of 'six provinces', including the whole of the Punjab. Almost at once the Akali Dal retaliated with a territorial demand of its own: for the creation of a new British Indian province of East or, as the Dal provocatively described it, 'Azad' Punjab with a demographic composition 40 per cent Muslim, 40 per cent Hindu and 20 per cent Sikh—ratios which, the Sikhs figured, would leave them with the communal 'balance of power'. On 4 June 1943 the Dal formally adopted this scheme as party policy; at the same time the Akalis firmed up their definition of the proposed province, which was described as encompassing Ambala, Lahore and Jullundur divisions, the districts of Lyallpur and Montgomery and a part of the district of Multan. Fourteen months later this demand was overwhelmingly endorsed by a massed 'Panthic meeting' at the holy city of Amritsar, a verdict watching British observers interpreted as reflecting a 'growing demand that the Sikhs should be regarded as a separate nation'.[90]

As we have seen, the Akalis harboured no romantic illusions about the Sikh royal families, but they realised their value to the Sikh cause. For one thing the Sikh states housed a significant slice of the Sikh population. Without them the so-called Sikh homeland would be barely 20 per cent Sikh; with the states included, the proportion would rise to a more respectable quarter. For another, the states had police, small but efficient armies, supplies of weapons, resources that could mean the difference between victory and defeat, if it came to a showdown. Last but not least, the princes were a useful conduit to the GOI, which would have a substantial say in determining where and in whose hands the Punjab ended up. After a frank talk with Akali MLA Baldev Singh in July 1946, Punjab governor Sir Evan Jenkins wrote: 'I think that the Sikh States might form a rallying point for the Sikhs...and enable them, if they so desired, to carve out a Sikh unit for themselves.'[91] This was not an original thought; years earlier Master Tara Singh had come to exactly the same conclusion.

Nevertheless, in putting forward this grand vision for a Sikh homeland, the Akalis had to ask themselves: Did they really want the aristocratic and autocratic Sikh princes to be a core part of it? Truth is, many—including Tara Singh—were unsure. However, thanks to the War, the Akalis and the Sikh rulers found themselves by 1942 sharing a common recruiting platform, paving the way for a closer structural association at a time when the Panth desperately needed to present a unified face to the world to combat the growing threat to Panthic territorial aspirations posed by the Muslim League's plan for Pakistan. Meanwhile, the Dal's perception of the Sikh princes as adversaries was blunted by the death, in 1938, of their most formidable and persistent princely critic Bhupinder Singh of Patiala. Another long-time *darbāri* foe of the Akali Dal, Jind Chief Minister B.L. Dhingra, passed on a year later. As we shall see, these changes paved the way for the emergence in the early 1940s of a much more populist and seemingly pliable princely cohort in the Punjab.

The Akali Dal and the Hindu Mahasabha—it goes without saying—were wholly distinct and separate organisations. Nonetheless as time went by they found they had much in common ideologically. Specifically, they found that they were of exactly the same mind in the matter of the Muslims and their scheme for Pakistan. Accordingly, in 1941, the Sabha floated the idea of the two parties entering into a loose anti-Muslim collaboration:

> The Mahasabha . . . is going ahead with its plans to isolate the Muslim community through political agreement with the other minority communities. Dr Moonje has written to Master Tara Singh, the Akali leader, inviting the views of his party on the possibility of holding a joint conference of all those who are opposed to the Pakistan idea—a suggestion which Tara Singh may possibly accept.[92]

In the event the conference idea was scrapped; but in July, Malaviya hosted a private meeting in Benares of Mahasabha leaders, which was attended by Tara Singh. Intelligence reports suggest that Moonje used the meeting to push the Mahasabha's plan for the 'wholesale militarization of the Hindus', and that the Master went away keen to involve the Sikhs 'in these endeavours'.[93] Tapping into the military resources of the Hindu and Sikh princes figured prominently in this joint agenda.

The princes were already well accustomed to talking to provincial politicians. More specifically, the *darbārs* for years had been discreetly feeding money to provincial parties and newspapers as a way of purchasing their goodwill. By the late 1930s, therefore, an informal but extensive web of interpersonal contacts and institutional arrangements connected the princes and their nominal adversaries. To open up a dialogue with the target *darbārs*, the Dal and the Sabha had only to activate this network.

The Akalis were the first to move. Around 1935, they approached the government of Patiala with the offer of a truce in their long-running feud. We do not know precisely what their terms were but a deal *was* struck; and despite some minor irritations, the peace held.[94] By 1940 a Congress worker was reporting: 'The Akali Party is in League with the various rulers of the Punjab States.'[95] But the Mahasabhites were quick to follow suit. In 1937, Savarkar and Moonje launched a systematic campaign to persuade the Hindu rulers and princes to 'take a lively interest in the affairs of the Hindu Mahasabha'.[96] Invitations were issued to rulers and senior *darbāris* to preside at Mahasabha functions; Sabha leaders found excuses to visit Hindu states and pay court; sympathetic notables such as Virendra Shah, raja of Jagmanpur in the UP, the son-in-law of the ruler of Datia, were induced to canvass other chiefs; and flattering letters were sent to ministers judged to carry weight with their masters.

For various reasons the princes generally responded warmly to these overtures. As we have seen, making friends among the politicians was a key element of their strategy to survive the demise of the Raj. Additionally, there were appreciable short-term benefits of reaching an understanding with popular parties such as the Mahasabha and the Akali Dal. Notably, a deal with the Akalis offered the Sikh rulers the possibility of a welcome reprieve from the periodic cross-border agitation by the Dal's minions—an agitation that by the 1930s was beginning to place a fairly serious financial strain on the Punjab states. Patiala's Home Minister Raghbir Singh put the argument succinctly:

> M[aster] Tara Singh is the only man amongst the Sikhs who has got a following...amongst the masses...others are leaders in name only...now, if we make him hostile, he [may]...be able to excite our public.... A man of his strong will can bring about such things, especially when time favours.[97]

Still, while all the Hindu and Sikh rulers stood to benefit, in the event most kept their options open; only a handful, chief of whom were Tej Singhji (r.1937–48) of Alwar, Brijendra Singh (r.1929–49) of Bharatpur, Ganga Singh (r.1887–1943) and his son Sadul Singhji (r.1943–48) of Bikaner, Anand Chand (r.1927–48) of Bilaspur, Jagendra Singh Deo (r.1944–48) of Charkhari, Vikram Sinha Rao Puar (r.1937–48) of Dewas Senior, Har Inder Singh (r.1918–48) of Faridkot, 'George' Jayaji Rao Scindia (r.1925–48) of Gwalior, Bhim Singhji (r.1940–48) of Kotah, Yadavindra Singh (r.1938–48) of Patiala and Martand Singh (r.1946–48) of Rewa, seized the olive branch proffered by the Sabha and the Dal enthusiastically. What made these princes more eager than the rest?

One reason was their youth. Except for the two Bikaner princes, they were all men in their twenties or early thirties, impressionable, idealistic, keen to make their mark. Another was the weight of expectation on their shoulders. Tej Singhji, Sadul Singh, Jayaji Rao Scindia and Yadavindra and Bhim Singh all succeeded illustrious predecessors and found it tough trying to fill their giant shoes. Yadavindra, for instance, was said to be 'sensitive to the verge of an inferiority complex'.[98] Thirdly, the need to be noticed by the world was heightened, in the case of several of these young rulers, by profound psychological scars carried over from childhood. Sadul Singh's growing up was impaired by the 'extreme' jealousy of his father, which often expressed itself in physical brutality.[99] Rewa's Martand Singh, also saddled with an overbearing father, grew up wrestling with sexual problems. Francis Wylie's diagnosis was that Rewa was 'either an H[omo]-S[exual], like [his] father, or impotent'.[100] Brijendra Singh of Bharatpur, despite, or more likely because of, the indoctrination given him by the well-meaning British, which included three years abroad at Swiss and English public schools, grew up sickly, indolent and intensely conceited, once remarking to a courtier: 'I must have committed some sin in my previous life for instead of remaining God I have been sent back a Maharaja.'[101] Saddled with the forename George (a sycophantic gesture to the King-Emperor by his Anglophile father) Jayaji Rao Scindia of Gwalior had to contend in early life with a possessive mother, the junior maharani, an ignorant woman steeped in fanciful superstition, who ensured that his every move was watched and recorded by spies, with the ministrations of callous court doctors who pumped him full of libido-suppressing drugs in an effort to stop him developing the sexual lusts that had 'in the end proved fatal to his Father', and with the accident of an extremely short stature, which accentuated his sense of himself as emasculated and physically unworthy of his Maratha warrior heritage.[102] In 1945 the resident at Gwalior noted bluntly: 'The Maharaja seems to be a psychopathic case and I have heard it suggested that his mental condition is not unusual...in the son of a syphilitic father.'[103] These were men who were likely either to place an unwarranted trust in their own judgement or to put too great a store on the advice of courtiers.

Of course there is nothing wrong with advice—so long as it is sound. And by and large the leading *darbāri* bureaucrats of the late colonial era were well fitted to provide it: faithful servants gifted with intelligence and acumen. Many of these civil servants, however, including some of the brightest, had become deeply influenced by communal ideas and values. Gwalior's newly appointed Home Minister, the veteran Manubhai Mehta, although still committed to the policy of reform that had marked his long tenure at Baroda, had become obsessed, by the late 1930s, with the project of organising the states into a 'buttress against pan-Islamism';[104] while his colleague Sardar Angre, the Political Minister, was described as 'communally-minded, and...strongly anti-Mohammedan'.[105] Pandit Sharma, the Prime Minister of Kishengarh, brazenly took the state's minor ruler along to an RSS rally. The Barwani court was allegedly thick with Brahmin intriguers.[106] And at Jaipur one of the chief topics of conversation at court in the late 1930s was said to be the 'causes of the downfall of the Hindoos'.[107]

Yet the key player in the initial princely intrigue with the Mahasabha, Maharaja Ganga Singh of Bikaner, was quite a different type altogether—neither youthful nor wayward nor especially a case for treatment. Indeed it is quite difficult to say, in the absence of any clues in the archives or in his biography, exactly what drove him in the matter—unless it was a desire to prove to his peers that, even at 60 years of age, he could not be taken for granted. Nevertheless, Ganga Singh's quixotic flirtation with the Mahasabha is strangely of a piece with the other great and perverse political crusade of his last years, his attempt to persuade the princes to reject the federation scheme he had helped to design a decade earlier.

At any rate, it was Bikaner who drew these like-minded rulers together and put them formally in touch with the Hindu Mahasabha. In 1941 he invited Savarkar, Moonje and S.P. Mookherjee to Bikaner for a private visit, and in March of the following year had the three Sabha leaders back for a round-table with Kotah, Jaipur, Gwalior, Alwar and Dholpur. British intelligence learned 'that the Mahasabha leaders succeeded in making a good impression' on the rulers, in that they had been able to convince them that the party had no wish to restrict their independence.[108] Further informal, clandestine contacts followed, and continued throughout the War. Meanwhile, as noted earlier, the younger Sikh princes were cementing ties with the Akali Dal. Of course, the convergence between the rulers and the communal parties never got to the stage of a publicly proclaimed 'alliance'. The princes were far too cagey (and wary of possible imperial repercussions) to take sides openly. But this did not worry the party leaders too much. 'Circumstances oblige the Princes to be dumb and perhaps even deaf publicly', B.S. Moonje acknowledged, 'but that is all the more reason to attach overwhelming importance to what they say when they break their silence within closed doors.'[109]

The developments described above would have far-reaching consequences for the future of the princely order; however, they posed a particular and immediate challenge to its Muslim members. The

Muslim princes found themselves, to their dismay, increasingly excluded from the confidences of their Hindu peers and former friends. 'Your Highness knows that in the good old days, when there was some intimate problem to be tackled,' Taley Mohammad Khan of Palanpur wrote to his friend Hamidullah Khan of Bhopal, 'the Princes used to have informal conferences...and the Standing Committee...took great pains to understand everyone's point of view....Why can't this be done now?'[110]

But while some older hands like Taley Khan merely complained, others, with perhaps a keener appreciation of the political implications of this growing schism—rulers like Saiyyid Reza Ali Khan of Rampur, and Hamidullah himself—reacted in kind. In 1940, Rampur broke away from the largely Hindu 'Central India group' of princes, of which he had been a co-founder, proclaiming that a platform for 'intimate friends' to swap ideas had been turned into a nakedly communal forum.[111] And Bhopal threw down the gauntlet in a big way—first by recruiting Punjab MLC and Muslim Leaguer Sir Hisamuddin Khan as his chief of staff,[112] and secondly by successfully contesting, in 1944, for the chancellorship of the COP with a view to capturing that organisation for 'the moslem cause'.[113]

But these gestures merely served to widen the fissure. Although Hamidullah tried hard to play down the communal angle during his campaign for the chancellorship no one was fooled. Gwalior's Kailash Haksar circulated a memorandum 'in which he endeavoured to convey the impression that His Highness [of Bhopal] was [an] out and out... Pakistani, and that if he were elected...the Chamber would be turned into a Pakistan strong-hold'; while Yadavindra Singh of Patiala pointedly informed the maharaja of Indore that voting for Bhopal would be tantamount to voting for the League.[114]

And these apprehensions were strengthened by a series of nakedly partisan appointments made by the new chancellor. As part of a general overhaul of the Chamber, Hamidullah Khan jockeyed the Nawab of Chhattari into the chairmanship of the strategic Committee of Ministers, selected Sir Sultan Ahmad (over excellent candidates in V.T. Krishamachari and Sir C.P. Ramaswamy Aiyer) for the new post of Constitutional Adviser to the Chamber, and jobbed a dozen of his co-religionists into senior administrative positions in the secretariat. For the next three years the COP would function, to all intents and purposes, as a sleeping partner of the AIML.

The image of the princely order projected by the spin doctors of the COP was one of brotherly solidarity. In fact there had always been a hierarchy of wealth, power and status within the order. A crude but revealing index of this ranking was the gun-salute table, which determined how much official deference each ruler was entitled to. To these long-established cleavages was added, in the 1940s, that of religion. Whilst the COP under Bhopal's leadership continued to present a bold face to the world, and in some ways improved its administrative performance, its political effectiveness was increasingly sabotaged by sectarian jealousy. After January 1944 the Chamber was, to all intents and purposes, an organisation of two distinct and separate factions, a larger Hindu–Sikh combine and a smaller, mainly Muslim one, loyal to the chancellor. Significantly, when matters finally came to a head early in 1947 over the question of the states joining the Indian Constituent Assembly, among the first *darbārs* to break ranks were the confederates of 1942: Bikaner, Gwalior, Jodhpur, Patiala and Rewa.

But we are getting ahead of our story. We shall return to the climactic events of 1947 in the next chapter; but in the meantime the domestic implications of the princes' covert alliance with the Mahasabha and the Akali Dal need to be considered. The rulers had entered into an understanding with the communal parties in the expectation that the latter would throw their influence behind the princely states in their fight to preserve their autonomy. As we shall see, this confidence was not misplaced. However, the Sabhite and Akali leaders would exact a high price for this service—and ultimately it was the states' subjects who paid.

Rājadharma revisited

The Hindu Mahasabha, in particular, proved a robust advocate for the states and their rulers as well as a vigilant 'watchdog for their rights and interests', arguing strongly in public forums and in representations to the government in New Delhi that the states should be allowed to remain in existence as internally autonomous entities within a loose-knit Indian federation. At the same time both parties worked hard, in public and behind the scenes, to discourage agitation against the princely governments. Akali Dal leaders, for example, several times intervened in SGPC debates to skittle proposals for anti-monarchical demonstrations. And Mahasabha spokesmen strove diligently to fill the hearts and minds of their supporters inside the states with royalist sentiments. Speaking at the South Kanara District Hindu Conference at Udipi in June 1944, Moonje called on 'all Hindus to respect and love their Hindu Princes as embodiments of Hindu pride and...achievements'; whilst Savarkar bluntly advised followers in Baroda not to take part in any 'subversive movements aimed at destroying the Princes'.[115] As to the impact of this propaganda, in 1944 the Sabha claimed that its intervention had substantially checked the growth of Congress' influence amongst the subjects of the Hindu states.[116] While there is no way of assessing the veracity of this bold claim, one cannot dismiss it either.

However, in discharging what they perceived to be their obligations under the pact made with the Hindu and Sikh princes, the communal parties expected to reap reciprocal benefits. In particular, they expected their new royal allies to act in ways that conformed to their vision of *rājadharma*. The Mahasabha's blueprint for a free India was one that privileged and entrenched the values and hegemonic power of the majority Hindu community; and the Dal's, one that envisioned a reconstituted Punjabi Sikh state—the so-called Khalistan. Implicit in the princes' compact with the communal politicians was an understanding that the states would be rated, and judged, by how closely their administrations approximated to this rarified ideological standard.

Trouble was, as we saw in Chapter 2, the *darbārs* typically cultivated a more pragmatic view of the world—one that put stability before orthodoxy. Given their commitment to policies of religious toleration, their preference for selecting their advisers according to merit rather than belief, and the eclectic and/or secularist tastes of many of the ruling families, it is no wonder that some were found wanting. As the prospect of Indian independence drew nearer, substantial pressure was applied to make these deviant governments shape up.

The Akali Party was first off the mark. 'The first step of our preparations to face the coming crisis', Master Tara Singh told an Akali War Conference in April 1940, 'is to finish [the] Panthic traitors.'[117] Within weeks, the young maharaja of Nabha found himself the target of a vitriolic campaign of abuse and innuendo; over the next five years further campaigns 'exposed' un-Sikh practices in Jind, Kapurthala and Patiala, focusing especially on non-Sikh officials. 'It appears', mused Jagatjit Singh of Kapurthala, that 'Tara Singh has formed an ambition to play the role of a King-maker in Sikh States'.[118] But the Mahasabha soon followed suit, putting into effect what Moonje called a policy of 'constructive criticism' of the Hindu *darbārs*.[119] At the Madhya Bharat Mahasabha annual session held at Indore in late 1941, resolutions were passed calling upon the Hindu states to reduce their employment of Muslims, adopt Hindi as their language of record, and collaborate in the establishment of a Hindi radio station and a regional Hindi-medium university. After the conference letters were sent to all the Central Indian Hindu States inviting them to implement these resolutions, without delay, 'in the interests of the Hindu public'.[120] School textbooks and official codes containing 'Persianised Urdu' words and phrases were other frequent targets.[121] But the Mahasabha reserved its biggest guns for Mirza Ismail's Jaipur. In 1944, Savarkar wrote to the maharaja of Jaipur demanding that he 'eliminate the moslem influence' from his state. Specifically he nominated for attention the state insignia, which needed to be redesigned to bring out 'the stamp of Hindutva, of Hindu culture', and the prime ministership. Shortly afterwards, the Mahasabha launched what its president termed the 'first campaign' in the 'war on Urdu',[122] which culminated in party zealot Pandit Ram Chandra Sharma staging an indefinite fast in Delhi in the cause of Nagri reform.

The natural instinct of the princes was to resist outside dictation, and especially where Muslim *dewans* held sway, as in Jaipur and Kapurthala, the communal demands of the Sabha and the Dal were, at first, vigorously rebuffed. Asserting that Kapurthala was 'on trial', Chief Minister Sir Abdul Hamid urged his master to hold fast both for the sake of communal harmony and in the interest of good relations with the British. 'If we show weakness or yield', he wrote, 'we shall, by our example, teach other communities to indulge in similar tactics.'[123] And the Jaipur government dug its heels in too. Worried by Sharma's apparent determination to starve himself to death, the *darbār* eventually conceded the Pandit's lesser demand for an allocation of public grazing land for cows, but stood firm on Urdu and the future of the *dewan*, who in June 1944 further irritated the Mahasabha leaders by externing its secretary Kharpade for delivering inflammatory speeches.[124] Dholpur, ruled by the irascibly conservative and politician-hating Udaibhan Singh, was another state that turned a deaf ear to the Mahasabha's appeals.

Yet most of the core states identified above as partners to the original compact with the communal parties, perhaps because they were already staffed at key points with officials who shared something of their sociopolitical philosophy, soon fell obediently into line. The result was the unleashing across the north Indian princely states of a process of what might be called respectively 'Sikhisation' and 'Hinduisation' that greatly reinforced the majoritarian aspects of their polity and society. The growing conformism of the Sikh princes to religious *diktat* was one manifestation of this trend. Having in his youth wedded a Hindu woman, in 1938 Yadavindra Singh of Patiala remarried, but this time chose a woman from within the faith, and the daughter of a prominent Akali to boot; and in March 1945 he offered a similar pledge in regard to his children. In April 1943 Jagatjit Singh of Kapurthala won a truce with the Akalis by pledging to raise his grandson in the orthodox *keshadhari* tradition. Even the secular Ranbir Singh of Jind bowed to the trend in 1947, announcing that he had taken a New Year's resolution to grow his hair and beard.

Another symptom was the progressive elimination of minority bureaucrats from senior posts in all the northern states in favour of men from the communities of the rulers. Several senior Muslim officials were sacked from Gwalior in 1937 at the start of the new reign, accused on probably trumped-up charges of bribery and cheating. Jaipur and Jodhpur, in 1940, replaced Muslim members of council with Hindus. In the same year, the maharaja of Patiala resumed the *jagir* of his Muslim Prime Minister Nawab Liaquat Hyat Khan and hinted that he might replace Liaquat with a Sikh if a suitable man could be found. The search for a replacement in fact took several years, but in 1945 the old retainer was given his marching orders. One of the first acts of his successor, H. Singh Malik, was to persuade the maharaja to elevate his brother to the post of Military Secretary in place of Colonel Hamid Hasan Khan. D.K. Sen of Patiala, Abdul Hamid of Kapurthala and Mohammad Sadiq of Jind also lost their jobs during this period; while the maharaja of Jaipur finally let his protégé Mirza Ismail go early in 1946. Last but not least, Datia's able if partisan Muslim *dewan*, Khan Bahadur Ainuddin, was turned out in November 1946 as the direct result of a protest movement coordinated by the local Hindu Sabha.

The loss of these men was a serious blow to the cause of communal harmony in the states. Luminous role models of pluralism, their presence had exerted a check on communal tendencies lower down. However, the purge of minority bureaucratic elements in the early 1940s went much further and much deeper than the above shortlist would suggest. The overall picture with regard to Muslim employment, so far as one can reconstruct it from published reports, is summarised in Table 3.4. It shows two things: first, a steady decline, over time, in the number and proportion of Muslims employed in high-level jobs in Hindu- and Sikh-ruled states; secondly, a corresponding rise in the number and ratio of Muslims employed by Muslim-ruled states (though the impetus in this case seems not to have come so directly from external pressure groups, e.g., the Ahrars or the Muslim League). But even this summary misses the full impact of the cleanout. Statistical evidence tendered to the States Ministry suggests that by the War's end, 88 out of the 97 top positions in the Bhopal civil service and approximately 1060 out of 1120 posts in the Bhopal police were held by Muslims.[125] Likewise Ministry officials who visited Junagadh, after it had been taken over in

Table 3.4 Proportion of senior bureaucrats belonging to the Muslim community, selected states

	c.1925		c.1945	
	Number	Per cent	Number	Per cent
Hindu-ruled states				
Bhavnagar	0/34	0.0	0/23	0.0
Bundi	1/24	4.3	3/59	5.1
Chhatarpur	3/22	13.6	0/19	0.0
Chhota Udaipur	0/15	0.0	1/24	4.2
Dhar	1/40	2.5	0/43	0.0
Gwalior	21/123	17.1	24/332	7.2
Indore	5/41	12.2	3/58	5.2
Jammu and Kashmir	4/30	13.3	12/68	17.7
Jhalawar	1/15	6.6	0/19	0.0
Khilchipur	4/12	33.3	1/19	5.3
Kotah	4/47	8.5	4/48	8.3
Maihar	2/15	13.3	2/34	5.9
Nawanagar	1/25	4.0	1/28	3.6
Panna	1/24	4.2	1/21	4.8
Shahpura	1/23	0.0	0/18	0.0
Total/Average	48/490	9.80	52/813	6.39
Muslim-ruled states				
Cambay	0/17	0.0	5/19	26.3
Janjira	5/23	21.7	8/23	34.8
Junagadh	7/27	25.9	12/27	44.4
Rampur	30/40	75.0	55/82	67.1
Tonk	26/36	72.2	33/42	78.6
Total/Average	68/143	47.6	113/193	58.5

Source: Selected state annual administrative reports for 1925/26, 1945/46.

1947, found about half of all places in the state's public service filled by Muslims.[126] Unfortunately, there are no equivalent figures in the government records I have seen for Hindu or Sikh states; however, to judge from anecdotal reports the trend there was similar.

At the same time, and perhaps even more importantly, communal thinking started to affect *darbāri* adminstrative decisions. For as long as anyone could remember, it had been the practice of Muslims in the Jodhpur town of Jaswantpura to place their *tazias*, during Mohurrum, on a *chabutra* revered by Jaswantpura's Hindus. However, in 1947 the *hakim* (senior official) of the district ordered the practice to stop, citing anonymous Hindu objections.

The Kabutran-ka-Chabutra, as the name suggests, is a place where pigeons are fed. Places like this have a very great sentimental importance and possess almost a religious significance for the Hindus. The fact that the Muslims were allowed [in the past] to place their Tazia [*sic*] over a sacred place like this goes to show the catholicity and magnanimous tolerance of the Hindus. . . . In the context of the present general changed situation, in my opinion it will be in the interest of Public Policy that the Tazia[s] should not be allowed to be placed on this chabutra.[127]

And Bikaner's police officers exhibited a similar spirit of partisanship when, in July 1946, a complaint of criminal assault was lodged by two Hindu shopkeepers, Shiv Dayal and his nephew Shankar, at the City Kotwali. The police took the complainants at their word and filed a first information charge naming four Muslims as the assailants. Later they frivolously dismissed a counter-charge of assault lodged by two of the Muslims named on the charge sheet. Reading between the lines of the police report of the incident, it is clear that they believed the Muslims— members of the Chippa caste, a subaltern group with a history of lawlessness—had lied. Unsurprisingly, this display of official partisanship infuriated the Chippas; and as night fell on 8 July some of their young men started attacking Hindu shops located in the *mohulla*. Frightened shop owners telephoned the police, who on arriving at the scene, promptly opened fire on the rioters. Two Muslims (one of them a woman) were killed and 40 others wounded in the ensuing fusillade. Although the police were outnumbered, even the state's Superintendent of Police (SP) afterwards conceded that their action had been hasty and out of all proportion to the danger posed by the unruly crowd. Nevertheless, while mildly censuring the officer in charge for shooting without real cause, the SP put most of the blame on the Chippas for breaking the peace.[128] The attitudes and mentalities revealed in these examples may not have been typical, even in the 1940s, but they were certainly not confined to a few maverick individuals. Besides, it is unlikely that the men concerned would have taken the line they did if they had thought their superiors would disapprove; and in fact, as we saw, no real disapproval was registered.

Discrimination was starting to become entrenched at the level of policy, too. Muslims in Hindu-ruled states such as Gwalior had their share of education grants sliced and in Muslim-ruled Bhopal the proportion of the ecclesiastical budget allocated to Hindu religious institutions was further reduced from an already low level. And several states, including

Kishengarh and Kapurthala, ceased in the early 1940s to use Urdu as their administrative language, the former going over to Nagri-based Hindi, the latter Punjabi written in the Gurumukhi script. Even the pro-Hindi AISPC recognised in these changes a 'policy of aggressive communalism'.[129]

Meanwhile, other states introduced programmes deliberately favouring the community of the ruler. Under the umbrella of its war-powers legislation, Bahawalpur in 1942 proclaimed a new licensing scheme for the cloth trade—which traditionally had been dominated by Hindus—reserving 50 per cent of licences for Muslims. As a result, a number of Hindu dealers were forced out of business. And similar favouritism was exhibited by the Bahawalpur *darbār* in the distribution of contracts for the supply of sugar. For its part, Bhopal spent lakhs funding a scheme for attracting Punjabis to settle in the state, whereby approved applicants (almost all of whom seem to have been Muslims) were given cheap loans to purchase land and tax-rebates on it for up to ten years, depending on how quickly it showed a profit. Eventually, some 100,000 Punjabis moved to Bhopal under this scheme—a demographic shift that prompted a Gwalior minister to exclaim: the state 'is being progressively muslimized'.[130]

Last but not least, the new orientation in princely governance was reflected in an extensive, and increasingly open, *darbāri* patronage of communal parties and allied grass-roots organisations. Having long resisted registering the Hindu Mahasabha as a legal organisation in the state on the plausible suspicion that many of its members were public servants, the Gwalior government in 1941 withdrew its objection, the Law and Justice Member minuting:

> In the present time, every religion and community is trying to develop itself. Therefore sanction for registering this society may be given without any such condition.[131]

Following Gwalior's lead, one by one, between 1941 and 1945, Baroda, Barwani, Bhavnagar, Alwar, Kotah, Jaipur and Dhar all opened their doors to the Mahasabha. In two of the above cases, the *darbārs* not only gave permission for the party to operate lawfully, but provided local organisers with assistance in getting new branches set up and deputed village teachers to do propaganda work on behalf of the organisation.

But that was just the beginning. After 1945, several Hindu states brought Mahasabhite cadres into their councils. Despite winning only two seats in the 1945 Raj Sabha elections, the Gwalior Hindu Sabha was allocated one of four non-official places in the state council. Shortly afterwards, the Mahasabha was given representation in the Bharatpur cabinet; and in 1946 Pandit Harihar Swarup Sharma, the elder brother of a future president of the BJS, was appointed to the staff of the maharaja of Alwar. These postings were followed in April 1947 by the even more consequential elevation of Mahasabha deputy-president N.B. Khare to the premiership of Alwar.

The RSS, too, benefited handsomely from the solicitude of communal state officials. In Kashmir, the ruler's personal *guru* Swāmī Sant Dev encouraged the opening of RSS offices in Jammu City and several other provincial towns during the early 1940s; and early in 1947 some 2000 trained RSS cadres entered the state apparently by arrangement with the *darbār*. In Sarila and Charkhari, the RSS benefited from the support of Deputy Superintendent of Police Ishwari Prasad and senior revenue officer Raghunandra Prasad respectively. By early 1947 high officials of Kapurthala were often to be seen presiding at local RSS gatherings.

Comparatively the Akali Dal fared less well at the hands of the Sikh *darbārs*, not simply because there were comparatively few Sikh-ruled states, but because none of the latter was yet prepared to share power— even with their fellow Sikhs. But the Dal was not greatly fussed by its exclusion from high office; it was content to be able, finally, to work inside the Sikh kingdoms openly, without constant official interference. As its deputy-president Giani Kartar Singh noted with satisfaction, the signs coming from the Sikh princes were now mostly positive, pointing to 'better days' ahead for the party.[132]

In their defence, the *darbārs* probably considered their co-option of the communal organisations a form of insurance against the increasingly strident demands of the Congress. Alternatively, they may have thought they could control them more easily from the inside than from without. If so, they grievously miscalculated. Misreading the signs, the communalist leaders in the states convinced themselves that their cause had the full blessing of the princely authorities; and they took this as an open licence to campaign. Inevitably, a major dividend of this intensified proselytisation by the communal parties was an upsurge in collective Hindu–Muslim violence. As we have seen, communal riots became, during the 1930s, an entrenched feature of life in many parts of princely north India; but it was only in the mid-1940s that the phenomenon became general and endemic. Before 1945 the peak year for communal incidents in the north Indian states was 1932, when there were nine such events (Table 1.4). As late as 1943 (the last relatively quiet year) there were just three. But in 1945 there were eleven riots and in 1946 no less than 15, four of them large-scale clashes resulting in fatalities and injuries requiring hospitalisation. At least 39 persons died in communal riots in princely north India between February 1946 and January 1947; and a further 247 were seriously injured. Property damage was also considerable, with a mosque (in Gwalior City), several temples (in Bhopal), and dozens of shops and houses destroyed.[133] With the vantage of hindsight, one can say that 1946 was the year that communalism in princely north India entered its climactic phase.

Moreover many of the above outbreaks appear to have been triggered by the provocative behaviour of communal party cadres. The *darbārī* report into the outbreak at Gwalior in April 1946 indicates that 'feelings had become strained among the millworkers' of the city as a consequence of agitation by rival Muslim League and Hindu Sabha activists.[134] Similarly, the official report on the Jammu outbreak makes it clear that most of the Muslims who took part in the affray were Punjabis deliberately trucked in to stir up trouble;[135] whilst information given to the resident at Bhopal suggests that the trouble there was caused directly by Mahasabha *agents provocateurs* planting wild rumours to the effect that 400 Hindus had been killed and 40 women 'violated' in the disturbances at Gwalior.[136] Indeed, the Sabhites as good as acknowledged the connection themselves. 'The Bhopal...riot', wrote the party general secretary, 'provides a good field for our work and [an opportunity to]...rehabilitate ourselves in public estimation.'[137]

Belatedly, some of the *darbārs* tried to put the genie back in the bottle. One of them was Gwalior. As soon as news of the 1946 riot broke, the government imposed an indefinite ban on meetings, processions and the carrrying of weapons in the capital and the towns of Lashkar and Morar. During the days that followed, several local Mahasabha leaders were detained (but not tried, for lack of hard evidence) and 'goonda elements' in Gwalior City and Lashkar 'rounded up'.[138] Later, a post-mortem was convened, which led to the *darbār* reviewing its 1939 riot containment plan and issuing a tough new Communal Disturbances Prevention Ordinance, which conferred enhanced powers of search and detention on the police and created a raft of new criminal offences relating specifically to communal riots, including offences of abetting, harbouring suspects, possession of firearms or explosives in areas proclaimed as 'disturbed', abduction of women and forced religious conversion—for all of which draconian jail terms were prescribed.[139] And the maharaja weighed in too. In an address on 1 December, he told his subjects that he was deeply ashamed by the manner in which

Gwalior's 'peace and tranquillity' had been disturbed by 'the unhealthy influence of parties [based] in other parts of India'.

> Gwalior has always been proud of the fact that the government of the State has regarded every sect and community with equality and while safeguarding the life and property of every class has given each community full freedom for the practice of its religious rites...our religious dealings have been so for centuries....Everyone must remember that in this country Hindus and Muslims have lived together for centuries and will do so in future. It is altogether impossible to eliminate each other by indulging in this senseless bloodshed.[140]

Yet if we believe the account left by his last *dewan* M.A. Sreenivasan, Jayaji Rao had to be prompted to make the speech and did so reluctantly. And the Sabhites seem to have understood this. On the second day of the Mohurrum festival, which followed closely upon the maharaja's intervention, Sabhite and RSS militants led by branch secretary Bhagwant Prashad launched a savage and unprovoked attack on Muslim processioners in the capital. Prashad himself stabbed one Muslim to death and inflicted fatal injuries on another, before he himself was overpowered and beaten. When in January, local RSS leader Dr Pachure was carpeted before Sreenivasan and asked for an explanation, he replied leeringly: 'We have hand grenades.'[141] But at least Gwalior had the admirable Sreenivasan. In some other states, such as Kotah, the official response was nothing short of craven. Although it was generally agreed that the Mahavir Dal had deliberately provoked the altercation at Baran that precipitated the town's first-ever communal riot in January 1947, its leaders were never charged. The *dewan* attributed this to the 'Hindutva' sympathies of his bitter rival, the IG of police.[142]

During the early twentieth century, outbreaks of collective violence triggered by disputes over religious or communal issues were few and far between in the princely states of northern India. They were not entirely absent, as the case study of the 1927 riot in Indore offered in Chapter 1 shows. But they were far less numerous, and less severe, *per capita*, than similar incidents in the provinces of British India. What is more, relations between the major religious communities in the states in this period seem to have been, in the main, quite harmonious—characterised by considerable friendly reciprocity, and by what Mark Peel has called 'practical toleration'. It was a different story by the 1940s. Communal riots had become numerous and widespread across the region. States such as Gwalior, Bikaner and Kotah, riot-free before 1940, had become major arenas of contestation. The gap between the states and the provinces in this respect had begun to narrow.

And communalism was starting to destroy *communitas* in the neighbourhoods. More and more, Hindus, Muslims and Sikhs in the states were keeping to themselves and shunning formal contacts with the members of other communities. When in July 1946, the president of Bikaner's Praja Mandal was arrested, the 'Mussalmans of the State were asked... to observe hartal', but they declined to take part in the demonstration, claiming that the Mandal was 'purely a Hindu organisation which cannot claim to have even a single Muslim member'.[143] Cooperation across communal boundaries was waning; and so, too, was the old spirit of tolerance. Every year, for as long as anyone could remember, the Mohurrum procession in the Jodhpur town of Bhimal had followed the same route, which included several approved halting places. According to the state's chief of police, there was 'no dispute between Hindus and Mohammedans over these places whatsoever'. However at Mohurrum 1944, Hindus contested the right of the masons' and spinners' *tazias* to halt at the chabutra in the Malaniyon-ka-Chouhata, and this position was reaffirmed the following year. It was a small meanness but one that rankled with the Muslims, who refused to renew their processional licences until the Jodhpur *darbār* had agreed to append a list of recognised stopping-places to the licences.[144] As Conrad Corfield, resident for the Punjab states, noted dismally after a fruitless attempt to persuade the Malerkotla authorities to intercede in the interminable quarrel between the state's Hindus and Muslims over predence in respect of evening prayer times: 'Communal rivalries [here] are endemic, and almost as explosive as in the Punjab proper.'[145] In 20 years, popular mentalities in the princely states of northern India had undergone a sea change.

The current chapter has sought to uncover the reasons for that metamorphosis in popular thinking. In the course of that exploration, it made three basic arguments. First, it demonstrated how the structural factors which had served historically to restrict intercourse between the states and British India—their economic backwardness, their physical isolation, their monarchical polity and the overarching mantle of British paramountcy—were gradually neutralised, over the second quarter of the century, by the insistent and ultimately ineluctable forces of progress, development and subcontinental integration—exposing them to provincially centred communal ideas and animosities, and opening them to increasingly extensive penetration by communalist-minded individuals and organisations: by evangelical missionaries, especially Arya Samajists; by British Indian Muslims looking for work in their mushrooming factories and canal colonies; above all by party politicians linked to the Mahasabha and the Akali Dal. Secondly, it showed how the transformation of the princely polity during the 1930s and 1940s— under pressure of external political events, and in response to the rulers' attempts to shore up their patrimony by reaching out to the progressive elements amongst their subjects—into something approaching a representative one, weakened its ability to defend against communalism by acting arbitrarily and ruthlessly against its agents. Thirdly and lastly, the chapter documented how the royal commitment to *rājadharma* was undermined by the attempt of some of the princes to try to purchase a future for themselves and their states by entering into a covert alliance with the communal parties.

Nevertheless, if the story of communal relations in the northern states between c.1920 and 1946 is a somewhat bleak one, we need to keep their fall from grace in perspective. Bad as they had become in Jammu, Kotah and Gwalior, conditions across the border in UP, Punjab, and CP were still worse, by several degrees, in 1946. Gwalior City was no Calcutta, Cawnpore or Bombay. Moreover, while the incidence of communal violence in the states had proliferated, sizeable pockets and residues of the old culture still survived there in the mid-1940s. In Kotah, for example, the *praja mandal* in September 1946 sent a delegation to greet Muslims returning from 'Id celebrations in September with gifts of cold drinks and expressions of communal fraternity; and later in the year the Mandal persuaded some leading Muslims to attend a public meeting to work out ways of reducing tension. At the end of the meeting, the parties issued a joint statement condemning rumours of communal trouble 'spread by school children and other irresponsible persons', and promising further cooperation in the task of peacekeeping. 'Neither community has anything against [the] other, and they should live in peace and harmony', the statement read.[146] Many more such 'peace committees' would be set up in the difficult days that lay ahead. It is clear, too, from election results, that, for all its high profile and noisy political posturing, the Hindu Right was still a long way short of capturing the hearts and minds of the landowning and professional classes of the states. For instance, Hindu Sabha candidates managed to capture just two of 55 elective seats in Gwalior in December 1945.

Finally, even as some of the northern *darbārs* compromised their adherence to the pluralist traditions of *rājadharma* in a bid to appease communalists within, they remained for the most part stalwart in their determination to keep the larger provincial infection at bay, and, what is more, confident of their ability, given proper vigilance, to do so.

> General conditions in British India and the strained relations between Hindus and Muslims everywhere outside Marwar are likely to have a bad effect upon the people [of] Marwar [a Jodhpur official noted]. It is therefore necessary to see that unsocial elements do not inflitrate and preach violence and hatred to members of either community. Makrana being the biggest town in this district, with a large industrial population, a large number of bad characters and a Muslim majority, is likely to take up this infection if precautions are not taken at an early stage.[147]

It was a brittle confidence, though, and, to the extent that it was based on the assumption that the situation had deteriorated so greatly that it could not possibly get much worse, unfounded. What we know through hindsight—but they did not—was that there was still a wild card left in the pack. Its name was 'partition'.

4

The Further Shores of Partition

There is a general feeling that the British Empire is fading away... When this happens, the group which is [best] organized for violence may succeed and a general state of disorder will help it succeed.

Jawaharlal Nehru, 1939

Imperial sunset

At the end of the War, in 1945, the popular movement in the princely states found itself facing a dramatically changed political situation replete with democratic opportunities; but its infrastructure in many states was still embryonic, and in others the transformation of the *praja mandals* into legal and constitutionalist bodies had robbed the movement of much of its earlier fire and enthusiasm. As for the AISPC, it had become almost moribund.

Nevertheless, the signs of an imminent British withdrawal from the subcontinent could not be denied; and thoughts of what this would mean for political stakeholders in the country galvanised the nationalists in the states into action. Everywhere, the *praja mandals* threw off their lethargy: recruiting drives were started; tired and compromised leaders dumped; and the demand for responsible government stepped up. When it inquired, in September 1945, as to the condition of its various regional affiliates, the AISPC discovered that the Punjab States Peoples' Conference had virtually ceased to exist. It had no paid-up members, its President was under restrictions, and its Secretary had died.[1] By 1947 the situation had been transformed. According to AISPC figures summarised in Table 4.1, organisational membership in the Punjab

Table 4.1 Praja Mandal membership in Punjab, 1947

Unit	Name of body	State population	No. of members
Patiala	Patiala State Praja Mandal	1,975,000	30,000
Malerkotla	Malerkotla State Praja Mandal	82,000	2,127
Fadikot	Faridkot State Praja Mandal	200,000	4,000
Dujana	Dujana State Praja Mandal	30,000	4,000(?)
Pataudi	Pataudi Rajya Praja Mandal	24,000	986
Loharu	Loharu State Praja Mandal	23,000	500
Jind	Jind State Praja Mandal	362,000	7,000
Nabha	Nabha State Praja Mandal	375,000	4,000
Punjab States Regional Council		5,100,000	c.53,000

Source: Note by Harbans Lal, Gen. Sec., Punjab Regional Council [March 1947], NMML, AISPC, file 138/1 of 1933–48.

region by March 1947 was pushing 50,000. And returns from other divisions reported similar gains. The Gwalior State Congress, for instance, claimed at the end of 1946 to have signed up 28,000 members—12,000 during the previous year.[2] In most places, too, parties affiliated to the AISPC fared well in post-War princely state elections. In the September 1945 poll in Jaipur, the RPM won 62 out of 93 elective seats in the Representative Assembly and 15 out of 28 such seats in the Legislative Council. Once looked down upon by the INC as an embarrassing drain on its resources, the *praja mandal* movement by 1946 was starting to assume the look of a real political force. 'They are becoming the counterpart of the National Congress in the States', acknowledged Jawaharlal Nehru admiringly.[3]

Yet the post-War explosion of nationalist sentiment across the northern states was not confined to the Congress-affiliated *praja mandals*. State-based Hindu sabhas also leaped on the post-War bandwagon; and conceded nothing to the Congress-*wallahs* in the shrillness of their patriotic evocations. But the notion of a single all-embracing nationalism remained, in the states as in the provinces, predominantly a Hindu attachment—and what is more, an unforgiving one. Modern nationalism of the Indian type has tended to have little patience with non-believers, or with those who dare to embrace an alternative vision. Thus, Muslims living in the states, who fell prominently into both categories, came increasingly to be viewed as 'anti-national' and targeted accordingly.

However, while rooted in exclusivist Hindu conceptions of the nation, the timing of these retaliatory attacks was largely dictated by the tempo of local Muslim political activity. Although for reasons already explained, the generality of Muslims in the states had shied away from the mainstream popular movement, this potential constituency was only belatedly and somewhat reluctantly tapped into by the AIML; and even the enthusiastic reception given to the Pakistan demand by most northern states Muslims did not immediately translate into an upsurge of regional support for its political sponsor. From 1943, though, the picture changed dramatically. From a base of 80 in 1940, membership of the Alwar state branch of the League rose steadily until, by mid-1947, it was touching 600. Nearby, the Jaipur State Muslim League grew from three score of members in 1940 to 30,000 in 1947. In Tonk, where the League surprisingly 'did not exist' until the mid-1940s, 150 sympathisers had been signed up by January 1947. Around this time, too, several *anjumans*, such as those at Kotah and Partabgarh, reconstituted themselves as League affiliates.[4] To be sure, the support for the League in the northern states still remained well behind that for the Congress; yet it was substantial enough by 1946 to command respect, particularly in the light of the parallel expansion there of the League's paramilitary Muslim National Guard.[5] Meanwhile, states Muslims evinced a growing affection for League causes. In January 1946, Muslim homes and businesses in CI were illuminated in celebration of the League's success in the recent provincial polls; and on 16 August, Muslims in a number of states turned out in answer to Quaid-i-Azam Jinnah's call for the observance of a day of 'Direct Action'. Further public gestures by Muslims across princely north India greeted the installation in September of a mainly Congress Interim Government in New Delhi.

The changing Muslim outlook in princely India reflected a growing anxiety on the part of Muslim subjects—especially in Hindu-majority states—about what the future held in store for them. As noted above, the rejuvenated *praja mandal* movement had revived its 1938 demand for the immediate establishment of full responsible government. Faced with this demand, many *darbārs* tried to meet it half way by allocating some government portfolios to party members occupying elected seats in the legislatures—replicating in effect the provincial dyarchy system of 1919–35. That sometimes sufficed to buy them breathing space—but it also established a precedent for further constitutional change. And other *darbārs* dug their heels in and rejected the demand outright. Eventually, the *mandal* leaders were left with no choice but to resort to mass agitation. During the autumn and winter of 1946–47, *satyagrahas* in the name of responsible government were launched in Kashmir, Alwar, Jind, Chhatarpur, Indore and a dozen other northern states.

Although unsuccessful, the scale and ferocity of these agitations—the Indore *satyagraha* climaxed in a march by 20,000 protesters on the palace, which was repulsed by a brutal police *lathi*-charge—sent shivers of alarm through Muslims in the affected states, who feared that they would sooner or later become a target for the mob's frustrations. Hardly less frightening for them, though, was the prospect that the *darbārs* might be forced, either by pressure from below or diplomatic pressure from New Delhi, to grant the *praja mandals'* demands. From a Muslim perspective, responsible government meant unalloyed Hindu *raj*, and in all likelihood an end to the governmental protection they had long come to expect and rely on for their security.

In part then they turned to the Muslim League in the hope that its political leverage, and street muscle in the shape of the National Guards, might afford them some shelter from Hindu aggression. And their vocal support for Pakistan—which, since it was not intended, according to the League, to include any princely states, seemingly had nothing concrete to offer the Muslims living there—can be similarly explained; it was a form of insurance. Once Pakistan had been established, its Muslim government would surely see to it that their rights were protected, one way or another.

Indeed, the Muslims were not the only minority group in the states to think this way. In early July 1946 a Sikh political conference attended by Akali leaders Master Tara Singh, Sardar Mangalsingh and Gyani Pratap Singh was held at Indore. The Akali visitors were 'greeted with an ovation on their arrival and taken in procession with Sikh and Khalistan slogans'. Later local Sikh leader Sardar Narayansingh of Indore assured Tara Singh that he had the full support of the Indore Sikh community 'in the Sikh struggle for existence'.[6] Again, one has to assume that the Indore Sikhs had little expectation of their state becoming part of any future Sikh homeland established in the central Punjab. Again, their response has to be understood in psychological terms, as a strategy of identity-reinforcement.

Ironically, though, such strategies only served to underline the fact that the minority communities generally nurtured different loyalties and goals to the Hindu majority community. In September 1946, *praja mandals* across the states celebrated the assumption of power by the Congress Interim Government with flag marches, rallies, speeches and fireworks; but in most places Muslims refused to attend. Indeed, the predominant Muslim response was to mark the event with very public displays of mourning:

> A suggestion had been made that a procession consisting of Muslims, Hindus and Sikhs carrying white flags should be taken out in the city to show that the State public had nothing to do with events outside State territory, but the Muslim League did not agree to join this procession. The position in the city therefore is that some black flags are visible and black arm bands are being worn by the Muslims.

So it went in Patiala. In Sujangarh town in Bikaner, Muslims actually attacked a Praja Parishad meeting, injuring two workers.

Congress and AISPC leaders, it must be said, did their level best to keep the lid on this incendiary situation. But the leaders of the Hindu Mahasabha and the Akali Dal added fuel to the fire. They refused to condemn violence in principle, and in fact endorsed its use as a political weapon by calling on their supporters to resist the Muslim-homeland scheme with all their strength. In June 1946 Master Tara Singh told a meeting of the Sikh faithful at Amritsar that they should be 'prepared to die in the struggle ahead'. In February 1947 he called for the formation of an Akal Fauj—an Akali army. On 3 March, standing on the steps of the legislative building at Lahore, he berated a hostile crowd of League supporters with the words: 'We may be cut to pieces, but we will never concede Pakistan.'[7] And a similar call to arms went out from the Mahasabha to the Hindus of Rampur, after the Muslim-ruled state controversially elected, in May 1947, to send a delegate to the Constituent Assembly in Delhi. Addressing a public rally in the capital, Chandra Saxena, secretary of the Bareilly Sabha, warned Hindu loyalists to expect a Muslim backlash and to be ready to 'guard their rights'.[8]

Inevitably, there were consequences: further street clashes in Kotah and Alwar, and a full-scale riot in Baroda City in the wake of Assumption Day, which left two people dead and 23 injured. But the worst aftershocks were felt in Gwalior. In February 1947 the embalmed corpse of the late Bhagwant Prashad, whose murder was described in the previous chapter, was paraded through the streets of Gwalior's capital 'with aggressive intent'. Predictably, Hindu emotions overflowed, a mob gathered, and Muslims were beaten. The assaults continued for three weeks; by which time the frenzy had spread to Lashkar and Ujjain, scene of the 1942 outbreak also described in Chapter 3. Here violence was shaped in part by collective memories of the earlier event, as well as by what had been happening in the capital. But again, the prime causal factor seems to have been the local Muslim League branch's determination to express publicly its support for Jinnah and Pakistan. Although the Hindu Mahasabha had maintained an office in Ujjain since the early 1940s, it had never held a meeting or staged a procession there. Despite the events of 1942, the town was not generally considered (like Gwalior, Lashkar, Morar and Guna) a stronghold of militant Hindudom. But in March 1947 the good Sabhites of Ujjain decided, in the light of this League propaganda, to make a statement. They organised an Anti-Pakistan Day. It was unexpectedly successful. Most Hindus in the town stopped work and many attended a public rally on the maidan. The Muslims did not interfere; they were intent on celebrating the League's triumph in the Punjab. Nevertheless they indicated their displeasure. Overnight, as if by arrangement, groups of Muslims gathered at several of the city's *dargahs* to hear poems read out, satirising Hindus and their religion.

The following day was Rang Panchami, the day of licensed mayhem that marks the climax of the Holi festivities. Around two o'clock in the afternoon, three or four Muslims were bicycling through the mainly Hindu neighbourhood of Bahadur Ganj when they were showered with coloured water, as happens in Holi, by some Hindu boys. Probably the water was thrown without political intent, given the age of the youths in question; however, their victims, who appear to have had League connections, took the prank as a challenge. Their leader got down from his bicycle, grabbed a stick and struck the boys several full-bodied blows. After that the Muslims decamped to the Bohra Bazaar and inflamed its residents with a lurid account of their recent misadventure, whereupon the Bohras hastened to defend their community's besmirched honour. Armed with various blunt implements, they waded into the Bahadur Ganj Hindus. By the time the police and the military appeared on the scene, six people lay dead in the *mohulla*'s dusty lanes.[9]

Driven largely by provincial political agendas, the communal fracas in Gwalior state had cross-border repercussions too. As the census data summarised in Table 5.1 indicates, the Muslim quantum of the population of north India in the early twentieth century was consistently higher in Muslim-ruled princely states than in all other places, whether neighbouring states or adjacent provinces. It would seem that, where possible, Muslims preferred to live under the rule of one of their own. Doubtless, they were influenced by the material benefits and opportunities (real) and the heightened security (perhaps imaginary, but nonetheless compelling) that the aegis of a friendly co-religionist could confer. Significantly, Table 5.1 also shows that the Muslim *share* of the population of the larger Muslim-ruled states rose appreciably during

1931–41, indicating that Muslims were starting to move there in search of safety. If a half-reliable census could have been taken in 1946, it probably would have revealed a sharp strengthening of this phenomenon.

In the absence of global data, however, we must make do with anecdotal evidence. This brings us back to Gwalior. After the second wave of rioting there in 1946, the state's Muslims began to emigrate; by early December the exodus had turned into a flood. Between the 1st and the 6 December, 1000 Muslims fled the capital and over the next seven days another 4000 followed. Where did they go? Mostly to Bhopal, although a few with the necessary means made the longer trip south to Hyderabad. Why Bhopal? According to refugees quizzed by Gwalior officials, it was because they believed they could find in Muslim-ruled Bhopal the security their own government no longer seemed able or willing to provide.[10] To underline the point, most of them bluntly rejected the *darbār*'s offer of repatriation.

Yet just when it appeared that all hell was about to break loose, the communal situation in the states stabilised. Even as the northern provinces succumbed one by one, like dominoes, to the spreading communal frenzy—first east Bengal and Bihar over the winter of 1946–47, then west Punjab and UP in the spring, and finally east Punjab in the early summer—an eerie kind of peace broke out in princely north India, one almost redolent of pre-War days. Even in Gwalior, violence abated after April. What was going on? Well, in some ways the lull was deceptive. As we shall see shortly, plans were already being laid, and preparations made, for ethnic cleansing on a large scale. At the same time, it appears that many people in the states had decided to hold their fire pending all-India developments.

The story of the efforts of the new Attlee Labour Government in Britain, from May 1945, to find a recipe for the transfer of power satisfactory to all the major parties and interest groups in the subcontinent is well known and requires no retelling here. Nevertheless, because some of its initiatives proved consequential for the communal situation in the states, we need to pause for a moment to consider how London proposed to deal with the thorny problem of their erstwhile allies, the princes. Surprisingly perhaps, given its socialist leanings, the Labour government took the line, inherited from its predecessor, that the 'paramountcy' which the Crown had exercised over the states was not morally or lawfully transferable and would therefore 'lapse' with the end of British dominion in India. As the Cabinet Mission explained, in a statement issued at the end of its two-month exploratory visit to India in the spring of 1946:

> This means that the rights of the [princely] States which flow from
> their relationship with the Crown will no longer exist and that all
> the rights surrendered by the States to the Paramount Power will
> return to the States. Political arrangements between the States on
> the one side and British India on the other will thus be brought to
> an end.[11]

Although the Mission's statement went on to make it clear that the
resultant 'void' would have to be 'filled' somehow, its perhaps deliberately elusive language left most contemporaries—not least among them
the princes—with the strong impression that the decision about when
and how would be one entirely for the states. The ambiguity left a copious
space for princely manoeuvre, as we shall discover in the next section.
More immediately, it raised the intriguing prospect of the princely
states becoming, to all intents and purposes, legally and practically
independent upon the British departure.

For the minorities, this was an important assurance because it
relieved them of the fear of being subjected to the rule of a rampant
Hindu-centred Congress government in New Delhi. The princely *darbārs*
may not have been, in every case, to their liking, but compared to the
GOI they were 'soft' states, which could be bargained with. Another
positive was that the Mission's Plan for the devolution of power
(published a couple of weeks after its statement on paramountcy)
favoured a federal India, in which the provinces and 'groups' would
control most of the functions of government, leaving only the powers
of defence, foreign affairs and communications to be exercised by the
Centre. A unitary India, with representatives from the Muslim-majority
provinces sitting in the federal legislature, was one much less likely to
be dominated at the Centre by the Congress; and a relatively weak
Centre had less capacity to cause problems. These features made the
Mission's scheme particularly attractive to Muslims living in the 'minority'
provinces; but Muslim subjects of Hindu-ruled states also found
them vaguely reassuring. Last but not least, the communal situation
in the states benefited from the continuing confusion in the public
mind about what—in the event of the British government changing
its mind—partition might actually involve. It is doubtful whether many
in 1946 and early 1947 thought in terms of fixed borders manned by
armed guards, or conceived of large transfers of population. Moreover,
thanks to the Muslim League's propaganda machine, most Indians, in
so far as they imagined Pakistan territorially, imagined it as consisting
of the so-called 'six Muslim provinces' in their entirety. Such a state if

created would be large, powerful, and would contain large Hindu and Sikh minorities—ingredients that would force the Congress to treat its residual Muslim population with kid gloves.

For months rumours and press speculation about these matters circulated; but the final picture did not become clear until 3 June, when the viceroy Lord Mountbatten announced over all-India radio that the Attlee government, on his advice, was preparing to transfer power to two successor authorities 'this year on a Dominion status basis'.[12] The announcement diplomatically avoided mention of Pakistan, but made it clear that the League's decade-old dream was about to be realised—that there would be a partition.

The 3 June statement said nothing about the states. Its brief was to address the problem of British India. Nevertheless, it had important implications for princely India because it ruled out some of the possibilities that had kept the hopes of the minorities there alive. By conceding Pakistan, the 3 June plan made it inevitable that the new India would have a strongly centralised government totally controlled by the INC. On the other hand, by mandating the partition of the Punjab along religious lines, it effectively pushed the eastern border of Pakistan west by some 400 kilometres, ensuring not only that it would be smaller, and therefore weaker, but that it would be far removed from the majority of the Hindu-ruled kingdoms. On both counts, the outcome was bad news for the states' Muslims, even as it strengthened the hand of the Hindu Right. The then premier of Alwar N.B. Khare contends in his memoirs that had 'the whole of the Punjab gone to Pakistan, Alwar State would have ... aligned itself with it'.[13] Coming from a pillar of the Mahasabha, the claim is difficult to credit; nonetheless it underlines how the 3 June decision closed off avenues that could have been exploited by the states to their advantage.

Understandably, the 3 June statement caused particular dismay among the Muslim elites of Muslim-ruled states. Two weeks after the announcement of the partition plan, the nawab of Bhopal called on Mountbatten. Agitatedly, he 'pointed out that his population included 150,000 warlike Muslims'. How could he expect them to tolerate his hooking up with 'a purely Hindu Dominion', he asked the viceroy.[14] Even more, though, it came as a shock to the Sikhs. Not only did the statement make no mention of Khalistan, the foreshadowed partition of the Punjab threatened to destroy the Panth as a political force by splitting it in twain. After 3 June the only way that the Akalis were ever going to attain their cherished goal of a Panthic homeland was by force of arms.

On the other hand the 3 June statement did provide one small consolation for the states' Muslims at least. It affirmed that London's policy towards princely India remained 'unchanged'. Evidently, the dictum of May 1946 on paramountcy still held good. This cheered the Muslims because it meant that when the British left, the princely states would regain their independence. They would no doubt continue to suffer local harassment, but would be shielded from the Hindu imperialism of New Delhi.

Thus as spring melted into summer, and the northern provinces of British India reeled under the impact of a tsunami of insensate communal violence, the north Indian states remained, for the most part, calm, seemingly once again, as of old, islands of refuge in a stormy sea. But the calm was a fragile one—a tissue of suppressed fears and unreliable hopes. It could not last. 'Here in Bhopal', an English officer serving in the nawab's army prophetically observed, 'we sit on the edge of a volcano.'[15]

Dreams and conspiracies

The official princely line, as articulated by the Standing Committee of the COP, was that the Cabinet Mission's statement on the extinction of paramountcy constituted the British government's pledged word— a guarantee that could be relied on absolutely:

> The States [after the transfer of power] will retain all subjects and powers other than those [voluntarily] ceded by them to the [Indian] Union. Paramountcy will terminate at the close of the interim period and will not be transferred to or inherited by the new Government of India. All the rights surrendered by the States to the Paramount Power will return to the States. The proposed Union of India will, therefore, exercise only such functions in relation to the States in regard to Union subjects as are assigned or delegated to the Union. Every State shall continue to retain its sovereignty and all rights and powers except to the extent that those rights and powers have been expressly delegated by it.[16]

In retrospect, this interpretation seems naïve. How could these little kings ever imagine that they would be allowed to get away with establishing even *de facto*, let alone *de jure*, independence in the midst of an independent Congress-ruled India? Well, naïve it may have been, but the princes had a right to think that the British government meant what it said; moreover until quite late in the piece—until mid-July in fact—both Whitehall and the viceroy held steadfastly to the literal Cabinet Mission line. Privately the Cabinet's thinking had already shifted. But they shied away from making their change of mind known to the princes, for fear that the Tory opposition might choose to make the future of the states an issue in the forthcoming parliamentary debate on the Indian Independence Bill. Mountbatten belatedly attempted to administer a reality-check in his address to the COP on 25 July, but by this time the hard-liners, with Chancellor Bhopal in the van, were already signalling their intention to push for full autonomy.

And even the viceroy's sober message contained a silver lining. While insisting that the states had no future except as partners of one or other of the new dominions, he promised that, at least so far as India was concerned, they would be required to accede only for the subjects of defence, foreign affairs and communications, and this without financial obligation, a position that as Mountbatten plausibly argued, left them with 'all the practical independence' they could 'possibly use'.[17] Also, the Congress seemed content with this compromise. 'We ask no more of them', declared Vallabhbhai Patel, 'than accession on these three subjects...In other matters we would scrupulously respect their autonomous existence.'[18] *Prima facie*, the three-subject deal looked like a fair one and most of the princes duly penned their signatures to Instruments of Accession (IOAs) on these terms.

A few of the rulers, however—most importantly Tej Singhji of Alwar, Brijendra Singh of Bharatpur, Hamidullah of Bhopal, Pratap Singh Gaekwar of Baroda, Yadavindra Singh of Patiala, Harinder Singh of Faridkot, Yeshwant Rao Holkar of Indore, Devi Singh of Barwani and Hanwant Singh of Jodhpur—many of them, significantly, rulers haunted by painful memories of humiliating Political Department reprimands and restrictions—declined to put their trust in these bland assurances. They did not trust the incoming government and did not believe that the British would be in any position after the transfer of power to hold the Congress to its promises. And they desired to wield real political power; to be proper independent sovereigns, not merely trumped up agents of the Indian Union. Indeed, in their more visionary moments they spoke of forging alliances and annexing additional territories, even of displacing the Congress from its perch in Delhi. Tej Singhji of Alwar told an 'All-India Kshatriya Conference' in April 1947: 'India's salvation lies in a Kshatriya Kingdom alone and the time has now come to establish such a kingdom.'[19] Encouraged by his mainly Jat Hindu advisers, Brijendra Singh of Bharatpur formed the view 'that the Jats from Bharatpur, right up to Delhi and beyond were with him in creating a [separate state of] Jatistan'; and as the date for independence neared, the maharaja had maps of his putative state made replete with 'borders'.[20] Pratap Singh of Baroda, not satisfied with the prospect of having his feudal right to levy tribute from the lesser rulers of Kathiawar restored to him with the extinction of paramountcy, aspired to become 'King of Gujarat'.[21] Across the way in CI, long-standing friends Bhopal and Indore dreamed of creating a separate Union of Rajasthan, and lobbied their neighbours to join them in the venture. Jodhpur, and a clutch of minor rulers including Barwani, Maihar and Sitamau appear to have given the idea serious consideration. Last but not least, both Patiala and Faridkot had their eyes set on becoming rulers (separately or jointly is not clear) of a Punjabi state with its capital at Simla, an aspiration given impetus, in Yadavindra Singh's case, by his court astrologer's discovery of a passage in an old Sikh text prophesying that in the next century a ruler would emerge to rebuild the Kingdom of Lahore—a ruler whose physical description in the book 'tallied' strikingly with that of the handsome Yadavindra.[22]

On the face of it, these dreams and schemes look like the products of delusional minds; and as *we* know, they were doomed to fail. But of course the contemporary actors of 1947 had no such knowledge; they were operating in the futuristic dark. Looked at from the perspective of the time, the plans of the dissident princes still appear hugely arrogant, but not wholly quixotic.

Today, we have grown used to the idea of the Union of India as a powerful, competently administered and highly centralised state; but that is not how it looked to most observers in 1947. The governmental infrastructure of India in 1947 had still not fully recovered from the enormous stresses and strains imposed upon it by four years of total war, and by the Bengal famine of 1943; many departments remained understaffed and were shortly to lose many of their most experienced personnel; and the reliability of the armed forces had been called into question by the INA affair and the naval mutiny of 1946. Then there was the imponderable of partition. Could the old imperial Raj survive a wholesale carve-up of its administrative assets—especially one of such an arbitrary nature as was demanded by the 3 June formula? To be sure, the incoming government was not completely untried; Congressmen had been involved in the running of the country, under viceregal supervision, since September 1946. Continuity in office was one of several advantages that the Congress had over the League as the latter prepared to take office in Pakistan. Yet it remained to be seen how the members of the interim government would perform in the absence of a guiding British hand. Would they have the mettle and the judgement to handle a major crisis? Some commentators were doubtful; and if it is true that Mountbatten (as Indian governor-general) was compelled on several occasions in later 1947 to step in and rescue an Indian Cabinet rendered moribund by panic and indecision,[23] they had good reason to be.

Last but not least, the future of the New Delhi government was clouded by the prospect of war with its soon-to-be neighbour Pakistan. On the one hand, it was widely believed in India that the new Muslim state—which no less an authority than the Cabinet Mission had pronounced 'unviable'—would swiftly become bankrupt and collapse, leaving northwest India ripe for re-conquest. 'One theory—very widely held—is that the Sikhs intend, possibly with the aid of Sikh units of the old I.A., . . . to march on Lahore and take it as well as the rich lands of Montgomery and Lyallpur', wrote Indian commander-in-chief Sir Claude Auchinlek.[24] On the other hand, rumours were rife that the Pakistan leadership was so desperate and so bitter about the 'moth-eaten' state they had been palmed off with that they intended, as soon as they could muster sufficient force, to launch a pre-emptive strike to recover the 'lost' districts of east Punjab and secure other border territories in Kashmir and Gujarat to provide themselves with an additional buffer. For instance, the jam saheb of Nawanagar claimed that he had 'learned some months ago [that Pakistan had a master plan for] invading India from Junagadh in the north and Hyderabad in the south'.[25] Lent a certain credibility by wild Pakistani rhetoric, these reports help to explain why, eager as he was to recover his independence, Sadul Singh of Bikaner was one of the first rulers to send delegates to the Constituent Assembly. For the Rajputana states, he explained to Lord Mountbatten, building a 'strong central government' was the first priority, because 'any weakening of the central authority will invoke us in chaos'.[26]

But Bikaner was not alone in forseeing the possibility of an Armageddon in north India once the restraining hand of the Raj, and its British troops, had been withdrawn. As the date of independence approached, rumours of a foreign invasion competed for space in the public mind, with *canards* about widespread administrative breakdown leading to anarchy in the streets. The princes heard the whispers doing the rounds; and made their plans accordingly. Some, with the maharaja of Bikaner, scurried to take shelter under the umbrella of the Union government; but the dissident rulers readied themselves to occupy the power vacuum they felt certain was about to develop:

While the Embassy has been unable to unearth any concrete evidence to support persistent rumours that the Sikh princes are behind a comprehensive plot to turn all or part of the Punjab into a single Sikh State, [American diplomat Howard Donovan reported to Washington in September 1947] there is no doubt in my mind that the leading Sikh princes would be entirely agreeable to such a project. In conversation with an officer of the Embassy some months ago the Maharaja of Faridkot predicted that neither the Government of Pakistan nor that of India would be able to survive without extensive foreign aid and implied quite clearly that certain Princes might fall heir to some of the territory involved.[27]

And it was not just the Sikh rulers who held this disparaging view of the incoming Congress-led government; the blue-blooded Rajput princes were, if anything, even more contemptuous of its bourgeois leaders. Blinded by their prejudices to the very considerable intellectual and material strengths of the Congress Raj, the dissidents thought that they would merely have to hold things together in their own territories in order to conjure a dramatic *coup d'etat*.

Nevertheless, for all that Alwar and company were driven by prejudice and ambition, they may not have acted so precipitously if they had not been encouraged to do so by external forces with axes of their own to grind. Only Hamidullah, perhaps, led; the rest followed, more or less knowingly, agendas mapped out by various anti-Congress political parties.

One of these was the British Conservative Party, which retained a sentimental affection for the Raj's faithful allies and wanted to ensure that the states were given a fighting chance of survival. In April 1947 Digvijaysinghji of Nawanagar had specifically sought Conservative help in this regard on a visit to London, drawing on links forged by his father, Ranjitsinghji, during the Churchillian campaign to torpedo the federation scheme. Lord Tweedsmuir, Walter Elliot and Sir Walter Monckton (who had professional ties with Hyderabad) had offered reassurances. Afterwards, Monckton informed the viceroy's chief of staff Lord Ismay that if the Cabinet stuck to its declared intention of refusing diplomatic recognition to the states which had opted for independence, the Conservatives might be compelled to use 'political channels' to assist them.[28] In the event, the services of several friendly ex-political officers, including the former Bhopal PA Lieutenant-Colonel G.B. Williams, were employed to help Bhopal and Indore rally their troops, Williams apparently serving as the clique's chief emissary to Jodhpur. The message conveyed to the rulers by these intermediaries was that they should dig in, pending a change of government in the United Kingdom at the next election.

Another would-be benefactor was the AIML. Having for decades ignored the states, the League leaders belatedly realised, in the wake of the 3 June debacle, that they represented an untapped resource—a way that Pakistan could yet add significantly to its territory and influence. Accordingly, they embarked on a feverish campaign to sell the idea of accession to Pakistan to the border princes. Initially, as one would expect, their efforts were concentrated on Muslim-ruled states. As Independence Day neared, Jinnah wrote to Hyderabad and Bhopal, Liaquat Ali Khan rushed off to Rampur, and Firoz Khan Noon was dispatched to Radhanpur, which had the strategic advantage of being proximate to Pakistani Sind. Their rulers were urged either to join Pakistan or declare independence from the Indian Union. When Reza Ali Khan the Shi'a nawab of Rampur demurred, saying that he regarded himself as 'an Indian first and a Muslim second', Liaquat, according to the nawab, insinuated that the latter might find himself in grave trouble if he 'deserted Pakistan'. This was not, as events would show, an idle threat. But the League did not confine its attentions just to co-religionist princes. Although they knew of the Mahasabha's covert overtures to the Hindu rulers, and the Akali Dal's to the Sikh princes, and the resultant entrenchment of Sabhites and Akali sympathisers in senior positions in a number of north Indian *darbārs*, the League leaders sensed that the princes' ideological commitment to the Hindu and Sikh causes remained shallow, and that they might be persuaded to change sides if a sufficient inducement was held out to them; hence the 'blank cheque' offer made by Jinnah to Hanwant Singh of Jodhpur, and the similar approach to Hari Singh of Kashmir in early July. Likewise, Firoz Khan Noon bent over backwards to convince the Hindu chiefs of Jhara, Diodar, Tharad and Suigam to sign up for Pakistan along with their erstwhile suzerain the nawab of Radhanpur. In of themselves, these tiny principalities offered little by way of additional territory; but they abutted directly on the Rann of Cutch, and Suigam boasted a direct motorable road link with Thar Parker in Sind. Their acquisition would put Radhanpur's accession beyond doubt, creating a wedge of Pakistan stretching into the heart of Gujarat.

Not surprisingly, though, the parties that pressed their demands most insistently were the princes' long-standing allies, the Akali Dal and the Hindu Mahasabha. As we have seen, the Akali Dal's dream was to win a territorial homeland for the Panth—Khalistan. When the Dal's fading hopes for a constitutional resolution of its claims were shattered by the 3 June settlement, it resolutely—and one has to say not all that reluctantly—fell back on the only other option available, which was direct action. From April 1947, *jathas* began to be assembled across the central Punjab, a process facilitated by the onset of the hot weather, which released the Jat Sikhs from farming duties. Initially, much of this organising was done by Giani Harbans Singh, an escaped criminal, under the overall direction of a Council of Action in Amritsar, whose members included Sardar Baldev Singh, Giani Kartar Singh, Master Tara Singh and Raghbir Singh, the former Patiala minister. The Committee also took on the job of raising money to buy arms and equipment for the *jathas*, eventually amassing a bulging war chest of between 10 and 12 lakhs. At the same time the Akalis re-activated their links with the Mahasabha and opened a dialogue with the Sikh states, in particular Patiala and Faridkot. The princes were the key players because, as noted previously, they commanded armies and supplies. Early in April, Master Tara Singh wrote to Yadavindra Singh and promised him the 'kingship' of the new Sikh state that would emerge from the ashes of the Punjab civil war in return for his assistance in driving the Pakistanis out. Yadavindra's answer was to announce, publicly, that his army was 'ever ready' to protect the community, a comment warmly applauded by Tara Singh.[29] A few days later Harinder Singh of Faridkot was invited by the Dal 'to undertake what would amount to military operations in his part of the Punjab'; one account has it that the maharaja was offered the district of Ferozepur by way of payment.[30]

The Hindu Mahasabha had a somewhat different agenda, since it was not in the position of having to seize territory; the framework of Hindustan already existed. Nevertheless it shared, with the Dal, a view that Muslims were the enemies of freedom: 'no Musalman can be trusted to be faithful to Hindustan', wrote Mahasabha deputy-president and Alwar premier N.B. Khare in July 1947. 'In case of any big emergency, the Musalmans will surely act as saboteurs...We need a United Hindu National Front, which will gather all the strength of the Hindus of India....All Hindus, princes and people, must...join it.'[31] But that still left the vexed problem of the Islamic 'fifth column'. What could be done to convince the Muslims in Hindustan their future lay elsewhere? By the spring of 1947 the Mahasabha leaders were reconciled to the view that, in the majority of cases, they would have to be driven out by force.

In framing this audacious scheme, however, the Mahasabha leaders well knew that it was far beyond their capacity to carry out unaided.

If the Muslims refused to take the hint that they were not wanted and insisted on staying put, substantial resources would be needed to pry them loose and move them across the border. Therefore they turned for help to their friends the Hindu princes and to the extensive Sabhite and RSS cohorts in the northern states. On the one hand, they encouraged the princes in their territorial ambitions as a means of fast-tracking their ultimate goal of establishing a Hindu *rashtra* in the subcontinent. On the other, they co-opted the RSS network to disseminate propaganda questioning the loyalty of Muslim minorities.

Yet in the event only a handful of the northern states embraced the ethnic cleansing plans of the Mahasabha—and the related Akali Dal project to push out the Muslims from the central Punjab—wholeheartedly; and they did not, strangely, include either Gwalior or Kotah and Jodhpur, all of which one would have marked down—on the strength of their track records of communal violence—as likely players. In fact a watertight case of complicity can be made only with respect to Alwar, Bharatpur, Patiala, Faridkot and Kashmir—just five *darbārs* out of several hundred. As to why these five succumbed and others like Gwalior and Kotah did not, it would seem that the main operative factors were four: the extent of the influence wielded by the communal parties; the sagacity of the ministerial advice tendered to the rulers; the size and temper of the locally domiciled Muslim population; and geographical location. All these five states either straddled or bordered, the contested lands of the eastern Punjab; and all possessed substantial numbers of Muslims—sufficient to pose a real or imaginary threat. Additionally both Bharatpur and Alwar contained sizeable populations of truculent Muslim peasants in the shape of the Meos. The Meos had shown in 1933 what they were capable of when aroused. In 1947 they remained a disgruntled and defiant body, barely under *darbāri* administrative control. The two governments (or elements therein) latched on to the Mahasabha's dire scheme as a way of finally ridding themselves of the Meo 'menace'.

And even these states harboured some lingering doubts about the wisdom of launching a pogrom against their own subjects. Reports would get out. Questions would be asked. What if the Union government survived and came seeking answers? Ethnic cleansing was not a job for the faint-hearted. As luck would have it, however, the Meos chose this very moment to launch another insurgency. During 1943 or 1944, two Meos with a background in Left-wing nationalist politics, Kunwar Muhammad Ashraf and Syed Mutalabi Faridabadi, came up with the idea for a locally self-governing Meo province comprising Alwar,

Bharatpur and Gurgaon district of the Punjab; and in December 1946 a mass meeting of Meos at the village of Teengaon in Bharatpur gave its blessing to the 'Meostan' project. This gathering was followed by a second, still larger one in February 1947, at which Unionist party MLA, Muhammad Yasin Khan, was chosen to head an interim Meostan executive. Although Mayaram, following the apologia left by Ashraf's colleague Abdul Haye, insists that these preparations had no hidden purpose and were designed simply to give a political expression to Meo ethnicity, they posed a clear threat to existing territorial arrangements in the region,[32] not least to the sovereignty of the Alwar and Bharatpur *darbārs*.

Moreover while the Mewati movement of the Meos may have started out as a nationalist project, Muslim communalists soon began jumping on board. In March 1946 a *maulvi* from the NWFP, one Abdul Qaddus, arrived in the small Alwar district town of Kishengarh and began 'spreading the Wahabi doctrine of Islam among the Meos'.[33] However, unlike the earlier *tablighī* missionaries, Qaddus did not limit his activities simply to imparting religious instruction. When the government excise on tobacco was raised, he convinced the Meos not to pay it; and when the *darbār* moved to recover the arrears by force, he persuaded 300 peasants to join him in offering armed resistance to the police. Some months later, one Shafat Meo Khan started up a similar campaign in Bharatpur, urging all who would listen to him 'not to pay Goverment dues, [and] to capture customs outposts, police stations and tehsil headquarters'. But, unlike Qaddus, Shafat managed to evade capture, and survived to play a key role in the calamitous events of the following spring and summer.[34] Meanwhile, elements within the Punjab Muslim League, still hopeful, perhaps, that the British would see fit to award the whole of the province to Pakistan, made contact with Shafat and the prominent Gurgaon Meo Sardar Muhammad, and convinced them to challenge Yasin Khan for the leadership of the Meostan movement. Whether this covert intervention led to the latter becoming, effectively, a League front, as would later be alleged, is dubious; but it was enough to persuade the Alwar and Bharatpur governments. The two *darbārs* began to crack down hard on the Meos, which triggered a spate of further violence: a clash with a contingent of Alwar troops on 3 April; an attack on a police patrol on 5 May; the ambushing of a motor car on 29 July; the looting of a village on 11 August and the razing of another on 13 August. There are also reports, although one cannot rely on them as being accurate since they come wholly from partial sources, of temples being desecrated and cows being slaughtered in the streets.[35]

While these acts of lawlessness hardly justify the Alwar council's claim that it was facing a rebellion,[36] they gave the Alwar and Bharatpur authorities the pretext they were looking for.

Likewise, the Kashmir government's pogrom against its Muslim subjects in Jammu was undertaken partly out of revenge for a formidable uprising in Poonch, a semi-autonomous *jagir* territory located in the state's southwest, abutting the district of Rawalpindi. The Poonchis, like the Meos, had a tradition of military service. Some 60,000 of them had volunteered to fight in the Second World War. They were strongly parochial, too, and had never accepted Srinagar's imposition of direct rule over the Poonch Jagir in 1936. In June 1947 they commenced a 'no-tax' campaign that rapidly escalated, courtesy of some heavy-handed reprisals by the *darbār's* police, into a widespread popular insurgency, spearheaded by a well-armed guerrilla force of Indian Army veterans led by local *zamindar* Sardar Qayyum Khan. This so-called Azad Army would eventually number in excess of 50,000. On 15 August, Independence Day, Pakistan flags were raised all over the region and shortly afterwards the movement's self-appointed political supremo, Muslim Conference MLA Sardar Ibrahim Khan, announced Poonch's secession from Kashmir. By the end of September 1947 Poonch town and its royal Dogra Rajput garrison were under heavy siege.

However, the ethnic cleansing events of 1947 in the north Indian states cannot be written off as a knee-jerk *darbāri* reaction to Muslim provocation. For one thing, there is the evidence, noted above, of ongoing contacts with the communal parties. For another, there is the sticking point that *darbāri* preparations in this matter were already well advanced when the Muslims struck in Alwar and Poonch. Over the winter and spring of 1947, many of the dissident north Indian states took steps to boost their strike power. Faridkot augmented its fledgling army with two battalions of paramilitary police, 45 jeeps and 20 trucks; Jind added motorised units to its forces; Bhopal brought in hundreds of Pathans from the NWFP; Indore assiduously stockpiled ammunition; Barwani recruited Gurkhas and Rajputs from eastern UP; and Bharatpur covertly set up a factory for the production of weapons and munitions. Much of this weaponry would end up in the hands of rogue militias linked to the Dal, the Mahasabha and the RSS.[37]

Finally, we have the pretty unambiguous testimony of two leading princely players that big plans were being discussed and concerted. On 8 July Alwar's Prime Minister, Khare, sent out a circular, under Tej Singh's name, to Hindu leaders and friendly rulers and officials from the Hindu states, inviting them to attend a convention in Delhi.

The purpose of the convention, the circular advised, was to make plans for the 'restoration of a Hindu Rashtra' in the capital following the transfer of power.[38] The brash Harinder Singh, maharaja of Faridkot, was even more forthright, telling British officers at Simla that the Muslims in east Punjab were about to be taught a sharp lesson and advising their wives to get out of India quickly as 'their turn might be coming soon'.[39]

They were not contemplating genocide. Aside from any moral scruples the dissidents might have entertained about such a course, it was simply not logistically feasible. In 1941 the Jammu region of Kashmir alone contained 1.2 million Muslims. Another million or so lived in the east Punjab states and nearly that many more in Rajputana. That was something like three million potential victims. A few years earlier, the Nazis had exterminated six million European Jews, but the Hitlerian Holocaust was effected through the agency of a giant state endowed with a technologically sophisticated infrastructure; princely states like Bharatpur and Faridkot did not command even a fraction of that capability. But they did not need to exterminate every Muslim living in their territories to accomplish their purpose. They needed only to kill some—enough to terrorise the rest into fleeing for their lives. With this comforting axiom in mind, the sanctioned killing squads of Alwar, Bharatpur and Kashmir, under cover of putting down rebellions against their lawful authority, began their grisly work.

The killing fields

No doubt the myriad shards of text and memory that have come down to us from 1947 will eventually be woven together into something approaching a total history of the Great Divide.[40] But before that happens, the histories of particular localities and regions will have to be written. This section tries to do that for the north Indian princely states. It does not pretend to be definitive, but it extends the historiography of the partition to areas that have not, hitherto, featured much in the discussion although they featured very prominently, as we shall see, in the sorry saga of the post-partition violence. Ironically the so far neglected, but comparatively accessible, archives of the princely states are quite rich sources of data on this subject.

Even reconstructing what happened within the more limited frame of the princely states, however, is no easy task. Widely distributed, the states' experience of partition violence varied considerably in scale and form. For instance, in some areas, *darbāri* elements played a direct and primary role in the killings, whereas in others, upright officials battled hard to contain the depredations wrought by undisciplined mobs. Likewise, the violence did not occur all at once. It moved to different rhythms, breaking out here, peaking there and subsiding somewhere else according to separate and unrelated timetables. The communalist princes and their party friends may have thought they had a master plan for the ethnic cleansing of Muslims, but there is little evidence even of inter-state cooperation in what transpired, let alone of close coordination. Our reconstruction must try to accommodate these multiple narratives.

Perhaps the best place to begin is with a snapshot. Overall the partition-related violence in the princely states of north India lasted about seven months. Although some scholars date the beginning of the ethnic cleansing in Rajasthan to the attack on the Muslim village of Hodad in Bharatpur on 23 March, it was the end of May before the campaign really got going there and in Alwar full-scale cleansing commenced only in June, precipitated in part by an influx of Meos fleeing the vengeance of the Bharatpur army. After a short lull in July, military operations in Mewat resumed on 7 August, with a pitched battle at Hasanpur in Alwar, and continued until the end of the month, by which time most of the Meos had either been killed or driven out of the two states. In the meantime, though, violence had spread to the Sikh-ruled states of eastern Punjab. In the latter part of August there was a general massacre of Muslims in Patiala City, and the same period saw the first of a gruesome succession of assaults on refugee trains passing through Patiala en route to west Punjab. Military action in the border districts of Jammu also appears to have started in mid-August, triggered, it would seem, by Radcliffe's boundary determination, although the full extent of it only became apparent in September, when Muslims fleeing the pogrom arrived at Sialkot. After that, the mayhem became general, extending as far afield as Bikaner and CI. But here the madness was quite short-lived. On 14 October an official at the Bikaner Home Ministry observed: the 'general situation in the country is much better . . . and is improving . . . [Soon] people will [start to] calm down'.[41] By the end of the year, order had been restored in most places. As to its geographical spread, the violence was intense and systematic in Mewat and Jammu, locally intense but not so systematic in the Punjab states, and scattered elsewhere. Only in Alwar, Bharatpur, Patiala, Kashmir and perhaps Faridkot did it coalesce into full-bodied ethnic cleansing.

Nevertheless violence against Muslims was certainly not confined to those five states, as was generally believed at the time. Dozens of Muslim refugees were murdered and thrown off trains passing through Gwalior, Bhopal and Kotah, while several score more perished at Hindu hands in Bikaner and Jaipur; and late in the day, when the situation had mostly cooled down in the Punjab and Rajputana, 24 were done to death in Dhar and Barwani in CI. And the victims of the partition violence in the states were not, by any means, all Muslims. Across the border in Bahawalpur, most were Hindus and Sikhs, done to death on the orders of Muslim League stalwart, PM Mushtaq Gurmani, as they tried to leave the state. Perhaps the only exception to this demographic rule (but a significant one, as Nehru acknowledged) was the Kashmir Valley where local Muslims—though vastly more numerous than the Hindu Pandits and Sikhs of the region—resisted the urge to even up the score for Jammu. Of course the rule of strength also applied to gender; women being considered, on all sides, legitimate spoils of war.

Finally, as to agency, contemporary English observers pretty much universally pointed the finger at the Sikhs. 'The Sikhs have throughout taken the major part in the orgy of murders, loot and rape which has been going on for weeks past . . . in the East Punjab', the commander-in-chief of the Indian Army, Claude Auchinlek, concluded emphatically in a report to the Cabinet and the Chiefs of Staff in September 1947.[42] But perhaps the real question is, which Sikhs? Or for that matter which Muslims and which Hindus?

For obvious reasons, individual killers are difficult to identify. Yet the evidence leaves no doubt that a substantial number were soldiers and policemen either in uniform or *mufti*. A report on the ethnic cleansing in Alwar provided to the AISPC asserted:

> we ourselves saw an Alwar soldier with a gun . . . driving away a herd of cattle. The State forces [have] not only put several hundred Meo villages to fire, killed several thousand Meos and . . . driven out the entire Meo population, but are with impunity perpetrating atrocities on Indian Union territory [as well].[43]

On the evidence of British eye witnesses in Sialkot, most of the killing in the border region of Jammu was 'carried out by Kashmir State troops, Dogras, Sikhs and Gurkhas [using] . . . mortar, grenade and automatic fire'.[44] And according to the English deputy commissioner of Ferozepur, who witnessed the derailment and loot of a 'Pakistan special' inside Patiala on the night of 9/10 August, 'this crime was [clearly] perpetrated by . . . men still in military service'.[45] These reports confirm that the partition violence in the north Indian states was to a large extent *darbāri*-sanctioned.

But what led thousands of Hindu and Sikh state subjects to sign up for these military-style pogroms; and what led thousands more to strike out on their own?

With respect to those princely subjects who were members of the Akali Dal, the Hindu Mahasabha and the RSS, one does not have to look very far for a motive. They were already sensitised to thinking of Muslims as enemies. The 'Praja Parishad people', a visiting Bikaner official reported from Chura, 'do not like the [prospect of] reconciliation between Hindus and Muslims. In fact their mind is that the Muslims have no place in Hindusthan.'[46] It would be safe to assume that the Punjabi *jathas*, of which I will speak shortly, were composed largely of hard-core members of this group. Again, some Hindu communities in the north Indian states had a history of unruly and truculent behaviour, especially towards Muslims. In Mewat, the pastoral Gujars were one such group. Some Mewati Gujars seized the opportunity provided by the Meo insurgency in Bharatpur and Alwar to settle old scores with their agriculturalist neighbours.

For the rest, their participation appears to have been, in the main, reactive—triggered by provocations (real or imagined) and by rumour-fed fears that they were themselves impending targets. In the days and weeks following the partition of 15 August 1947, it dawned upon the Muslims living in east Punjab and adjacent regions that they had become, in effect, displaced persons stranded in hostile territory. A British political officer, visiting Alwar in early August, found the state's Muslim officials 'thoroughly demoralised'; while Bohra Muslims in Barwani reported feeling 'terrorised'.[47] Many of these orphans now, understandably, looked to migrate to Pakistan; but the problem was getting there. Transport was scarce and expensive. There was talk of the Pakistani and Indian governments providing some, but it had not yet been organised. In the short term, therefore, Muslims in the states sought safety in numbers. Patrolling along the Punjab border, a Bikaner police superintendent found that the Muslims were

> deserting small villages and...collecting in thousands at Nawan P.S. Sangria and at Surewala P.S. Sikki – while in P.S. Hanumannagar Moh[amma]d[a]ns have gathered in thousands at Dabhi, Jandwala etc – in P.S. Lakhuwali at village Ludhana etc and in P.S. Suratgarh at Sardegarh...[48]

Elsewhere, they took refuge in towns and villages where there was already a sizeable Muslim presence, such as Malerkotla City, Bassi,

Samana and Sanaur in the Punjab, or congregated in accessible urban strong points. In Bharatpur City, Muslims took shelter in the jama masjid; and about 25,000 Muslims flocked to the famous Sufi shrine of Rosa Sharif at Sirhind in Patiala. But while these Muslims may have been frightened, they made it clear that they would fight, if necessary, to defend themselves and their loved ones. On the night of 13 August, Khan Ahsan Ali Khan, a kinsman of the nawab of Malerkotla and a Ludhiana Muslim League office-bearer, toured the state capital 'telling the Muhammadans that there was great fear of an attack from the Sikhs of Patiala and other places and that they should arm themselves and be on guard in groups for the whole night'. By the 15th virtually every adult male Muslim in the town had acquired at least a *lathi* for his personal protection.[49]

Predictably, the mere fact of the Muslims massing set alarm bells ringing. The majority of the groups might have comprised harmless refugees, but to Hindus and Sikhs living in the neighbourhood of the Muslim strong points, their inhabitants looked alarmingly like 'mobs' out for trouble. Hindus in Ganganagar, Bikaner police reported, 'are fearing that [the Muslims] might...attack them'.[50] And in some cases these fears proved justified. Around Sunam, nervous Muslim refugees gladly accepted an offer of protection from the notorious outlaw Subhan Khan, wanted by the Patiala government for armed robbery. Others, judging that they were in imminent danger of attack from the marauding Sikh war-bands, decided that they had little to lose and possibly much to gain by striking first, although initially most of their targets seem to have been poorly defended Sikh and Hindu villages rather than the jathas *per se*. Others again resolved, maliciously, to cause as much damage as they could before they were rounded up and expelled to Pakistan. One 25,000-strong Muslim formation, operating out of Badbar in Patiala, was alone considered responsible for 'more than sixty murders'.[51] Few as these atrocities were, compared to what the Muslims themselves had already suffered in places such as Bharatpur and Alwar, they fuelled a perception that the Punjab was facing a Muslim onslaught.

The result was an epidemic of panic. In Narwana, the non-Muslim railway staff became too 'badly frightened' to work; in Bhatinda, Hindu merchants hastily buried their valuables in 'apprehension of urban markets being plundered'; in Narnaul, an overtaxed sub-inspector wired, 'help us or we are finished';[52] in Ganganagar, a thousand *dandas* were sold in the marketplace on one day in late August to Hindus looking to protect themselves from attack. Soon, thousands of Hindus and Sikhs were in full flight.

But then a strange phenomenon occurred that bears comparison with the 'great fear' that swept rural France in 1789. Almost overnight, the mood among urban non-Muslims in the Sikh states of the Punjab changed from one of abject fear to insensate rage. In part this remarkable transformation was probably due to their humiliating realisation, with hindsight, that they had allowed themselves to be intimidated by a minority: Muslims were plentiful in rural Punjab but relatively few in its towns. In the main, though, it was a product of righteous anger. Over the previous weeks, stories had been circulating of massacres in west Punjab and the NWFP, some of them originating in overblown press-reports, many of them narrated personally to shocked audiences by Hindu and Sikh escapees. Wherever such tales of woe were heard, the effect was instantaneous. Barnala's SP reported that 'news of the atrocities in Lahore, Amritsar, Jullundur and Multan' had 'created a clear hatred in the minds of the [town's] Sikhs and Hindus for the Muslims'; while Ganganagar's district magistrate wrote of crowds driven to frenzy by 'harrowing tales of wholesale slaughter' in Sind.[53] Even officials in Patiala, where the bureaucracy was packed with diehard communalists, recognised the threat these activities posed to the maintenance of public order.[54]

In some instances the targets of this retributive rage were known Muslim predators such as the bandit-leader Subhan Khan, who was hacked to pieces, together with his son, by a knife-wielding Hindu mob in Sunam on 7 September, and Muslims who knowingly or inadvertently had given offence to their communal neighbours. In the latter category were the Rafiq family of Mathari village in Patiala, who were targeted for having slaughtered a cow to provide meat for a *chehlum* feast. Seven family members paid for this indiscretion with their lives and ten more suffered serious injuries. More commonly, however—like the movie-goers blown to bits by the bomb thrown into the Novelty Talkies Cinema, Bhatinda, on 20 August, or the nine passengers butchered at Maur railway station a week later—the victims were luckless bystanders; Muslims unfortunate enough to be in the wrong place at the wrong time.

Yet fear and blind rage were not the only motivations. Some killed simply because they could. Normally people in civil society are inhibited from committing acts of savagery both by moral reservations and because they know that they are likely to be caught and made to pay for their crimes. In the post-partition mayhem, these constraints were for many people swept aside. The post-partition anarchy and the threatening posture of Pakistan allowed the Hindu and Sikh perpetrators to convince themselves that they were acting as patriots—as volunteer soldiers. And, of course, soldiers are absolved by the rules of war from criminal responsibility for their actions. Moreover, they were buttressed in this misguided view by the flamboyant language employed during this period of crisis by some of India's national leaders. Accused later by the Union government of abetting criminal actions, RSS supremo M.S. Golwalkar flung back:

> Of course the R.S.S. members have been charged with being violent against Pakistan during the partition day troubles. But who was not violent during those days—and who could afford to follow the creed of non-violence during those days? Did not P[andi]t Nehru and Sardar Patel then exhort the people to become their own soldiers? Did not Dr Gopi Chand Bhargava [premier of east Punjab] urge the Punjabi youth to fight the Pak Goondas? . . . The sangh is proud of its work in the . . . Punjab. . . .[55]

All this loose talk, together with the quite visible collapse of lawful authority in many areas, led the more cynical perpetrators to conclude (rightly as it turned out) that they were unlikely ever to have to account for their actions in a court of law.

Nevertheless, while individual acts of vengeance by enraged Hindus and Sikhs certainly took place, they did not account for more than a fraction of the total Muslim death toll. Most of the killing was done, not in the heat of the moment, but with icy premeditation and ruthless calculation by large well-organised military-style formations. Some of these were, as previously mentioned, *darbāri* forces acting under military direction; but most were private formations of vigilantes sanctioned and supplied by senior *darbāri* officials—Sikh *jathas* in east Punjab, and Hindu *dhārs* in Alwar and Bharatpur.

Despite or perhaps because of their infamous reputation, not a lot is known about the composition and structure of these organisations. Even their total number is uncertain. But it is clear that the biggest of them were extremely large formations. Akali stalwart 'General' Mohan Singh's 'fauj' was estimated by the *Statesman* at 'about 12,000'; while Mayaram estimates that the *dhārs* which laid siege to the villages of Mandawar and Harsauli in Bharatpur were between 10,000 and 20,000 strong.[56] As regards makeup, it is likely that most of their members were Jat ex-servicemen, both regular army and INA. Finally, a few of the senior *jatha* leaders have been identified: the aforementioned Mohan Singh; Udham Singh Nagoke, who is said to have commanded on the

'Faridkot front'; Narijan Singh Gill and Raghbir Singh, who jointly oversaw the ethnic cleansing operations in and around Patiala; and Bacchu Singh, whose *dhar* carved a swathe through Mewat. But the names of their lieutenants and followers are shrouded in obscurity and will probably, in most cases, never be known.

About their methods, though, we can be more precise. Although loose aggregations and by definition undisciplined, they were, for the most part, capably and even daringly led, and, thanks to the patronage of the dissident *darbars*, well-armed and possessed of good intelligence, which was reflected in their discriminating choice of targets. Broadly speaking, the war-bands concentrated on Muslim villages and refugees on their way to Pakistan. But they did not attack all the Muslim settlements and every refugee train. By and large, they avoided tackling really big formations of Muslims, such as the one quartered at Rosa Sharif in Patiala, and they shied off attacking refugee convoys that their *darbari* sources indicated were guarded by regular troops, unless the same intelligence sources gave them reason to think that the latter had been suborned. Nevertheless when they did attack, they acted with foresight, energy and absolute ruthlessness. Attacks on refugee trains, for example, were planned with reference to the railway timetable and published updates on station billboards. Learning that an 'up', or westbound, train was due to arrive at a certain time, the raiders would simply wait for it either at a scheduled halt or at some convenient point along the line; if the latter, logs or stones would be placed across the tracks to force the driver to halt. Then, depending on what kind of train it was (whether a 'Pakistan Special' or a mixed local) it would either be strafed from fixed positions, or boarded and the Muslim passengers picked off individually.[57] Likewise, road convoys of refugees would be intercepted— often by prior arrangement with the authorities supposedly responsible for their safety—at secluded spots that offered a good field of fire and the prospect of a quick getaway.

Likewise, there was a set pattern to the war-band attacks on villages. First, the village or villages selected for cleansing would be encircled and all exit points closed to prevent the occupants from escaping. Then the attack proper would commence. Typically, in this phase, one group of assailants would spray the village with rifle and light machine-gun fire to dislodge the Muslims from the rooftops, while another lobbed grenades and petrol bombs over the walls. Finally, when the attackers judged that they had created sufficient confusion and panic inside, they would move in for the kill. In this last phase, a third group of hardened fighters, armed with *kirpans* or spears, would be delegated to finish off the surviving males while a second, smaller contingent, often composed of older *jathedars*, rounded up the village women. When all was secured, these trophies of battle would be carted off along with any other 'valuables' that had escaped the fires.

Indeed, while each war-band action was unique in its particulars, one is struck by how similarly all of them unfolded—by how remarkably *routinised* so much of the grisly work of ethnic cleansing was. One might even suggest, with Shail Mayaram, that it had a ritualistic or performative aspect. That fact that the Sikhs often used *gurudwaras* as assembly points, and that the Jat *dhārwalas* in Mewat 'began their day by offering the ritual sacrifice of a goat to their deity Sinsini',[58] certainly points in that direction.

Even the princely regimes involved in the ethnic cleansing project, which had much to lose by disclosure, were forced to concede that widespread disturbances had taken place within their dominions. Yet they disputed that many had been killed. For instance, when in late August Bikaner's IG of police visited Bahawalpur, to inquire about reports of Hindu and Sikh casualties there, he was told straight-faced by his opposite number in the Bahawalpur police that 'only about 20' non-Muslims had died in the state thus far, a figure the Bikaner man knew to be a lie. 'I fear', the latter reflected afterwards, 'that the Bahawalpur authorities [are] . . . disinclined to take a very serious view of these troubles.'[59] Not so, understandably, the intended victims. Meos interviewed by the Muslim League's Mian Iftikharudin and Daud Ghaznavi spoke of a 'general slaughter'; while survivors of the pogrom in Bahawalpur put the non-Muslim death toll there at 100,000.[60]

Such independent inquiries as were made at the time tended to agree with the survivors' version of events. Former Bengal Chief Minister Hasan Suhrawardy, who produced a series of detailed reports on the partition massacres based on 'thorough' on-the-spot inquiries, reckoned that 50,000 Muslims had been killed in Alwar, another 10,000 in Bharatpur. As for the Punjab, he concluded that:

> The Muslims have been [entirely] eliminated from the 5 Sikh States of Patiala, Kapurthala, Nabha, Faridkot and Jhind [sic].[61]

Similarly, Communist Party of India officials concluded after touring Mewat and interviewing Meo survivors that between 15,000 and 20,000 had been massacred in the two states and in Gurgaon district. British observers, meanwhile, provided a number of varying estimates of the extent of the massacres in the Punjab and Jammu in personal letters home, reports to superiors and articles written for the press. For example, the Eastern Command's General Tuker, drawing upon army intelligence, estimated the total loss of life in east Punjab at between 100,000 and 200,000; while the Kashmir correspondent of *The Times* in August 1948 filed a report which boldly asserted that 237,000 Muslims had been 'systematically exterminated' in Jammu by 'the forces of the Dogra State'.[62] Finally, the Indian government some seven or eight months after the event launched an inquiry into the allegations that the Alwar and Bharatpur *darbars* had set out to expunge Muslims from their territories. They interviewed the two maharajas and many of their officials and took possession of relevant documents. Former Chief Minister Khare brazenly volunteered under interrogation that as many as 15,000 Muslims 'might have been slaughtered' in Alwar.[63] New Delhi's guesstimate of Muslims killed in Bharatpur, also never made public, was 30,000.[64]

None of these figures, however, are authoritative. Although he had fallen out with Jinnah, Suhrawardy was still a stalwart of the Muslim League. And the *Times* man, too, seems to have harboured Pakistani sympathies and, more importantly, offers no clues as to the source of his information. As for the GOI team, by the time it got around to investigating much of the physical evidence had been destroyed and many eye witnesses gone to Pakistan. Needless to say, the conditions ruled out a comprehensive body count.

On the other hand, headcounts were made of survivors. Thus one can easily calculate, with reference to the 1941 census data, the net 'loss' of Muslims in each region. Theoretically a further subtraction of the number of Muslims from each region who migrated to Pakistan and other places, and a percentile adjustment to compensate for natural increase within the survivor population, should give us a rough approximation of the number of Muslims killed in 1947. In practice, however, there are grave problems with this method of accounting, most importantly a lack of comprehensive Pakistani migration data linked to specific localities, and the widespread lack of fit between pre- and post-independence administrative boundaries.

For instance, we have a fair idea, thanks to a headcount done in Pakistan in 1949, of the number of Muslim emigrants from Kashmir (almost all of them, it is safe to assume, escapees from the Jammu region). The figure given is 333,964. Subtracting the 1961 Muslim population of Jammu (598,492) from the 1941 Muslim population of the province (1,212,405) gives a subtotal of 613,913. Deducting the Kashmiris in Pakistan leaves a deficit of 279,949, which very roughly accords with the *Times* correspondent's 'precise' estimate of Muslim deaths in 1947.

But the Jammu of the 1961 census was not the same unit as the Jammu of the 1941 census; it no longer included large parts of Mirpur and Poonch, which had been lost to Azad Kashmir in the Indo-Pakistani conflict of 1947–49. Obviously an adjustment is required; the problem is to work out how big it should be, bearing in mind that if one removes all of the 310,000 Muslims recorded in the 1941 census as living in Mirpur from the equation, one is left not with a deficit but with a surplus (which of course cannot possibly be correct).[65] Interestingly, an early official calculation made in Pakistan, using headcount data, came up with a figure of 50,000 deaths, which may prove, in the light of future research, to be closer to the truth than the *Times* man's guesstimate or *Statesman* editor Ian Stephens' assertion that 200,000 Jammu Muslims were killed.[66]

For the present, however, we must make do with the information we have. Putting the claims of the refugees, the contemporary estimates, and such information as can be gleaned from the census data together, I think we can safely say that the death toll from partition-related violence in the princely states was in the vicinity of 50,000 in Alwar and Bharatpur, 80,000 in Jammu, 70,000 in the Sikh states, 10,000 in Bahawalpur and perhaps 5000 in Rajputana and CI—a total of 215,000. If this finding is even approximately correct, it casts considerable doubt on the accuracy of G.D. Khosla's oft-quoted estimate of half a million killed for all of north India.[67] Moreover, it identifies the princely states as absolutely central to the killing, rather than merely peripheral or ancillary to it—particularly when one takes into account the many cross-border raids carried out by Sikh *jathas* based in and supplied by the states, and the number of refugee trains and road convoys from Delhi and UP ambushed while passing through princely state territory (Map 4.1). Indeed, by far the greater part of the casualties suffered by the west-bound refugees in 1947 appear to have been sustained in transiting the territories of the Sikh princes—especially the initial, Patiala, sector that began at the Ghaggar bridges to the west of Ambala.

However, in giving due prominence to the obviously central question of the death toll, we must be careful not to lose sight of the bigger picture. The 1947 violence had many faces, and far more subjects of the princely states were touched by it than the 200,000 or so who were killed. In the course of the assaults by the vigilante squads and *darbāri* military forces some tens of thousands of women and girls (we will never, for obvious reasons, know the exact number) were raped or carried off to become the concubines of their assailants. On the fringes of the killing fields, minorities prevailed on by officials to stay put and remain in their homes were subjected to widespread physical harassment and verbal abuse; while in Jaipur and Bikaner, Muslim artisans and

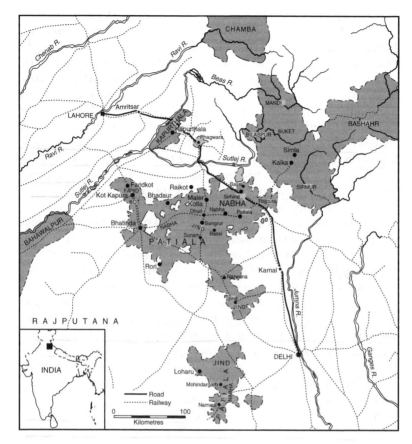

Map 4.1 The Punjab states on the eve of the transfer of power, showing major road and rail arteries.

service providers were boycotted for months by the Hindu buying public. A great deal of minority-owned property was destroyed; and Islamic institutions were hard hit, with as many as 132 mosques razed in Alwar alone.

The foregoing discussion has explained *why* violence and destruction erupted in the princely states of north India in 1947; but how was it *allowed* to happen on the massive scale documented above? One reason the vigilantes got away with it for so long is that they skilfully exploited the tactical advantages conferred by the terrain. Never staying for long in any one area, and constantly hopping backwards and forwards between different princely jurisdictions, the war-bands capitalised on the element of surprise, and, at the same time, made themselves difficult to catch. Units of the Indian army conscientiously pursued the Sikh *jathas* as far as they could within east Punjab, but were precluded from pursuing them beyond, the states being legally foreign territory. Pursuit was hampered, too, by flooding caused by heavier than average monsoonal rains, and by a shortage of petrol, which limited the response capacity of the state forces. Yet it must be said none of these elements would have counted for much if the private armies had been dealt with firmly by the princely authorities. Instead they were given protection and support. This begs, finally, the vexed issue of responsibility. How much of what happened was the doing (vicariously if not directly) of the rulers personally?

In a celebrated outburst in March 1948, AISPC President Pattabhai Sitaramayya accused the maharaja of Patiala of having 'innocent blood of two lakhs of...Muslims' on his hands.[68] Similar allegations were levelled against the rulers of Bharatpur, Kapurthala, Kashmir, Alwar and Faridkot. Needless to say, these charges were vigorously denied by the princes concerned; and for what it is worth, their denials are borne out by such documents as survive in the state archives, which contain no genocidal directives. Yet even if we give the rulers the benefit of the doubt and conclude that they did not specifically order their forces to help the war-bands carry out their grisly work—a position incidentally which the Muslim League's Suhrawardy urged on Gandhi—it is hard to accept that they did not know that such aid was, in fact, being rendered. At the beginning of November 1947, the Patiala Home Ministry issued a directive that weapons should be provided to Sikh and Hindu refugees—knowing full well that some of these weapons would be used to kill Muslims.[69]

In addition, we have fairly solid evidence linking at least three of these rulers directly to the war-bands. According to refugee accounts, corroborated by the testimony of English eyewitnesses, Hari Singh of Kashmir

> was seen with 4 truck loads of arms at Khana Chak (Jammu District), fired the first shot at the Jammu refugee camp on I'd day, gave orders to kill at Palahanwala, and again at Chhamb (Tahsil Bhimbar), distributed arms to the RSSS at Bhimbar, watched the slaughter of Muslims from his car at Narayana (Mirpur), and generally set an example of fanaticism and extreme sadism to his officers, to the troops and to assassins from outside the State...[70]

Brijendra Singh of Bharatpur also got caught out, observed witnessing massacres of Meos at Khumbar and Deeg. When some Muslims reproached him about this, he is said to have replied, 'Why come to me? Go to Jinnah.'[71] And Faridkot's ruler, Harinder Singh, actually interrogated a party of *jathādars* in the presence of a very distressed Sikh lady from Simla, admonishing one who confessed that he had come to think killing repugnant to his *dharma*, and asking the others for juicy details of the carnage.[72]

Finally, it has to be suspicious that, in the midst of one of the greatest human convulsions in modern history, several rulers elected to spend a good deal of the summer of 1947 away from their capitals, ostensibly to escape the hot weather of the plains. At the very least, one could suggest that by leaving at this time they were turning their backs on duty; but to my mind, they were not so much trying to dodge hard work as attempting to evade responsibility. Being away gave them an alibi. If they were not there, how could they be held responsible?

But others, perhaps, bear an even heavier burden. A knowledgeable source on Punjab affairs, the Indian Army's Major Short, firmly believed that the Sikh rulers had been 'carried along' by bad advisers.[73] While this view seems, in the light of the foregoing discussion, overly generous in respect of the culpability of the princes, Short is certainly justified in spreading the blame. In Chapter 3 we noted how communalists were starting to penetrate the ranks of the administrative services of the north Indian states, in some states even to the extent of capturing executive-level jobs. This trend continued, unabated, through 1947. Consequently, when the leaders of the war-bands approached the *darbārs* looking for support, they found many sympathetic listeners. Bikaner's Public Works minister, touring Chura in October 1947, was embarrassed to discover

> that the Inspector [of Police] had strong communal views and definitely anti-Muslim views though nothing was proven against him. I was surprised [too] during my recent visit to find the Tehsildar P[andi]t Chand Ratan Misra and the Sub-Inspector [of] Police, Lala Anup Chand, also holding strong anti-Muslim views. They gave vent to their anti-Muslim feelings [openly] in the presence of Munshi Birdha Chand, Nazim Sujangarh.[74]

In Bikaner, however, the rot seems to have been confined mainly to the district level, whereas in Alwar and Bahawalpur senior officials including both Prime Ministers, Khare and Gurmani, are credited with planning and directly overseeing the ethnic cleansing in those states.[75] Barwani was another place where communalist attitudes extended right to the top of the administration. As for Patiala, the partisan character of the senior bureaucracy is reflected in the following memorandum penned by the head of the state's Criminal Investigation Department (CID), Bir Davinder Singh:

> Pakistan has got an eye upon [us]...and it is not unlikely that an attack in force will be launched by that dominion on the East Punjab. In that emergency every able bodied man and woman will be required to put up strong resistance to save the Province from being over-run and devastated by the Muslim Marauders. In that case...the meek and appeasing policy of the Congress will not stand in their stead.[76]

Not surprisingly, Bir Davinder Singh's is one of the names most often mentioned by contemporary witnesses, along with that of the Patiala army's Colonel Bhagwan Singh, when the issue of *darbāri* logistic support for the *jathas* is brought up.

That said however, two caveats need to be entered. First, official attitudes and practices within and between the states varied considerably. Even in Patiala, where the fury of the mobs threatened, in places, to swamp the forces of law and order, some district officials managed to keep their heads. As a measure of this, one conscientious district nazim was roundly attacked by local Hindus for his allegedly 'pro-Muslim policy'.[77] Conversely, several officials in Bikaner were transferred, and one subsequently dismissed, for lending their support to an economic boycott of Muslims. As regards states, Dholpur's record was much better than that of its Jat neighbour Bharatpur; while in east Punjab, Muslims fared better in Jind and Kapurthala than in Faridkot, Nabha, Kalsia or Patiala. For instance, there were very few killings in the Jind capital, Sangrur, a remarkable record considering the size of the town and its large Muslim population. Not surprisingly, though, the east Punjab states in which Muslims suffered the least were Malerkotla and Loharu, both ruled by Muslim princes.

The second caveat is that the behaviour of all the *darbārs* improved after September, most markedly that of Bahawalpur and Patiala. In both cases the improvement coincided with a renaissance of royal authority—Yadavindra Singh returning from his summer palace of Chail in middle of the month and Sadiq Mohammad Khan arriving back in his capital after a shortened European vacation on 1 October. For the first time,

Yadavindra publicly distanced himself from the Akali ethnic cleansing project. However, this turnaround stemmed less from a belated moral awakening than from a recognition that circumstances had changed. Unexpectedly both Pakistan and the Nehruvian *raj* in Delhi had survived. What is more, they had begun to bring the divided Punjab back under control. This raised the stark possibility that there might be a reckoning for the violence. Prudence told the dissident rulers that the time had come for them to mend their bridges with the Indian government. Besides, further ethnic cleansing was hardly necessary. By the end of October 1947, most of the Muslims of the east Punjab states, Alwar and Bharatpur had been killed or were on their way to Pakistan. As a bitter Hasan Suhrawardy reflected in a letter to the Mahatma: 'What is the use now of the Maharajah of Patiala, after all the Muslims have been eliminated from his State, standing up as the champion of peace and order?'[78]

By late 1947 the dissident princes were resigned to the continuance of the Congress *raj* in New Delhi, and the prospect of a re-institution in some form of paramountcy. But the scars of their ill-fated bid for autonomy and power remained. The ethnic cleansing unleashed in their name, and with their support, had in a matter of months transformed society and social relations in northwest India. The region's Muslims had mostly died or fled. As Alwar's Judicial Minister noted complacently, but with scant exaggeration: 'the Meo problem...which was troubling the State for several centuries has been solved'.[79] Indirectly, too, ethnic cleansing had prepared the ground for an even larger social revolution, by making room for an influx of Hindu and Sikh settlers from west Punjab and Sind. This gave the region a defining non-Muslim character such as it had never possessed historically. More particularly, the immigration of large numbers of Sikhs lifted the proportion of Sikhs in the population of east Punjab from around one-fifth to over a third, and in some areas to more than a half, most of them, significantly, located in the Sikh states. Although the Sikh politicians, too, like the dissident princes, had failed to realise their dream of autonomy, it gave them a persuasive claim for constitutional recognition within the Union—one that Delhi would be eventually forced to concede.[80] Yet possibly the most lasting legacy of the massacres of 1947 was not their demographic impact but the psychological wounds they inflicted on millions of individual minds. This was true even for people who for years had lived peacefully alongside Muslims. After the partition holocaust—even though it was widely recognised that in east Punjab and the states the Muslims had been the main victims of that holocaust—most of them found it difficult to resume formal social relations with their erstwhile neighbours. Symptomatic of this hardening of social attitudes was a dramatic rise in the membership of Hindu communal organisations, especially the RSS. In Bikaner the RSS was reported to be 'spreading all over the State'.[81] Still more unforgiving were the refugees—who did indeed have much to forgive, but looked, instead, to exact revenge.

The price of survival

Terrible though the death toll in 1947 was, the fact remains that the large majority of north Indian Muslims survived the holocaust, as did most of the Hindus and Sikhs. This was true both of the erstwhile British-ruled provinces and of the princely states. Some made it through thanks to the protection of sympathetic neighbours; others were just plain lucky. Chiefly, however, vulnerable minority groups held on to life and limb by following strategies of accommodation in respect of the goals and desires of the regional communal majority. By definition, all these strategies involved a measure of humiliation; but that was usually the least of their physical and psychological costs.

One of them was religious conversion. It is believed that as many as 45,000 to 50,000 people in Mewat and a similar number in Bahawalpur changed their religion during the partition mayhem.[82] Whilst many of these reportedly converted under extreme duress—in other words as an alternative to being slaughtered—others seem to have tried to anticipate events by converting of their own accord. At Chura 17 Muslims 'applied to the Tehsildar, saying they wanted to be converted'; at Patta Braore in Patiala, a number of Muslims 'recently embraced Sikhism and converted their mosques into Gurudwaras'; and at Teh Narwana, another Patiala village, all the 'Moola Jats and Kamins...were converted as Hindus of their [own] free will'.[83] Some of these people actually received certificates from local officials, attesting to the fact that proper procedures had been followed. These actions can be considered 'strategic', first, because they were initiated in advance of a direct threat, and, secondly, because they were undertaken in the vast majority of cases with the expectation that they could be reversed when conditions had normalised. By 1948, Meo 'converts' were telling Vinobha Bhave that they were 'Mussalmans' and that their conversion to Hinduism had been made 'under coercion'.[84] In August 1947, Jani, the Muslim gatekeeper at the Malwa Cinema on Patiala's Mall Road, suddenly announced to the world that he had become 'Man Singh', a Sikh; in 1948 he quietly re-converted, and later became manager of a nearby *dargah*.

Likewise, while one cannot pretend that the thousands of Muslim women abducted from their villages during 1947 had any sort of a choice in the matter, since, in most cases, they were simply dragged away by main force, some, nevertheless, appear to have gone with their captors willingly. At the height of the troubles in Bikaner, a 20-year-old Muslim woman Mot Khudijan was apprehended by police in the company of a Hindu man named Buthram. Questioned by a Muslim head constable, she explained that Buthram had 'saved her life', and that she had repaid the debt by marrying him.[85] Again, while the phenomenon of abducted women refusing out of shame to return to their natal families or, conversely, being rejected by them as soiled goods is now well-documented, more attention needs to be given to the motive of self-interest. Some Muslims in this predicament appear to have accepted their fate stoically, and in a few cases even gladly, because it allowed them to stay on in familiar surroundings. Even Jawaharlal Nehru, who certainly cannot be described as a hard-line Hindu, was moved by the case of the 176 abducted women 'recovered' from Hindu and Sikh households in Patiala, who were so distressed at the prospect of imminent evacuation to Pakistan, that they broke out of the camp where they were being detained, and—on being recovered a second time—threatened, in several cases, to commit suicide.[86]

But the most common survival strategy deployed in 1947 was flight. As conditions in the princely states began to deteriorate in the spring of 1947, vulnerable minorities of all colours reacted instinctively and looked around for places of refuge, intending, in most cases, to stay there only for so long as it took for the violence to subside. Some in the first instance opted for local strong points or places where co-religionists were known to be numerous—such as the aforementioned Rosa Sharif in Patiala. Others, particularly Muslims from CI, sought the protection of nearby states governed by reputedly friendly princes, such as Dholpur, Jaora, Hyderabad and—especially—Bahawalpur and Bhopal. By the end of October, at least 100,000 Muslims from the states had been resettled in Bahawalpur; and about the same number, mostly from Gwalior and Indore, had found refuge inside Bhopal. By 1949 nearly two million Muslim princely subjects, chiefly from Rajasthan, Kashmir and the east Punjab states, had become citizens of Pakistan.

One should not, however, be deceived by these big numbers into underestimating the challenges that migration as a survival strategy posed. First, it meant a huge break with things familiar and reassuring. Secondly, it meant undertaking a long, arduous and risky journey into the unknown. Thus the Muslims who left first and most eagerly were generally those who had close League connections, or who were otherwise ideologically committed to the Pakistan ideal, or who had little to lose. The Kunjras of Sujangarh in Bikaner, for instance, who departed at the start of October in what onlookers described as considerable haste, left behind personal debts of two lakhs of rupees.[87] Others who opted to go early were influenced by reports of governmental incentives being offered to new settlers, by invitations from relatives and by the pre-emptive actions of respected or wealthy community leaders.

But of course, many Muslims were given no choice at all: they had their minds made up for them by the *darbāri* authorities. When in October the Bharatpur government finally stopped hunting the Meos down and started putting them on trains instead, it was so much in a hurry to get the evacuation underway that it did not bother to make any arrangements for their onward passage. Similarly, Muslims in Patiala's Sunam district, having been told by local officials that they 'should go to Pakistan', were refused permission to detour to collect personal property, and were fired on and *lathi*-charged when some of them demurred.[88]

As for the journey itself, in the event, the large majority of Muslims from the Indian states who set out across the Punjab bound for Pakistan (and almost all of those who headed for Bhopal and Hyderabad), eventually reached their chosen destinations. So did most of the Sikhs and Hindus who fled Khairpur and Bahawalpur. Very few, however, arrived unscathed. The Muslims who volunteered to leave states such as Bharatpur, Patiala and Kashmir were subjected to 'prolonged searches' by *darbāri* police and generally stripped of all valuables, most of which they never saw again.[89] Then, once on the road, refugees had to run the gauntlet not only of the war-bands but also of greedy border officials. Some refugee columns were actually preyed upon by the military escorts appointed to 'protect' them. Refugee convoys originating in Bahawalpur, for example, were forced to pay protection money to their escorts before the latter would agree to let them move off; and during the journey to India the soldiers helped themselves to personal items and the favours of 'beautiful girls'.[90]

And even when they eventually reached safety, beyond the new international border, the problems continued. Most of the refugees spent weeks or months housed in camps similar to the ones they had vacated; and to these physical discomforts was added the trauma of adjusting to a new habitat and the shock of discovering that many local officials and residents—although their co-religionists—viewed them, respectively, as a nuisance and a potential economic threat. Some became so disillusioned by their reception that they actually packed up their meagre belongings and went back, braving the rigours of the borderlands all over again.

One such group were the Meos from Alwar and Bharatpur. Some three lakhs of Meos or about half the community, initially ended up in Pakistan; but many soon grew disgruntled and left. By April 1948 the exodus was running at 'about 1000 a day', and by June over 20,000 Meos had quit Pakistan for the refugee camps of Gurgaon district, where they joined 200,000 others still in limbo.

They were not welcomed back. When N.B. Khare was summoned to a meeting in New Delhi in September 1947, he went with some trepidation, expecting to be hauled over the coals for what his government had done to the Alwar Muslims. Instead, he received a patient and friendly hearing, which ended with the representative of the Home Department remarking: 'Dr Khare is right... I think all these Muslim refugees should be sent to Pakistan.'[91] This comment mirrored a growing conviction in official circles in India that, having demanded the creation of Pakistan on the basis that there were 'two nations' in the subcontinent, Muslims had made their bed, and should as far as practicable be encouraged to lie in it, through assisted relocation. In the case of the Meos, the belief was alloyed with irritation at the group's apparent vacillation. At one point they had seemed bent on going to Pakistan; now, it appeared, they wanted to stay.

However, since Congress policy specifically forbade compulsory repatriation, the hard-liners tried to pressure the Meos into leaving voluntarily—a strategy that culminated in the Dr Gopichand Bhargava-led east Punjab government threatening to withdraw rations from all Meos in transit camps 'not starting for Pakistan'. Eventually 50,000 were coerced by this means into agreeing to go, and were duly packed off in a huge convoy at first light on 10 November. The following day, however, the caravan was intercepted by Union officers on the direct order of the Prime Minister, Jawaharlal Nehru, who had been alerted to its departure by his agent in the region, former Kashmir Chief Minister Gopalaswamy Aiyengar. Returned to camps in Gurgaon, the Meos were given assurances of protection by the deputy commissioner of the district and by several visiting Congress Party heavyweights, including Gandhi who promised he would include them in his prayers.[92]

But this still left the problem of what to do with the remaining Meos from Bharatpur and Alwar, of whom some 200,000 had taken shelter with relatives in Gurgaon. The obvious policy was to send them back to their villages and this was what the Meos themselves wanted. 'They say they should be allowed to go back to Alwar and Bharatpur,' Hasan Suhrawardy reported.[93] Against that the *darbārs* concerned had made it abundantly clear, through their policy of ethnic cleansing, that they did not want the Meos around; and a year later they were still adopting a rigid stance. When Aiyengar told Khare that Nehru wanted him to accept the Alwar Meos back, he replied curtly: 'once they enter the Alwar State they will be tried [*sic*] as rebels and shot'.[94] Similarly blunt messages emanated from neighbouring Bharatpur. Despite these warnings, some 25,000 Meos did attempt, over the following months, to return to their ancestral villages—only to discover on arriving there that the greater portion of their lands had been allocated to Hindus, primarily (it was probably meant as an insult) to menial Chamars. While a few Meos managed to get their lands back through the expedient of paying *phirothi* (in effect, extortion) money to corrupt officials, the majority were held off at gunpoint. Early in April, the Alwar government instructed the Meos squatting in its territory to leave or 'be driven out'.[95]

Apprised of these ominous developments, the Union government in Delhi was divided about how it should react. Nehru thought the issue clear-cut. Alwar and Bharatpur were in clear defiance of the government's refugee policy; besides which Muslim opinion was watching the situation in Mewat closely. Pushing out the Meos who had returned 'would have a disastrous repercussion in Kashmir'.[96] Officials in the Relief and Rehabilitation ministry, however, put a rather different spin on the issue: 'on a strict interpretation of the facts', minuted departmental secretary V.D. Dantyagi, they 'are not really entitled to stay on in India'.[97] In turn, this hard-line approach was strongly endorsed by Vallabhbhai Patel as the minister responsible for Home and States. Echoing Khare, Patel characterised the Meos as communistic Muslim Leaguers who had forfeited the government's consideration by engaging in a rebellion against lawful authority. As he told the deputy high commissioner for Pakistan:

> the return of Meos to Alwar and Bharatpur would cause great bitterness and discontent and might lead to serious breaches of the peace... there was little chance of the Meos being received in Alwar and Bharatpur with that degree of peace and security which would be essential for their rehabilitation... in as much as the *atrocities committed by them* were still fresh in the minds of the non-Muslims of ... [those] States[s].[98]

Without consulting the PM, Patel directed the commissioner of Gurgaon to arrange for the evacuation of all the remaining Meos to Pakistan. On learning of this order, Nehru at once countermanded it, and issued one of his own, directing the government of Rajasthan to rehabilitate all the Alwar and Bharatpur Meos on their original lands.

But the latter order it appears was never passed on. After a lapse of three weeks, marked only by a suspicious silence, Nehru asked the head of the Rajasthan rehabilitation programme, B.G. Pradhan, for a progress report. Pradhan was surprised. Rehabilitation of the Meos? As far as he knew, there was no such programme in place. However, he took the precaution of first consulting Khemchand Mathur the Collector of Alwar. Mathur confirmed Pradhan's impression that no orders with respect to the Meos had been received and offered to accompany him to Delhi to testify to that fact in person. Arriving at South Block, the two men first paid a courtesy call on Patel, who urged them not to worry; but the effect of this reassurance lasted only so long as it took them to cross the passage to the office of the prime minister.

> I sat as an accused in front of him [Mathur remembers]. Nehru said 'You don't work', [to which] I replied, 'I do what I am asked to do'. 'But four to six days [*sic*] ago, I sent an order to restore the Meos' lands. What have you done about it?' 'I have not received it.' 'Who says so?' Nehru [then] called up the movement file – asked Vellodi [the I.C.S. officer from the States Department], 'What has happened to my order?' It was discovered [that] the order was still lying in the file – [it] had not been sent. Nehru lost his temper. 'Nobody works!' He threw the paperweight [on his desk] at Vellodi, who ducked. After that he said, 'You all get out. You are not a penny's worth.'[99]

EX. INTERVIEW.

Following this outburst, Nehru went to see Patel, who tried to reason with him. Another row ensued. But eventually the deputy prime minister gave way and agreed to support a staggered programme of resettlement. The Rehabilitation Ministry duly fell into line.

Progress remained slow; nevertheless by May 1949, 43,000 Alwar and Bharatpur Meos had been resettled on their original, or equivalent, lands or, where neither option was available, awarded cash compensation. The remainder still stranded in the camps—some 62,000—were resettled, progressively, during the latter part of 1949, in accordance with the decision of a ministerial summit in June.

In deciding belatedly to rehabilitate the Meos rather than expel them, the New Delhi government rationalised its action by proclaiming smugly that it was 'fulfil[ling] the ... wishes of Gandhiji'.[100] Would the Mahatma have approved? Probably. But by then he was long dead.

During the first three decades of the twentieth century, ethno-communal violence was not a serious problem in the princely states of north India. But the structural and cultural bulwarks that had protected the states from rampant manifestations of communal hostility earlier, began to erode during the 1930s and 1940s, as British Indian-based communalist parties and organisations increasingly penetrated their flimsy border defences and as some of the princes sought to form alliances with these groups in a bid to shore up their political futures. The jockeying for power in north India set in motion by the British withdrawal in 1947 and the accompanying partition of the country to form a 'homeland' for Muslims greatly intensified the impact of these influences: first, by stereotyping the Indian Muslims who remained outside the boundaries of Pakistan as a people who really belonged elsewhere; secondly, by tempting a group of dissident princes into embracing the mad ethnic cleansing schemes of the Hindu Mahasabha and the Akali Dal, which for the first time in the history of the region gave communal violence a veneer of governmental legitimacy; and thirdly, by triggering a massive exodus of traumatised Hindus and Sikhs from west Punjab and Sind, bent on revenge.

In the early twentieth century the 'two Indias' had stood apart. In 1947, they merged in a dark apotheosis of ambition and bloodlust. Although the states still remained separate entities, their borders meant little in the midst of the Punjab holocaust, as refugees flooded across the region looking for places of safety. What is more, the territorial schemes of the dissident *darbārs*—and the logistic support they provided to the ethnic cleansing activities of the *jathas*—represented an explicit repudiation of the existing borders that for a century and more had separated them from 'British India'. Most of the big Sikh war-bands were based in the states, and largely supplied by them, but much of their grim work was executed in the Punjab proper. Conversely, much of the violence unleashed against Muslims within the Punjab states and in Jammu was carried out or at least provoked by Hindu and Sikh immigrants from Punjab and NWFP. One is tempted to say that in the Punjab, in autumn 1947, the communal trajectories of the Indian princely states and of British India finally intersected.

However, such a conclusion would be too facile, for what happened in the Punjab states, Kashmir, Alwar and Bharatpur was exceptional; nowhere else, in the north Indian states, did the communal violence attain anything like the same proportions; nor was it annexed to any projects of ethnic cleansing. And even the Sikh rulers, in the end, stepped back from the brink, if only out of fear that they might be held to account for their actions. Embedded in the *darbāri* files for this period are hints of plots and dark designs, but overwhelmingly the written record testifies to the continuing commitment of the north Indian princes and their officials to policies of pluralism and toleration. It remained to be seen how far these traditional principles, the principles of *rājadharma*, would commend themselves to their newly acquired populations of Hindu and Sikh refugees.

RATHER LAME
CONCLUSION.

5
The New India

Dr N.B. Khare: Whether it is a mosque, or whether it is a temple, in both places God is worshipped and God is one.

Maulana A.K. Azad: No, Doctor, God has become two now.
Conversation, 1947

Bluster on the right

The systematic ethnic cleansing of Muslims from east Punjab, Jammu and eastern Rajputana during the spring and summer of 1947, the mass exodus of survivors for safe havens in Pakistan and other parts of India, and the arrival of an even larger number of Hindu and Sikh refugees from west Punjab, Bahawalpur and Sind transformed the ethnic landscape of north India. What had for centuries been an area of rich ethnic diversity, inhabited, especially in rural areas, by dense concentrations of Muslims, became, almost overnight (although in actuality refugees from Pakistan continued to trickle across the border until the early 1950s) a dominantly Hindu region except in east Punjab where, as noted in the previous chapter, Sikhs now formed a substantial minority. In 1941 Muslims had been 27 per cent of Alwar's population; ten years later they comprised scarcely 6 per cent. During the same period the segment of the population of the east Punjab states professing Islam plummeted from 12.7 to 1.8 per cent, while that of Bikaner dropped from 15 per cent to a little over 11. The effects of this demographic revolution are still evident today, and it is unlikely that they will ever be reversed. Nevertheless, even as Khare's killing squads failed to eliminate Muslims entirely from Alwar, so in other states too some Muslims managed to hang on—a handful in the east Punjab states, rather more in Rajputana and Gujarat and an overwhelming majority in CI (which was more distant from Pakistan and where attacks on Muslims in 1947 were less frequent and in the main less savage). Indeed in several Muslim-ruled states the Muslim population share actually remained constant or, more remarkably still, increased, as Table 5.1

Table 5.1   Muslims as a percentage of the total population, provinces, agencies and Muslim-ruled states, 1901–51

Unit	1901	1921	1931	1941	1951
Punjab states/PEPSU	20.5	19.9	18.2	12.7	1.5
Pataudi	16.2	16.0	16.8	17.0	0.6
Loharu	12.9	14.1	13.4	14.2	0.3
Malerkotla	35.1	35.4	37.8	38.5	7.8
Bahawalpur	83.0	82.8	81.2	81.9	–
Sind	76.2	73.4	72.8	71.0	
Khairpur	81.7	81.1	82.1	83.0	–
Rajputana	9.5	9.1	9.5	9.7	6.2
Tonk	11.7	13.2	13.9	14.6	9.4
UP/Rohilkhand	24.4	25.8	27.0	27.9	14.4
Rampur	45.2	47.0	46.7	49.4	49.0
Kathiawar/Saurashtra	13.9	13.1	13.6	12.2	11.2
Janagadh	n/a	19.4	19.3	20.0	12.2
Cambay	13.4	12.9	11.7	12.0	5.7
Gujarat states	n/a	4.6	4.1	4.0	4.5
Balasinor	n/a	n/a	10.2	10.0	5.7
Palanpur	9.7	10.6	10.9	9.9	6.8
Radhanpur	n/a	n/a	12.0	12.6	6.2
Sachin	n/a	n/a	12.0	11.5	6.7
Central India	6.1	5.5	5.7	5.9	4.8
Bhopal	10.5	9.4	12.3	14.1	15.4
Baoni	n/a	n/a	12.9	12.3	6.8
Jaora	n/a	n/a	15.9	16.7	11.2
Kurwai	n/a	n/a	13.7	n/a	n/a
Madras	6.5	6.7	7.1	7.9	5.0
Hyderabad	10.4	10.4	10.6	16.5	11.8
All states	13.9	13.4	13.5	13.9	–

Sources: *Census of India*, 1901, Vol. 1, Pt 2, pp. 58–61, Vol. 9A, Pt 2, pp. 52–3, Vol. 16A, Pt 2, pp. 37–40, Vol. 17A, Pt 2, Table 6, Vol. 19A, Pt 2, pp. 14–15, Vol. 25A, Pt 2, pp. 30–5; *Census of India*, 1921, Vol. 1, Pt 2, p. 40, Vol. 8, Pt 2, pp. 57–61, Vol. 13, Pt 2, pp. 37–8, Vol. 16, Pt 1, p. 62 and Pt 2, pp. 52–64, Vol. 17, Pt 2, p. 14, Vol. 18, Pt 2, p. 20, Vol. 20, Pt 2, p. 14, Vol. 21, Pt 2, pp. 22–3, Vol. 22, Pt 2, pp. 16–17, Vol. 24, Pt 2, p. 26; *Census of India*, 1931, Vol. 1, Pt 2, p. 514, Vol. 8, Pt 2, pp. 403–10, Vol. 10, Pt 1, p. 122 and Pt 2, p. 276, Vol. 14, Pt 2, p. 299, Vol. 17, Pt 2, pp. 278–9, Vol. 18, Pt 2, pp. 493–7, Vol. 20, Pt 2, p. 310, Vol. 27, Pt 1, p. 118; *Census of India*, 1941, Vol. 1, Pt 1, pp. 98–9 and Pt 2, pp. 128–9, Vol. 2, pp. 44–5, Vol. 3, pp. 86–93, Vol. 5, pp. 88–92, Vol. 12, p. 26, Vol. 18, p. 33, Vol. 5, pp. 58–60, 64–5, Vol. 22, Pt 2, p. 338.

shows. To be sure (except for the significant exception of Kashmir), the Muslims who remained in the Union at the end of 1947 constituted only a small minority of the total population, barely 10 per cent as against almost a third in undivided India. Yet, altogether, there were over 45 million of them, of whom about eight million were resident in the states. This was no small number. Moreover its visibility was enhanced by the fact that Indian Muslims lived predominantly in urban areas. In Jamnagar, Muslims still make up about a fifth of the population; in Malpura, a *mofussil* town once part of Tonk, they number a third; in Rampur City they constitute a healthy majority.

For many Hindus and Sikhs living in the northern states, the continued presence of Muslims in their midst, after what had transpired in 1947, was a source of great irritation. The Muslims were generally reckoned to have 'caused' the partition of 1947, and its attendant violence, through their demand for a homeland. More specifically, it was widely believed that the Muslims had begun the cycle of killing in the Punjab and should be made to pay for that crime. Again, most Hindus and Sikhs found it difficult to comprehend why any Muslims would want to stay in India when they had 'Islamic' Pakistan to go to. Blinded by prejudice, many came to the conclusion that the Muslims who had stayed on had done so in order to wreak havoc against the Union at the instigation of their masters in Pakistan. As a Hindu medical practitioner in Bhopal gravely informed Gandhi: 'The Muslims of India have amassed huge stores of arms and ammunition in many places . . . In the event of a war between India and Pakistan these so-called loyal Muslims will resort to sabotage, create chaos in the country and Paralyse the whole machinery of Government.'[1]

These inchoate suspicions and fears sparked numerous excesses. In Udaipur and Kotah, Bohras received 'threatening letters . . . urging them to leave for Pakistan'.[2] In the capital of Nawanagar, Hindus called for an end to the tradition of employing Arabs in the maharaja's bodyguard. In Jammu, mosques were attacked and desecrated, and posters put up denouncing the state's recently installed Muslim Chief Minister, Sheikh Abdullah, as a 'rascal' and Pakistan stooge.[3] Closer to the border, where cattle-raids by Pakistani militias from Sind and Bahawalpur kept the villagers of Jodhpur and Bikaner constantly on edge, alleged Muslim 'fifth columnists' were named in local newsletters and their houses attacked. At the end of the year, Hindu mobs attacked Muslim refugees camped in the city of Ajmer, killing 56 and injuring several hundred others.

Convinced that the Muslims could never be trusted, some Hindu zealots called for them to be deported *en masse* on grounds of national security. Even the Hindu Mahasabha hesitated to go that far; but it did challenge their automatic right to Indian citizenship, suggesting that Muslims who wanted to remain in the country should be required to prove their loyalty—either by signing a written pledge of allegiance or, better still, by shedding blood for the nation when the expected open war with Pakistan eventually erupted.[4] After one of these Sabhite outbursts, American consul-general in Bombay John Macdonald commented sardonically that it looked as if Muslims who wanted to remain in the country would have to get used to the idea of living meekly as second-class citizens 'under the domination of Hindus'.[5]

To be sure, these extreme attitudes were unrepresentative; yet contrary to popular and much scholarly opinion they were not confined to the fanatical fringe of Hindudom; indeed even the Congress at this time had its share of mavericks eager to push the Hindu communalist line. Party President and first Indian President, Rajendra Prasad, took a prominent public stance on the issue of cow-protection and vigorously opposed state intervention in the area of Hindu personal law. Nehru's deputy, Vallabhbhai Patel, argued forcefully in Cabinet for a pre-emptive strike against Pakistan; sacked several senior Muslim advisers in the Home ministry; opposed, as we have seen, the return of the Meos; and in a widely reported speech to a Muslim gathering at Lucknow on 6 January 1948 told the audience that the government had the right to demand of them 'practical proof' of their loyalty.[6] Sitaramayya, who succeeded Prasad as party president, tried to broker a *rapprochement* between the Congress and the RSS, which, he insisted, was 'not the enemy'. And the Congress Chief Minister of UP, G.B. Pant, echoed the Mahasabha in suggesting that the Muslims could best demonstrate their fidelity to the nation by shedding their blood for it. Similarly tendentious comments were expressed by party heavyweights Charan Singh, Rehabilitation Minister Mohanlal Saxena, Purushottamdas Tandon, K.M. Munshi, Ravi Shankar Shukla and J.B. Kripalani, who could not forget, or forgive, the loss of his native Sind.

Misled by the continuing electoral failures of the Hindu Mahasabha, which captured a miserable three (out of 1585) in the provincial poll of 1946, and only one more in the first democratic elections of 1951 in which it secured less than 1 per cent of the national vote, most historians have discounted the Right as a political factor in early independent India. However, veteran Mahasabha leader, B.S. Moonje, advised the British not to be deceived about the party's 'status and importance' from the 'mere fact' that it had not fared well at the ballot box,[7] and the anecdotal evidence supports that proposition. Early in 1949 a crowd estimated at over 40,000 flocked to hear V.D. Savarkar speak at a rally in north Calcutta; later in the year the RSS's Golwalkar attracted an audience of perhaps 200,000 to another in Delhi. Around the same time, the Congress central office was receiving over 20,000 petitions, letters and telegrams per day in support of a legislative ban on cow-slaughter, which both the Mahasabha and the RSS supported. Interestingly this view was also shared by staffers at the American embassy in New Delhi, who reported to Washington in December 1948 that the Mahasabha was an underrated factor in Indian politics since its 'communalistic, bigoted' principles were 'accepted, at least in part, by a large section of the members of the Indian National Congress'.[8] Given the latter point it would not be an exaggeration to characterise the dominant trend in Indian politics in the late 1940s as a 'swing to the Right'.

There were several reasons for this radical shift—all connected with the partition and its aftermath. As Christophe Jaffrelot points out, the 'situation in India after 15 August 1947 was *a priori* favourable to Indian nationalism', because of the 'tangible focus' that Pakistan provided for anti-Muslim feeling.[9] Secondly, as noted above, the mass exodus of Muslims after August 1947 made India much more uniformly, and conspicuously, Hindu than it had been in British days, thereby validating, in an ironic sort of way, the Right's insistent demand that India should unselfconsciously embrace its Hindu identity. Thirdly, the RSS won widespread respect through its assistance to homeless Hindu and Sikh refugees. As Bikaner's IG of Police minuted, with grudging admiration: 'It is, however, a fact that the Sangh has won considerable popularity among the Hindus [here] who credit them with having saved the lives and honour of innumerable Hindus and exacted an eye for an eye.'[10] Fourthly, the Mahasabha and the Dal both drew plaudits for having steadfastly opposed partition—a principled position the INC, burdened with the responsibilities of negotiating a smooth transfer of power, was unable to replicate. Lastly, and perhaps most importantly, the Right garnered many new supporters from among the ranks of the traumatised Hindu and Sikh refugees from Pakistan.

The refugees who settled in the north Indian princely states during the late 1940s arrived with little more than the clothes on their backs. Some were able to put up with relatives, but the vast majority were consigned to hastily constructed barracks offering only the barest of essential services and where fire was a constant hazard. And if that was not bad enough, the refugees had to negotiate their way around a ponderous and capricious rehabilitation bureaucracy. When Sikh retailer Jagir Singh arrived in Kapurthala from west Punjab in 1947, he approached the local rehabilitation committee for help in finding a new shop. They did not disappoint. Within weeks, Singh had been allocated a handsome building once owned by a Muslim. He paid the required deposit and moved in. The rest of his meagre capital, he invested in the new shop. Two months later, he was informed that the government had decided to put all the shops in the town formerly owned by Muslims up for auction. Unable to raise the asking price, Singh was forced to vacate the shop.[11] And many would-be agriculturalists experienced similar difficulties. The process of rural rehabilitation worked efficiently in Patiala and Kapurthala, but grindingly slowly in Nabha, Alwar, Bharatpur, Faridkot and the Punjab hill states, where, 15 months after the partition, three-quarters of the lands formerly occupied by Muslims remained to be redistributed.

But even when officials helped, rather than hindered, the refugees found great difficulty adjusting to their new surroundings. Although the authorities tried, as far as possible, to send people to places similar to those they had vacated (urban dwellers to cities, peasants to villages, for example), the initial experience of the refugees was invariably one of severe dislocation and culture shock. Elderly cultivators in Alwar interviewed by Miriam Sharma and Urmila Vanjani, for instance, still recall vividly their first impression of the Mewat hills: how dry and harsh they looked, compared to the lush, canal-irrigated west Punjab. They were given land—but neither as much nor of the same quality as the lands they had vacated—and found it necessary to supplement its meagre bounty by taking work as day-labourers on the farms of richer peasants. To this day they 'still think of themselves as *sanarthis*, refugees, and contrast themselves to the *local log* (using the English word) among whom they live'.[12]

In turn, the refugees often appeared strange, even threatening, to their new neighbours, which further retarded the process of assimilation. A Jaipuri Hindu recalls:

> There was something of a problem in that the habits of these people were different from [those of] the local inhabitants.... for example people coming from a place like Karachi, they are not used to going out for their morning [ablutions]...they would do it on the rooftops, and people didn't like it.[13]

It seems that the Durgapur camp on the outskirts of the city quickly acquired a reputation as 'a place of ill-repute', inhabited by people of 'lax morals'.[14] Likewise, immigrants to Banswarra came with strange deities and processional rituals, which the local Nagar Brahmins and Neemas found offensive. As for the Punjabis who came to Alwar, they reportedly brought 'drinking and drunkenness'.[15]

Furthermore, the refugees aroused local resentment by putting pressure on scarce public resources, such as schools; while the Sindhis, more particularly, ruffled the feathers of the local business community with their entrepreneurial drive, sharp business practices and inclination to behave arrogantly towards competitors.[16] Jaipuris joked bleakly among themselves that someone menaced simultaneously by a Sindhi and a snake, would be better off killing the Sindhi first! Rootless and alienated, refugees were ripe for political mobilisation, and their experiences pre-disposed them towards the Mahasabha and the RSS, or in the case of the Sikhs, the Akali Dal.

Learning in September 1949 that Union Rehabilitation Minister Mohanlal Saxena had ordered the sealing of all Muslim-owned shops in Delhi and UP, a furious Jawaharlal Nehru exploded: 'All of us seem to be getting infected with the refugee mentality.'[17] There can be little doubt as to what sort of 'mentality' Nehru meant. Everywhere the refugees settled, communal trouble erupted. On 5 December 1947 a dispute in the Dargah Bazaar area of Ajmer between a Sindhi shopkeeper and a Muslim customer over the return of an allegedly defective gramophone led to widespread rioting, in which three persons died. During the following week mobs of refugees attacked Muslims living in the nearby villages of Khanpura and Kalyanpura, killing six. On 15 January 1948 the Muslim village of Jahangirpur in the Ujjain district of Gwalior was overrun, its inhabitants beaten, houses burnt and crops levelled. On 30 January an elderly Bohra man was found dead of stab wounds in a street in Mandsaur, in the same state, close to where a Sindhi boy had gone missing two days before. In February, Punjabi Hindu refugees 'committed arson and looting' in the village of Phikhanwala in Kalsia. On 1 March, a Muslim butcher was fatally stabbed by a Sindhi in Nasirabad and later in the same month a Sindhi hawker in Ajmer was apprehended for wrapping his wares in the leaves of a *Qur'an*. After a political meeting in Sirmur at the start of April, Hindu refugees boasted that the remaining 'Muhammadans' were going to be 'slaughtered and driven out of the State'. In December a wrangle over the ownership of an Indore house that a Sindhi refugee had occupied illegally sparked the biggest communal riot in the town since the 1927 disturbance described in Chapter 1.[18] Altogether, there were 30 major communal incidents in Gujarat, Rajasthan and CI during 1948, and nearly as many during 1949, most of them products of refugee aggression (Table 5.2).

Table 5.2 Major communal clashes in selected former princely ruled regions, 1948–50

	Gujarat		Rajasthan		Central India	
	I	C	I	C	I	C
1948	8	57	19	88	3	29
1949	7	12	19	96	3	14
1950	3	4	12	108	3	22

I = incidents; C = casualties (deaths and injuries requiring hospitalisation)
Source: Fort. Intelligence and police reports for: Rajasthan, Bikaner, Ajmer, Madhya Bharat, the Matsya Union, Madhya Pradesh, Gujarat, Saurashtra and Central India, 1948–50.

These numbers not only make a mockery of contemporary official claims that communal disorders had practically ceased in the country,[19] but put a question mark over the agreed historical consensus that communal incidents in the country 'declined markedly' between 1947 and 1954.[20]

To be sure, these developments were not unique to the states; refugees went to every part of the Indian dominion, and their behaviour was no less communalist there—as Nehru's aside to Saxena suggests and as Paul Brass' recent work on UP amply demonstrates.

Nevertheless, because the GOI sent comparatively more refugees per head of existing population to the princely areas than to the former Union provinces—apparently on the grounds that the former still remained, on the whole, more sparsely populated and less economically developed (and therefore ripe for an injection of human capital)—and because most of the refugees, especially in Gujarat and CI, gravitated to the towns, their impact on communal relations there was magnified. Gwalior's population, for example, increased by a third between 1941 and 1951, swelled by over 20,000 migrants from Pakistan. Bikaner, essentially a frontier town notwithstanding its grand status as a princely capital, added 5000 refugees to its population in the same period. Jamnagar and Bhavnagar, still smaller places, took in over 3000 refugees each. Of provincial cities, perhaps only Delhi and Ludhiana underwent a greater social transformation.

Meanwhile, the Right continued to receive legitimation and support from a number of Hindu and Sikh princes and ministers. Despite failing in his pledge to rid the state of the Meos, Khare retained the affection of Tej Singhji and, wherever possible, he used his dominant position at the Alwar court to further the communal agenda of the Mahasabha. Revenue Minister Lal Singh and influential court identity Mauli Chandra Sharma assisted him in this propaganda.[21] On 17 January 1948 the raja of Barwani dismissed his existing crop of advisers and appointed a new ministry consisting largely of 'out and out Hindu Sabhaites'.[22] At nearby Piploda, the mother of the minor Rawat used her authority as Regent to elevate RSS cadre V.V. Kulkarni to a senior post in the state judiciary, and other RSS and Mahasabhite appointments followed. Official patronage also helped the RSS to flourish in Sarila and Charkhari, while the Bharatpur *darbār* is said to have supplied the Sangh with guns and ammunition manufactured at a secret installation and stored in a cave near Baretta. Both Tej Singhji of Alwar and Jayaji Rao of Gwalior presided over Mahasabha and RSS functions, and in 1948 the young maharana of Udaipur, Bhagwat Singh, became RSS *sanghchalak* for southern Rajputana.

The dissident princes encouraged the Mahasabha, the Akali Dal and the RSS to expand in their states because their presence constituted a useful counterweight to the increasingly well-organised *praja mandals*, some of which were starting to call for the end of the monarchies and a full merger with the Indian Union. For the same reason, some of the northern rulers began to cultivate political links with their extended kinfolk and more generally, with the Rajput and Jat communities, leading to the setting up of what the *praja mandalis* disdainfully labelled 'king's parties'. The raja of Bilaspur organised his Chandela Rajput clansmen around the slogan 'Jai Kheloor'.[23] The Jodhpur *darbār* lent its backing to the creation of a Rashtriya Kisan Sangh, described by local Lok Parishad officials as the 'RSS . . . in new guise'.[24] Yadavindra Singh of Patiala established the Panthic Party in October 1947 and presided over the formation of the loyalist Sikh Students Federation early the following year. Sadul Singh gave funds to the Bikaner Rajput Sabha and staunchly defended the Rajputs' right to organise 'for their self-preservation', against criticism from the Union States Ministry.[25] The maharaja of Jaipur sponsored a 'parallel movement' of *jagirdars* to oppose the *praja mandal* in the upcoming state elections.[26] Khilchipur's officials organised a Rajput Sangh, Dungapur's a Kshatriya Parishad and Banswarra's a Prithvi Rajput Hitkarini Sabha.

It is easy, given the above, to form an inflated estimate of the importance of the Right in the immediate post-independence period. Although it certainly enjoyed very great popular support—and certainly more such support than most historians have allowed—the Right never commanded the loyalty of the majority of even the Hindu and Sikh population of the country. Moreover it was a scattered force, and a divided one. Nowhere, except perhaps in New Delhi, inundated with refugees, did it attain a critical mass. And despite repeated attempts by the Mahasabha to cobble together strategic alliances with other like-minded formations, the Right remained split on the issues of what kind of Indian state they wanted and how it should be achieved. Nevertheless, while the Right's limitations as a political movement are clear enough in hindsight, they do not seem to have been widely appreciated at the time. On the contrary, quite sensible people in the Union government saw the Right as a serious threat to the stability of the new Indian state. What made them so worried?

Partly, it was the nature of the Right's agenda. The Akali Dal's minimum demand was for a Punjabi-speaking—essentially Sikh—state within the Union; the Mahasabha's goal was a Hindu India in which Muslims would have few (or even no) rights; the Rajput Sangh opposed *zamindari* abolition, a central plank in the INC programme; the maharaja of Patiala's desire was to see India become something like a constitutional autocracy—an ambition not shared, one hardly needs to say, by the large majority of the members of the Indian Constituent Assembly. Mainly, though, it was fear of what the Right might do, in concert with the dissident princes, if its demands were rejected. The northern princely states were already in the grip of a menacing lawlessness. In Banswarra a meeting of the Kshatriya Mahasabha in January 1948 opened with a 'volley of 100 shots' and concluded with the presentation of a ceremonial sword to the presiding officer as a symbol of that organisation's determination to 'live and rule with Aid of Sword'. In Jodhpur in April, a 2000-strong body of Rajputs confronted members of the local *praja mandal* 'with guns'. Around the same time a conference of the Patiala Praja Mandal was broken up by armed Akali Sikhs. Over the winter of 1947–48, *jagirdars* belonging to the Dungapur Kshatriya Parishad carried out raids on villages where Congress workers had been active; and early in the new year, Meo villages in Bharatpur were ravished by a posse of Jats under the command of the ruler's younger brother, Raja Mansingh.[27]

This was low-level thuggery, to be sure, and in itself no direct threat to the integrity of the Union. Nevertheless it was clear, from the kinds of things that police spies picked up at RSS and Rajput Sangh rallies, that elements of the Hindu and Sikh Right had the Nehru government firmly in their sights. At a meeting of the Khilchipur Rajput Sangh, presided over by the *dewan*, the national flag was burned; afterwards the Rajputs—many of them, by this stage, drunk on country hooch—marched through the capital brandishing swords and shouting slogans ridiculing the Union prime minister. Another Rajput rally in Jodhpur concluded with cries of 'Pakistan Zindabad'.[28] At a Mahasabha meeting in Alwar, Khare pilloried the Union government leaders as 'an incompetent lot whose rule was bound to fail soon', at which point former Tehri minister M.C. Sharma, who was sitting beside him on the platform, interjected that a better description would be 'traitors'.[29]

Clearly the Right held the government in contempt. Would it attempt to overthrow it? Bizarre as it was, this notion haunted the policy makers in Delhi throughout the winter of 1947–48. Why else, they asked themselves, were the Akali Sikhs secretly manufacturing weapons at Tarn Taran? For what other reason would the RSS be stashing away ammunition in Bharatpur and Jammu? Further to these ruminations, the Indian intelligence service reported that a number of central Indian rulers had been meeting regularly with 'communal organisations' at Katra in Rajgarh to formulate a plan 'to overthrow the Nehru Gov[ern-men]t'.[30] The Home Minister, Patel, concluded on viewing these reports that a section of Rajput society 'still dreamt of the power of their sword[s] and still thought of carving out a kingdom for themselves'.[31] Later he likened the situation facing the government in early 1948, particularly in eastern Rajputana, to 'a powder magazine, which a single spark may set ablaze'.[32]

Even in this nervous and gloomy frame of mind, however, the Nehru ministry was mentally unprepared for the tragedy that struck the country at the end of January 1948. For some months Union police intelligence officers had been keeping a close watch on the activities of the Hindu Rashtra Dal, and, early in the new year, they learned that some disaffected members of the Dal were intending to take revenge on Gandhi for his stand over the sterling balances issue. But the police did not know precisely who the plotters were, or when or where the assassination was due to take place. In the event, on 30th January, one member of the cabal, a brooding 37-year-old Brahmin newspaper editor from Poona named Nathuram Godse managed to slip past the heavy police cordon ringing the capital and infiltrate Gandhi's late-afternoon prayer meeting at Birla House. Moving slowly so as not to attract attention, Godse wormed his way through the crowd until he stood almost face to face with the Mahatma. Then he pulled out his Beretta automatic and fired point blank, injuring the great man fatally.

The shock to the nation was visceral. Anger and grief overflowed. In Kolhapur, mobs vented their rage in a very un-Gandhian orgy of destruction. But in some quarters of the Right there was scarcely concealed jubilation. The Kotah RSS, for example, celebrated the event with a distribution of sweets to its members. In Alwar, the Mahasabha offered its 'condolences', but in a manner that reeked of insincerity. The authorities in New Delhi took careful note of these obscenities and vowed that the people responsible for them would be made to pay.

The Union strikes back

The countrywide revulsion occasioned by the Mahatma's murder rebounded on the Hindu Right. 'When it was known that the assassin... was a Hindu Mahasabhite', the chief commissioner (CC) of Ajmer reported, 'a feeling of hatred' arose amongst the general public against the Mahasabha–RSS combine.[33] Anticipating this reaction, moderate elements in the Mahasabha leadership clustered around its President, S.P. Mookherjee, persuaded the party's WC, on 15 February, to voluntarily suspend political activity. Although this decision was later partially reversed, under pressure from Moonje, in August, by then things had cooled down sufficiently for the party to escape further penalty. Nevertheless the party lost credibility and membership slumped. Datia Sabha President, Ghanshyam Napith, resigned the day after the assassination; and over the following months many other party cadres 'busy in exculpation' followed his example.[34]

The RSS, on the other hand, was singled out for exemplary retribution. Convinced that 'Bapu's murder was not an isolated business but part of a much wider campaign organised chiefly by the R.S.S.', Nehru overrode civil libertarian objections from Leftist ministers and Patel's scepticism about the extent of the alleged conspiracy and demanded that the cabinet ban the organisation. He got his way. The Sangh was proscribed and arrest warrants issued for its leaders and senior full-time workers. Within weeks 20,000 *swyamsevaks* were behind bars. But the witch-hunt did not end there. Public servants across the country were forbidden to 'maintain any kind of connection' with the organisation on pain of 'severe action'; school principals were called upon to report staff believed to have RSS sympathies; and students found to have drilled with the Sangh had their certificates stamped accordingly.[35] This crackdown would last until July 1949.

As the government's noose tightened, sobering revelations about the Hindu and Sikh Right piled up. Most of this information confirmed Nehru's darkest suspicions. However, what had not been guessed before, and only emerged clearly following the police investigation into the conspiracy to kill the Mahatma, was the extent to which the Right was entrenched in the north Indian princely states. As the inquiry into Gandhi's assassination unfolded, information came to light from several witnesses that Nathuram Godse and a second conspirator, Narayan Apte, had lodged in Gwalior City at the house of the local Hindu Sabha leader Dr S.D. Pachure on their way to Delhi, and had returned there on 27 January in search of a more reliable pistol after the revolver they had brought from Poona misfired in a test. Although Pachure vigorously contested these allegations, the Gandhi murder trial judge accepted the police evidence that the weapon that killed the Mahatma was in fact procured by him from a friend in Gwalior.[36] It was also revealed during the inquiry that Nathuram Godse had earlier called on the chief minister of Kishengarh, a man known to the police as a strong RSS sympathiser.

More damning still, was the information gleaned by Union Intelligence that the states had become a refuge for RSS renegades. Early in February 1948 it was discovered that as many as 35 wanted RSS-men, including the *pracharak* of Agra, were hiding out in remote villages of Bharatpur.[37] Other RSS cadres, it was claimed, were holed up in Alwar, Dhar, Dholpur, Dewas Senior, Barwani, Piploda, Dungapur and Faridkot. 'The R.S.S. movement is recovering both at Rewa and Satna, and some of the [Vindhya Pradesh] ministers are secretly flirting with this movement', observed the Regional Commissioner (RC) for CI, in a report of September 1948.[38]

For months the Union government had been fielding persistent allegations that a number of north Indian states, Alwar and Bharatpur in particular, had conducted, or provided logistic support for, attacks on Muslims during the spring and summer of 1947. It had shrugged them off, pleading a lack of hard evidence. However, the discovery that some of the *darbārs* were in cahoots with Rightist extremists added an entirely new dimension to the case against the states and convinced even the conservatives in the Indian cabinet that they would have to be reined in. Eight days after Gandhi's murder the rulers of Alwar and Bharatpur were presented with 'prima facie evidence' of their 'complicity…in R.S.S. activities',[39] and forced to step down from their *gaddis* pending a full investigation. Rightist officials in the two states were sacked and replaced by Union administrators.

Yet the move against the Alwar and Bharatpur states was proceeded with cautiously and with some trepidation. The States Minister prepared the ground thoroughly, consulting a number of other rulers in advance about what was proposed, and seeking advice from the governor-general, Mountbatten. And he persuaded the Cabinet to pass over the issue of genocide and to focus on the maharajas' RSS connections, leaving the issue of their complicity in the murder of Muslims to emerge incidentally: with 'these two States under our influence and, if necessary, under our control', he hazarded, the government 'would be able to unearth all that has happened and the part which each State and its officials have taken in various crimes'.[40]

On further reflection, however, Patel began to wonder whether deposing the maharajas and putting them in the dock, as it were, had been the right course. Committed though he was to bringing the states and their rulers into line with Congress policy, he did not want to destroy root and branch the traditional values and loyalties embodied in the system of monarchical rule. And as a conservative and religious man he was also deeply conscious of the important place the princes already occupied within the Hindu and Sikh communities, and of the useful public role they could still play, with proper handling, on the government's behalf. These considerations prompted the States Minister to think that a better way forward might be by means of a general constitutional change imposed on the princely states at large—one that would bring them more directly under the Centre's control. This approach would have the advantage of keeping the lid on potentially embarrassing information and would not put the Union government in the difficult position of having to discriminate between 'good' and 'bad' rulers.

Since coming into office, Congress had mellowed its stand on the states. It no longer ranted about 'feudal anachronisms', and indicated that it was prepared to allow some of them to remain under certain conditions, most importantly the early adoption by the states of full responsible government, and their satisfying New Delhi that they had the capacity to deliver 'efficient administration and . . . provide adequate social and health services'.[41]

A year on, however, it was beginning to look as if even this limited autonomy option might be unsustainable. Despite the passage of further constitutional measures enlarging the powers and functions of legislative councils, and the installation in many states of 'popular' ministries, the progress of democratisation in princely India remained slow and by 1948 was everywhere still a long way short of the criterion of full responsible government based on adult franchise. Moreover, few of the new 'popular' ministries were performing with great distinction. There were reports from Indore of a 'constant array of shortages', particularly of cloth and food grains.[42] One of veteran nationalist Jai Narain Vyas' first acts as head of the new ministry in Jodhpur was to give the state's railway employees an unaffordable pay rise. Armed robberies in Udaipur rose from 928 to 2026 in the space of a year. The newly installed chief minister of Rajgarh was observed 'blackmarketting in Bombay'.[43] After receiving a flood of unfavourable notices about the conduct of Sheikh Abdullah's government in Kashmir towards the people of Jammu, Nehru chastised him: 'People appear to be starving, including children.'[44] Returning from a visit to Punjab and East Punjab States Union (PEPSU), Union Health Minister Amrit Kaur wrote despondently:

> The police is very corrupt. High police officials keep trucks for transporting forbidden goods from one province to another, e.g. wheat, cement, opium...S. Dalip Singh, I.G.P., is very communal...The Premier, Gian Singh, is weak and made to be communal. The other Ministers are inefficient, ignorant...and corrupt.[45]

Ironically, these developments appeared to lend credibility to the dire warnings of rulers like Hamidullah and Udaibhan Singh of Dholpur about the dangers of democracy.

It was the issue of national security, though, that finally clinched the argument for the hawkish States Minister. Already the two dominions were engaged in an unofficial but intense military conflict in Kashmir, and many Indian strategists thought it only a matter of time before the Pakistan government attempted to compensate for the setbacks its forces were suffering in the Kashmir Valley by launching a strike into east Punjab. By January 1948, reports from the border suggested that such an attack might be imminent:

> Ahir regiments have been replaced by tribal Pathans and Arabs in Bahawalpur State. This concentration of troops in Bahawalpur is significant. Apart from this, the Muslims are crossing the border in Military lorries and are going to Malerkotla and some to Loharu. It is very much suspected that these people are being infiltrated to do spying against the Indian Union...in case of attack.[46]

Patel, and Baldev Singh, the defence minister, were both concerned about the strategic and logistic implications of an agglomeration of weak, independent states strung out along what would become, in the event of an all-out war with Pakistan, 'the front line defence of the Indo-Gangetic Plains'.[47] Clearly the states' forces would be insufficient in themselves to resist a full-scale Pakistan incursion, and any joint forces sent to the front would suffer from problems of divided command. Briefly, the government considered adopting a suggestion from Bikaner

Prime Minister K.M. Panikkar that each of the states of Jodhpur, Jaisalmer and Bikaner be asked to cede a 15-mile wide strip of territory along their western borders to the Union. But on reflection, Patel decided that the government's defence needs would be served better by a comprehensive scheme of integration.

Historians have rightly emphasised the enormity of the constitutional and administrative changes set in motion by this decision. The States Minister himself later characterised them as constituting a 'bloodless revolution'. However, the few official documents on the development of the policy open to scholars rather give the impression that even Patel—who initiated the policy without prior reference to the Union Cabinet—did not initially intend it to be as far-reaching as it eventually turned out to be. Initially the focus was only on the smaller states of Orissa and Chhattisgarh, which almost everyone agreed were not viable, and when, in January 1948, a clutch of maharajas called at the States Ministry to seek Patel's assurance that their states would not suffer the same fate, departmental secretary V.P. Menon told them, on his behalf, 'that the principle of merger would not be applied to those States which had individual representation in the Constituent Assembly and which obviously had a future'.[48]

Clearly, at some point, Patel and Menon changed their minds. Perhaps the catalyst was Gandhi's murder. Certainly, Patel felt more confident after that tragedy about tackling the larger states in the wash of the popular fury against the RSS and the Hindu Mahasabha unleashed by Nathuram Godse's misplaced heroics.[49] Doubtless, too, what the Ministry learned then and later about the support being afforded to Rightist organisations by many of the north Indian Rajput and Jat princes also figured prominently in their thinking. At any rate, in March 1948, the States Ministry moved against Alwar and Bharatpur, taking advantage of the fact that they were both under temporary Union administration pending the outcome of the Ministry's inquiry. The two states were merged into one under the title of the Matsya Union. Shortly afterwards, it was the turn of Gwalior and Indore—both, significantly, considered hotbeds of the Right. In April they were combined with 20 smaller states to form the Union of Madhya Bharat. Over the following months Udaipur (and, at intervals), Jaipur, Jodhpur, Jaisalmer and Bikaner were incorporated in the Union of Rajasthan, the Kathiawar states in the Saurashtra Union, the Sikh states, together with Malerkotla and Loharu in PEPSU,[50] and Baroda and the Gujarat states in the province of Bombay. As a condition precedent, the princes appointed to head these new units were required to sign covenants binding them to act constitutionally, and new Instruments of Accession ceding to the Union the power to pass laws in respect of all matters falling within the purview of the federal and concurrent lists included in the seventh schedule of the GOI Act of 1935.

By 1950 the Indian states as they had existed during the colonial period had passed through the trapdoor of history; in this sense Patel's summation was correct—he had overseen a political revolution. Despite this, the princes lived on. As we shall see in the next section, many of the ex-rulers confounded popular expectations by adapting fluidly and with great effect to the demands and opportunities of democratic politics.

But after 1948–49, they no longer ruled. A few of the more important princes, it is true, were co-opted to serve as *rajpramukhs* and *uprajpramukhs* (governors and lieutenant-governors) of the so-called 'Part B' states created by the States Ministry's merger policy; however, these were appointed positions and did not carry the same cachet as hereditary kingship. Thus, while many ex-rulers continued to speak out in support of pluralism and toleration, after 1948–49 these interventions carried less weight than formerly. At the same time, the abolition of the institution of monarchy absolved them from their formal kingly responsibilities for religious management and ritual performance—roles which had enabled them to stand up to and where necessary gainsay the priesthood. Some, to be sure, tried to keep up these traditions, at least to the extent of continuing to preside at important festivals; but others, angered and humiliated by their un-throning, gave up the game altogether and retreated into doleful isolation. For the first time in nearly half a century, Dholpur in 1948 absented himself from his capital during the autumn Dasehra festival, while Alwar avoided both Dasehra and Diwali that year, sending his son to preside in his stead. Likewise, when the maharana of Udaipur learned that some Rajasthan Congress ministers were planning to attend the 1949 Gangor festivities in Mewar he cancelled the event. These Quixotic gestures further undermined the residual charismatic appeal of the princely order. When he rid India of the venerable institution of monarchy, Sardar Patel unwittingly destroyed yet another of the bulwarks that had helped keep the erstwhile states, for long, relatively free from the scourge of communal violence—the code of *rajadharma*.

But that was not all. Although the States Minister persuaded the Cabinet to award the 'covenanting' rulers generous lifetime pensions, paid for from the public purse, integration cut off their access to tax revenues and the state bureaucracy. They no longer possessed the capacity to appropriate state resources or issue directives to further the needs of particular communal groups of subjects. This change particularly hurt Muslims living in the former Muslim-ruled kingdoms of Bhopal, Rampur, Junagadh and Tonk.

For a century and more these Muslims and their forebears—though in each case only a small minority of the population—had been favoured in the disbursement of scholarships, educational places, government contracts and money for the upkeep of religious buildings. They had enjoyed virtually complete freedom of worship—even in respect of Islamic rites mortally offensive to members of other religions, such as cow-slaughter. With integration, local Hindus and Sikhs naturally expected these discriminatory policies to end. Thus, when Tonk was merged into Rajasthan, Hindus in Chabra village immediately got up an agitation to overturn the old *darbāri* ruling that music could not be played within a 50 yards of a mosque, day or night. As an ostensibly secularist government, the Congress regime in New Delhi was compelled to view such requests sympathetically.

Nevertheless, mindful of the possibility of a Muslim backlash, it instructed its officers to move circumspectly. Accordingly, in October 1949 the newly appointed CC of Bhopal, N. Bonarjee, placed a ban on the killing of cows during the Muslim festival of 'Id but exempted the city slaughterhouse, thereby ensuring that 'beef was available to Muhammadons [*sic*]' during that period. Unsurprisingly, this forbearance angered the local Hindu Sabha, and when in January 1950 a large consignment of cattle arrived in the city, bound for the municipal slaughterhouse, the communalists took their protest on to the streets. On 12 January some 1000 demonstrators, mostly Sindhi refugees, taunted the police with cries of 'Gau Mata ki jai', and 'Hindu Dharam ki jai'. This was followed by a general *hartal*. Nervous about the way events in the city were unfolding, Bonarjee sought advice from the States Ministry, and was authorised to impose further restrictions, which effectively brought Bhopal's cow-slaughter rules into line with those of Delhi and UP.[51]

Meanwhile, other influential voices were raised in support of a tougher stance on the 'Muslim question', loudest among them the Commissioner of Meerut's:

As you know, the line we have taken throughout the Bareilly Division has been that cow-sacrifice should be discouraged as much as possible, and if necessary prohibited . . . It is discouraging to have in this island State in the heart of the Division cow-sacrifice being performed in the same old way. The result has been to encourage the ... Muslims in the Bareilly Division to look to Rampur as the area where they are sustained in what they regard as their full freedom. ...

There is a definite tendency throughout the Bareilly Division for Muslims to regard the Rampur State as a sort of 'keep' for them. This is one of the things retarding their adjustment to the new set of things in the country. From the point of view of internal security, and in terms of the home front in case of a show down with Pakistan, there is a quite real, and I think reasonable, apprehension in the minds of people in the Bareilly Division that Rampur may provide (whether the ruler ... likes it or not) a directing centre for sabotage and disruption deep within the country. This is the view also of my Deputy Magistrates.[52]

These views resonated with the Rightist Congress leaders in New Delhi. Patel's States Ministry directed the chief ministers of the Part B states to undertake an urgent and sweeping review of their 'ecclesiastical' rules and expenditures to eliminate all remaining vestiges of communal (by which they meant Muslim) privileges. The result was a raft of new regulations and edicts that significantly eroded the rights of all Muslims living in the Part B states, but particularly those of Muslims who had previously enjoyed the protection and patronage of Muslim princes.

One early target of this communal assault was the Shariat Court of Tonk, which was closed in December 1948. Another was the beef trade. First in Saurashtra, then in other states, slaughterhouses were compelled to cease operating during Hindu holy days, and then altogether during the holy month of Shraven. Some were shut down permanently. More importantly, the new unions began to divert money away from heavily subsidised Muslim charities into other areas of need. Deemed a 'communal institution', the State Orphanage for boys at Junagadh was closed in June 1950. Around the same time, the Saurashtra government terminated its support for a free food programme run by the Dargah of Hazrat Shirazi Sahib at Dhanphulia and cancelled the stipends of at least half a dozen important mosques in Junagadh and Mangrol.[53] Again, particularly in Rajasthan, Muslims were adversely affected by new ideologically driven educational policies, which led to Urdu being phased out of the primary curriculum in Jodhpur and Jaipur. Last but not least, in 1949 the Saurashtra and Rajasthan unions legislated to ban the slaughter of cows, including old and ailing animals except under veterinary direction. The laws carried hefty penalties—fines and prison terms of up to ten years. The Rajasthan government had wanted also to prohibit the importation and sale of beef (which is of course a staple of the Muslim [BUT NOT NECESSARY] diet in South Asia); however, the States Ministry refused to assent to this draconian proposal.

When the Muslims living in the Muslim-ruled states realised that integration was coming, and pondered its implications, they initially thought they might be lucky even to survive. Not only did they expect to be short-changed by the popular governments that integration would inevitably bring to power, they feared that, without a friendly police force to protect them, they could easily fall prey to Hindu mob violence. Soon after the creation of PEPSU, a delegation of Muslims from Malerkotla called on the Indian PM in Delhi. Afterwards Nehru recorded: 'The small Muslim minorities [in PEPSU] are terribly afraid of the Sikhs who are often aggressive and even violent [towards them].'[54] And Sirmur's Muslims, too, felt insecure—refugee elements in the state had threatened to wreak vengeance on them the moment the state was integrated into Himachal Pradesh; while the Muslims of Tonk were discomforted by Rajasthan union Chief Minister Manak Lal Verma's pronouncement that disloyalty to the new regime would be severely 'dealt with'.[55] Fearing the worst, Muslims in some states turned in desperation to their former rulers for protection—interestingly they included the Muslim elite of Indore, who retained more faith in the goodwill of Yeshwant Rao Holkar, though a Hindu, than in the good offices of the new Madhya Bharat government.[56]

Thankfully, the Muslims' fears that they might become the victims of a bloodbath proved, in the event, exaggerated. Still, Muslims living in the new unions did experience violent attacks, particularly from Sindhi refugees. Some examples were provided in the previous section. Many Muslim-owned properties were also damaged in these communal attacks, including mosques—as at Mangrol, in Kathiawar, in September 1949. At the same time, the Muslims' socio-economic position deteriorated as a result of the policy changes mentioned above; and they suffered considerable harassment at the hands of the police, a number of Muslim hotel proprietors losing their licences just for allowing their patrons to listen to radio broadcasts from Karachi. Bit by bit, the weight of these setbacks began to take its toll on the confidence of the community.

Proud of their culture and acutely conscious of their former dom-inance, the Muslims clinging on in the former *nawabi* capitals at first tried to deal with their plight by keeping themselves aloof and holding on to their dignity; but gradually they came to realise that as a disparaged and friendless minority they would have to make adjustments to the way they lived if they were ever to prosper in the new India. In particular, they came to accept that they would have to start giving way in religious disputes, instead of, as in the past, insisting on precedence. So, wholly without fanfare (but with much private gnashing of teeth), a communal retreat in the former princely domains of north India began. Sensing this change in the wind, Hindu leaders in Tonk City opened a branch of the Mahasabha. The Muslims complained, but otherwise held their peace. In September 1949, for the first time in living memory, a Dol Yatra procession in Tonk was allowed to pass, unhindered, by the city's main mosque with drums beating and conches blaring. Even before the bill banning cow-slaughter had been passed, Saurashtra officials noticed that Muslims in the region had begun to substitute goats for cows in the annual Bakr 'Id sacrifice. Similarly, Bhopal CC Bonarjee was struck by the generally limpid reaction accorded to his proposal for a limited ban on cow-slaughter in what had been previously one of the custom's great strongholds. The only explanation that made any sense to him was that the Bhopal Muslim community had become resigned to occupying, henceforward, 'a position of . . . complete inferiority'.[57]

In Chapter 2 we commented on the tendency of vulnerable minorities in the princely states to exercise restraint in matters of religious expression as a way of purchasing the toleration of the majority, and we suggested that this constituted a principal reason for the relative infrequency of violent communal encounters in the states during the late colonial period. The responses on the part of the former *nawabi* state Muslims outlined above could be construed as a reversion to this earlier defensive strategy. If that interpretation is correct, it would help to explain why the incidence of Hindu–Muslim riots in these places dropped off after 1949, and remained at a low level for most of the following decade.

With the extinction of the princely polity, India lost a valuable systemic prop of communal harmony. Meanwhile, former princely subjects found themselves, as a result of integration, in an unfamiliar landscape. For long decades they had been accustomed to looking to their rulers for boons and to their local *darbars* for the provision of welfare services such as education and public health care. Virtually overnight, they had to get used to negotiating with much more remote and bureaucratic authorities for these same bounties—authorities based in far-off state capitals or in New Delhi. And if this transformation was not unsettling enough, they also had to come to terms with the jarring fact that they were no longer, legally speaking, subjects of discrete units known as princely states—Jaipuris or Bhopalis or Patialans—but citizens of a vastly greater national state called India. To be sure, all these adaptations took time; old habits are resilient. As Narain and Mathur remind us, even today regional loyalties in places like Rajasthan have not entirely broken out of their centuries old 'moulds'.[58] Certainly, people living in the former kingdoms were not going to reconfigure the way they imagined their surroundings simply because someone in the corridors of power far away had decided that different arrangements should apply! Nevertheless, Patel's 'bloodless revolution' did make a significant difference in this respect, albeit gradually. By eliminating state boundaries, it encouraged the former princely subjects to look outwards—encouraged them to seek and forge extended contacts with like-minded others. In turn, this out-reach slowly changed the ex-subjects' mental map of the world, sensitising them to the idea that complete personal fulfilment could only be achieved within the framework of those modern collectivities, 'community' and 'nation'. Through these processes, the erstwhile states, and their peoples, became more and more exposed to the forces of political modernity we have identified as productive of communal violence.   *TOO GENERALIZED A STATEMENT*

Starting over

The rapid rise of the Hindu and Sikh Right in India during the 1940s was brought to an abrupt halt by the furore unleashed by Gandhi's assassination. For two years thereafter the Right as an organised movement struggled, weighed down by guilt, Union repression, infighting over strategy and money problems caused by the drying-up of *darbari* patronage following the integration of the states. Meanwhile, Patel's death in December 1950 helped Nehru get the better of his Right-wing opponents within the Union government and the Congress Party. He convinced the Cabinet to support the enactment of a secularist Hindu Code Bill, persuaded the party to change its constitution to prohibit dual membership with other organisations (explicitly the RSS) and in September 1951 moved Purushottamdas Tandon out of the Congress presidency and forced another orthodox stalwart D.P. Mishra to resign from the party.

Arguably the Hindu Mahasabha never recovered from these reversals. Although it resumed political work in November 1948, the Sabha almost immediately shot itself in the foot by vetoing a WC recommendation to open up party membership to all Indian citizens 'irrespective of caste or religion'.[59] S.P. Mookherjee, its most popular leader in the absence of Savarkar, who had retreated into semi-retirement, resigned in protest, plunging the party into a succession-crisis. By December, new party President L.B. Bhopatkar was privately predicting a drubbing at the next parliamentary polls, due in December 1951, which in the event proved a fairly accurate forecast. (The party managed to capture just four Lok Sabha seats.) Since then it has struggled to win even a 5 per cent share of the popular vote in parliamentary elections.

But to the chagrin of the Nehru government, the Right refused to fade away. In the summer of 1950 Mookherjee came up with a proposal for the formation of a new Hindu political party, which he canvassed with a number of prominent Hindu activists in Delhi, Punjab and PEPSU, and with RSS leader M.S. Golwalkar. Although Golwalkar seems to have had some misgivings, the idea was generally well received and in the end even the RSS leader pledged assistance on the organisational side. The first units of the BJS, or Indian People's Party, were set up in mid-1951, and in October the BJS held its first national conference. Likewise, the Union failed utterly in its attempt to get rid of the RSS by declaring it an unlawful organisation. Highly disciplined and dedicated, the *swayamsevaks* by and large defied the ban and continued to drill; and when Golwalkar in December 1948 called on them to join in a mass *satyagraha* designed to force the Union government into rescinding the ban unconditionally, some 60,000 responded by courting arrest. Unnerved by the scale of this protest, New Delhi abandoned coercion in favour of diplomacy and re-opened negotiations with Golwalkar, which resulted in the ban being formally lifted in July 1949.

Formed only just in time to put up candidates, the BJS, not surprisingly, made little impression on the 1951–52 Lok Sabha polls, capturing just three seats and three per cent of the national vote. But thereafter the new party experienced steady growth, winning 14 seats in the parliamentary elections of 1962 and 35 in the 1967 polls, which saw a significant drop in popular support for the Congress; and in 1977 helped the Jayaprakash Narayan-led Janata Party coalition topple the Congress in elections that had been intended to provide retrospective legitimation for Indira Gandhi's Emergency. Meanwhile the creation, in April 1964, of the VHP, or World Hindu Congress, gave a voice and imparted an added sense of purpose to the cause of evangelical Hinduism. These precocious developments paved the way for the meteoric rise of the BJS's lineal successor, the BJP, as documented in Chapter 1.

More remarkably, the princes, too, survived the Union's retribution. Somewhat to the amusement of the country's nationalist newspaper columnists, a number of ex-princes and members of princely families, including Karni Singh of Bikaner, Anand Chand of Bilaspur, Narayan

Singh Deo of Patna, Daulatsinghji of Idar, Hanwant Singh of Jodhpur, Giriraj Singh, the brother of the maharaja of Bharatpur, and Jodhpur's uncle, Ajit Singh, cast their hats into the ring at the first general election of 1951. By 1957 the trickle had become a flood. According to William L. Richter's calculations, 43 members of princely families contested parliamentary and state assembly seats during the period 1957–60, 51 during the period 1961–66, and 75 during the period 1967–70.[60] Anecdotal evidence suggests that this high participation rate continues. Moreover, the ex-princes adapted to the hurl-burly world of electoral politics with considerable aplomb. Not only helped by Patel's financial generosity, but also well served by administrative experience, and ingrained habits of feudal deference, they have proved consistent vote-winners. Comparing data from the 1962 to 1967 general elections, Richter found that the effect of a party endorsing a princely candidate for a constituency was, first, to raise the overall voter turnout, and secondly, to increase the chances of that party emerging victorious from the contest.[61] At the 1951–52 polls the former maharaja of Jodhpur not only won his home Lok Sabha seat handsomely, with a more than 62 per cent vote share, in a head-to-head contest with his long-time nationalist adversary Jai Narain Vyas, but 31 Rajasthan Assembly seats into the bargain. In the 1962 Lok Sabha poll, Maharani Gayatri Devi of Jaipur set a new world record when she won her constituency by a margin of 175,000 votes. During the period 1951–71, Richter calculates, princely candidates enjoyed a success rate at the polls of almost 85 per cent— a remarkable record by any standards.[62] Of course this popularity with the voters made the ex-princes a very bankable political asset, and soon all the major parties, except the CPI, were lining up to secure their services. By the end of the 1950s the princely order found itself in a stronger bargaining position than any of the erstwhile rulers could have imagined possible early in 1948.

Initially, the princes for the most part entered politics with limited ambitions. While some doubtless saw a legislative career as a way of continuing to protect and serve those they had ruled over as subjects, most first-timers had a more pragmatic and self-interested motive for seeking political power: they hoped to use it to defend themselves, their families and their privy purses from possible spoliation at the hands of future national and state governments. Thus a sizeable number of former rulers in 1951 accepted tickets from the Congress, on the sensible ground that it was the governing party and was certain to be returned. (Several went on to hold portfolios in Congress state governments.)[63] Many others stood as independents.

Even in 1951, though, most of the princes felt more comfortable on the Right side of politics. A few, perhaps out of gratitude for past services rendered, signed up with the Mahasabha, which continued during the 1950s to campaign vigorously for the protection of princely 'rights'.[64] Rather more joined the BJS. The maharajas of Patna and Kalahandi in Orissa, finding none of the existing Rightist parties quite to their liking, founded their own, the Ganatantra Parishad, which was later merged with the Swatantra Party.

And as time went by this correlation increased. In 1959 a number of ex-rulers and consorts, including Bhagwat Singh, the maharana of Udaipur and Gayatri Devi of Jaipur, joined the newly formed Swatantra Party. Shortly afterwards the nawab of Malerkotla took up with the Akali Dal. In 1967 Harish Chandra, the former ruler of Jhalawar, left Congress for the Jana Sangh; with him, went the maharajas of Kotah and Bundi. About the same time the formidable rajmata of Gwalior finally ended her uneasy relationship with the ruling party when the MP Provincial Congress Committee refused to accept her slate of candidates for the upcoming elections. Rewa and Panna also took up with the BJS in 1970; and in 1971 the influential maharana of Udaipur switched to the BJS from Swatantra. Altogether six princes stood for parliament on a BJS ticket at the 1971 polls. Admittedly, there are several ways of reading this princely defection to the Right, and on close examination some defectors appear to have been moved more by personal or career-ist reasons rather than by ideology *per se*. When I asked the maharaja of Kotah why he deserted Congress in 1967, I hoped he would say something to the effect that he had come round to thinking the BJS had better policies for the country; instead he responded simply: 'because Jhalawar did'.[65] As noted above, Vijayaraje Scindia's departure followed a falling out with the provincial Congress high command. More importantly, the timing of the drift away from Congress had a lot to do with the Indira Gandhi government's decision to cancel the privy purses granted to the families of the covenanting rulers in 1948. On the other hand, politicians do not usually join parties they do not approve of. When they crossed over to the BJS, the princes knew exactly what it stood for and were not in the least deterred by that knowledge. Moreover, several of these new recruits went on to become very active party members. The rajmata, notably, became BJS vice-president and a founding member, in 1980, of the BJP national executive.

Political scientists interested in South Asian governance have long accepted that the British Raj left a significant imprint on the administrative framework of post-1947 India: for example, on the country's

1950 republican constitution, which was heavily influenced in its federal features by the GOI Act of 1935. More recently, scholars have begun to identify political continuities of a broader kind between pre- and post-1947 South Asia—similarities in the public behaviour of governing elites, similarities in strategic thinking (especially towards China and central Asia) and continuities in local and regional political culture. Few Indianists, these days, would seek to quarrel with S.N. Eisenstadt's once provocative assertion that 'within many of the New States, older traditional models of politics have tended to reassert themselves after the initial phase of independence'.[66]

With the coming of integration in 1948, most contemporaries thought that they had seen the last of Indian 'feudalism'. They were mistaken. Integration destroyed the princely states—but it stopped short of 'liquidating the Princes'.[67] Thanks in part to Sardar Patel's generosity, and in part to their unique social position, the princes, as a class, not only survived the abolition of the institution of monarchy but remained an influential political force, both within the regions they had formerly ruled over as kings, and more widely. In turn, the continuing importance of the princes as political actors served as a reminder of what had once been, and thereby helped to keep alive, in popular consciousness, memories of those former times.

6
Conclusion

Where the BJP rules, there are no riots.

The United Front's Ramakrishna Hegde, 1998

Communalism revisited

During the last half century, a very considerable amount of scholarly time and effort in South Asian studies has been spent on discovering the roots of collective ethno-nationalist violence involving Muslims and non-Muslims—'communal' violence in local parlance—in the region. In the process much has been learned both empirically and theoretically.

For instance, we now know a great deal about how Hindu–Muslim communal riots in South Asia begin and escalate. While no two riots are ever exactly alike, the vast majority involve disputes over public ritual and contests for access to, and control over the use of, sacred space. According to the *SCR* of 1930, the most frequent precipitating cause of riots in colonial times was the issue of Hindu processional music—specifically, whether Muslims were entitled to insist that the Hindus keep quiet in the vicinity of mosques. This is probably still the case.[1] Likewise, for all their ferocity, communal riots in India usually do not last long or spread very far from their point of origin. They are rarely spontaneous events and often exhibit signs of elaborate pre-planning. Although individuals join riot-crowds for various and often complex psychological reasons, once involved they generally follow the lead of shadowy manipulators whose motives are almost always in the largest sense political—men (riots are overwhelmingly a masculine domain) that Stanley Tambiah evocatively calls 'riot-captains'.[2]

However, while religious contestations are ubiquitous in India they do not always lead to riots. In late colonial princely north India, the focus

194

of this study, Hindus and Muslims were forever testing the boundaries of each other's civic tolerance, but these contestations rarely spilled over into physical violence. Most remained transient and verbal. Of the rest, many ended with one or both of the parties agreeing to back down; while others were resolved formally through the mediation of responsible community elders. The evidence from the states is that Indians in colonial times were keenly aware of the destructive potential of collective violence and strove to organise their religious practices in such a way as to minimise, as far as possible, the risk of it. The message I get from field studies is that this spirit persists in many South Asian villages and towns.[3] Communal rioting may now be an endemic phenomenon in the region; yet the incidence of such riots, in India at least, is scattered and erratic.

It is easy to understand why, despite their relative rarity, most scholarship on communalism has focussed on riot events rather than on the times and places where they are absent. Violence is dramatic and lends itself to a good story. Moreover, because riots are usually widely reported, often generating official inquiries and court cases, they offer glimpses into the deeper recesses of society. This makes them a handy analytical entry point for scholars looking to provide a 'thick' description of local social structures and processes. However, in concentrating on riot events, we miss what was, and is, typical about communal relations in South Asia. More importantly, we risk becoming blinded to the many ties that bind face-to-face communities in the region together. Indeed, one wonders whether our efforts to understand the phenomenon of communalism as it affects the region, worthy as they are, have not, ultimately, been directed towards the wrong goal.

Nevertheless, the work done on riots is important because it has forced scholars to contemplate the factors that transform some (but not all) everyday disputes over sacred space in South Asia into major confrontations. Why do some disputes lead to riots and others not? Why, despite this, has the number and severity of riots in the region continued to increase over time?

Several theories have been advanced over the years to account for the rise of communal conflict in South Asia. One, initially proposed by Indian nationalists, holds that the communal differences which emerged during the colonial period were a product of Machiavellian British 'divide-and-rule' policies—such as the government's concession of separate electorates to Muslims in the Morley–Minto Reforms of 1909. Another, the Marxist view, maintains that communal conflict—though a species of 'false consciousness'—is nonetheless, like the class struggle proper, rooted in poverty and deprivation and the monopoly control by the capitalist class of the means of production. A third theory is that communalism is a by-product of urbanisation and industrialisation. Conflicts about religious rituals and competitions for sacred space, the government's statistics show, are most likely to escalate into large-scale violence in big cities—or more precisely in their local neighbourhoods (*mohullas*). The correlation is explained, according to this view, by the fact that industrialised urban environments contain large numbers of lumpen elements, such as itinerant labourers and coolies, a cohort easily mobilised for action and one to a certain extent conditioned by the rigour and anomie of subaltern life to violence. Fourthly, and more broadly, Ashis Nandy and others have drawn attention to the role played by institutional modernisation in creating more efficient mechanisms for communal mass-mobilisation—print capitalism, schools, railways and the telephone—and a reason for it, in the shape of representative bodies and 'democratic' elections. Lastly, communalism has been seen as a substitute for older forms of social bonding disrupted by the onset of modernity.

The modernisation theory, in its several variants, now pretty much dominates the scholarly debate on communalism in South Asia. Yet while it seems to fit well with what we know of the larger diachronic picture, namely that since the nineteenth-century riots in the region have tended to increase steadily in number and severity, it fails to account for the sharp rises and falls that have occurred in the rate of growth during that time—for example, what Gopal Krishna has called the 'great divide' of 1964, when riots suddenly surged all over the country after a long period of relative quiescence.[4] Nor can modernisation, alone, adequately explain why comparable regions and cities appear to exhibit a markedly different propensity to communal violence. Ashutosh Varshney concludes his critique of the modernist argument by suggesting:

> If there are enough places that, in spite of modernity, do not have communal violence, and communities in such towns have found a way to solve or coexist with inter-religious problems, the explanatory focus will have to shift from modernity to...factors that make it possible for communities to live together...[5]

His point is well taken.

But then, until Varshney took the trouble to dig into the newspaper files, all we had to illuminate what was going on was annual Home

Ministry data that told us about the aggregate performance of the various states—the so-called riot table. There is still no easy way for scholars to learn what is currently happening in contemporary South Asia, city by city, on the communal front. And detailed information about riots in India during colonial times is equally scarce. In the absence of such data, it is perhaps understandable that scholars until now have concentrated on anatomising individual riots, or charting changes in the incidence and nature of communal conflict over time within particular regions or towns. And of course this scholarship has been immensely useful. Yet the glaring fact remains that there have been precious few attempts to study communalism in South Asia comparatively from a spatial perspective. Even the large and rather rich literature that has been produced over the last 30 years for the colonial period has been almost all focussed on the provinces of British India, and that too mostly on UP and Bengal.[6] As for the Indian princely states, which during the late colonial era collectively occupied about a third of the subcontinent and housed about two-fifths of its people—surely a significant segment— they have received virtually no attention from scholars of communalism.

The comparative data for the 1920s and 1930s on riot frequency and intensity as between princely and British India, summarised in the Introduction, demonstrates the benefits that comparative analysis can offer the study of communalism. There were only a handful of what could be termed serious Hindu–Muslim riot-episodes in the states during the decade 1920–30, and not many more for the one following (Table 1.4 and Figures 1.1 and 1.2). Yet in the provinces of British India—separated from the states by only the flimsiest of borders—it was quite another story. Militant communalism had been a fact of life in British India since the 1880s. During the 1920s there was a further surge in the level of communal violence—prompting worried government officials in New Delhi to canvass the views of provincial governments on ways to deal with what they now referred to as the 'communal problem' in the subcontinent. Why was the communal temperature in these two neighbouring parts of India so different? What kept the states relatively immune from communal violence?

Unimpressed by the grand theories that have been advanced to explain the 'growth' of communalism, Ashutosh Varshney has tried to pinpoint the factors and conditions that limit and mitigate its spread. His conclusion is that communal violence can be contained, even in unpromising indus-trial neighbourhoods, if they possess a flourishing civic life. Specifically, he points to the conciliating and bonding potentialities of community organisations that cut across religious and other ethnic divides; but in their absence, he suggests, the same result can be achieved through the simple expedient of people of different religions interacting in their daily lives. To Varshney almost anything that brings Hindus and Muslims together socially is valuable. He pins his hopes especially, though, on the gradual growth of more formalised exchanges, such as 'Hindu and Muslim families visiting one another, jointly participating in festivals, and allowing their children to play together in the neighborhood'.[7] The fact that such links are easier to build up in small, self-contained communities than in cities, 'which tend to be less interconnected and more anonymous', goes a long way to account, Varshney reckons, for the fact that communal riots in South Asia occur much more frequently and with far more devastating effect in urban centres than in villages.

Varshney's vision of the Indian little community as a holistic work-in-progress brings to mind work done, a generation ago by sociologist Victor Turner and social historians E.P. Thompson and George Rudé. In his classic anatomy of religious pilgrimage, Victor Turner observes that while pilgrims might start their journey as total strangers, they soon experience a spontaneous sense of bonding, a 'non-utilitarian experience of brotherhood and fellowship'. But that is just the beginning. Over time, members of the group come to realise the value of the bonds they have struck up—how they can assist in the mobilising and organising of the resources needed to keep them 'alive and thriving'—and look for ways to perpetuate and entrench them. By this means, Turner argues, fellowship—or as he prefers to characterise it, 'communitas'—eventually becomes a *normative* condition in society.[8] Thompson and Rudé, in their work on urban neighbourhoods in pre-modern Europe, start with a less optimistic premise about human nature, but their findings also lend support to the view that communities are sustained by mutual benefit. Studying English towns in the eighteenth century, Thompson discovered that people living there had a sharply developed sense of 'moral economy', at the core of which was a belief that the urban poor had an entitlement to basic subsistence.

Shortly after their foundation, the villages and urban *mohullas* that comprised the basic living spaces for the subjects of the north India princely states must have gone through a similar process to that envisaged by Victor Turner. At some point in time, each embryonic community would have been obliged to devise a liveable 'constitution' in order to maintain its viability. Not surprisingly, people living there in the early twentieth century retained little if any memory of these original compacts; nevertheless, they still displayed a robust sense of belonging to an integrated community and a clear understanding (as their petitions testify) of what was allowed, and not, within its boundaries. They may not have been able to point to a *Magna Carta* of municipal government, but they carried in their minds a staggering array of 'time-honoured' precedents that defined acceptable behaviour, which they did not hesitate to invoke in defence of their own public conduct or deploy in criticism of that of others. The village or the *mohulla* was their naturalised domain, and they felt an obligation to respect and help to enforce the unwritten conventions that allowed the community to co-exist.[9] On the other hand, they expected that correct behaviour in this respect entitled them to live and work and worship as full members of the community, free from molestation. Clearly there are shades, here, of Thompson's 'moral economy'; however, the communal consensus in early twentieth-century princely India seems to have extended more widely and covered more elements than in his case study. For our purposes, the crucial thing perhaps is that it appears to have embraced the accommodation of religious difference. On the evidence presented in Chapter 2, the villages and *mohullas* in the states were sites where people routinely and quite unself-consciously interacted across religious boundaries—in other words, they were places that possessed in larger measure the preconditions that, according to Varshney, serve to limit and in some cases prevent outbreaks of communal violence.

But these little communities also exhibited another residual tendency that Varshney oddly ignores, but which I believe played almost as important a role in keeping them free of communalism as their ethic of interdependence. Often given to rivalry and disputation, the inhabitants of the villages and *mohullas* of early twentieth-century princely north India invariably rallied together to present a common front against unwelcome outsiders—and one gets the distinct impression from the archival sources that in this period *most* non-kin outsiders were unwelcome—whether local *darbāri* officials or itinerant missionaries or nationalist politicians from British India. By the early twentieth century, communalism was already rampant in the provinces and especially in the large metropolitan capitals of the Raj; and in retrospect, one can see that the further spread of the virus was probably inevitable. Yet for a brief while, the innate hostility of the grass-roots communities towards outsiders helped to insulate them from contamination.   So WHAT ?

Face-to-face communities and neighbourhood networks were not, however, unique to princely India in the early twentieth century. They were ubiquitous in pre-modern Europe, too, as Thompson's work shows, and in other parts of Asia as James Scott has made clear in his studies of moral economy in the villages of colonial Southeast Asia. Arguably, they are a feature of all pre-modern societies; if so, one would expect to find them wherever pockets of the old order remained. Certainly, British India, which in the early twentieth century was very much a transitional society, contained many such places. Does this present a problem? Not really. As the statistics provided in Table 2.5 make clear, the princely states in this period were considerably less developed, on aggregate, than the provinces. They were more rural, their towns less industrialised and proletarian, and their populations less literate. What is more, most states remained at this point relatively isolated, cut off from one another, and from British India, by distance, topography and poor communication links. 'Sheltered for a long time from the great changes which have taken place in other parts of India, the States of the Central region have lived in isolation from those currents which have stirred or motivated the actions of Indian people outside the States', the Union government's Commissioner for CI observed perspicaciously in a report of 1948.[10] A liability in other ways, this remoteness served—in concert with the aforementioned spirit of parochialism—to delay the exposure of the peoples of the states to the unsettling influence of the political and ideological battles that were starting to divide Hindus and Muslims in British India.

The hypothesis that the backwardness of the princely states helped to insulate them against communalism is further confirmed by the way events unfolded during the period under study. Between 1900 and 1940, the isolation of the states was gradually broken down. This opened them to penetration by the heady new doctrines of ethnicity and nationality that were doing the rounds of the provinces. As these subversive ideas took root, first in the cities and towns on major railway routes, then in other cities and finally, to a limited extent, in the countryside, people accustomed to operating as functioning members of small localities and thinking of themselves first and foremost as subjects of particular states, began to find points of contact with groups of imaginary others outside the bounds of their lived communities and the borders of their states, groups which were increasingly defined in terms of religious affiliation. In turn this identification of nationality with religion reinforced the tendency, always present in Islam and at work in Hindu thought since the late nineteenth century, towards orthodoxy and the eradication of syncretism. By the 1930s these trends had begun to affect grass-roots relations between Hindus and Muslims in princely India.

Concurrently, but particularly from the 1930s, British Indian communal organisations and political parties began to take an active interest in the states in ways that greatly exacerbated the communal situation there also. At the most basic level, their involvement provided a pool of battle-hardened zealots eager to take to the streets for religious causes. Groups like the Punjabi Ahrars turned what might otherwise have been small-scale communal events—such as the MYA agitation in Srinagar in 1931—into much more extensive and bloody ones. More importantly, perhaps, the intervention of the communal parties had the effect of turning particularist disputes over religious space and ritual into issues about the oppression of minorities by majorities, which in turn linked them to other similar disputes elsewhere, as when Sheikh Abdullah threatened in 1933 to 'make an Alwar' of Kashmir.[11] The process was similar to the one that Tambiah has identified in his examination of communal riots in post-colonial South Asia, which he labels 'transvaluation'. It had the twofold effect of making subsequent localised confrontations between Hindus and Muslims in the states appear more significant than they actually were, and of making it much harder for the parties immediately concerned to settle their differences amicably without loss of face.

Finally, in the early 1940s, the princely states of north India began to experience some of the communal costs of economic development. Canal irrigation projects and a war-led expansion of industry in the states attracted a flood of economic immigrants, many of them Muslims. Delicate communal balances in the cities of princely north India were upset, which awakened the slumbering paranoia of local Hindu elites in the same way that revelations of Muslim population growth in British India had done earlier. More importantly, the new arrivals put a strain on the 'moral' equilibrium or consensus of their adopted neighbourhoods—the fount of their communitas. Although many undoubtedly brought a sense of moral equation with them from their natal places, they had no immediate way of tapping into the local code—that was something one only learned by living there. Lacking the code, they tended, initially, to treat everybody in their village or *mohulla* not closely related to them with suspicion, which, inviting a like response, delayed their integration into the community. Last but not least, many of the migrants who came to the states in this period were labourers and factory hands from the cities of the Punjab and UP—provinces that had long been awash with communal propaganda. Toting this cultural baggage, they tended to make for awkward and troublesome neighbours.

As the princely states of north India developed economically and opened up to the world, their communal situation progressively deteriorated. From the early 1930s, Hindu–Muslim riots proliferated yearly, spreading across the region. This grim march culminated, during 1947, in large-scale massacres of Muslims in Jammu, Mewat and the states of east Punjab.

It is not a progression. It is episodic, a very important difference. Also regional.

The case of the states therefore lends support to the argument that, other things being equal, the likelihood of communal conflict is enhanced by modernisation.   A MEANINGLESS GENERALIZATION.

Yet it was not so much less developed character of the states that set them apart from the provinces (which, as observed above, also contained large pockets of 'underdevelopment') as their style of governance. By the early twentieth century the British Raj had evolved into a quasi-responsive government. Bureaucracy still held sway, but it was held in check by a separate and reasonably independent judiciary, public opinion and an organised national movement, and ultimately by the authority of Parliament. Especially at the provincial level, representative forms of government were starting to intrude. The princely states, on the other hand—certainly in north India—remained very much as they had always been—autocratic monarchies. Did this make a difference? Was the monarchical polity of the states better suited to managing communal disputation than the bureaucratic polity of the provinces?

It is almost an axiom of scholarship on Hindu–Muslim riots in post-colonial India that governments can and periodically do stir the communal pot, either with a view to improving their chances in elections or in the hope of distracting the attention of the public from their administrative failings. Typically, a recent analysis of Hindu–Muslim disturbances in Surat concludes: 'To put it plainly, it was state-sponsored rioting.'[12] More particularly, a number of studies have pointed the finger at the (inevitable) involvement of the police in riots. The perception—shared by many Muslims—is that the police often intervene in disputes on the Hindu side. What has not been looked at so much, though—since the question does not really arise in the context of post-independence India—is the nature of the ruling polity. Varshney, for example, concludes that the role of governance cannot be an important variable, for while 'the political system and institutions are the same right across the country' different parts of India 'tend to have very different patterns of ethnic violence and peace'.[13] Nevertheless, while eager to play down the role of governance as a factor in riots, Varshney accepts that partisan governments have in the past fuelled communal conflict—for example, Hyderabad under the last nizam; and he allows that it lies within the capacity of states to curb communal conflict if they are so minded.[14] This latter point marks a significant departure from most scholarly interventions in this area, yet there is solid empirical evidence in its favour—possibly as much as there is for the stock view that governments invariably act self-interestedly. 'There clearly have been incidents in Bijnor which generated intense feelings,' the Jeffreys observe, 'but

[margin note:] NOT ENOUGH ATTENTION TO THIS.

successive district magistrates seem to have been willing (and able) to control potentially explosive events.'[15]

Likewise, the riot statistics for the princely states and the British provinces summarised in Chapter 1 provide *prima facie* support for the view that governments matter. No other explanation can really account for the very marked divergence in riot propensity between these thoroughly interlocked parts of India that the figures display. This global finding is borne out, locally, by the case of the riot-prone city of Ajmer—culturally an integral part of the princely region of Rajputana, but separately administered during the colonial period by a British CC. Ajmer was the first town in Rajputana to blow up, communally speaking, in the modern period, and the only one to explode three times during the first half of the twentieth century.

I argue the point further in Chapter 2, which looks at ways in which the monarchical polity of the states may have made a difference. I suggest there were three. First, although the states were not, properly speaking, autocracies, at least in the period covered by this study, compared to the British-style governments of the provinces, the princely *darbārs* were much less constricted, in the maintenance of civil order, by bureaucratic inertia or interference from the judiciary, which in the states was invariably a subservient arm of government. Secondly, because they were hereditary kings reputedly connected to the gods, the rulers were able to exert a restraining personal influence over their subjects in a way that the 'secularist' British administrators could not. They were also, in their own right, 'natural' communal leaders, widely looked up to for guidance. As a police chief of Patiala, accused by the local *praja mandal* of favouring Sikhs over Hindus, declared passionately in 1948: the state 'has inseparable ties with the Sikh Religion. Nowhere else in a religion is found such a precedent, where a prophet or Guru has owned a royal family as exists in Sikh religion in respect of Phulkian States, which are situated... in...the home land of the Sikhs.'[16] Generally, the Indian princes used their charismatic authority to promote the ideal of religious toleration and often reinforced this by co-opting members of minority communities as senior advisers. Thirdly, *darbāri* culture conditioned the minorities to accept restrictions on their civic rights. While it warmly embraced the principle of freedom of worship, the polity of the princely states was not even-handed. Almost everywhere, *darbāri* administration privileged the community of the ruler—privileged it in secular matters of employment and education and in the matter of public religious rituals, such as processions and sacrifices—which in turn nurtured the perception that subjects who did not belong to the community of the ruler could expect

BUT WHAT ARE THE IMPLICATIONS OF THIS?

little sympathy from the authorities if they tried to disturb the hierarchy by challenging the dominant majority's control over sacred public space. Theoretically, the latter could have protested their implicit relegation to a position of inferiority and tried to challenge it in the streets. But until the 1940s, knowing that the system was stacked against them, they mostly kept any sense of grievance they may have felt to themselves. Ultimately, I believe, it was this self-policing that kept the states in the early twentieth century free from serious communal violence.

Peter van der Veer perceptively observes: 'When a pluralist state can no longer project its transcendent, arbitrational image, conflicts can only be resolved through violence.'[17] Over time, the gradual introduction by the *darbārs* of constitutional reforms, and their adoption of new pre-emptive strategies to ward off the threat to their position posed by the rising forces of Indian nationalism under the leadership of the INC, undermined the effectiveness of the above monarchical constraints on communal conflict. As the states liberalised, their freedom of action in the public domain was reduced. This made it harder for them to coerce communal malcontents. Paradoxically, liberalisation also eroded the princes' legitimacy. Although many rulers continued to speak out nobly and courageously against communal violence, as time went by, fewer among their subjects paid heed. In a sad, reflective speech to mark the end of his reign in 1948, the raja of Phaltan recalled that religious pluralism had been a watchword in Maharashtra since the time of its seventeenth-century ruler Shivaji. He went on:

> I too in my humble sphere used to carry on the State administration in the same way... But, though this [pluralist] policy of the Durbar found favour with the people of my State for a number of years, I must admit, with regret, that there has been of late a noticeable change in the attitude of, at any rate, a section of the public.[18]

By 1948 the Indian princely states were crumbling states, still capable of lashing out against their perceived internal and external enemies, but no longer possessed of sufficient authority simply to *command* respect for the rights of communal others.

Some rulers, however, had already given up trying. Worried about what might happen to them if and when the British finally departed the subcontinent, the princes began, in the 1920s, to cautiously put out feelers to provincial political leaders and parties they judged to be sympathetic to the states and the system of monarchy. Initially they focussed their efforts on trying to strike a bargain with the more moderate leaders of the INC; but after 1940, realising this was a fairly hopeless pursuit, they turned their attention to the communal parties. In 1941, Patiala held out an olive branch to the Akali Dal's Master Tara Singh. The following year a clutch of north Indian Hindu rulers opened negotiations with the Hindu Mahasabha. Shortly afterwards, well-connected chamber secretary Mir Maqbool Mahmud put Bhopal in touch with the League. These approaches were well received: in part because the communal parties compared to the Congress were weak and sorely in need of the kind of material support and influence in high places that the *darbars* could provide, but mainly because they saw in the majoritarian polity of the states a reflection of their cultural vision for the future Indian nation. Deals were struck.

In the short term at least the hook-up with the communal parties proved of considerable benefit, politically, to the states concerned. Communally, though, its results were disastrous, for it opened the door to the entry into the northern states during the early 1940s of a phalanx of Sabhite, Akali, Leaguer and Sanghite militants, whose rabid warnings against the 'plots' being hatched by communal Others predictably incited a bellicose response from lumpen elements in the towns.

By this time, moreover, many of the states had started to introduce representative institutions. The arrival of elections not only gave a spur to the establishment there of political parties, but made it necessary for these nascent parties to find and connect with a friendly constituency. Communal propaganda served this purpose well, for it was not dependent on hard-to-keep promises. Yet minorities, Muslims in particular, seeing in these developments the thin end of the wedge of democracy, felt uneasy. Vulnerable to the tyranny of numbers, they closed ranks and set up community organisations—*anjumans*—for self-protection. With Hindu communalist parties in the lists, and with the Muslims suspicious of the whole process, elections in the states soon became regular occasions YES. for communal riots. By the mid-1940s, populist violence had become widespread across the region.

Communalism, then, appears to be, in large measure, a by-product of NO. modernisation—perhaps especially of political modernisation. It may be thought of, therefore, as one of the many societal banes that afflict modern life, like stress, congestion and crime—things we would rather do without, but which we have accepted as part and parcel of modern living. It is tempting to suggest—pushing the argument a step further— that communal conflict is one of the social costs that we *must* pay, if we want to continue to enjoy the fruits of technological progress and liberal democracy. VERY BAD CONCLUSION,

But is communalism an *inevitable* outcome of modernisation? Paul Brass's recent work on Aligarh suggests that it is not—and so does the experience of the erstwhile north Indian princely states. Communalism is not something born of nature; it is a societal construct. So, too, is communal violence a product of human agency and action. People take on identities that suit them. They can be active or passive participants in communal affairs. When a riot breaks out they can join it or stay away. Even more power in this respect rests with communal elders or charismatic opinion-makers, such as the princes were in colonial times (and their descendants perhaps still are today).

What this study of communalism in princely India highlights, though, is the extent to which communalism and communal violence can be constrained (or not) by the discourses, policies and acts of governments. Authoritarian governments, of the princely type, appear better placed to keep the lid on plebeian violence than democratic ones. Managed pluralism is a much more difficult policy option for democratic governments locked into the competitive business of vote-winning, which requires, these days, the active appeasement of numerous ethnic constituencies. Significantly, in this context, the incidence of communal riots dropped sharply during the period of Indira Gandhi's Emergency.

Nevertheless, as Varshney's work has shown, the spread of the communal virus remains, as it was in the colonial period, erratic. Some places have a history of communal riots; others have managed to stay almost riot-free. Even in 1947, when much of north India, including a number of princely states, went up in flames, some states stayed quiet—largely because their *darbārs* chose to be guided by the traditional obligations of *rājadharma*, and actively enforced the peace. Kishengarh was one: 'due to the wise statesmanship and foresightedness of His Highness the Maharaja', a petition of the state's prominent citizens proudly proclaimed, '...there have been no disturbances or trouble here'.[19] Moreover, to the extent that trouble did come to the states, generally it came by way of external agency, in the shape of Sikh *jathas* or organised cadres belonging to the RSS, or posses of vengeful refugees, rather than as a result of a breakdown of communitas at the grass roots. 'There was trouble in the village', a Hindu survivor of the Mewat tragedy remembers, 'but generally it was not the people who lived in our village—the Muslims—who tried to attack us, but...the Muslims who came from outside.'[20]

Deeply embedded traditions are not easily eradicated. Although the states by the end of the colonial period were no longer the havens of communal co-existence they had been 30 years earlier, they remained, in aggregate—even at the height of the partition riots—more peaceful

BACK 8 FORTH —
WISHY-WASHY

than the British-ruled parts of the country. When the American political scientist Irene Tinker-Walker arrived in the newly integrated state of Rajasthan in 1951 to monitor the first general elections there, she expected that 'this backward and highly religious area' would be awash with religious dissentions and conflicts. She found none: 'militant communalism', the puzzled writer concluded, was 'absent'.[21] Modernisation may have weakened the *darbārī* culture of pluralism, but it had not managed to obliterate it.

The tradition continues. Published Home Ministry data indicates that those parts of the Indian Union forged wholly, or largely, out of the territories of former princely states—MP, the Saurashtra region of Gujarat, Rajasthan, Himachal Pradesh (HP) (and for that matter, although it falls outside the scope of this study, Kerala)—have experienced proportionately less ethno-communal violence, over the past 60 years, than those that once comprised British India.[22] Kerala's good record is usually put down to Communism. MP's and Rajasthan's are generally ascribed to their relative 'backwardness'. These explanations overlook the crucial point that before 1948–49—and for a century and more before that—these parts [NO,] of the subcontinent had a monarchical polity that actively fostered communal co-existence.

Yet as Tables 1.1 and 1.2 show, Gujarat, Rajasthan, HP and MP have been happy hunting grounds since the 1960s for the BJS/BJP. This brings us back to the paradox of Middle India.

Legacies

Eisenstadt claims that New States often incorporate, within their institutional and organisational frameworks, older models of politics. Today, few scholars of modern South Asia would quibble with this judgement. It has long been accepted that the Indian Republic owes much in respect of its institutions, laws and procedures to its predecessor, the British Raj. More recently, scholars such as Pamela Price have remarked on the persistence of kingly (or perhaps one should say *darbārī*) styles of behaviour among modern Indian political elites [WHAT ABOUT] operating in what is a supposedly democratic arena. Yet the extent of [QR G?] the specific political legacy of the princely states remains, despite William Richter's pioneering work on princely politicians, understudied and unappreciated. In particular, little attention has been given to the legacies left by the *darbārī* culture. By way of rounding off the narrative, I want to draw attention to some of the ways in which I believe the princely monarchical past has imprinted itself on the post-colonial

Indian political system, particularly in those parts I have designated Middle India.

As we remarked in Chapter 5, the integration of the Indian princely states into the Indian Union in the late 1940s did not, contrary to what is commonly believed, and as Sardar Patel boasted disingenuously at the time, amount to a 'revolution'. Certainly, Patel and Menon oversaw big changes. The princes were forced to step down from their *gaddis*, and most of the states ceased after 1948 to exist as separate administrative units. Nevertheless, parts of the old order survived. In particular, there was a significant continuity in terms of personnel. Most former *darbāri* bureaucrats were kept on, albeit sometimes in different jobs. Generally what happened was that 'the ex-princely *diwans*...became collectors and deputy collectors', while 'lesser executive officers became *mamlatars*, *mahalkaris* (sub-district revenue officers) and so on'.[23] More importantly, the former rulers, for the most part, continued to play an active political and pastoral role within their erstwhile domains. Ironically, this latter 'neo-feudal' transition was given a significant head start by the Congress government, which on Patel's recommendation granted the princes handsome tax-fee stipends and put pressure on the Part B states to allow the princes to continue to 'go out in procession for worship' in their former capitals—a concession that helped to keep them in the public eye and maintain their hold on the affections of the religious masses.[24]

The entrenched wealth and residual charisma of the ex-rulers ensured that they would remain powerful regional brokers. But these same assets also set them up nicely to stake out a claim in the new arena of electoral politics. In the event most who stood won—handsomely. According to William Richter's analysis, princely candidates at the second, third and fourth general elections captured a higher percentage of the vote than non-princely candidates, won by higher margins than non-princely winners and attracted additional voters to the polls. Not surprisingly, most Indian political parties have been only too happy to include ex-rulers and other princely family members on their tickets—even their once harsh critic, the Congress.

Nevertheless, while the princes have been, on the whole, pragmatic in the distribution of their electoral favours, since the 1960s they have gravitated to the Right side of politics. Of recent times, they have clustered under the banner of the BJP.

Despite Richter's honest scepticism on the point,[25] it is clear from the work of Bruce Graham and others that the Right's ability to call on the services of increasing numbers of princely candidates gave it a significant electoral lift. As Graham points out, the BJS achieved its best-ever parliamentary results, in the Kota and Gwalior constituencies in the 1967 poll, fielding high-profile princely candidates.[26] Additionally, the Right's access to the patronage and endorsement of powerful princely families helped many of its non-princely candidates get over the line—as when Hanwant Singh masterminded a rout of Congress in the Jodhpur division in the 1952 Rajasthan Assembly elections, and Man Singh gave the royal nod on the eve of the 1967 poll in the Jaipur City seat to an aspiring Rajput politician named Bhairon Singh Shekhawat, telling the voters he was a 'good man'.[27] In particular the BJS benefited greatly in this way from its pact with the Scindias, which delivered no less than 23 Vidhan Sabha seats in and around Gwalior in the MP election of 1967.

Princely support helped the Rightist parties entrench themselves in the constituencies carved out of their former domains. Even during the so-called 'one party dominance' period in India, Congress struggled to win in Rajasthan and MP. In the 1952 Vidhan Sabha poll in Rajasthan, the Congress polled 38.8 per cent of the vote and won only 74 out of the 153 contested seats—barely enough to put it in office. It recovered in 1957 but again fell over the line in 1962. Similarly, in MP, the Congress vote share during the 1950s and 1960s hardly ever exceeded 40 per cent— well below its national average. On the other hand, parties like the Swatantra and the BJS while never really managing to take off nationally, established significant bridgeheads in some of the former princely regions, such as Orissa, Gujarat and MP. In the 1962 Rajasthan poll, Swatantra won 36 seats and 17.2 per cent of the vote. At the 1967 Assembly election in Gujarat, it won 66 seats and 38.2 per cent of the vote. As for the BJS, over a third of the party's 116 Assembly victories in 1962, and nearly half of its 35 Lok Sabha victories in 1967 were won in MP. To a large extent this regional pattern of Hindu-Right voting has continued under the BJS's lineal successor—the BJP.[28]

Again, the princely connection seems self-evident. Yet the fact that these areas have produced such a plethora of senior BJS and BJP leaders—from Atal Behari Vajpayee and Lal Kishanchand Advani downwards—suggests that there is more to this connection than simply the pulling power of princely candidates. Could it be that the real explanation for the consistent support tendered to Rightist parties by the voters of Middle India lies in the political values imparted to the region by centuries of *darbāri* rule?

Election-watchers in India have long been intrigued by the success-rate of the Right in the former princely regions of India, but early commentators were content to offer somewhat simplistic explanations that turned on the hypothesis of their 'backwardness'. 'In the State of Rajasthan the "value pattern" of the people is traditional. Besides illiteracy and poverty, there is a strong hold of religion over the masses', wrote C.P. Bhambhri in 1963.[29] As Richter has shown, the claim of backwardness is hard to sustain, given that Middle India was not, even in the 1950s, significantly more backward than other parts of north India where the Right has done less well. Nevertheless the point about tradition remains moot and it has recently been canvassed again by Rob Jenkins. According to Jenkins, the success achieved by the BJP in Rajasthan has been due to a successful wedding of 'nationalism to regionalism'. The party co-opted a 'pre-existing regional identity—one heavily imbued with what has been called the Rajput ethic—and reinvented it for its own purposes'.[30] Following Iqbal and Mathur, he locates the core of this identity in the hegemonic values bequeathed to the region by its long history of Rajput governance.

Jenkins himself provides numerous examples, drawn from his personal observations of BJP electoral campaigns in the state, of 'Sangh Parivar foot soldiers' invoking 'fragments of history for partisan purposes'. Interestingly, the stuff of this propaganda, Jenkins shows, usually involved stories—some true, others false, almost all highly coloured—that celebrated the liberality, magnanimity and inclusiveness of the old regime and its Rajput kings. He describes the approach as one of 'crudely-packaged hagiography'.[31] But the BJP was not the first party to selectively evoke the princely past in a search for votes. Swatantra, as Wood remarks, made considerable use of this strategy in the 1967 Gujarat poll: 'During the election campaign...an attempt was made to evoke nostalgia for the princely past and to capitalize on residual loyalties.'[32] There seems little doubt that nostalgic folk-memories of *darbāri* rule, skilfully co-opted and reshaped, have contributed in a major way to the Right's electoral successes in Middle India.

But if the princely era has helped to shape the electoral choices of post-colonial Indian voters, and thus, indirectly, the nature and political affiliation of the country's post-colonial governors, has it also affected, more directly, the policy agenda? Specifically, has princely polity influenced the policies of the Right?

Iqbal and Mathur, while noting the important role that ex-rulers have played within the non-Congress opposition in Rajasthan, conclude that they have exerted a moderating influence on the Right's promotion of 'revivalist interpretations of Hindu orthodoxy'.[33] At first sight this conclusion is hard to reconcile with the stridently evangelical postures adopted by some of the aforementioned princely politicians. Consider, for example, Rajmata Scindia—an extremely pious person, she had at one stage thought of exchanging the world of politics for the reclusive life of the *sannyasin*.[34] She regularly sought guidance from Hindu *gurus*. Not surprisingly, on entering politics, Vijayaraje at once adopted a strongly fundamentalist and communalist policy line, telling a joint meeting of MP and Rajasthan VHP units in 1968, 'The greatest need of the time is to make people understand the true meaning of Hindutva and to carry its glorious light to every corner of the world.'[35] Indeed, the Rajmata's hard-line stance became still more pronounced after the BJS's reincarnation as the BJP, when she concerted with Murli Manohar Joshi to put an end to the new party's brief flirtation with 'Gandhian socialism'.[36] Vijayaraje, it is true, was unusually religious. Yet other princely recruits such as Panna and Jhalawar were not far behind her in advertising their commitment to Hindutva. As Jaffrelot observes, 'some notables and even some princes proved to be deeply committed to Hindu nationalist ideology. In certain cases, they embodied the qualities of the most dedicated cadres of the RSS.'[37] Likewise, many ex-rulers have been warm supporters of the VHP. Those who have been closely associated with that organisation include Karan Singh, son of the last ruler of Kashmir, the maharaja of Jhalawar and Bhagwat Singh of Udaipur, who served a term as VHP president.

Moreover, just as the Mahasabha justified its support for the princes, in part, on the perception that they were connected with the ancient god-kings and thus with the divine, so the Sangh Parivar, since the 1980s, has subtly and effectively infused these elements into its propaganda. But just as Savarkar once did, the Parivar reserves its most fulsome plaudits for the King of Nepal, and for a similar reason: Nepal is an independent and avowedly Hindu kingdom. For instance, in 1983 the VHP organised an *ektamaja yājna* in Nepal in honour of the royal family. Adorning the *rath* was a picture of the king accompanied by a sign, which read: 'I want to keep Nepal and [sic] Ideal Land Of Hindus.'[38]

On the other hand, many of the former rulers and princely family members, in keeping with the traditions of *rājadharma*, have come out strongly in support of religious toleration—in particular, toleration of Muslims. In 1964, Maharaja Jai Man Singh publicly excoriated the local BJS for playing the communal card in a bid to carry the Jaipur City municipality. And in 1989 when riots broke out in the city in the wake of a BJP election victory, his son 'went out in his car to where the trouble was, in an attempt to stop it'.[39] Likewise, politicians in the former princely regions—Right and non-Right alike—have frequently invoked the salutary example set by the *darbārs* in this respect. Setting out the new Rajasthan government's policy towards Muslims, Chief Minister Jai Narayan Vyas in 1951 'advised the people to maintain the traditions of brotherhood and fellowship established by many States before integration'.[40] BJP stalwart Bairon Singh Shekhawat has made similar statements.

At first glance, these positions are hard to reconcile. It would appear that some princely families inherited different pasts from others. Yet while the past is always subject to selective interpretation, I would suggest that the differences in emphasis in this case arose because the tradition of princely pluralism itself—as the discussion of *rājadharma* in Chapter 2 attempted to show—was deeply ambiguous about minorities, at once inclusive and majoritarian. The point may be illustrated further with reference to the princely impact on the evolution of the core BJS/BJP ideology of *Hindutva*.

If one compares what V.D. Savarkar said about Hindutva in the 1920s and 1930s with what the BJP polemicists were saying about it in the 1980s and 1990s, it is immediately apparent that the idea has undergone a subtle but important shift during the past half century. In his 1922 essay, Savarkar drew a sharp line between the communities he felt belonged, as Indian citizens, and the rest. In the first group were Hindus, Jains, Sikhs and even Parsis, in the second Indian Christians, Eurasians—and, most particularly, Muslims. Muslims, he asserted, might claim, with Hindus, 'a common Fatherland and . . . an almost pure Hindu blood and parentage', but they could not be recognised as Hindus since they had 'ceased to own Hindu civilization (Sanskriti) as a whole'. 'They belong, or feel they belong', he went on (in a vein uncannily redolent of Jinnah's 'two-nation' speech of 1940) 'to a cultural unit altogether different from the Hindu one.' 'Their heroes and hero worship, their fairs and their festivals, their ideals and their outlook on life, have now ceased to be common with ours.'[41] In his December 1937 speech to the Mahasabha's annual session, Savarkar made a similar point but put it even more bluntly: 'there are two nations in the main', he declared, 'the Hindus and the Moslems . . . there are two antagonistic nations living side by side in India'.[42] Following this line, the Mahasabha's 1934 constitution, re-affirmed in 1948, stated that membership was open only to Hindus (although the term was generously interpreted to include anyone who professed a religion of Indian origin). By contrast the BJS from the start opened its doors to anyone willing to abide by its rules and principles; and the party's election manifesto of 1957 spoke inclusively of 'nationalizing' the country's non-Hindu minorities by 'inculcating in them the ideas of Bharatiya culture'.[43] And this more liberal interpretation of *Hindutva* has carried over into the discourse of the BJP. As senior BJP leader Vijay Kumar Malhotra put it in February 1996: '*Hindutva* and Indian nationhood

LIBERAL?

are synonymous terms. All those living in the country are Bharatiyas or Hindus. There is no contradiction between the two.'[44]

The shift has been driven partly by the BJP's determination to win government. When Vinayak Savarkar wrote *Hindutva* he was a prophet preaching in the political wilderness. Prophets are by nature inflexible. More surprisingly, he remained so even after he became in 1937 an orthodox politician. But then, the Mahasabha was a party resigned never to winning an election. As bit players, Savarkar and company had little to lose by sticking rigidly to principle. By contrast, the leaders of the BJS and especially of the BJP from the start had their eyes fixed on political power. This meant adapting the party policy to the aspirations not merely of middle-of-the-road voters, but of voters from backward castes traditionally aligned to the Congress. It meant courting Muslims. That the BJP especially has been fairly successful in roping in these groups is to a large extent due to its re-packaging of Hindutva. But this has in turn created problems for the BJP leadership with the other members of the Sangh Parivar. As the *Indian Express* noted in February 1998, 'the saffron brigade... has been perplexed by the moderate statements of the party's prime minister-in-waiting and a series of political compromises'.[45] In an effort to rebuild these crucial bridges, the party infused its 1998 election manifesto with a strong dose of Hindutva rhetoric. But the adverse speculation continued. During late 1998 and 1999, RSS conclaves repeatedly criticised the BJP-led Union government. The tenor of these criticisms was that the Sangh Parivar had not made the kind of gains it had expected from the BJP exercising power at the centre. Another critic, former BJP Chief Minister of Uttar Pradesh Kalyan Singh, remarked acidly in 1999 that there appeared to be 'two Congress parties' functioning in the Lok Sabha.[46]

However, the shift on Hindutva began well before 1995, in fact it was already underway when the BJS became the BJP. This suggests that it sprang from much deeper roots than the need to conciliate a set of unruly coalition partners. As I read it, the process of reinterpretation began in the 1960s, when the BJS inducted a number of ex-princes and princely family members—men and women who had grown up surrounded by *darbari* culture. These carriers of the culture of the erstwhile states—Jhalawar, Panna, Udaipur, and above all, perhaps, the Rajmata of Gwalior—brought to the BJS a vision of the state as a powerful, paternalistic institution with the moral and physical capacity to enforce a Hindu majoritarian compact that would, at the same time, minimise social violence by guaranteeing the right of non-Hindus to reside and work and worship in their local communities. That is exactly the vision of the state that the BJP is currently trying to sell the Indian people. As party leader Balraj Madhok put it in 1987: 'To recognize India as primarily a Hindu Nation if not State, might give the majority enough security to be generous and tolerant towards the largest minority than it has been in recent years.'[47]

And it is a vision that, until recently, many, if not most, Indian Muslims have glumly embraced for want of practical alternatives. Even the Indian branch of the Jamaat-e-Islami advised its followers in 1960 that it would be 'terribly suicidal' for them 'to strive for some communal rights'.[48] Indian Muslims are comfortable with the idea of a strong state willing to protect them—thus their consistent support for the Congress when it was the dominant party. This being so, the Muslims living in the Union—like the Muslims who, before 1948, lived in the princely states—have been prepared, for the most part, to accept a less privileged social position as a tradeoff for the majority community's tolerance and the state's protection.

Fittingly, perhaps, the humble driver of Lal Kishanchand Advani's 'chariot' in the *rath yātrā* of 1990 was—a Muslim.

Rulers come and go. But the administrative legacy of decades and centuries is not easily undone. Although it is now approximately 60 years since little kings governed in India, grass-roots communal relationships—especially in places like Gujarat, Rajasthan and MP—still bear the imprint of courtly examples and policies.

Notes

1   Introduction

1. Ger Duijzings, 'The End of a "Mixed" Pilgrimage', in the *International Institute for the Study of Islam in the Modern World Newsletter*, Vol. 3 (July 1999), p. 1.
2. Key Robinson essays on this theme can be read in his *Islam and Muslim History in South Asia* (New Delhi: OUP, 2000).
3. The progenitor of the thesis was Karl Deutsch. See his *Nationalism and Social Communication: An Inquiry into the Formation of Nations* (Cambridge, Mass., 2nd edn, 1966). Its leading exponent in the South Asian context has been Paul Brass. See his *Language, Religion and Politics in North India* (Cambridge, 1974), Ch. 1; and 'A Reply to Francis Robinson', in the *Journal of Commonwealth and Comparative Politics*, 15 (1977), pp. 231–4.
4. For a brief history of the term, see Gyan Pandey, *The Construction of Communalism in Colonial North India* (Delhi, 1992), Ch. 1.
5. Presidential address by Sir Muhammad Iqbal to the annual session of the All-India Muslim League, December 1930, in Sir Maurice Gwyer and A. Appadorai (eds), *Speeches and Documents on the Indian Constitution 1921–47* (Bombay, 1957), Vol. 2, p. 439.
6. B. Anderson, *Imagined Communities: Reflections on the Origin and Spread of Nationalism* (London, 1983).
7. Paul R. Brass, *The Production of Hindu–Muslim Violence in Contemporary India* (Seattle, 2003), p. 70.
8. The propaganda of the BJP avows a brand of Hinduism that gives prominence to Rama and deities associated with him such as Hanuman. Ironically, Advani's *rath* was more evocative of the image of Krishna than of Rama, since in both major versions of the *Ramāyana* Rama fights on foot. It is the demon-king, Ravana, who, in the epics, fights from a chariot. See Shail Mayaram, 'Communal Violence in Jaipur', in *Economic and Political Weekly*, 13–20 November 1993, pp. 2529–30.
9. Ibid., p. 2529.
10. Susan B. Devalle, 'Social Identities, Fundamentalism and Politics in India', in David N. Lorenzen (ed.), *Bhakti Religion in North India: Community, Identity and Political Action* (Albany, 1995), pp. 315–16.
11. Hafiz Nomani, quoted in *The Times of India*, 12 January 1998. For another defence of the BJP's record on the score of riots, see Prakash Nanda, 'Trial by Secularists: BJP Perpetually in the Dock', in *The Times of India*, 22 January 1998.
12. Ashutosh Varshney, *Ethnic Conflict and Civic Life: Hindus and Muslims in India* (2nd edn, New Haven, 2002), p. 98.
13. This is one of several issues in respect of communalism about which Brass and Varshney fundamentally disagree. Brass, *Production of Hindu–Muslim Violence*, p. 377.

14. Dick Kooiman, *Communalism and Indian Princely States: Travancore, Baroda and Hyderabad in the 1930s* (New Delhi, 2002).
15. Bipan Chandra, *Communalism in Modern India* (Delhi, 1984), p. 292.
16. C.A. Bayly, 'The Pre-History of "Communalism"?: Religious Conflict in India, 1700–1860', in *Modern Asian Studies*, Vol. 19 (1985), p. 201.
17. Ibid., p. 180.
18. Cynthia Keppley-Mahmood, 'Rethinking Indian Communalism: Culture and Counter-Culture', in *Asian Survey*, Vol. 33, No. 7 (1993), p. 726.
19. Achin Vanaik, *The Furies of Indian Communalism: Religion, Modernity and Secularization* (London, 1997), pp. 145–9.
20. Peter van der Veer, *Religious Nationalism: Hindus and Muslims in India* (Delhi, 1996), pp. 36, 52.
21. Chandra, *Communalism*, p. 4.
22. Roger Jeffrey and Patricia M. Jeffrey, 'The Bijnor Riots, October 1990: Collapse of a Mythical Special Relationship?', in *Economic and Political Weekly*, 5 March 1994, p. 551.
23. Rajendra Prasad, *Autobiography* (Bombay, 1957), pp. 13–14.
24. Bipan Chandra, *Communalism*, p. 199.
25. See also Dick Kooiman, 'Communalism and Indian Princely States: A Comparison with British India', in *Economic and Political Weekly*, 26 August 1995, pp. 2123–33.
26. Interview with Brigadier Bag Singh, Bikaner, 12 March 1998.
27. *Hindustan Times*, 18 February 1998.
28. Roger Jeffrey and Patricia M. Jeffrey, 'The Bijnor Riots, October 1990', p. 551.
29. Brass, *Production of Hindu–Muslim Violence*, p. 9.
30. Speech at Lallgarh Palace, 1 January 1932 [British Library] I[ndia] O[ffice] R[ecords], L/P&S/13/603.
31. Minutes of the RTC Consultative Committee, dated 3 March 1932 N[ehru] M[emorial] M[useum and] L[ibrary], Moonje Papers, Subject file 21. Mehta was responding to a Muslim League demand that a fixed quota of states' seats in the proposed federal legislature should be set aside for Muslims.
32. Announcement on behalf of the Maharaja by the Maharajkumar of Karauli, issued on 4 November 1946, IOR L/P&S/13/1422.
33. Mustansir Naqui to Gandhi, 31 October 1947, AISPC, Pt I, file 11 of 1947–48.
34. R.S. Azad to Gandhi, 25 September 1938, AICC, file G-35 (3) of 1938.
35. I have tried to compensate for this by supplementing the information on communal violence gained from newspapers with information from police reports and other sources. In so doing I may have overcompensated, but if that is true it merely reinforces the point made below.
36. S.N. Roy, Dep. Sec., Govt. of Bengal to Home Sec., GOI, 7 September 1926, N[ational] A[rchives of] I[ndia], Home (Pol.) file 219 of 1926. For a typical example of a minor encounter which stopped short of developing into a riot, see R[ajasthan] S[tate] A[rchives] B[ikaner branch], Jodhpur, Social C 1/5 of 1936–47 on the Holi festival at Riyan village in March 1938.
37. IG Police, Jodhpur, to Chief Minister, Jodhpur, 26 May 1937, RSAB, Jodhpur, Social, C 2/21 of 1928–46.
38. Kooiman posits a similar trajectory for the Southern states. After 1924, he writes, 'there was a gradual increase communal riots' in Hyderabad, but these

continued to be 'local and fewer than in contemporary British India'. Kooiman, *Communalism and Indian Princely States*, p. 220.

39. *Kalsia Administration Report* for 1925–26, p. 8.

40. Fort. report on Rajputana for period ending 15 June 1933, IOR L/P&S/13/1404.

41. H. Wilberforce-Bell, AGG, Punjab States, to Pol. Sec., GOI, 20 May 1935, and report by J.C. Donaldson, ICS, dated 21 September 1935, IOR R/1/1/2687.

42. Resdt, Jaipur to AGG, Rajputana, 30 January 1926, IOR L/P&S/10/947.

43. The presence of a small mosque on the third side of the compound added weight to the Muslim claim, but it was the Dargah that drew the crowds, particularly at the time of the annual fair held to mark the 'urs of the Sufi saint. The parties being unable to agree on a compromise, the state eventually intervened and built a wall, at its own expense, across the middle of the compound. The wall left the disputed well in the possession of the Muslims, but the *darbār* compensated the Hindus by digging a new well for their exclusive use. Chief Minister Kishengarh to Administrator Kishengarh, 23 November 1940, and Resdt, Jaipur to Resdt, Rajputana, 20 August 1940, IOR L/P&S/13/1423.

44. *The Times*, 2 September 1924. *The Times'* observation was occasioned by a serious Hindu–Muslim clash in Gulbarga, Hyderabad which left 4 persons killed and 12 badly injured. Although the Gulbarga riot falls outside the geographical scope of this inquiry, it was in its own way a landmark event—it was the first serious Hindu–Muslim disturbance in the premier state in the twentieth century.

45. Interview with R.G. Verma, Patiala, 1 February 1998.

46. Interview with Jaswant Singh, Kota, 17 February 1998, and interview with Dr Jagat Narayan Srivastava, Kota, 18 February 1998. According to a Muslim builder interviewed by Ashis Nandy in Ayodhya, the practice was common there too. Nandy, *Creating a Nationality*, p. 172.

47. Teja Singh never went inside the mosque, but that was not for lack of respect for Islam. Islam too was a force for good and a path to salvation. 'What he wanted was that I should be a better Sikh; what I wanted for him was to be a better Muslim.' Interview with Teja Singh Tiwana, Patiala, 30 January 1998.

48. Chaudhury Abdul Aziz to Sardar Bishen Singh, 3 July 1936, PSA, Kapurthala, Sadar Office, M/3–38–36. See also interview between G. Wingate, Dep. Pol. Sec., GOI, and Subedar Major Sardar Mohammad Khan, Presdt of the Meo Indian Officers Conf., Nuh, 12 January 1933, on the communal situation in Alwar. IOR R/1/1/2325.

49. Report from Dist. SP, Sujat, to Mekhma Khas, 19 March 1935, RSAB, Jodhpur, Social, C 2/21 of 1928–46.

50. Office note on telegram from 'the Muslims of Mekrana' to the Chief Minister, Jodhpur, dated 14 April 1937, RSAB, Jodhpur, Social, C 2/21 of 1928–46.

51. Petition from the Beldars of Jodhpur, dated 7 November 1938, RSAB, Jodhpur, Social, C 2/21 of 1939–45.

52. Gurdial Singh to J.W. Johnston, Administrator Nabha, 17 July 1928, P[unjab] S[tate] A[rchives Patiala], Nabha, P[rime] M[inister]'s Office, 2349/2503E.

53. Toleration in this instance was doubtless made easier by the fact that, on average, only one or two cows a day were killed, and those too in secluded locations well away from Hindu residential areas. Mangrol's Muslims were also able to access supplies of beef through neighbouring Junagadh. Ishaq

Mahomed Chhapra, Sec., Mangrol Muslim Seva Mandal, to Sir Fazli Husain 18 September 1934, IOR R/1/1/2595.

54. The custom was for the Malerkotla Jains to compensate the butchers for their loss of trade, but in some years the butchers gallantly refused to take the money. Fort. reports on the Punjab states for the periods ending 30 September 1940 and 15 September 1943, IOR L/P&S/13/1345.

55. Fort. report on Rajputana for the periods ending 15 and 30 September 1926, IOR R/1/1/1448.

56. Chief Minister of Kapurthala to the Sec. to the AGG, Punjab States, 9 March 1932, PSA, Kapurthala, Sadar Office, E/5-1-32.

57. Quoted in Janet McCalman, 'In the Heartland of the Poor, One Nation Still Fails to Appeal', in *The Age* [Melbourne], 24 June 1998, p. 13.

58. Evidence of Police Special Prosecutor to the Indore Riots Inquiry Commission, *The T[imes] o[ff] I[ndia]*, 28 June 1927.

59. Evidence of Harnarain, *TOI*, 26 June 1927.

60. Evidence of Sub-Inspector Harprasad, Investigating Officer, *TOI*, 1 June 1927.

61. *TOI*, 17 February, 28 June 1927.

62. Brass, *Production of Hindu–Muslim Violence*, p. 16.

63. Quoted in *TOI*, 12 April 1927.

64. In 1945, Indore police dealt with 30 cases of riotous assembly, compared with 26 cases of murder, 15 of attempted murder, 18 of culpable homicide, 224 of grievous hurt, 40 of abduction, 28 of rape, 26 of dacoity, 29 of robbery, 1481 of housebreaking, 3884 of ordinary theft and 509 of cattle theft. *Indore Administration Report 1945*, p. 40.

2 Islands in the storm

1. Gopal Krishna, 'Communal Violence in India: A Study of Communal Disturbances in Delhi – I', in *Economic and Political Weekly*, 12 January 1985', p. 65; and Achin Vanaik, *The Painful Transition: Bourgeois Democracy in India* (London, 1990), p. 139n.

2. *Report*, Vol. 1, p. 26.

3. Report by Sub-Inspector of Police, Hindumal Kote, Bikaner, dated 27 April 1935, RSAB, Bikaner, Home Dept, 154/1935.

4. Quoted in Ashis Nandy, Shikha Trivedi, Shail Mayaram and Achyut Yagnik, *Creating a Nationality: The Ramjanmabhumi Movement and Fear of the Self* (Delhi, 1995), p. 83.

5. Stanley J. Tambiah, *Leveling Crowds: Ethnonationalist Conflicts and Collective Violence in South Asia* (Berkeley, 1996), p. 274. Tambiah here is drawing upon the pioneering sociological work of Elias Canetti, particularly his *Crowds and Power* (New York, 1984), pp. 15–16.

6. M.S. Gill and Gaganjot Deol, 'Patterns of Riots in India', in *Asian Profile*, Vol. 23, No. 1 (February 1995), pp. 65–6.

7. Barbara Daly Metcalf, 'Imagining Community: Polemical Debates in Colonial India', in Kenneth W. Jones (ed.), *Religious Controversy in British India: Dialogues in Indian Languages* (Albany, 1992), p. 230.

8. Note by Muddiman, dated 28 September 1924, N[ational] A[rchives of] I[ndia], Home (Pol.) file 140 of 1925.

9. James Manor, 'The Failure of Political Integration in Sri Lanka (Ceylon)', in *Journal of Commonwealth and Comparative Politics*, Vol. 17, No. 1 (1979), p. 38. Manor opines that it is surely 'less than accidental that elections in Sri Lanka have tended to bring in their train [outbreaks of] communal, criminal or insurrectionary violence'.

10. Richard G. Fox, 'Communalism and Modernity', in David Ludden (ed.), *Contesting the Nation: Religion, Community and the Politics of Democracy in India* (Philadelphia, 1996), pp. 237–9.

11. Nandy, *Creating a Nationality*, p. 13.

12. Report by Resdt, Punjab States, dated 21 April 1941, IOR L/P&S/13/1345.

13. Sir Saiyyid Reza Ali Khan, Nawab of Rampur, to Major Saloway, 18 September 1941, IOR R/1/1/3822.

14. In a pioneering study, Edward Haynes compared the Alwar state with the neighbouring Gurgaon district. He found that in 1921, in Alwar, 119.07 of every thousand workers worked in industry, 5.70 in transport and 48.71 in trade; whereas in Gurgaon the equivalent figures were 151.90, 19.25 and 54.20 respectively. Haynes, 'Comparative Industrial Development in 19th- and 20th-Century India: Alwar State and Gurgaon District', in *South Asia*, n.s., Vol. 3, No. 2 (December 1980), p. 30. Earlier, John Hurd used 1931 census figures for the 28 largest states to build a case that indirect rule in India had retarded economic development there. See John Hurd II, 'The Economic Consequences of British Rule in India', in *The Indian Economic and Social History Review*, Vol. 12 (1975), pp. 169–82; and 'The Influence of British Policy on Industrial Development in the Princely States of India, 1890–1933', ibid., Vol. 12 (1975), pp. 409–24.

15. G.T. Fisher, Resdt, CI, to Sir Kenneth Fitze, Sec. to Crown Rep., 14/15 July 1942, IOR L/P&S/13/1109.

16. Lord Irwin to Lord Peel, 21 March 1928, Br. Lib., Irwin Coll., Sec. State's Letters, Vol. III; and R.A. Holland, AGG, Rajputana, to Pol. Sec., GOI, 1 February 1924, IOR R/1/1/1566.

17. Note by G.K.S. Sharma, Crown Finance Officer, dated 8 May 1946, IOR R/1/1/4245; and Lord Linlithgow to Lord Zetland, 13 December 1939, Br. Lib., Zetland Coll., Vol. 18.

18. Bikaner Council Proceedings, 21 December 1935, RSAB, Bikaner, PM's Office, A 1021–1122 of 1935.

19. My understanding of *communitas* is informed by the work of Victor Turner. Turner defines *communitas* as a 'non-utilitarian experience of brotherhood and fellowship'. *Dramas, Fields and Metaphors: Symbolic Action in Human Society* (Ithaca, 1974), p. 45.

20. Interview with Dr Jagat Narayan Srivastava, Kota, 18 March 1998.

21. Nandy, *Creating a Nationality*, p. 126.

22. E.P. Thompson, 'The Moral Economy of the English Crowd in the Eighteenth Century', in *Past and Present*, No. 50 (February 1971), pp. 78–9.

23. James C. Scott, *The Moral Economy of the Peasant: Rebellion and Subsistence in Southeast Asia* (New Haven, 1976), esp. pp. 170–4, 180–92. For a discussion of some of this literature, see Arjun Appadorai, 'How Moral Is South Asia's Economy? – A Review Article', in the *Journal of Asian Studies*, Vol. 43, No. 3 (May 1984), pp. 481–97.

24. Note by Hakim, Phalodi, dated 9 November 1931, RSAB, Jodhpur, Social, C 2/21 of 1928–46.

25. Petition from the Hindu Chhipas of Pali to the Chief Minister, Jodhpur, dated 10 December 1942, RSAB, Jodhpur, Social, C 2/1 of 1928–45.
26. Typescript copies of the diaries of Thakur Amar Singh Kanota, Jaipur, 1902, p. 530 (entry for 10 April), 1908, p. 9 (entry for 26 June), 1924, p. 21 (entry for 25 February), and 1935, p. 227 (entry for 17 August).
27. Interview with HH of Dhrangadhra, 28 January 1998.
28. Nandy, *Creating a Nationality*, p. 152.
29. The *Tribune*, 28 October 1931. See also the letter from Sita Ram, Saresht Singh and Habib-ul-Rahman of the 'Jind Law and Order Committee' to the editor of The *Tribune*, 20 November 1931.
30. Note on the Muslim deputation that met the maharaja of Bharatpur on 2 June 1924, IOR R/1/1/1570. The deputation had heard that mosques in Bharatpur were being demolished.
31. Note by Col. G. Kirkbride, dated 28 December 1944, IOR L/P&S/13/1436.
32. Statement tendered by Rashid Khan's illegitimate son to Major R.J. Mcnabb, PA, Haraoti and Tonk, dated 25 September 1928, encl. in L.W. Reynolds, AGG Rajputana to B.J. Glancy, 28 September 1928, IOR L/P&S/13/1434.
33. Dholpur to M.K. Vellodi, Sec., MOS, 16 March 1949, and Dholpur to N.M. Buch, Jt Sec., MOS, 20 February 1949, MOS 5(1)-P/49.
34. Note by Menon, dated 24 November 1941, IOR R/1/1/3770.
35. Interview with Brigadier Bag Singh, former state Army Commander, Bikaner, 13 March 1998; Amar Singh Kanota's diary, 1904, p. 948 (entry for 8 January 1904); and report on Tonk by Major D. Fraser encl. in Fraser to the P.A. Haraoti and Tonk, 6 February 1931, IOR L/P&S/13/1434.
36. *Cambay Adminstration Report 1941–42*, p. 9.
37. On this see Denis Vidal, *Violence and Truth: A Rajasthani Kingdom Confronts Colonial Authority* (Delhi, 1997), esp. Chs 2, 4 and 6.
38. *The Holkar Sirkar Gazette*, No. 223–4, June 1930, p. 10.
39. *The Servant of India*, 31 May 1934.
40. Order dated 20 October 1929, RSAB, Bundi, Mahakma Khas, English Office, file 8A.
41. Around 1929 relations between Hindus and Muslims in Junagadh were disturbed by a dispute over a sacred site near Una. When in 1931 a Muslim boy was killed at Verawal, suspicion immediately fell on the Hindu community; and in due course charges were laid against the *purohit* of a temple and four other young Hindu males. These charges were later upheld at trial by the presiding sessions judge. However, the verdicts were overturned on appeal by the judicial assistant, which 'created further communal feelings'. On 18 July 1931, six Hindus including the Nagar Seth who was believed to have funded the appeal, were killed in a revenge assault. Note by Capt. G.B. Williamson, member of council, Junagadh, dated 29 January 1932, IOR R/1/1/2184.
42. C.S. Ranga Iyer, *India in the Crucible* (London, 1928), p. 296.
43. Speech of September 1930, *Indian Annual Register*, 1930, Vol. 2, p. 472.
44. Quoted in Sharma, 'On Hindu–Muslim Brotherhood', p. 35.
45. Speech of 11 September 1939, IOR L/P&S/13/1406; and statement of 9 September 1942, quoted in *The Times of India*, 10 September 1942.
46. *Extraordinary Gwalior Government Gazette*, dated 30 September 1941.
47. Note dated 5 December 1928, RSAB, Jodhpur, Social, C 2/1 of 1928–45.
48. Diary of Amar Singh Kanota, 1923, p. 108 (entry for 19 October 1923).

49. Resolution of the GOI, Education Dept, dated November 1920, NAI, F&P, Intl.B, November 1920, 302–18.
50. Freitag, *Collective Action and Community*, p. 53.
51. Arjun Appadorai, *Worship and Conflict in Colonial Rule: A South Indian Case* (Cambridge, 1981).
52. At one stage the maharaja of Kishengarh also participated in the discussions. *The Times of India*, 10 September 1932.
53. Gurdial Singh, Dulat, to J. Wilson-Johnston, Administrator, Nabha, 25 August 1927, and note by Gurdial Singh, dated 4 February 1928, PSA, Nabha, PM's Office, 3315/3452E.
54. Deohri Mualla Dept note, dated 18 January 1944, PSA, Patiala, Dharam Arth, 42/2. For a retrospective summary of the situation in the Punjab states see note, Home Dept, PEPSU, dated 22 September 1951, PSA, Patiala, Dharam Arth, 415/74.
55. Resdt, Rajputana, to Pol. Sec., GOI (teleg.), 6 September 1924, Home (Pol.), 310 of 1924; and diary of Amar Singh Kanota, 1935, p. 198, and 1936, p. 196 (entries for 28 June 1935 and 13 June 1937). Alwar claimed that his road-widening schemes went through 'without protest'. By comparison, when the civic authorities in Cawnpore in 1913 attempted to remove a small portion of the surrounds of a mosque in order to widen the adjacent thoroughfare, a major riot resulted.
56. Joanne Punzo Waghorne, *The Raja's Magic Clothes: Revisioning Kingship and Divinity in England's India* (University Park, Pennsylvania, 1994), p. 9.
57. Maharaja of Rewa to Col. Campbell, Resdt, CI, 15 September 1944, NAI, Jayakar Papers, p. 780.
58. Sir Jadunath Sarkar, *A History of Jaipur, c.1503–1938* (rev. and ed. Raghubir Singh, Hyderabad, c.1984), p. 17. For details of princely roles in other festivals, see Sardar Sahib Deohri Mualla, Patiala, to Director of Agriculture, Patiala, October 1939, PSA, Patiala, Dharam Arth, 186/92; fort. report on the Gwalior Residency for period ending 31 October 1939, IOR L/P&S/13/1197; Mekhma Khas office order, Jodhpur, dated 21 September 1948, RSAB, Jodhpur, Social, C 1/3 of 1948; and N.B. Khare, *My Political Memoirs: Or Autobiography* (Nagpur, 1959), p. 318.
59. Narayan Mahadev Parmanand, *Letters to an Indian Rajah from a Political Recluse* (2nd edn, Bombay, 1919), p. 21.
60. Max Weber, *The Theory of Social and Economic Organization* (trans. A.M. Henderson and Talcott Parsons, Glencoe Illinois, 1947), p. 328.
61. Address by the maharaja of Bikaner to the Carlton Club, 29 May 1935, *Asiatic Review*, Vol. 31 (January–October 1935), p. 447.
62. Narada quoted in Thomas R. Trautmann, 'Traditions of Statecraft in Ancient India', in R.J. Moore (ed.), *Tradition and Politics in South Asia* (New Delhi, 1979), pp. 95, 137; and Pratap Chandra Roy (trans.), *The Mahabharata of Krishna-Dwaipayana Vyasa* (Calcutta, 1963), Vol. 1, p. 101.
63. Specifically, it was the power of the goddess that resided in the throne. The installation rituals usually lasted three days, and included worship of titular deities, worship of state emblems, sacrifices, the feeding of brahmins, circumambulation, the making of the forehead of the ruler with a *rāja tilak*, an effusion (the *abishekha*), and, lastly, enthronement. Ronald Inden, 'Ritual, Authority and Cyclic Time in Hindu Kingship', in J.F. Richards (ed.), *Kingship and Authority in South Asia* (2nd edn, Madison, Wisconsin, 1981), pp. 37–8;

222 *Notes*

and Adrian Mayer, 'Rulership and Divinity: The Case of the Modern Hindu Prince and Beyond', in *Modern Asian Studies*, Vol. 25, No. 4 (1991), pp. 767–70.

64. Note, n.d. on 'Some Salient Points about Benares State', NAI, Rajendra Prasad Papers, 8-P/48.

65. Chief Sec., Tehri Garhwal, to PA, Tehri Garhwal, 17 January 1930, IOR R/1/1/2129.

66. *The New York Times*, 11 April 1942.

67. Letter from HH of Dhrangadhra to the author, 21 February 1998.

68. K.M. Panikkar, *His Highness the Maharaja of Bikaner: A Biography* (London, 1937), p. 385.

69. Forster to his mother, 3 August 1921, *Hill of Devi*, p. 104; and ibid., p. 113. And see also pp. 106–10 for further descriptions of the festival. The birth of Lord Krishna is celebrated as Gokul Ashtami. Dewas is not far from Krishna's reputed birthplace at Mathura.

70. Lt.-Col. G.D. Ogilvie, AGG, Rajputana, to Pol. Sec., GOI, 23 April 1933, Br. Lib., Lothian Coll., 6; Lord Willingdon, Viceroy of India, to Sec. State, 30 April and 22 May 1933, Br. Lib., Templewood Coll., 6; *The Times*, 22 May 1933; and Iris Butler, *Viceroy's Wife: Letters of Alice, Countess of Reading from India, 1921–5*, p. 52 (entry for 7 November 1921).

71. Interview with HH of Dhrangadhra, Pune, 23 January 1998.

72. The guru bequeathed a number of items to the Phul family living in the Jungly Ilaqa district of the Punjab as a reward for their sheltering him from the soldiers of the Mughal viceroy. When subsequently the family split, they were shared between its three branches. The Patiala branch obtained custody of the *hukumnama* which spelt out the guru's debt to the Phul house. The Nabha branch got the *saropa* and the guru's *kirpan* or dagger, 'the origin[al] of all kirpans' that Sikhs are enjoined to carry. Afterwards they also acquired Gobind Singh's comb, with some strand of his hair attached to it. So valued were these items by the Nabha rulers that they were kept locked in a private room of the Nabha fort to which only members of the Phul family had admittance. However, in a desperate bid to avert deposition, Ripudiman Singh in 1923 approached the Akalis with an offer to transfer the relics to Amritsar. Two Akali emissaries told him that if this were done, 'no less than four lacs of Sikhs would be prepared to sacrifice their lives in the cause of the Maharaja'. But the scheme was foiled when the Prime Minister Daya Kishen Kaul, got wind of it. Sir Daya Kishen Kaul to Lt.-Col. A.B. Minchin, AGG, Punjab States, 3 July 1924; and note encl. in Administrator, Nabha, to AGG, Punjab States, 8 September 1923, NAI, Home (Pol.), 401 of 1924.

73. *Danta Administration Report 1944–5*, p. 66.

74. Note encl. in K.S. Sheikh Mohammad Zahid of Mangrol to HH of Dhrangadhra, 21 November 1996. (I am indebted to HH of Dhrangadhra for letting me see this correspondence.)

75. Speech at Lallgarh palace, 1 January 1932, IOR R/1/1/2234.

76. *The Times of India*, 26 February 1936.

77. Iqbal Narain and P.C. Mathur, 'The Thousand Year Raj: Regional Isolation and Rajput Hinduism in Rajasthan Before and After 1947', in Francine Frankel and M.S.A. Rao (eds), *Dominance and State Power in Modern India: Decline of a Social Order*, Vol. 2 (Delhi, 1990), pp. 31–3.

78. Patrick Hanks (ed.), *Collins Dictionary of the English Language* (Sydney, 1982), p. 1319.

79. Note by Sir Charles Watson, dated 1 February 1932, IOR R/1/1/2184.
80. Household Minister to Master Tara Singh, 5 December 1942, PSA, Kapurthala, Sadar Office, P/3-3-43.
81. Two of my informants exemplified this tradition. The family of Dr Sahai, Director of the Palace Museum, Jaipur, served the maharajas of Jaipur faithfully from 1777 to 1948, and Vaduendra still sees himself as a dynastic retainer; while Khemchand Mathur followed his father and great uncle into the service of Alwar. Interview with Vaduendra Sahai, Jaipur, 7 November 2000; and interview with Khemchand Mathur, Jaipur, 10 November 2000.
82. As noted above, in 1931 six Hindus were murdered in the Junagadh town of Verawal. The perpetrators, all Muslims, were duly arrested, tried and convicted. But many people remained convinced that the murderers had been put up to it by two notoriously communal state officials. However, despite repeated representations from the Hindu public, the two men were allowed to continue in their posts. On the other hand Chelshankar Dave, the Hindu chief of police, who had led the successful murder investigation, was summarily sacked a few months later without explanation. Note by Capt. G.B. Williams, Member of Council, Junagadh, dated 29 January 1932, IOR R/1/1/2184.
83. V. Vishwanath, CC, Bhopal, to V.P. Menon, Sec., MOS, 20 April 1950, NAI, M[inistry] O[f] S[tates], 9 (8)-P/50. At one stage in the 1930s the Bhopal government approached the GOI with a proposal that the state become a major supplier of meat to the Indian Army. Note by K. Fitze, AGG, CI, on talk with the nawab of Bhopal, September 1936, IOR R/1/1/2891.
84. Note by Gurdial Singh, Home Member, Nabha, dated 22 February 1929, PSA, Nabha, PM's Office, 4133/4224E; 'Bye Laws for the Control and Regulation of the Slaughter-House, Nabha', issued on 14 August 1926, PSA, Nabha, PM's Office, 5703/5768E; and note on press conf. at Mahakma Khas, Kotah, dated 16 November 1944, RSAB, Kotah confdl file 27A.
85. Fort. report for Rajputana for period ending 15 September 1945, IOR L/P&S/13/1442; and office note dated 5 January 1941, RSAB, Jodhpur, Social, C 2/6A of 1929–41.
86. As Thursby shows, elaborate rules governed the slaughter of animals in the provinces too. But there was no equivalent to the bans that applied in the states. In the provinces, the guiding principle with the authorities was what was customary. Thursby, *Hindu–Muslim Relations in British India*, pp. 89, 106.
87. F.V. Wylie, PM, Alwar, to PA, Eastern Rajputana, 19 September 1933, NAI, F&P, Intl., 621 of 1933.
88. And these disparities increased with seniority. In the police force, for example, Muslims in 1932 comprised half the cadre, but held only 35 per cent of ranking positions; while just two of 37 men of inspector grade and above were Muslims. Christopher Snedden, 'Paramountcy, Patrimonialism and the Peoples of Jammu and Kashmir, 1947–1991' (Unpublished PhD dissertation, Latrobe University, Melbourne, 2001), pp. 2, 29–30.
89. Memo by the All-India Riyasti Hindu Hitarshi Mandal, New Delhi, dated April 1932, IOR R/1/1/2234. In 1947, out of a budgetary allocation of close to four lakhs, all but Rs 7400 was spent on Islamic charities and institutions. MOS office notes dated 7 May, and 14 and 18 September 1950; and CC, Bhopal to V.P. Menon, 2 Dept 1950, MOS, 9 (16)-P/50.
90. Statement by Dr M.A. Ansari quoted in the Bombay Chronicle, 23 May 1924.

91. Robert W. Stern, *The Cat and the Lion: Jaipur State in the British Raj* (Leiden, 1988), p. 276.
92. In 1921, Sikhs were 18.41 per cent of the population in princely Punjab, 11.09 per cent in British Punjab. There was an even wider divergence in the proportion of the Muslim population as between Muslim-ruled Jaora and Bhopal and the rest of CI. *Census of India 1921*, Vol. 1, Pt 1, p. 70, and Vol. 18, Pt 1, p. 23.
93. 'Petition to Maharaja From the Chaudhuries of the Hindu Communities of Ladnun', dated 17 April 1937, RSAB, Jodhpur, Social, C 2/21 of 1928–46.
94. T.R. Bhatt to the Maharaja of Tehri-Garhwal 3 October 1946, AISPC, Pt I, file 165 of 1946.
95. Telegram from 'Loyal Hindus of Tijara', 25 December 1932, quoted in maharaja to Col. G. Ogilvie, AGG, Rajputana, 27 December 1932, NAI, Home (Pol.) 43/3 of 1933.
96. Satirical attack on maharaja of Patiala in the *Kirpan Bahadur ji Sangat* of Amritsar, 19 September 1929, quoted in L.F. Rushbrook-Williams, Foreign Minister, Patiala, to AGG, Punjab States, 21 November 1927, PSA, Patiala, Hist. Section, file H-89B. Sikh historian and man of letters Khushwant Singh recalled recently how shocked he was to see Bhupinder Singh of Patiala smoking outside the Chamber of Princes building in Delhi. Review by Khushwant Singh of K. Natwar Singh, *Magnificent Maharaja*, *Outlook*, 6 April 1998, p. 79.
97. Giani Kartar Singh to Chief Sec., Kapurthala, 9 February 1943, PSA, Kapurthala, Sadar Office, P/3-3-43.
98. Trilakchand Mathur to B.S. Moonje, 27 October 1932, NMML, Moonje Papers, Subject File 21; and Vidal, *Violence and Truth*, pp. 187–9.
99. Beneshiam Wahie to Moonje 28 May 1933, Moonje Papers, Subject File 33.
100. Charles Allen and Sharada Dwivedi, *Lives of the Indian Princes* (London, 1984), p. 310; interview with HH of Dhrangadhra, Pune, 26 January 1998; and R.E. Holland, AGG, Rajputana, to Pol. Sec., GOI, 16 March 1921, NAI, F&P, Dep. Intl. (Secret), May 1921, 12.
101. E.H. Kealy, AGG, Western India, to Pol. Sec., GOI, 21 November 1931 and 25 January 1932, IOR R/1/1/2184.
102. Maharaj Rana of Jhalawar to PA Kotah of Jhalawar, 7 April 1920, NAI, F&P, Intl. B, November 1920, 302–18.
103. Office note, Revenue Dept, Jodhpur, quoting letter from Manager, Kuchaman Thikana, dated 17 October 1928, RSAB, Jodhpur, Social, C 2/1 of 1928–45.
104. In Baria, CI, there were just three offences against the cow-killing prohibition rules in 1924–25, two in 1925–26. *Baria Administration Report 1925–6*, p. 11.
105. Speech by a Mr Ramzan in the Chhipas' Mosque, Bikaner, 3 September 1946, quoted in note by IGP, Bikaner, dated 4 September 1946, RSAB, Bikaner, Home Confdl file 60 of 1946.
106. Petition from the 'Hindu subjects of Bahawalpur', dated June 1933, IOR R/1/1/2433.
107. Krishanasavan Arya, member CWC Rampur, to Rajendra Prasad (teleg.), 26 September 1948, NAI, Rajendra Prasad Papers, 8-P/48.
108. Home (Public) dispatch, 27 December 1893, NAI, Foreign Dept, Intl. A, December 1894, procs 113–55.

3 Metamorphosis

1. Interestingly, communal leaders on both sides—still committed it would seem to the code of peaceful co-existence—did their best to prevent violence, even going to the length of throwing their turbans at the feet of the rioters. Petition to maharaja of Patiala dated [June] 1932, PSA, Patiala, Ijlas-i-Khas, 353.

2. The Muslims had taken out a *chaddar* ('offering') procession as part of their Mohurrum celebrations. The Hindus were inaugurating a new Shiva temple. Although the rioters included some people from the surrounding villages, Shail Mayaram has proved that Meo participation in, and support for, the May riot was minimal. The majority of the crowd evidently comprised Julahas (weavers). Nor can we follow Pema Ram when he suggests that the urban Muslims were behind the Meo agitation of November 1932. They made use of it (see p. 92–3) but they did not start it. CID reports dated 27 May, 28 December 1932, NAI, Home/Pol. 43/3 of 1933; and Pema Ram, *Agrarian Movement in Rajasthan, 1913–1947* (Jaipur, 1986).

3. For example, *The Ahrar* (Lahore), 21 January 1932 and 17 February 1932, quoted in PSA, Kapurthala, Sadar, E/5-1-32.

4. Report by J.C. Donaldson, ICS, dated 21 September 1935, IOR R/1/1/2687.

5. Petition from the 'Muslims of Bikaner', dated 28 April 1934, RSAB, Bikaner, PM's Office, B 363–368 of 1934.

6. Donaldson report, loc. cit.

7. Note by R.E.L. Wingate, dated 22 June 1933 on phone call from the Chief Sec., Punjab, relaying information received from Jammu, IOR R/1/1/2424.

8. Tambiah, *Leveling Crowds*, p. 192.

9. Chief Sec., Punjab, to Pol. Sec., GOI, 5 December 1932, NAI, Home (Pol.) 42/3 (Pt 2).

10. Some 10,000 Muslims emigrated from Alwar in late 1932. There were several smaller emigrations during the period, including one of some 900 Muslims from Kot Putli in Jaipur in 1935.

11. Note by IGP, Bikaner, dated 18 April 1938, RSAB, Bikaner, Home/Confdl file 17 of 1938.

12. Quoted in 'Resumé of Events in the Indian States for the Fortnight Ending 31 May 1934', IOR L/P&S/13/1375.

13. Press statement by nawab of Rampur, [November] 1931, RSAB, Kotah Confdl file 48; and speech by maharaja of Bikaner, November 1931, IOR R/1/1/2234.

14. Note by J.M. Ewart, Director, IB, GOI, dated 12 January 1939, IOR R/1/1/3322.

15. Presidential address to the Bhopal Hindu Conf., delivered 27 May 1938, AISPC, I, file 18, Pt II of 1938–42. On the genesis of the 'dying Hindus' thesis, see Pradip Kumar Datta, 'Dying Hindus: Production of Hindu Communal Common Sense in Early-20th Century Bengal', in *Economic and Political Weekly*, June 1993, pp. 1305–25.

16. *The Times*, 25 January 1922.

17. In Gwalior, for example, the literate population expanded by 113,281 between 1931 and 1941. *Census of India 1941*, Vol. 20, Pt 2, p. 251 and Vol. 22, Pt 2, pp. 253–5.

18. Details of constitutional changes in individual states down to 1944 can be read in IOR L/P&S/13/886 and IOR L/P&S/13/993.

19. Quoted in Reginald Coupland, *Indian Politics 1936–1942: Report on the Constitutional Problem in India Part II* (London, 1943), App. IV, p. 330.
20. *Mayubhanj Administration Report, 1925–26*, p. 106.
21. Press statement by Sayer Zaheer Hashmi, Gen. Sec., and Govind Prasad Srivastava, Sec., Bhopal SPC, 6 January 1946, AISPC, Pt I, file 19, Pt II of 1945–48.
22. Jawaharlal Nehru to Saifuddin Kitchelew, 20 December 1946, NMML, Nehru Papers, Ist Instalment, file 1.
23. Coupland, *Indian Politics*, p. 178.
24. 'Report on Constitutional and Administrative Reforms in Indian States for the Period Ending 15 May 1941', IOR L/P&S/13/993.
25. Seth Jamnalal Bajaj to Raja Gyan Nath, Praja Mandal, Jaipur, 3 May 1940, IOR L/P&S/13/1406.
26. Note by R.R. Burnett, Resdt, Rajputana, dated 19–21 July 1946, IOR L/P&S/13/1434.
27. Note by Sapru, dated 7 June 1942, NAI, Jayakar Papers, file 763.
28. Nazim, Barnala, to Pindi Dass Sabharwal, Minister for Law and Justice, Patiala, November 1931; and IG Police, Patiala, to Revenue Minister, Patiala, 28 March 1933, PSA, Patiala, Ijlas-i-Khas, p. 344.
29. Martin E. Marty and R. Scott Appleby, *The Glory and the Power: The Fundamentalist Challenge to the Modern World* (Boston, 1992), p. 34.
30. *Aligarh Gazette*, 4 May 1923; and note by F&P Sec., Bharatpur, on 'The Shudhi Movement Relating to the Malkanas', dated 23 July 1923, IOR R/1/1/1430 (1).
31. *Morvi Administration Report, 1925–6*, p. 8.
32. *Jaipur Administration Report 1922/3–1925/6*, p. 8; and Sec., Jamiat Tabligh-ul-Islam, Delhi, to Presdt, State Council, Jaipur, [January 1926], quoted in *Muslim Outlook* (Lahore), 4 January 1926.
33. IG Police, Jaipur, to IG Police, Bundi, 4 June 1935; and Sheikh Munshi Khadim Hussain, Member Bundi Council, to Major W.F. Webb, Dewan of Bundi, 11 July 1935, RSA, Bundi, Mahakma Khas, English Office, file 20A.
34. This is at any rate the view of Majid Siddiqi, 'History and Society in a Popular Rebellion: Mewat, 1920–1933', in *Comparative Studies in Society and History*, Vol. 23 (1986), esp. p. 443. It is only fair to add that it is a view strongly disputed by the most careful sociologist of the Meos, Shail Mayaram. See her *Resisting Regimes: Myth, Memory and the Shaping of a Muslim Identity* (Delhi, 1997), p. 226.
35. 'Note on the Muslim Delegation Received by the Maharaja of Bharatpur at the Golbagh Palace, 2 June 1924', IOR R/1/1/1570.
36. Pandit Shiva Kumar Chatevedi to Prof. G.L. Dhanopiya, 19 November 1932, RSA, Karauli, State Council, file 3 of 1933.
37. *Vijaya* (Delhi), 24 March 1920, quoted in NAI, F&P, Deposit Intl., July 1920, p. 38.
38. C.W.C. Harvey, PA, Alwar, to Resdt, Jaipur 11 January 1939, IOR R/1/1/3223; and Mohammad Hassan, Sec., Jamiatul Muslimin, Bahawalpur, to K.B. Menon, 16 December 1940, NMML, A[ll] I[ndia] S[tates] P[eoples'] C[onference], file 138-I.
39. NMML, Oral History Transcript 313, pp. 42, 53.
40. Mohammad Hassan, Sec., Jamiatul Muslimin, Bahawalpur, to K.B. Menon, 16 December 1940, AISPC, file 138-I.
41. 'Facts about Charkari Movement', n.d., AISPC, Pt I, file 36 of 1946–48.

42. In 1938 the Bhopal Hindu Sabha merged with the *Anjuman* Khuddam-e-Wattan to form the Bhopal SPC; but it remained effectively a Hindu body. Chaturnarayan Malaviya, Sec., Bhopal SPC, to Balwantray Mehta, Sec., AISPC, 2 August 1938, AISPC, Pt I, file 18 (Pt II) of 1938–42; and 'Report on Work Done by the Rajputana Provincial Hindu Sabha, 1944–45', NAI, Jayakar Papers, file 833.

43. *The Times of India*, 14 June 1927.

44. The Sabha leaders knew they were being manipulated but did not know how to respond. 'The Growth of the Indore Public Meetings Act', by Hajarilal Jadia, convener, Indore Public Meetings Act Prevention Committee, n.d., NMML, AICC, G-35 (3) of 1938.

45. Nehru quoted in Coupland, *Indian Politics*, p. 178.

46. Report by the Chief Justice, dated 11 April 1946, PSA, Patiala, Ijlas-i-Khas, 2105.

47. Gandhi to N.C. Kelkar, July 1934, AICC, G-27 (1) of 1934–35.

48. Nehru to S. Malappa, 9 July 1936, AICC, file G-27 of 1936.

49. Gandhi to Mirza Ismail, 5 October 1941, NMML, Mirza Ismail Papers, Serial No. 365.

50. Quoted in Richard Gordon, 'The Hindu Mahasabha and the Indian National Congress, 1915–1926', in *Modern Asian Studies*, Vol. 9 (1975), p. 161.

51. *The Times of India*, 24 November 1936.

52. Quoted in Kenneth W. Jones, 'Politicized Hinduism: The Ideology and Program of the Hindu Mahasabha', in Robert D. Baird (ed.), *Religion in Modern India* (3rd edn, New Delhi, 1995), pp. 256–7.

53. Chief Sec., Punjab, to Resdt, Kashmir, 2 November 1931, IOR R/1/1/2155 (1).

54. Intercepted letter from Swami Rama Anand Sannyasi, Dayanand Dalit Udhar Sabha, Delhi, to Bhai Parmanand, 27 November 1931, IOR R/1/1/2234; and resolution of joint meeting of WC of the Hindu Mahasabha and members of the Central Hindu Committee of the CLA, 7 November 1931, B.S. Moonje Papers, SF 21.

55. Ganpat Rai, Gen. Sec., Hindu Mahasabha, to B.S. Moonje, 4 July 1932, Moonje Papers, subject file 21.

56. The *Daily Herald* (Lahore), 11 December 1931.

57. Intercepted letter from Tehri Singh Vidyarthi, Nagpur, to Lala Khushal Chand Kursand (ed.), *Milap*, Lahore, 24 December 1931, IOR R/1/1/2234.

58. Procedings of the Hindu Riyasti Hiteshi Sammelan, Lahore, 28 December 1931, IOR R/1/1/2234.

59. Quoted in Chief Sec., Punjab, to Pol. Sec., GOI, 5 December 1932, NAI, Home (Pol.) 42/3 (Pt 2).

60. Ganpat Rai to R.E.L. Wingate, Dep. Sec., Pol. Dept, GOI, n.d., NMML, Moonje Papers, subject file 34.

61. J.A.O. Fitzpatrick, AGG, Punjab States, to Pol. Sec., GOI, 14 June 1933, IOR R/1/1/2433.

62. C.G. Prior, Praja Mandal, Alwar, to J.H. Thompson, Resdt, Jaipur, 25 July 1938, IOR R/1/1/3131.

63. Editorial in *Harijan*, 3 December 1938.

64. See Ian Copland, ' "Congress Paternalism": The "High Command" and the Struggle for Freedom in Princely India', in Jim Masselos (ed.), *Struggling and Ruling: The Indian National Congress 1885–1985* (New Delhi, 1987), pp. 127–9.

65. 'Lawless Limbdi', NMML, Jai Narain Vyas Papers, file 1.

66. See Amrit Kaur to Jawaharlal Nehru, 6 July 1939, NMML, Nehru Papers, 2/128.
67. Sir Richard Tottenham to the PA, Eastern Rajputana States, 25 March 1940, IOR R/1/1/3545.
68. Jai Narain Vyas to Sir Donald Field, Chief Minister of Jodhpur, May 1940, NMML, Vyas Papers, file 3.
69. Mirza Ismail to Hiralal Shastri, 4 September 1942, NMML, Hiralal Shastri Papers.
70. Although Muslims comprised a substantial minority of Sirohi urban population, particularly in Abu Road, they failed to carry a single ward in the state's first municipal elections in 1940. *Sirohi Administration Report, 1940–41*, pp. 78–9.
71. Yeshwant Rao Holkar famously suggested that if the Japanese invaded he would declare Indore an 'open city'. Later he published an open letter to American President Franklin Roosevelt urging him to use his influence with Whitehall to speed up the pace of devolution. Memo. by Kanji Dwarkadas, dated 28 January 1945, encl. in US Consul-General, Bombay, to Sec. State, Washington, US State Dept decimal file 845.00/4–1947.
72. Political Dept note [July 1941], IOR R/1/1/3706; and note on the AISML by Int. Bureau, Home Dept, dated 15 March 1943, NAI, Home (Pol.) 17/2 Pol (I) of 1943.
73. AIML Papers, Karachi University, file 214, Pt IV of 1940.
74. Jinnah to Gandhi, 17 September 1944, in L.A. Sherwani (ed.), *Pakistan Resolution to Pakistan, 1940–1947: A Selection of Documents* (Karachi, 1969), pp. 78–9.
75. Note prepared for the League's Council of Action, dated 24 January 1944, AIML Papers, Karachi University, file 155, Pt I of 1944.
76. Press statement by Hindu Mahasabha, n.d., CI Agency, Confdl file 70-A of 1940.
77. G.V.B. Gillan, Resdt, Gwalior, to Sec. to CR, 15 July 1941, IOR L/P&S/13/1192.
78. Unsigned report by an officer of the Gwalior Praja Mandal on 'Hindu–Muslim Riot at Ujjain', NMML, AISPC, file 60 of 1946–47; and *Jayanti Pratap*, 20 August 1942.
79. *Jayanti Pratap*, 6 August 1942.
80. Speech of 15 February 1939, in K.M. Munshi (ed.), *Indian Constitutional Documents: Munshi Papers*, Vol. II (Bombay, 1967), p. 355.
81. The 1937 election results are very difficult to interpret accurately, in part because different sources give slightly different figures. I have erred probably on the side of optimism in allocating 17 victories to 'Hindu Sabha' candidates.
82. Speech by Moonje to the South Kanara Dist. Hindu Conf., Udipi, 3 June 1944, NMML, Hindu Mahasabha Papers, C-48.
83. Speech by Moonje to the Baroda Hindu Sabha, 1944, quoted in *The Times of India*, 3 May 1944.
84. Savarkar's presidential address to the 22nd session of the Hindu Mahasabha, Madura, 1940, NAI, Jayakar Papers, file 709.
85. *Samagra Savarkar Wangmaya*, Vol. VI, pp. 353–4.
86. Gurbachan Singh and Lal Singh Gyani, *The Idea of the Sikh State* (Lahore, c.1946), p. 17.
87. Quoted in Rajiiv A. Kapur, *Sikh Separatism: The Politics of Faith* (London, 1986), p. 207.

88. Sadhu Swarup Singh, *The Sikhs Demand their Homeland* (Lahore, c.1946), p. 82 (my italics).

89. Unnamed Sikh officer to Col. Spencer, 19 September 1947, Br. Lib., Rees Coll., file 50 (my italics).

90. Rajwant Kaur Dhillon, 'Demand For Pakistan: Role of Master Tara Singh', in Verinder Grover (ed.), *The Story of Punjab, Yesterday and Today*, Vol. 1 (New Delhi, 1995), p. 538; fort. report from Punjab for second half of September 1944, in P.S. Gupta (ed.), *Towards Freedom: Documents on the Movement for Independence in India 1943–1944* (New Delhi, 1997), Pt 3, p. 3270.

91. Sir Evan Jenkins to Lord Wavell, 4 July 1946. Nicholas Mansergh (editor-in-chief), *Constitutional Relations Between Britain and India: The Transfer of Power 1942–7* [Hereafter TOP], Vol. VIII (London, 1979), p. 6.

92. Weekly report by director, IB, Home Dept, dated 22 February 1941, IOR L/P&J/12/483.

93. Weekly report from director, IB, Home Dept, dated 5 July 1941, IOR L/P&J/12/483.

94. There are only stray references to the deal in the Patiala archives, which give no hint as to its terms, although we may suppose that they included a promise by the princes to direct their nominees on the SGPC to support the Tara Singh faction. It was a rocky courtship, however. Soon Tara Singh was accusing Bhupinder Singh of going back on his word. The cause of this (temporary) rupture was the sacking of Tara Singh's brother, Professor Niranjan Singh, one of the people who had helped arbitrate the settlement, from his chemistry teaching job at Khalsa College. The maharaja of Patiala as college chancellor could have intervened to prevent the dismissal, but chose not to do so. This, in Tara Singh's view, constituted 'a breach of the understanding between the State and the Akali Party ... almost a betrayal'. Message from Tara Singh to Raghbir Singh, Home Minister, Patiala, sent via S. Gurjit Singh on 11 August 1937, PSA, Patiala, Ijlas-i-Khas, file 2055.

95. Chunan Singh Bavar, Gen. Sec., City CC, Ferozepur, to Maulana A.K. Azad, 30 December 1940, NMML, AICC, file G-35 of 1940.

96. Circular letter from Moonje to various rulers, dated 10 December 1938, NMML, M.S. Aney Papers, subject file 7; and see also Savarkar's presidential address to the 22nd annual session of the Mahasabha at Madura, 1940, NAI, Jayakar Papers, 709.

97. Raghbir Singh to Prime Minister of Patiala, 27 August 1937, PSA, Patiala, Ijlas-i-Khas, 2055.

98. Report by J.H. Thompson, Resdt, Punjab States, dated 26 November 1945, IOR L/P&S/13/1358.

99. Note by G.V.B. Gillan, Resdt, Rajputana, 11 March 1943; and note by C.C.H. Smith, PA Rajputana States, dated 16 August 1946, IOR L/P&S/13/1396.

100. Note by S. Owens, tutor to the maharajkumar of Rewa, on talk with Wylie at the residency, Bangalore, dated 6 February 1945, IOR R/1/1/4259.

101. J. Thompson, Resdt, Jaipur, to Maj. A.A. Russell, sec. to Resdt, Rajputana, 16 September 1940, IOR R/1/1/3500.

102. Aide-memoir by Col. G.T. Fisher, Resdt, Gwalior, dated 21 November 1937, IOR R/1/1/2947. Born in 1916, Jayaji Rao Scindia was only nine years of age when his father died. Accordingly the state experienced an extended period of

British 'minority rule', from 1925 until 1937, when Jayaji Rao (already two years into his majority) was invested with full powers. During this time the Political Department was responsible not only for the welfare of the state but also for the maharaja's education; hence their anxiety about his mental fitness.

103. H.M. Poulton, Resdt, Gwalior, to CR, 17 June 1945, IOR L/P&S/13/1192.

104. Draft of newspaper article on 'Hindus and Federation: Do Not Fall Unwitting Victims to Pan-Islamism' by Mehta, written in December 1937, Jayakar Papers, file 65.

105. Aide-Memoir by Fisher, dated 21 November 1937, IOR R/1/1/2947.

106. Note by Col. G.T. Fisher, Resdt, CI, dated October 1942, IOR R/1/1/3882.

107. Diary of Amar Singh Kanota, 1937, p. 416 (entry for 12 December 1937).

108. Secret report received in Home Dept, IB, dated 2 April 1942, NAI, Home (Pol.), 222/42.

109. B.S. Moonje to the Viceroy, 3 October 1940, IOR L/P&J/8/683.

110. The nawab of Palanpur to the nawab of Bhopal, 13 January 1944, B[hopal] R[ecord] O[ffice], Bhopal, Pol. Dept, Chamber Section, file 94, 10/1 of 1943. One story doing the rounds in Delhi just before independence was that Rampur was pointedly left out of a meeting chaired by the maharaja of Patiala. Nehru to the maharaja of Patiala, 25 July 1947, in S. Gopal (ed.), *Selected Works of Jawaharlal Nehru*, 2nd series, Vol. 3 (New Delhi, 1986), p. 263.

111. The nawab of Rampur to the maharaja of Dewas Junior, 6 April 1940, IOR R/1/1/3556.

112. Sir Olaf Caroe attributed the appointment to the nawab of Bhopal's desire to acquire a conduit into 'the inner circles of the Muslim League'. Caroe to Sir Bertrand Glancy, 4 April 1940, IOR R/1/1/3533.

113. Hamidullah was persuaded to stand by Chamber secretary Maqbool Mahmud, brother-in-law of Punjab Unionist premier Sir Sikander Hyet Khan (mover of the Lahore Resolution) and by Sikander's brother Liaquat. The fact that both Maqbool and Liaquat had in the past worked for non-Muslim rulers (Jhalawar and Patiala respectively) suggests that something quite fundamental was happening to the once proudly ecclectic *darbāri* polity. Maqbool to Liaquat, 26 June 1943, BRO, Bhopal, Pol. Dept, Chamber Section, 94, 10/1.

114. Liaquat to the nawab of Palanpur, 20 January 1944, BRO, Bhopal, Pol. Dept, Chamber Section, 94, 10/1; and memo. By Kanji Dwarkadas, dated 28 January 1945, encl. in Consul General Bombay to Sec. State, Washington, 10 April 1947, US State Dept decimal file 845.00/4–1047. K.M. Panikkar saw him as 'a Muslim partisan and enemy of the Hindus'. K.M. Panikkar, *An Autobiography* (Madras, 1977), p. 138.

115. Speech of 3 June 1944, NMML, Hindu Mahasabha Papers, file C-48; Savarkar quoted in *The Times of India*, 23 and 24 April 1945.

116. Savarkar to the maharaja of Jaipur, 19 July 1944, NMML, Hindu Mahasabha Papers, file C-39.

117. Speech at Pherala, Lyallpur district, 6 April 1940, IOR R/1/1/3554.

118. Maharaja of Kapurthala to Resdt, Punjab states, 17 April 1940, IOR R/1/1/3554; and report of meeting of the SGPC on 18/19 November 1944, PSA, Patiala, Dharam Arth, 286/50.

119. Moonje to M.R. Jayakar, 24 September 1943, NAI, Jayakar Papers, 724.

120. For example, Jamuna Prasad Mukhraiyya, Sec., Madhya Bharat Hindu Sabha, to F&P Member, Gwalior, 8 April 1942, M[adhya] P[radesh] S[tate] A[rchives], Gwalior, Home Dept, file 74 of 1941.

121. Sharda Bhai Pachure *et al.* to the Sec., Education Dept, Gwalior, 8 December 1944, MPSA, Gwalior, Home Dept, file 43 of 1944; and *The Jayanti Pratap* (Gwalior), 29 April 1943.

122. Press statement by Savarkar, dated 28 June 1944, NMML, Hindu Mahasabha Papers, C-39.

123. Note dated 28 January 1943, PSA, Kapurthala, Sadar Office, P/3-3-43.

124. By the time the truce was brokered, Sharma had subsisted for 54 days on nothing but water—a feat, he claimed, that even Gandhi had not equalled. The government made 54,000 *bighas* of crown land available for cattle grazing.

125. Verma, *Bhopal*, p. 99.

126. Fort. report from Regional Commissioner, Western India, for the period ending 31 December 1947, NAI, RCO, Rajasthan, file 18-P/48-D. Mahasabhite sources put it at more like 80 per cent. *The Mahratta*, 16 June 1944.

127. Hakim, Jaswantpura, to Chief Sec., Jodhpur, 13 October 1947, RSA, Jodhpur, Social, file C 1/2 of 1947.

128. Memorandum prepared for the maharaja of Bikaner by Chunilal Kapur, IG Police, Bikaner, dated 11 July 1946, RSAB, Bikaner, Home Dept, 35/1946.

129. Note by Jai Narain Vyas, Gen. Sec., AISPC, dated [August 1945], AISPC, 86 (Pt II) of 1945–48.

130. Kamtaprasad, Presdt, Sehore Praja Mandal, to Vallabhbhai Patel, 11 September 1947, AISPC, Pt I, file 19/1 of 1945–48.

131. Minute [in Hindi] by Bapurao Pawar, Law and Justice Minister, Gwalior, dated 14 April 1941, MPSA, Gwalior, Home Dept, 11/1941.

132. 'Patiala Administration and the Position of the Sikhs', n.d. [1942], IOR R/1/1/3884.

133. The worst clashes occurred in Jammu City on 15 February; at Balotra (Kotah) on 18 March; in Gwalior City on 3 April; at Halvad (Dhrangadhra) on 10 April; at Bhopal on 12 April; at Sheoganj (Sirohi) on 26 June; at Bikaner on 8 July; at Baroda on 3 September; at Dholidub (Alwar) on 24 September; at Gwalior again in late November, and at Baran (Kotah) on 24 January 1947. The Bikaner riot has already been discussed at some length.

134. Resdt, Gwalior, to Pol. Sec., GOI, 12 April 1946, IOR R/1/1/4421.

135. The resident afterwards counted eight Punjabi Muslims among the 28 rioters admitted to hospital. Another 200 Punjabis arrived by train the day after the riot, again, presumably, by arrangement, but were turned back at the station. W.F. Webb, Resdt, Kashmir, to Sec. to the CR, 19 February 1946, IOR L/P&S/13/1266.

136. Pol. Dept, New Delhi, to Resdt, Gwalior (teleg.), 12 April 1946, IOR R/1/1/4421.

137. Gen. Sec., Hindu Mahasabha, to S.P. Mookherjee, Presdt, Hindu Mahasabha, 24 April 1946, NMML, Hindu Mahasabha Papers, file C-140.

138. Resdt, Gwalior, to Pol. Sec., GOI, 12 April 1946, IOR R/1/1/4421.

139. Penalties ranged from six months imprisonment to life, but most offences under the Ordinance carried jail terms of seven to ten years. Penalties were generally harsher than for comparable offences under the Gwalior Penal Code. *Communal Disturbances Prevention Ordinance: Gwalior State*, Ordinance

No. 3 of Samvat 2004 (1946), MPSA, Gwalior, Bundle No. 15, Serial No. 22, file No. 104/11.

140. Statement issued by the maharaja of Gwalior on 1 December 1946, IOR R/1/1/4509.

141. M.A. Sreenivasan, *Of the Raj, Maharajas and Me* (Delhi, 1991), p. 220.

142. Tour note by L.A.G. Pinhey, PA, Eastern Rajputana, dated February 1947, IOR R/1/1/4590.

143. 'Representation by Bikaner Muslims to Liaquat Ali Khan in Delhi, [July] 1946', RSA, Bikaner, Home Dept, file 35/1946.

144. IG Police, Jodhpur, to Chief Minister, Jodhpur, 11 February 1945, and Judicial Supt, Mallam, to Chief Minister, Jodhpur, 25 December 1945, RSA, Jodhpur, Social, file C 1/2 of 1947.

145. Note by Conrad Corfield, dated 30 January 1942, IOR L/P&S/13/1345. This was the same problem that had triggered the disturbances of 1935 in Malerkotla, discussed above.

146. Fort. police report for first half of September 1946, RSA, Kotah, Confdl file 36; and IG Police's confdl weekly diary for period ending 15 November 1946, RSA, Kotah, Confdl file 39.

147. Hakim, Parbatsar, to Sub-Inspector of Police, PS, Parbatsar, 19 October 1946, RSA, Jodhpur, Social, file C 1/1 of 1944–49.

4   The further shores of partition

1. Harbans Lal Gupta, Gen. Sec., Punjab SPC, to Jai Narain Vyas, 10 October 1945, AISPC, file 138/1 of 1933–48.

2. Membership statement, n.d., NMML, AISPC, file 60 of 1946–47.

3. Nehru to Sir T. Vijayaraghavashari, PM, Udaipur, 13 June 1946, NMML, Nehru Papers, 1st Instalment, file 1.

4. Chief Minister, Alwar, to PA, Alwar, 8 May 1942, PM, Jaipur, to PA, Jaipur, 9 September 1943, PM, Alwar, to PA, Jaipur, 5 March 1945, Home Minister, Jaipur, to PA, Jaipur, 4 April 1945, PM, Jaipur, to PA, Jaipur, 2 January 1947, and Vice-Presdt, State Council, Tonk, to PA, Jaipur, 25 January 1947, IOR R/2/150/123; IG Kotah's confdl diary for period ending 9 December 1946, RSA, Kotah, Confdl file 39; fort. report on Rajputana for period ending 28 February 1947, IOR L/P&S/13/1442; and Shail Mayaram, 'Speech, Silence, and the Making of Partition Violence in Mewat', in Shahid Amin and Dipesh Chakrabarty (eds), *Subaltern Studies: Writings on South Asian History and Society*, Vol. 10 (Delhi, 1996), p. 131.

5. Fort. report on CI for period ending 31 January 1947, IOR L/P&S/13/1181.

6. Fort. report on the CI Agency for period ending 15 July 1946, IOR L/P&S/13/1181.

7. Quoted in Bal Raj Nayar, *Minority Politics in the Punjab* (Princeton, N.J., 1966), p. 91; and Sir Penderel Moon, *Divide and Quit* (Berkeley, 1962), p. 77.

8. Fort. report on the Gwalior residency for the period ending 15 May 1947, IOR L/P&S/13/1197.

9. A.A. Russell, Resdt, Gwalior, to Sec. to the CR, 15 February 1947, IOR R/1/1/4509; and report on 'The Hindu–Muslim Riots at Ujjain', n.d. [by Sec. Gwalior State Congress], NMML, AISPC, file 60 of 1946–47.

10. Note by T.B. Creagh-Coen, dated 21 December 1946, IOR R/1/1/4509.
11. 'Memorandum on States Treaties and Paramountcy', dated 12 May 1946, quoted in Gwyer and Appadorai, *Speeches and Documents*, Vol. 2, pp. 768–9.
12. 'Statement Containing the Final Decision of His Majesty's Government Regarding the Method of the Transfer of Power', 3 June 1947, quoted in Gwyer and Appadorai, *Speeches and Documents*, Vol. 2, pp. 671–4.
13. Khare, *Memoirs*, p. 298.
14. Viceroy's personal report No. 10, dated 29 June 1947, *TOP*, Vol. XI, p. 689.
15. Letter from 'a senior officer in the Bhopal State Forces', encl. in Admiral E.A. Taylor to Arthur Henderson, 5 December 1946, IOR L/P&J/7/132.
16. Resolution of the Standing Committee of the COP, 29 January 1947, in C.H. Philips (ed.), *The Evolution of India and Pakistan 1858–1947: Select Documents* (London, 1962), pp. 435–6.
17. Address by the viceroy to the special session of the COP, 25 July 1947, in Munshi, *Indian Constitutional Documents*, Vol. 2, p. 417.
18. Statement issued by Patel on 5 July 1947, in Gwyer and Appadorai, *Speeches and Documents*, Vol. 2, p. 771. This went well beyond the policy agreed upon between the Congress and the AISPC in 1946, which was that only the 20 or so largest states could expect to retain a quasi-separate existence, and then only as fully constitutional monarchies. Note by Hiralal Shastri, Sec., Rajputana Regional Council, dated 6 February 1946, AISPC, Pt I, file 2 of 1945–48.
19. Quoted in the *People's Age* (New Delhi), 14 September 1947.
20. Maps of the greater Bharatpur kingdom were reportedly discovered by government invesigators. Fort. report on the Matsya Union from dep. chief intelligence officer, Bharatpur, for the period ending 15 October 1948, NAI, RCO, Rajasthan, file 263-P/48-I; *The New Nazis* (Lahore, 1948), p. 21, Br. Lib., Mudie Coll., 31; and Mayaram, 'Speech, Silence, and the Making of Partition Violence in Mewat', p. 135.
21. Maharaja of Baroda to V. Patel, 2 September 1947, cited in V.P. Menon, *The Story of the Integration of the Indian States* (Bombay: Orient Longmans, 1956), p. 399.
22. General Claude Auchinlek, C.-in-C. India, to Sir Geoffrey Scoones, 5 October 1947 [marked 'top secret and personal—destroy when read'], Manchester University Lib., Auchinlek Papers, No. 1263; interview with R.G. Verma, Patiala, 1 February 1998; and statement by former SP, Narnaul, Patiala, quoted in *The Sikhs in Action* (Lahore, 1948), p. 51.
23. Larry Collins and Dominique Lapierre, *Freedom at Midnight* (London, 1975), pp. 314–15.
24. Auchinlek to Sir Geoffrey Scones, 5 October 1947, Auchinlek Papers, No. 1263.
25. Interview given by the jam saheb, as quoted in the *Hindustan Times*, 23 September 1947.
26. The Maharaja of Bikaner to Mountbatten, 3 April 1947, *TOP*, Vol. X, p. 110; and see also Sadul Singh's earlier inquiry, to his resident, about the availability of 'outside forces' in the event of trouble: Note on Bikaner by R.R. Burnett, Resdt, Rajputana, dated 30 December 1946, IOR L/P&S/13/1396.
27. Donovan to Sec. of State, Washington, 23 September 1947, US State Dept, decimal file 845.00/9-2347.
28. US Ambassador New Delhi to Sec. State, Washington, 24 April 1947, US State Dept, decimal file 845.00/4-2447; Monckton to Ismay 9 June 1947, *TOP*, Vol. 11, p. 214; and Ismay to Mountbatten 19 June 1947, *TOP*, Vol. 11, p. 504.

29. Address to the 1st Sikh regiment, Patiala, 3 April 1947, and press statement by Tara Singh of 15 April 1947, as recorded in the diary of Ganda Singh, in Mushirul Hasan (ed.), *India Partitioned: The Other Face of Freedom* (New Delhi, 1995), pp. 31, 34–5.

30. Sir E. Jenkins to Lord Mountbatten, 9 April 1947, *TOP*, Vol. 10, p. 173.

31. Khare, *Memoirs*, pp. 321–2; and B.S. Moonje to A. Lahiri, 14 July 1947, NMML, Hindu Mahasabha Papers, file C-156, Pt 1.

32. Mayaram, 'Speech, Silence', pp. 136–7; and Haye, 'The Freedom Movement in Mewat', pp. 311–15.

33. Fort. report on the Rajputana Agency for the period ending 15 March 1946, IOR L/P&S/13/1442.

34. Fort. report on the Rajputana Agency for the period ending 28 February 1947, IOR L/P&S/13/1442.

35. Fort. report on the Rajputana Agency for the period ending 15 May 1947, IOR L/P&S/13/1442.

36. Khare, *Memoirs*, p. 302.

37. Entry in the diary of Major-General Hamid for 29 April/1 May 1947, Hamid, *Disastrous Twilight: A Personal Record of the Partition of India* (London, 1986), p. 169; and report by Major-General T.W. Rees, commander Punjab Boundary Force, dated 15 November 1947, Br. Lib., Jenkins Coll., 2.

38. Khare, *Memoirs*, pp. 321–2.

39. Auchinleck to Sir Geoffrey Scones, 5 October 1947, Auchinleck Papers, No. 1263.

40. Historians have only recently begun to probe the dark underside of the partition, and all these pioneering accounts focus on the provinces. Some of the more important are Swarna Aiyer, '"August Anarchy": The Partition Massacres in Punjab, 1947', in D.A. Low and Howard Brasted (eds), *Freedom, Trauma, Continuities: Northern India and Independence* (New Delhi, 1998), pp. 15–38; Paul Brass, 'The Partition of India and Retributive Genocide in the Punjab, 1946–47: Means, Methods, and Purposes', in *Journal of Genocide Studies*, Vol. 5, No. 1 (2003), pp. 71–101; Urvashi Butalia, 'Community, State and Gender: On Women's Agency During Partition', in *Economic and Political Weekly*, 24 April 1993, pp. 12–24; Mushirul Hasan, 'Partition: The Human Cost', in *History Today*, Vol. 47, No. 9 (1997), pp. 47–53; Hasan, *India Partitioned*, esp. Vol. 1, pp. 15–42; Ayesha Jalal, 'Nation, Reason and Religion: Punjab's Role in the Partition of India', in *Economic and Political Weekly*, 8 August 1998; Rita Menon and Ramla Bhasin, *Borders and Boundaries: Women in India's Partition* (New Brunswick, N.J., 1998); and Gyanendra Pandey, *Remembering Partition: Violence, Nationalism and History in India* (Cambridge, 2001).

41. Note by Col. Narayan Singh, ADC to the Prime Minister, Bikaner, dated 14 October 1947, RSA, Bikaner, Home Dept, file 26/1948.

42. Report by Auchinleck dated September 1947, Auchinleck Papers, No. 1262.

43. Report by Brish Bhan, Syed Muttalabi and Tara Chand Gupta, n.d. [1947], NMML, AISPC, Pt I, file 223/47.

44. High Commissioner, Karachi to CRO, London (teleg.), 6 November 1947, IOR L/P&S/13/1845B.

45. He deduced this 'From the fact that new cable wire was used, gelignite which is only a military supply was employed, a new battery and telephone were amongst the equipment taken to the spot, [and] a khaki coloured Jeep was the means of transport'. Report by D.W. Macdonald, addl. DC, Ferozepur, cited in *The Sikhs in Action*, Appendix VI.

46. Note by Jaswant Singh, Public Works Minister, Bikaner, dated 5 October 1947, RSA, Bikaner, Home Dept, file 26/1948.
47. Report by DC, Sialkot [October 1947], quoted in *Kashmir Before Accession*, p. 23; PA, Jaipur to CR (teleg.), 7 August 1947, quoting former Alwar Minister Gen. Abdul Rehman Khan, *TOP*, Vol. XII, p. 571; and 'unfortunate residents of Barwani' to PA, CI (teleg.), 18 October 1947.
48. Confdl report by SP, Sog, dated 2 September 1947, RSA, Bikaner, Home Dept, file 21/1947.
49. Batoo Ram Sood, Presdt, Malerkotla Riasti Praja Mandal, to Presdt, AISPC, 25 August 1947, NMML, AISPC, file 108 of 1945–48.
50. Confdl report by SP, Sog, dated 2 September 1947, RSA, Bikaner, Home Dept, file 21/1947.
51. SP Barnala to IG Police, Patiala, 7 September 1947, PSA, Patiala, Ijlas-i-Khas, file 2028.
52. Telephone message from Gurbachan Singh, IG Police, Sunam, to IG Police, Patiala, 26 August 1947, PSA, Patiala, NAI Ijlas-i-Khas, file 2028.
53. Note by SP, Barnala, dated 9 March 1947, PSA, Patiala, Ijlas-i-Khas, file 2233; and note by DM, Ganganagar, dated 20 August 1947, RSA, Bikaner, Home Dept, file 38/1947.
54. Interview with Teja Singh Tiwana, Patiala, 30 January 1998; and PM, Patiala, to Food Member, Govt. of Pakistan (teleg.), 4 September 1947, PSA, Patiala, Ijlas-i-Khas, file 2029.
55. 'A Plea to Pause and Ponder: Misunderstandings about the R.S.S. Clarified', encl. in B.R. Madhoke to Rajendra Prasad, NAI, Prasad Papers, file 6-R/48.
56. The *Statesman*, 4 March 1948; and Mayaram, 'Speech, Silence', p. 155.
57. Identifying Muslims on the mixed local trains was more difficult than one would suppose, since Muslim refugees often tried to evade the *jathas* by travelling in disguise. Sikh student Teja Singh Tiwana was journeying home to his village on a train bound for Bahawalpur, when it was stopped and boarded near Nabha. Initially, he was not disconcerted, as all the people in his compartment appeared to be Sikhs or Hindus; but when the *jathedars* entered they quickly established by dint of a body search that three were Muslim males. Without a moment's further reflection they beheaded the three in full view of the horrified youth. Interview with Teja Singh Tiwana, Patiala, 30 January 1998.
58. Mayaram notes that this deity is supposed to have been beheaded by Turks. 'Speech, Silence', p. 144.
59. A staff officer in the Bahawalpur Army had previously informed him privately that at least 150 Hindus had already perished. Report by Chunilal Kapur, IG Police, Bikaner, dated 26 August 1947, RSA, Bikaner, Home Dept, file 38/1947.
60. Gurdhari Lal *et al.* to maharaja of Patiala 12 January 1948, encl. a 'Brief Statement of Bahawalpur State Situation', PSA, Patiala, Ijlas-i-Khas, file 2275.
61. Suhrawardy to Charles O. Thompson, US Consul-General, Calcutta, 4 November 1947, encl. in Consul-General to Sec. State, Washington, 28 November 1947, US State Dept decimal file 845.00/11-2847.
62. Lt.-Gen. Sir Francis Tuker, *While Memory Serves* (London, 1950), p. 489; and *The Times*, 10 August 1948.
63. Interview with N.B. Khare by Dr H.D. Sharma, 16 July 1967, NMML, Oral History Transcript No. 230, pp. 71–4.
64. On advice received, according to Mayaram, from the CC of Ajmer who headed the Bharatpur investigation. 'Speech, Silence', p. 149.

65. The 1949 census is described in Snedden, 'Paramountcy', p. 94. Details come from *Dawn*, 2 January 1951.
66. Ian Stephens, *Pakistan* (London, 1963), p. 200.
67. For a sample of the range of opinion, see Andres Bjorn Hansen, *Partition and Genocide: Manifestation of Violence in Punjab 1937–1947* (New Delhi, 2002), p. 193.
68. Sitaramayya to Nehru, 4 March 1948, NMML, AICC, file 1 of 1948.
69. Note, Ijlas-i-Khas, dated 3 November 1947, PSA, Patiala, Dharam Arth, file 1205/117.
70. *Kashmir Before Accession*, p. 35. See also the report of Hari Singh's involvement in the Jammu incident in the *Civil and Military Gazette* of 18 December 1947, quoted in Snedden, 'Paramountcy', p. 92.
71. *The New Nazis*, p. 26.
72. The Sikh lady was travelling with the maharaja and maharani in their car. Suhrawardy to Gandhi, 19 November 1947, encl. in Consul-General Calcutta to Sec. State, Washington, 28 November 1947, US State Dept decimal file 845.00/11-2847.
73. Howard Donovan, US Embassy New Delhi, to Sec. State, Washington, 12 December 1947, US State Dept decimal file 845.00/12-1247.
74. Note by Jaswant Singh, Public Works Minister, Bikaner, dated 5 October 1947, RSA, Bikaner, Home Dept, file 26/1948.
75. Khare's role in the planning of the pogrom against the Meos has already been documented. On Gurmani's role in the Bahawalpur killings, see notes of a conversation between Lt.-Col. Sardar Narinder Singh, formerly of the Bahawalpur army, and the private sec. to the maharaja of Patiala on 3 December 1947, PSA, Patiala, Ijlas-i-Khas, file 2275.
76. Note by Supt. Police, CID, Patiala, dated 26 November 1947, PSA, Patiala, Ijlas-i-Khas, 2028.
77. Situation report, HQ, east Punjab, to Army HQ, India and Pakistan, 3 September 1947, Br. Lib., Rees Coll., 64; telegrams from refugees encl. in SP, Barnala, to IG Police, Patiala, 30 August 1947, PSA, Patiala, Ijlas-i-Khas, 2028; Chanan Singh, pleader, *et al.*, Sunam, to maharaja of Patiala (teleg.), 20 September 1947, PSA, Patiala, Ijlas-i-Khas, file 2032.
78. Suhrawardy to Nehru, 6 November 1947, encl. in Charles O. Thompson, US Consul-General, Calcutta, to Sec. State, Washington, 28 November 1947, US State Dept decimal file 845.00/11-2847.
79. Memorandum by Judicial member of Council, dated [1948], quoted in Khare, *Memoirs*, p. 331.
80. In 1962, Indian Punjab was further partitioned along linguistic lines to create the Punjabi-speaking state of Punjab and the Hindi-speaking state of Haryana. This was consistent with the GOI's decision in 1956 to accommodate some language-based territorial demands but not territorial demands based on other ethnic criteria, especially religion. The post-1947 story of the Punjab is touched on briefly in my article, 'The Master and the Maharajas: The Sikh Princes and the East Punjab Massacres of 1947', in *Modern Asian Studies*, Vol. 36, No. 3 (2002), pp. 695*et seq.*
81. Note by Jaswant Singh, Public Works Minister, Bikaner, dated 5 October 1947, RSA, Bikaner, Home Dept, file 26/1948. See also the description of the RSS rally at Kotah City on 28 October 1947 in the Confdl diary of the IG Police, Kotah, for the week ending 31 October 1947, RSA, Kotah, Confdl file 39.

82. Memoir by Judicial Member, Alwar Council, dated [1948], quoted in Khare, *Memoirs*, p. 331; and report by deputy IG Police, Ganganagar, dated 4 October 1947, RSA, Bikaner, Home Dept, file 38/1947. See also Khare's testimony in his interview with Sharma, 16 July 1967, NMML, Oral History Transcript No. 230.

83. IG Police, Bikaner, to Chief Sec., Bikaner, 4 November 1947, RSA, Bikaner, Home (Confdl) file 27 of 1947; and Sardar Boor Singh, Presdt, Himalaya Sikh Missionary Soc., to General Gurdial Singh Harika, PM, Patiala, 18 October 1947, and 'residents of Teh Narwana' to Vallabhbhai Patel (teleg.), 11 November 1947, PSA, Patiala, Ijlas-i-Khas, file 2035.

84. Rajendra Prasad to Patel 26 June 1948, Valmiki Choudhary (ed.), *Dr Rajendra Prasad: Correspondence and Select Documents*, Vol. 9 (New Delhi, 1988), p. 163.

85. Statement by Mot Khudijan, alias Ram Piaire, aged 20, appended to note by IG Police, Bikaner, dated 5 January 1948, RSA, Bikaner, Home (Confdl) file 27 of 1947.

86. Nehru to Mrs Rameshwari Nehru, Women's Section, Ministry of Relief and Rehabilitation, 1 March 1948, NMML, Nehru Papers, 1st Instalment (master file).

87. Note by Jaswant Singh, Public Works Minster, Bikaner, dated 5 October 1947, RSA, Bikaner, Home Dept, file 26/1948.

88. Nazim, Sunam, to PM, Patiala [rec'd], 24 October 1947, PSA, Patiala, Ijlas-i-Khas, file 2032.

89. This, despite some of them receiving 'promissory notes' from state officials for the safe keeping of their property. UK High Commr., Karachi, to Sec. State for Commonwealth Relations (teleg.), 7 October 1947, IOR L/P&S/13/1358; and Syed Jamil Hussein, advocate, Lahore, to PM, Patiala, 11 March 1948, PSA, Patiala, Ijlas-i-Khas, file 2032.

90. Report by Deputy IG Police, Ganganagar, dated 4 October 1947, RSA, Bikaner, Home Dept, file 38/1947.

91. Khare, *Memoirs*, p. 317.

92. Rajendra Prasad to Bhargava, 15 February 1948, Prasad Papers, file 1-C/48; and Mohammad Yasin Khan to Vinobha Bhave, 13 April 1948, NAI, Prasad Papers, file 5-R/48.

93. H.S. Suhrawardy to Charles O. Thompson, US Consul-General, Calcutta, 4 November 1947, US State Dept decimal file 845.00/11-2847.

94. Khare, *Memoirs*, p. 305.

95. Hari Lal Bhargava, member, PPCC, to Gandhi, 12 January 1948, Mohammad Yasin Khan to Vinobha Bhave, 13 April 1948, and note by M.N. Masud, n.d., encl. in Mridula Sarabhai to Nehru, 15 April 1948, NAI, Prasad Papers, file 5-R/48.

96. Nehru to C.M. Trivedi, Gov. of East Punjab, 5 July 1948, Gopal, *Selected Works*, 2nd series, Vol. 7, p. 39.

97. Note by Dantyagi, dated 18 June 1948, NAI, Prasad Papers, file 5-R/48.

98. Dep. PM to Dep. High Commissioner for Pakistan, 26 February 1948, NAI, Prasad Papers, file 5-R/48 (emphasis added).

99. Interview with Khemchand Mathur, Jaipur, 10 November 2000.

100. 'Note on [the] Rehabilitation of Meos in Alwar and Bharatpur', encl. in Mohanlal Saxena, Rehabilitation Minister, to Prasad, 18 June 1949, Choudhary, *Prasad*, Vol. 11, p. 100.

5   The new India

1. B.K. Vaidya to Gandhi, [1947], NMML, Hindu Mahasabha Papers, file C-92.
2. Fort. report on the Pol. situation by CIO, Jaipur, for period ending 15 September 1949, NAI, RCO, Rajasthan, file 164-P/50-R.
3. 'Hindus of Kashmir' to Vallabhbhai Patel, 1 November 1947, NAI, MOS, file 118(1)-P.R. of 1947; and Nehru to maharaja of Kashmir, 30 December 1947, NMML, Nehru Papers, 1st Instalment, file 4.
4. Statement by Ashutosh Lahiri, Gen. Sec., Hindu Mahasabha, quoted in the *Bombay Chronicle*, 10 January 1948.
5. John J. Macdonald, US Consul-General, Bombay, to Sec. State, Washington, 15 January 1948, US State Dept decimal file 845.00/1-1548.
6. *Hindustan Times*, 7 January 1948. See also Sarvepalli Gopal, *Jawaharlal Nehru: A Biography*, Vol. 2 (London, 1979), p. 77; Mushirul Hasan, *Legacy of a Divided Nation: India's Muslims Since Independence* (London, 1997), p. 148; and Christophe Jaffrelot, *The Hindu Nationalist Movement and Indian Politics 1925 to the 1990s* (London, 1996), p. 84.
7. B.S. Moonje to the Viceroy, 3 October 1940, IOR L/P&J/8/683.
8. Howard Donovan, counselor, US Embassy New Delhi, to Sec. State, 29 December 1948, US State Dept decimal file 845.00/12-2948.
9. Jaffrelot, *Hindu Nationalist Movement*, p. 81.
10. Note by Chunilal Kapur, IG Police, Bikaner, dated 3 December 1947, RSA, Bikaner, Home Dept, file 12 of 1948–49.
11. Petition from 'Jagir Singh and others' to maharaja of Kapurthala, dated 25 February 1948, AISPC, file 91 of 1946–48.
12. Miriam Sharma and Urmila Vanjani, 'Remembrances of Things Past: Partition Experiences of Punjabi Villages in Rajasthan', in *Economic and Political Weekly*, 4 August 1990, p. 1728.
13. Interview with Wing-Commander Rawat Ghanshyam Singh, Jaipur, 10 November 2000.
14. Interview with Vaduendra Sahai, Jaipur, 7 November 2000.
15. Zenah Banu, *Immigrants: A New Virus for Communal Violence in India* (Delhi, 1998), p. 67; and Sharma and Vanjani, 'Remembrances of Things Past', p. 1733.
16. Interview with Justice I.S. Israni, Jaipur, 11 November 2000; and Howard Donovan, Chargé d'Affaires, US embassy, New Delhi, to Sec. State, Washington, 23 December 1947, US State Dept decimal file 845.00/12-2347.
17. Nehru to Saxena 10 September 1949, quoted in Gopal, *Jawaharlal Nehru*, Vol. 2, p. 77. Nehru made a similar remark to Patel about the Hindu Punjabi refugees in Kashmir. They were of 'a different type' to the local Hindus, he opined. Nehru to Patel 30 December 1947, NMML, Nehru Papers, 1st Instalment, file 4.
18. Fort. reports from CC, Ajmer, for first half of December 1947, and first half of March and second half of March 1948, NAI, RCO, Rajasthan, file 18-P/48; Mamsor Khan, Jahangirpur to Lord Mountbatten (teleg.), 20 January 1948, NAI, MOS, file 2(25)-P.R./47; SP, Mandsaur, to IG Police, Gwalior, 1 February 1948, MPSA, Gwalior, file 104–11 of 1947; Ghasituram Rickhanwala to Nehru (teleg.), 1 March 1948, AISPC, file 138 Pt 1; Fort. report from RC Gujarat for period ending 31 March 1948, NAI, RCO, Rajasthan, file 18-P/48-D; Report by Dep. IG Police, Bikaner, dated 26 March 1948, RSA, Bikaner, Home Dept, file 26/1948; CC, Himachal Pradesh to Under-Sec., MOS, 26 April 1948, NAI, MOS, file 4(61)-P/48; and RC, CI to MOS (teleg.), 29 December 1948, NAI, RCO, CI, file 177-Q of 1948.

19. Fort. Appreciation from Ministry of Information and Broadcasting No. 35, dated 22 May 1948, NAI, RCO, Rajasthan, file 100-P/48.

20. Krishna, 'Communal Violence in India', p. 65.

21. Press statement by Bolanath Master, Sec., Alwar RPM, dated 1 January 1948, AISPC, Pt 1, file 2 of 1945–48.

22. President, Barwani Rajya Lok Parishad to RC, Indore, 23 February 1948, AISPC, Pt 1, file 11 of 1947–48.

23. Report on Bilaspur by Brish Bhan, President, Punjab States Regional Council, dated 22 December 1946, AISPC, Pt I, file 25 of 1945–47.

24. Sec. Lok Parishad Jodhpur to Sec., AISPC (teleg.), 24 February 1948, AISPC, file 87, Pt 1 of 1945–48.

25. Note by Maharaja of Bikaner on meeting in Delhi, dated 19 June 1948, AISPC, Pt 1, file 141.

26. Hiralal Shastri to Maharaja of Jaipur, 12 July 1948, NMML, Shastri Papers.

27. Nanigram B. Trivedi, Gen. Sec., Banswarra RPM, to Gen. Sec., AISPC, 3 February 1948, AISPC, Pt 1, file 6 of 1945–48; Panalal Sharma, Sec., Jodhpur Lok Parishad, to Sec., AISPC (teleg.), 30 April 1948, AISPC, file 87, Pt 1, of 1945–48; press release from Hamideo Joshi, Dungapur, dated 12 January 1948, AISPC, file 51 of 1945–48; 'Bhasawar People' to Sec., MOS (teleg.), 17 March 1948, AISPC, Pt 1, file 15 of 1945–48; and Dep. High Commissioner, Lahore, to CRO, 7 March 1948, IOR L/P&S/13/1376.

28. Nehru to chief ministers, 1 July 1948, G. Parthasarathi (ed.), *Letters to Chief Ministers, 1947–1949* (Delhi, 1985), Vol. 1, p. 142.

29. Quoted in report by Brish Bhan, Syed Muttalabi and Tara Chand Gupta on a visit to Alwar, n.d. [1948], AISPC, file 223 of 1948.

30. Confdl report from DI, G.R.P. Bina, dated 20 December 1948, NAI, CI Agency, Confdl file 9-Q of 1948.

31. Speech by Patel at Alwar, quoted in press release by GOI Info. Bureau, dated 25 February 1948, IOR L/P&S/13/1387.

32. Patel to Prasad 24 June 1948, Choudhary, *Prasad*, Vol. 9, p. 152.

33. Fort. report from CC, Ajmer, for the first half of February 1948, RCO, Rajasthan, file 18-P/48.

34. Fort. report from CC, Ajmer, for the second half of February 1948, RCO, Rajasthan, file 18-P/48.

35. Note by S.N.P., Bikaner, dated 23 March 1948, and Home Ministry, New Delhi, to provincial govts. (teleg.), 12 December 1948, RSA, Bikaner, Home Dept, file 12 of 1948–49; and M.R. Thosar to Rajendra Prasad, 7 July 1948, Choudhary, *Prasad*, Vol. 9, pp. 205–6.

36. Deposition of Madhukar Keshav Kale of Lashkar, Gwalior given on 14 July 1948; and summing up by special judge Atma Charan on 19 February 1949, East Punjab High Court, *Gandhi Murder Case*, Vol. 1, p. 67 and Vol. 3, p. 78. Pachure was sentenced to transportation for life, ibid., p. 109, but the sentence was subsequently overturned on appeal.

37. R.G. Iyengar, Supt., E. Rajputana States Agency, to MOS (teleg.), 6 February 1948, and Iyengar to MOS, 11 February 1948, NAI, RCO, Rajasthan, file 83-P/48.

38. Fort. report from the RC, CI, for the second half of September 1948, NAI, RCO, Rajasthan, file 18-P/48-E.

39. 'India news' release from the Ministry of Information and Broadcasting for the week ending 12 February 1948, IOR L/P&S/13/1393.

40. Patel to Nehru 6 February 1948, Choudhary, *Prasad*, Vol. 8, p. 197.

41. The States Ministry's V.P. Menon in conversation with staffers at the American embassy, New Delhi. Ambassador, New Delhi, to Sec. State, Washington, US State Dept decimal file 845.00/12-3147.
42. Ibid.
43. Fort. report from RC, CI, for period ending 31 December 1947, NAI, RCO, Rajasthan, file 18-P/48-E.
44. Nehru to Sheikh Abdullah, 21 May 1948, NMML, Nehru Papers, 1st Instalment, file 9.
45. Rajkumari Amrit Kaur to Nehru, 12 September 1949, NMML, Nehru Papers, 1st Instalment, file 29, Pt 1.
46. Intelligence report received in Patiala, 10 January 1948, PSA, Patiala, Ijlas-i-Khas, file 2028.
47. 'Proposal for the Formation of the United State of Gwalior, Indore and Malwa', as summarised for the Cabinet by V.P. Menon, 25 April 1948, Br. Lib., Mountbatten Coll., file 147.
48. V.P. Menon, *The Story of the Integration of the Indian States* (Bombay, 1961), p. 164.
49. Patel to Prasad, 24 June 1948, Choudhary, *Prasad*, Vol. 9, p. 152.
50. The Patiala and East Punjab States Union.
51. Note by N. Bonarjee, CC, Bhopal, dated 18 October 1949, NAI, MOS, file 344-P/49; Bonarjee to V.P. Menon, Sec., MOS, 23 January 1950, and V.P. Vishwananth, CC, Bhopal, to Menon, 20 April 1950, NAI, MOS, file 9 (8)-P/50.
52. Commissioner, Meerut-Rohilkhand Division, to Chief Sec., UP, 8 November 1948, NAI, MOS, file 606-P/48.
53. Suleman Haji Pirmohamed Diwan to Maulana A.K. Azad, Education Minister, GOI, 12 May 1950 and B.R. Patel, Chief Sec., Saurashtra, to RC, Saurashtra, 2 August 1951, NAI, MOS, file 1(67)-P/50.
54. Note by Nehru, dated 25 September 1948, NMML, Nehru Papers, 1st Instalment, file 13, Pt 3.
55. Intelligence report for Rajputana for second half of June 1948, NAI, RCO, Rajasthan, file 18-P/48-I.
56. Howard Donovan, US Ambassador, New Delhi, to Sec. State, Washington, 4 June 1948, US State Dept decimal file 845.00/6-448.
57. Note by N. Bonarjee, dated 18 October 1949, NAI, MOS, file 344-P/49.
58. Narain and Mathur, 'The Thousand Year Raj', p. 23.
59. Howard Donovan, US Chargé d'Affaires, New Delhi, to Sec. State, Washington, 11 August 1948, US State Dept decimal file 845.00/8-1148.
60. William L. Richter, 'Princes in Indian Politics', in *Economic and Political Weekly*, 27 February 1971, p. 537.
61. Richter, 'Electoral Patterns', pp. 37–8.
62. Richter, 'Princes in Indian Politics', p. 537.
63. The first was Harish Chandra, the former ruler of Jhalawar, who became a member of the Mohanlal Sukadia-led government of Rajasthan in 1960.
64. Resolution passed at special session of the Mahasabha at Jaipur, April 27–29, under presidency of N.B. Khare, quoted in Fort. report on Rajasthan for the second half of April 1951, NAI, RCO, Rajasthan, file 44-P/51-B.
65. Interview with HH of Kotah, Kotah, 18 March 1998.
66. S.N. Eisenstadt, 'Post-Traditional Societies and the Continuity and Reconstruction of Tradition', in *Daedulus*, Vol. 102 (1973), p. 3.

67. The phrase is Nikita Khruschev's. The Soviet premier met a number of princely politicians during his state visit to India in 1956. He found their incorporation within a supposedly egalitarian political system at once fascinating and puzzling. Quoted in B. Krishna, *Sardar Vallabhbhai Patel: India's Iron Man* (New Delhi, 1995), p. 434.

6 Conclusion

1. See Varshney, *Ethnic Conflict and Civil Life*, Table 8.1, p. 208, for a summary of the reported causes of riots in Hyderabad City, 1978–95.
2. Tambiah, *Leveling Crowds*, p. 236.
3. See, e.g., Jeffrey and Jeffrey, 'The Bijnor Riots', p. 552.
4. Krishna, 'Communal Violence in India', p. 65.
5. Varshney, *Ethnic Conflict and Civil Life*, p. 111.
6. One of the more comprehensive studies of this type is Suranjan Das, *Communal Riots in Bengal, 1905–1947* (Delhi: OUP, 1991).
7. Varshney, *Ethnic Conflict and Civic Life*, p. 3.
8. Turner, *Dramas, Fields and Metaphors*, pp. 45, 169, 174–5.
9. Compare Sukeshi Kamra, *Bearing Witness: Partition, Independence, End of the Raj* (Calgary, 2002), pp. 117–19. Kamra notes how testimonials from refugees forced out of their homes by partition violence often articulate a sense of having lost not only hearth and home, but the *capacity* ever again to 'belong', so closely had they identified with their natal community.
10. Fort. report from RC, CI, for the period ending 31 January 1948, NAI, RCO, Rajasthan, file 18-P/48-E.
11. Resdt, Kashmir to Pol. Sec., GOI (teleg.), 28 May 1933, NAI, Home (Pol.), 43/2/33.
12. Dr Satyakam Joshi of the Centre For Social Sciences, Surat, on the September 2000 Surat riots, quoted in *Frontline*, 10 November 2000, p. 41.
13. Varshney, *Ethnic Conflict and Civil Life*, p. 38.
14. Ibid., p. 192.
15. Jeffrey and Jeffrey, 'The Bijnor Riots', p. 552.
16. Note by IG Police, Patiala, dated 1 March 1948, PSA, Patiala, Ijlas-i-Khas, file 2242.
17. Van der Veer, *Religious Nationalism*, p. 23.
18. Statement by the raja of Phaltan, 7 March 1948, NAI, Rajendra Prasad Papers, file 8-P/48.
19. Petition from 'The People of Kishengarh State', dated 27 February 1948, NAI, RCO, Rajasthan, file 46-P/48.
20. Testimony of Sona Devi, as quoted in Sharma and Vanjani, 'Remembrances of Things Past', p. 1730.
21. Tinker-Walker, 'Rajasthan', in S.V. Kogekar and Richard L. Park (eds), *Reports on the Indian General Elections, 1951–52* (Bombay, 1956), p. 225.
22. Some of this data is summarised in Table 1.1. Ashutosh Varshney provides fuller figures of deaths by state expressed as a proportion of the state urban population, which suggests that Gujarat may have had the worst communal record of any state of the Union between 1950 and 1995—but most of this violence was centred in Surat and Ahmedabad, which were never part of princely India. Varshney, *Ethnic Conflict and Civic Life*, p. 97.

23. John R. Wood, 'British Versus Princely Legacies and the Political Integration of Gujarat', in *Journal of Asian Studies*, Vol. 44, No. 1 (November 1984), p. 76.

24. States Minister to RC, Indore (teleg.), 13 October 1948, NAI, RCO, CI, file 136-Q of 1948.

25. Richter, 'Electoral Patterns', p. 31.

26. Bruce D. Graham, *Hindu Nationalism and Indian Politics: The Origins and Development of the Bharatiya Jana Sangh* (Cambridge, 1990), p. 229.

27. S.P. Verma and C.P. Bhambhri (eds), *Elections and Political Consciousness in India: A Study* (Meerut, 1967), p. 64. Victory in Jaipur launched Shekhawat on a brilliant political career that culminated in him becoming a most successful chief minister of Rajasthan.

28. For example, Nasir Tyabji has done a detailed district-by-district analysis of the 1991 election. His figures suggest that the BJP did significantly better in former princely state areas than in former provincial areas. Interview, Nasir Tyabji, New Delhi, 30 January 1996. Himachal Pradesh, a state formed, in part, out of the 'Punjab Hill States Agency', has always been, like Rajasthan and MP, a fertile field for the Rightist parties. The major exception, perhaps, is that the BJP has managed to carve out a substantial constituency in Gujarat—a feat that eluded its predecessor.

29. C.P. Bhambhri, 'Rightist Parties and Traditional Society in Rajasthan: A Viewpoint', in the *Political Science Review*, Vol. 2 (October 1963), p. 33.

30. Rob Jenkins, 'Rajput Hindutva, Caste Politics, Regional Identity and Hindu Nationalism in Contemporary Rajasthan', in Thomas Blom Hansen and Christophe Jaffrelot (eds), *The BJP and the Compulsions of Politics in India* (New Delhi, 1998), pp. 102, 104.

31. Ibid., pp. 111–12.

32. Wood, 'British Versus Princely Legacies', pp. 91–2.

33. Iqbal and Mathur, 'The Thousand Year Raj', p. 33.

34. Scindia, *Princess*, p. 253.

35. Organiser, 3 May 1968, quoted in Jaffrelot, *The Hindu Nationalist Movement*, p. 247.

36. Malik and Singh, *Hindu Nationalists*, p. 44.

37. Jaffrelot, *The Hindu Nationalist Movement*, p. 344.

38. McKean, *Divine Enterprise*, p. 121.

39. Interview with Mrs Chandra Mani Singh, Jaipur, 10 November 2000.

40. Speech of 31 May 1951, NAI, RCO, Rajasthan, file 44-P/51-B.

41. Savarkar, *Hindutva*, pp. 100–1.

42. *Samagra Savarkar Wangmaya*, Vol. VI, p. 296.

43. Quoted in McKean, *Divine Enterprise*, p. 100.

44. *Hindustan Times*, 2 February 1996, quoted in Partha S. Ghosh, *BJP and the Evolution of Hindu Nationalism: From Periphery to Centre* (New Delhi, 1999), pp. 114–15.

45. Editorial, *Indian Express*, 4 February 1998.

46. The *Hindustan Times*, 7 December 1999.

47. Quoted in Thodore p. Wright Jr, 'The Babri Masjid Controversy in India', in André Wink (ed.), *Islam, Politics and Society in India* (New Delhi, 1991), p. 47n.

48. *Radiance* (the official journal of the Jamaat-e-Hind) 17 December 1960, quoted in Balraj Puri, 'Indian Muslims Since Independence', in *Economic and Political Weekly*, 2 October 1993, p. 2141.

Select Bibliography

Unpublished sources

Private papers

British Library, London

Harrington Hawes Collection, MSS Eur. D1225.
Jenkins Collection, MSS Eur. D807.
Moon Collection, MSS Eur. F230.
Mountbatten Collection, MSS Eur. F200.
Mudie Collection, MSS Eur. F164.
Reading Collection, Pt I, MSS Eur. E238, and Pt II, MSS Eur. F118.
Templewood Collection, MSS Eur. E240.

John Rylands Library, University of Manchester

Auchinlek Collection.

Nehru Memorial Museum and Library, New Delhi

M.S. Aney Papers.
Seth Jamnalal Bajaj Papers.
Sir Mirza Ismail Papers.
Correspondence and Papers of Dr B.S. Moonje.
Jawaharlal Nehru Papers, and Jawaharalal Nehru Papers, 1947– (First instalment).
Hiralal Shastri Papers.
Jai Narain Vyas Papers.
Oral History Transcripts 310 (N.B. Khare), 313 (Hiralal Shastri) and 330 (Ganpat Rai).

National Archives of India, New Delhi

Jayakar Papers (Correspondence and papers of M.R. Jayakar).
Prasad Papers (Correspondence and papers of Rajendra Prasad).

Quaid-i-Azam Academy, Karachi

Quaid-i-Azam Papers (Correspondence and papers of Muhammad Ali Jinnah).
Shamsul Hasan Collection.

Personal collection of Mr Mohan Singh Kanota, Jaipur

Diaries of Thakur Amar Singh Kanota.

Official records

India Office Library, London

Crown Representative Records (R/1).
Private [India] Office Papers (L/PO).
Records of the Political and Secret Department of the India Office (L/P&S).
Residency Records (R/2).

National Archives of India, New Delhi

Foreign and Political Department Records.
Home Department (Political Section) Records.
Ministry of States Records.
Regional Commissioners' Offices Records.

Nehru Memorial Museum and Library, New Delhi

Akhil Bharat Mahasabha Papers.
All-India Congress Committee Files.
All-India States Peoples' Conference Papers.

Bhopal Record Office

Records of the Political Department, Bhopal.

Madhya Pradesh State Archives, Bhopal

Records of the Huzur Office, Indore.
Records of the Home Department, Gwalior.

Punjab State Archives, Patiala

Records of the Dharam Arth, Patiala.
Records of the Ijlas-i-Khas, Patiala.
Records of the Prime Minister's Office, Patiala.
Records of the Chief Minister's Office, Nabha.
Sadar English Records, Kapurthala.

Rajasthan State Archives, Bikaner

English Office Records, Bundi.
Records of the Home Department, Bikaner.
Records of the Prime Minister's Office, Bikaner.
Confidential Records of the Prime Minister's Office, Bikaner.
Social and Ecclesiastical Records, Jodhpur.
Confidential Records, Kotah.
Council Records, Sirohi.
Political Records, Sirohi.
State Council Records, Karauli.

History of the Freedom Movement Office, Karachi University, Karachi

All-India Muslim League Papers.

Monash University Library, Melbourne

Microfilm copies of US State Department Records: India, 1945–48 (Decimal files 845.00–845.30).

Dissertations

Snedden, Christopher, 'Paramountcy, Patrimonialism and the Peoples of Jammu and Kashmir, 1947–1991' (PhD dissertation, Latrobe University, Melbourne, 2001).

Interviews

Rani Laxmikumari Chunderwat of Thikamgarh, head of one of Jaipur's noble families.
Sharvan Dutt, grandson of bodyguard to Maharaja Ganga Singh of Bikaner.
Bhajan Grewal, Sikh academic, Melbourne.
Justice I.S. Israni, member, High Court of Rajasthan (refugee from Sind).
Mian Safraz Mahmood, former councillor, Lahore Metropolitan Corporation.
Khemchand Mathur, former Alwar collector and senior official in the government of Rajasthan.
Ajmer Singh Siddhu, long-time resident of Patiala.
HH Mayurdhwaj Sinhji, ruler of Dhrangadhra, 1942–48.
Brigadier Bagh Singh, former Chief of Staff, Bikaner State Forces.
HH Brijraj Singh, son of the last ruler of Kotah, Congress/PJS politician.
Mrs Chandra Mani Singh, Director, Jawahar Kala Academy, Jaipur.
Mohan Singh, Curator, Patiala Museum.
Wing-Commander Rawat Ghanshyam Singh, member, Rajput princely family of Central India.
Thakur Jaswant Singhji, son of general Officer Commanding, Kotah State Forces.
Vaduendra Sahai, Director, Palace Museum, Jaipur and scion of a leading *darbāri* family.
Dr Jagat Narayan Srivastava, retired professor of history, Kota.
Tej Singh Tiwana, raised Nabha, former president, PEPSU Socialist Party.
R.G. Verma, Resident of Patiala since the 1920s.

Published sources

Official publications

Indian Statutory Commission Report (London, 1930), Vols 1, 4, 6 and 7.
Memoranda on the Indian States 1930 (Calcutta, 1931).
Indian states administration reports (various).

Newspapers and periodicals

Hindustan Times (New Delhi), 1945–50.
Jayanti Pratap (Gwalior) (English/Hindi), 1939–45.
Peoples' Age (New Delhi), 1946–47.
Statesman (Calcutta) (weekly edition), 1930–50.

The New York Times, 1900–50.
The Times (London), 1900–50.
The Times of India (Bombay), 1920–40.
The Tribune (Lahore), 1946–47.

Collections of documents

Choudary, Valmiki (ed.), *Dr Rajendra Prasad: Correspondence and Select Documents*, Vols 4–9 (New Delhi, 1985–88).

Gupta, P.S. (ed.), *Towards Freedom: Documents on the Movement for Independence in India 1943–1944* (New Delhi, 1997).

Gwyer, Sir Maurice and Appadorai, A. (eds), *Speeches and Documents on the Indian Constitution 1921–47*, Vol. 2 (London, 1957).

Mansergh, Nicholas, Lumby, E.W.R. and Moon, Sir Penderel (eds), *Constitutional Relations Between Britain and India: The Transfer of Power, 1942–7*, 12 Vols (London, 1970–83).

Munshi, K.M. (ed.), *Indian Constitutional Documents: Munshi Papers*, Vol. 2 (Bombay, 1967).

Parthasarathi, G. (ed.), *Letters to Chief Ministers, 1947–1949* (Delhi, 1985).

Shah, Muhammad, *The Indian Muslims: A Documentary Record*, Vol. 6 (Meerut, 1983).

Memoirs, diaries and collected letters

Ackerley, J.R., *Hindoo Holiday: An Indian Journal* (Harmondsworth, 1983).

Ashraf, K.M., 'K.M. Ashraf on Himself', in Horst Krüger (ed.), *Kunwar Muhammad Ashraf: An Indian Soldier and Revolutionary 1903–1962* (Delhi, 1969), pp. 291–336.

Campbell-Johnson, Alan, *Mission with Mountbatten* (London, 1951).

Coupland, R., *Indian Politics 1936–1942: Report on the Constitutional Problem in India Part II* (London, 1943).

Das, Durga (ed.), *Sardar Patel's Correspondence, 1945–50*, 10 Vols (Ahmedabad, 1974).

Fitze, Sir Kenneth, *Twilight of the Maharajas* (London, 1956).

Forster, E.M., *The Hill of Devi: Letters from Dewas State Senior* (London, 1953).

Gopal, S. (ed.), *Selected Works of Jawaharlal Nehru*, 2nd series, Vols 1–10 (New Delhi, 1984–90).

✓ Hamid, Major-General Shahid, *Disastrous Twilight: A Personal Record of the Partition of India* (London, 1986).

✓ Khare, N.B., *My Political Memoirs: Or Autobiography* (Nagpur, 1959).

Moon, Penderel, *Divide and Quit* (London, 1961).

Panikkar, K.M., *An Autobiography* (Madras, 1977).

Scindia, Vijayaraje, *Princess: The Autobiography of the Dowager Maharani of Gwalior* (London, 1985).

Sreenivasan, M.A., *Of the Raj, Maharajas and Me* (New Delhi, 1991).

Troll, Christian W., 'Five Letters of Maulana Ilyas (1885–1944), The Founder of the Tablighi Jama'at, Translated, Annotated and Introduced', in Troll (ed.), *Islam in India: Studies and Commentaries*, Vol. 2 (Delhi, 1985), pp. 138–76.

Tuker, Sir Francis, *While Memory Serves* (London, 1950).

Zeigler, Philip (ed.), *The Personal Diary of Admiral the Lord Louis Mountbatten, Supreme Allied Commander, Southeast Asia 1943–1946* (London, 1988).

Monographs

Baxter, Craig, *The Jana Sangh: A Biography of an Indian Political Party* (Philadelphia, 1969).

Brass, Paul R., *The Production of Hindu–Muslim Violence in Contemporary India* (Seattle, 2003).

——, *Theft of an Idol: Text and Context in the Representation of Collective Violence* (Princeton, N.J., 1997).

Chandra, Bipan, *Communalism in Modern India* (New Delhi, 1984).

Copland, Ian, *The Princes of India in the End-Game of Empire, 1917–1947* (Cambridge, 1997).

Fox, Richard G., *Lions of the Punjab: Culture in the Making* (Berkeley, 1985).

Freitag, Sandria B., *Collective Action and Community: Public Arenas and the Emergence of Communalism in North India* (Berkeley, 1989).

Ghosh, Partha S., *BJP and the Evolution of Hindu Nationalism: From Periphery to Centre* (New Delhi, 1999).

Gold, Daniel, *The Lord as Guru: Hindu Sants in North Indian Tradition* (New York, 1987).

Graham, Bruce D., *Hindu Nationalism and Indian Politics: The Origins and Development of the Bharatiya Jana Sangh* (Cambridge, 1990).

Hasan, Mushirul, *Legacy of a Divided Nation: India's Muslims Since Independence* (London, 1997).

Jaffrelot, Christophe, *The Hindu Nationalist Movement and Indian Politics 1925 to the 1990s* (London, 1996).

Kooiman, Dick, *Communalism and Indian Princely States: Travancore, Baroda and Hyderabad in the 1930s* (New Delhi, 2002).

Malik, Yogendra K. and Singh, V.B., *Hindu Nationalists in India: The Rise of the Bharatiya Janata Party* (New Delhi, 1995).

McKean, Lise, *Divine Enterprise: Gurus and the Hindu Nationalist Movement* (Chicago, 1996).

Menon, V.P., *The Story of the Integration of the Indian States* (Bombay, 1961).

Nandy, Ashis *et al.*, *Creating a Nationality: The Ramjanmabhumi Movement and Fear of the Self* (Delhi, 1995).

Panikkar, K.M., *His Highness the Maharaja of Bikaner: A Biography* (London, 1937).

Price, Pamela G., *Kingship and Political Practice in Colonial India* (Cambridge, 1996).

Stern, Robert W., *The Cat and the Lion: Jaipur State in the British Raj* (Leiden, 1988).

Tambiah, Stanley J., *Leveling Crowds: Ethnonationalist Conflicts and Collective Violence in South Asia* (Berkeley, 1996).

Thursby, G.R., *Hindu–Muslim Relations in British India: A Study of Controversy, Conflict and Communal Movements in British India 1923–1928* (Leiden, 1975).

Vanaik, Achin, *The Furies of Indian Communalism: Religion, Modernity and Secularization* (London, 1997).

Van der Veer, Peter, *Religious Nationalism: Hindus and Muslims in India* (Delhi, 1996).

Varshney, Ashutosh, *Ethnic Conflict and Civil Life: Hindus and Muslims in India* (New Haven, 2002).

Vidal, Denis, *Violence and Truth: A Rajasthani Kingdom Confronts Colonial Authority* (1st English edn, Delhi, 1997).

Waghorne, Joanne Punzo, *The Raja's Magic Clothes: Re-Visioning Kingship and Divinity in England's India* (University Park, Pennsylvania, 1994).

Articles

Bayly, C.A., 'The Pre-history of "Communalism"?: Religious Conflict in India, 1700–1860', in *Modern Asian Studies*, Vol. 19, No. 2 (1985), pp. 177–203.

⌐Brass, Paul R., 'Elite Groups, Symbol Manipulation and Ethnic Identity Among the Muslims of South Asia', in David Taylor and Malcolm Yapp (eds), *Political
⌐ Identity in South Asia* (London, 1979), pp. 35–77.

Brennan, Lance, 'A Case of Attempted Segmental Modernization: Rampur State, 1930–1939', in *Comparative Studies in Society and History*, Vol. 23, No. 3 (1981), pp. 350–81.

Copland, Ian, 'Congress Paternalism: The "High Command" and the Struggle For Freedom in Princely India', in Jim Masselos (ed.), *Struggling and Ruling: The Indian National Congress 1885–1985* (New Delhi, 1987), pp. 121–40.

——, 'Islam and Political Mobilization in Kashmir, 1931–34', in *Pacific Affairs*, Vol. 54 (1981), pp. 228–59.

✓ ——, 'The Further Shores of Partition: Ethnic Cleansing in Rajasthan 1947', in *Past and Present*, No. 160 (August 1998), pp. 203–39.

✓ ——, 'The Master and the Maharajas: The Sikh Princes and the East Punjab Massacres of 1947', in *Modern Asian Studies*, Vol. 36, No. 3 (2002), pp. 657–704.

✓ ——, 'The Princely States, the Muslim League and the Partition of India in 1947', in *The International History Review*, Vol. 13 (1991), pp. 38–69.

Derrett, J.D.M., 'Rājadharma', in *Journal of Asian Studies*, Vol. 25 (1976), pp. 597–609.

Fox, Richard G., 'Communalism and Modernity', in David Ludden (ed.), *Contesting the Nation: Religion, Community and the Politics of Democracy in India* (Philadelphia, 1996), pp. 235–49.

Gill, M.S. and Deol, Gaganjot, 'Patterns of Riots in India', in *Asian Profile*, Vol. 23, No. 1 (February 1995), pp. 59–66.

Gordon, Richard, 'The Hindu Mahasabha and the Indian National Congress, 1915–1926', in *Modern Asian Studies*, Vol. 9 (1975), pp. 145–203.

Haye, Chowdhry Abdul, 'The Freedom Movement in Mewat and Dr K.M. Ashraf', in Horst Kruger (ed.), *Kunwar Mohammad Ashraf: An Indian Scholar and Revolutionary, 1903–1962* (Delhi, 1969), pp. 291–336.

Haynes, Edward S., 'Comparative Industrial Development in 19th- and 20th-Century India: Alwar State and Gurgaon District', in *South Asia*, n.s., Vol. 3, No. 2 (December 1980), pp. 25–43.

✓ Jeffrey, Roger and Jeffrey, Patricia, 'The Bijnor Riots, October 1990: Collapse of a Mythical Special Relationship', in *Economic and Political Weekly*, 5 March 1994, pp. 551–8.

Jenkins, Rob, 'Rajput Hindutva, Caste Politics, Regional Identity and Hindu Nationalism in Contemporary Rajasthan', in Thomas Blom Hansen and Christophe Jaffrelot (eds), *The BJP and the Compulsions of Politics in India* (New Delhi, 1998), pp. 101–20.

✓ Kooiman, Dick, 'Communalism and Indian Princely States: A Comparison with British India', in *Economic and Political Weekly*, 26 August 1995, pp. 2123–33.

Krishna, Gopal, 'Communal Violence in India: A Study of Communal Disturbances in Delhi – I', in *Economic and Political Weekly*, 12 January 1985, pp. 61–74.

Mahmood, Cynthia Keppley, 'Rethinking Indian Communalism: Culture and Counter-Culture', in *Asian Survey*, Vol. 33, No. 7 (July 1993), pp. 722–37.

√Mayaram, Shail, 'Communal Violence in Jaipur', in *Economic and Political Weekly*, 13–20 November 1993, pp. 2524–41.

√——, 'Speech, Silence, and the Making of Partition Violence in Mewat', in Shahid Amin and Dipesh Chakrabarty (eds), *Subaltern Studies*, Vol. 9 (Delhi, 1996), pp. 126–64.

Mayer, Adrian C., 'The King's Two Thrones', in *Man*, n.s., Vol. 20 (1985), pp. 205–21.

Narain, Iqbal and Mathur, P.C., 'The Thousand Year Raj: Regional Isolation and Rajput Hinduism in Rajasthan Before and After 1947', in Francine R. Frankel and M.S.A. Rao (eds), *Dominance and State Power in India: Decline of a Social Order* (Delhi, 1990), pp. 1–58.

Peabody, Norbert, 'In Whose Turban Does the Lord Reside? The Objectification of Charisma and the Fetishism of Objects in the Hindu Kingdom of Kota', in *Comparative Studies in Society and History*, Vol. 33 (1991), pp. 726–54.

Ramusack, Barbara N., 'Maharajas and Gurudwaras: Patiala and the Sikh Community', in Robin Jeffrey (ed.), *People, Princes and Paramount Power: Society and Politics in the Indian Princely States* (New Delhi, 1978), pp. 170–204.

Richter, William L., 'Electoral Patterns in Post-Princely India', in Jagdish N. Bhagwati *et al.* (eds), *Electoral Politics in the Indian States: Three Disadvantaged Sectors* (Delhi, 1975), pp. 1–77.

——, 'Princes in Indian Politics', in *Economic and Political Weekly*, 27 February 1971, pp. 535–42.

Robinson, Francis, 'Islam and Muslim Separatism', in Taylor and Yapp, *Political Identity*, pp. 76–112.

Wood, John R., 'British Versus Princely Legacies in the Political Integration of Gujarat', in *Journal of Asian Studies*, Vol. 44, No. 1 (November 1984), pp. 65–99.

Zutshi, Chitralekha, 'Religion, State and Community: Contested Identities in the Kashmir Valley, c.1880–1920', in *South Asia*, n.s., Vol. 23, No. 1 (2000), pp. 109–28.

Index

economic growth in, 1930s and
1940s, 72–3, 124
governmental spending in, 35, 57–8,
60–1, 117–18
integration of, 180–4
overtures to local political leaders, 127
patronage of communal
organisations, 118–19, 176
political agitation in, 85–6, 176
polity, 44–52, 63–5, 123, 212
regulation of religious worship,
59–60
religious demography, 28, 30, 74,
118, 130–1, 144, 147–8,
168–70, 175
role in Partition massacres of 1947,
144–60
use of divide-and-rule tactics by, 87–9
see also under communal riots
princes, Indian
anti-communal rhetoric of, 47–8, 121
as agents of communal
incorporation, 48–56, 203
attitude to outside agitators, 93–4
charismatic authority of, 51–2
links with provincial politicians,
101–2, 108–10, 114, 204–5
post-Integration political role of,
184, 190–3, 208–12
Punjab and East Punjab States Union
(PEPSU), 182–3, 187
Punjab States Agency, 25, 30, 78, 79,
82, 145–6, 168–9
death toll in 1947, 154
Punjab Riyasti Praja Mandal, 85
Punjab States Peoples'
Conference, 125

Qaddus, Abdul, 142
Qadian, 90
'Qadianis', *see under* Ahmadiyyas

Radcliffe, Sir Cyril, 145
Radhanpur (state), 43
Nawab Murtaza Khan Jorawar Khan
of, 139
Rai, Ganpat, 93
Rajasthan Sevak Sangh, 85–6
Rajgarh (state), 178, 182

Rajkot (state), 36, 95
Rajputana Agency/Rajasthan, 7, 8, 25,
26, 30, 44, 56–7, 79, 82, 83, 85, 146,
168–9, 183, 186–7, 191, 207, 209
death toll in 1947, 154
Rajputana Provincial Hindu Sabha,
87–8
Rajputs, 61, 83
political formations amongst, 176–8
Rajput culture, 210
Ramanandis, 83
'Ramjanmabhumi' movement, 7
see also Bharatiya Janata Party (BJP);
Vishwa Hindu Parishad (VHP)
Rampur (state), 29, 64, 93, 129, 186
Nawab Reza Ali Khan of,
71–2, 111, 139
Rampur city, 29, 170
Rashtriya Swayamsevak Sangh (RSS),
103, 119, 141, 143, 146, 160,
171–2, 176, 178–80, 190,
206, 213
refugees from West Punjab and Sind
guarded response to, 173–4
impact of their stories of horror
1947, 149, 166
problems of adjustment, 162–3,
172–3
'religious fundamentalism', 81–2
Rewa (state), 112, 180
Maharaja Gulab Singh of, 35
Maharaja Martand Singh of, 108–9
Richter, William L., 191, 207–8, 210
Robinson, Francis, 2
Rudé, George, 37, 198

Saiyyid Ahmad Khan, 3
sajjada nashins, 90
Sanatan Dharma Sabha, 54, 83
Sapru, Sir Tej Bahadur, 80
Sarila (state), 119, 176
Saurashtra Union, 183, 186–8
Savarkar, Veer Vinayak Damodar, 102,
104, 112–14, 172, 212–13
Saxena, Chandra, 129
Saxena, Mohanlal, 171, 174
Scott, James C., 38, 199
Sen, D.K., 115
separate electorates, 4, 97